Nationalism and War

Has the emergence of nationalism made warfare more brutal? Does strong nationalist identification increase efficiency in fighting? Is nationalism the cause or the consequence of the breakdown of imperialism? What is the role of victories and defeats in the formation of national identities? The relationship between nationalism and warfare is complex, and it changes depending on which historical period and geographical context is in question. In *Nationalism and War*, some of the world's leading social scientists and historians explore the nature of the connection between the two. Through empirical studies from a broad range of countries, they explore the impact that imperial legacies, education, welfare regimes, bureaucracy, revolutions, popular ideologies, geopolitical change, and state breakdowns have had in the transformation of war and nationalism.

JOHN A. HALL is the James McGill Professor of Comparative Historical Sociology at McGill University. His recent publications include *Ernest Gellner* (2010) and *An Anatomy of Power: The Social Theory of Michael Mann* (Cambridge University Press, 2006).

SINIŠA MALEŠEVIĆ is Professor and Head of the School of Sociology at the University College, Dublin. His recent publications include *The Sociology of War and Violence* (Cambridge University Press, 2010) and *Identity as Ideology* (2006).

Nationalism and War

Edited by

John A. Hall and Siniša Malešević

CAMBRIDGE
UNIVERSITY PRESS

CAMBRIDGE UNIVERSITY PRESS
Cambridge, New York, Melbourne, Madrid, Cape Town,
Singapore, São Paulo, Delhi, Mexico City

Cambridge University Press
The Edinburgh Building, Cambridge CB2 8RU, UK

Published in the United States of America by
Cambridge University Press, New York

www.cambridge.org
Information on this title: www.cambridge.org/9781107610088

© Cambridge University Press 2013

First published 2013

Printed and bound in the United Kingdom by the MPG Books Group

A catalogue record for this publication is available from the British Library

Library of Congress Cataloging in Publication data
Nationalism and war / edited by John A. Hall and Siniša Malešević.
    pages cm
    Includes bibliographical references.
    1. Nationalism–Psychological aspects.   2. War–Psychological aspects.
I. Hall, John A., 1949- editor of compilation.   II. Malešević, Siniša,
    1969- editor of compilation.
    JC311.N32275 2013
    320.54–dc23
                                                        2012033804

ISBN 978-1-107-03475-4 Hardback
ISBN 978-1-107-61008-8 Paperback

Contents

Figures

Tables

Notes on contributors

MIGUEL ANGEL CENTENO is Professor and Chair of Sociology at Princeton University. His publications include *Democracy within Reason: Technocratic Revolution in Mexico* (2nd edn. 1997), *Blood and Debt: War and State-making in Latin America* (2002), *The Other Mirror: Grand Theory and Latin America* (2000), and *Essays in Latin American Military History* (2006). His latest publications are *Global Capitalism* (2010) and *Discrimination in an Unequal World* (2010). He is currently working on book projects on liberalism in the Iberian world, and war and society.

RANDALL COLLINS is Dorothy Swaine Thomas Professor of Sociology at the University of Pennsylvania. He was President of the American Sociological Association, 2010–11. Previously he has taught at the University of Virginia, University of California Riverside, University of Chicago, Harvard, and Cambridge University where he was Pitt Professor of American History and Institutions. Among his books are *Macro-History: Essays in Sociology of the Long Run* (1999), *The Sociology of Philosophies: a Global Theory of Intellectual Change* (1998), *Interaction Ritual Chains* (2004), and *Violence: a Micro-Sociological Theory* (2008). His blog, *The Sociological Eye*, is at http://sociological-eye.blogspot.com/

JOSE MIGUEL CRUZ is a visiting assistant professor at Florida International University. He was the director of the University Institute of Public Opinion (IUDOP) at the University of Central America (UCA) in San Salvador from 1994 to 2006. His last edited book, *Street Gangs in Central America* (2007), summarizes an eight-year research project on gangs in Central America.

JOHN DARWIN teaches imperial and global history at Oxford University where he is a Fellow of Nuffield College. His recent publications include *After Tamerlane: the Global History of Empire since 1405* (2007), which won the Wolfson History Prize, and *The Empire Project:*

x   Notes on contributors

the Rise and Fall of the British World System 1830–1970 (2009), which won the Trevor Reese Memorial Prize in 2010.

RENE FLORES is a graduate student in the Princeton Department of Sociology. He received his undergraduate degree in Interdisciplinary Studies from the University of California-Berkeley in 2007. He was a research assistant at El Colegio de México in Mexico City.

JOHN A. HALL is the James McGill Professor of Comparative Historical Sociology at McGill University in Montreal. His books include *Powers and Liberties* (1985), *Liberalism* (1987), *Coercion and Consent* (1994), and, most recently, *Ernest Gellner* (2010). *The Importance of Being Civil* is in the press, and he is at work on a monograph dealing with the interactions between nations, states, and empires.

WESLEY HIERS recently received his Ph.D. from UCLA's Department of Sociology, where he wrote a comparative-historical dissertation on the relationship between political institutions and racial exclusion in the United States and other former European settlement colonies. He is currently working on a project with Andreas Wimmer that examines the historical roots of right-wing populism in Europe.

JAMES HUGHES is Professor of Comparative Politics at the London School of Economics. His research spans the study of political violence and terrorism, and national and ethnic conflict, with a focus on the relationship between communities and movements engaged in ideo-logically motivated violence. He graduated with a B.Sc. in Political Science and Ancient History from Queen's University Belfast in 1982, and then took his Ph.D. in Soviet history at the LSE (1982–87). He is the author, co-author, or editor of seven books, and his recent works include *The Myth of Conditionality* (2004), *Chechnya: From Nationalism to Jihad* (2007), and *EU Conflict Management* (2010). He is head of the international advisory board of the European Centre for Minority Issues based in Flensburg.

BILL KISSANE was born in the Republic of Ireland and educated at Trinity College Dublin (BA, MA) and the London School of Economics (M.Sc., Ph.D.). He is currently Reader in Politics at the LSE and teaches courses on civil wars, and on democratization. He has published *Explaining Irish Democracy* (2002), *The Politics of the Irish Civil War* (2005), and *New Beginnings: Constitutionalism and Democracy in Modern Ireland* (2011). His edited collection *Reconstructing National Identity after Europe's Internal Wars* and his *Civil War: the Contemporary Challenge* are scheduled for publication in 2014.

RICHARD LACHMANN (Ph.D. Harvard 1983) is Professor of Sociology at the University at Albany, State University of New York. His book *Capitalists in Spite of Themselves: Elite Conflict and Economic Transitions in Early Modern Europe* (2000) received the 2003 American Sociological Association's Distinguished Scholarly Publication Award. He is the author of *States and Power* (2010). He is currently writing a book examining the decline of dominant economic and military powers in early modern Europe and the contemporary United States. He is also researching media coverage of war deaths in the United States and Israel from the 1960s to the present.

MATTHEW LANGE is Associate Professor of Sociology at McGill University. His research explores the developmental legacies of colonialism and the causes of ethnic violence and uses comparative-historical methods. He is the author of *Educations in Ethnic Violence* (Cambridge University Press, 2012), *Comparative-Historical Methods* (2012), and *Lineages of Despotism and Development: British Colonialism and State Power* (2009). He is the co-editor of *The Oxford Handbook of the Transformations of States* (in press) and *States and Development: Historical Antecedents of Stagnation and Advance* (2005).

RENE LEMARCHAND is Emeritus Professor of Political Science at the University of Florida. He has written extensively on the Great Lakes region of Central Africa. He is the author of *Rwanda and Burundi* (1970), which received the Herskovits Award of the African Studies Association. His latest books include *The Dynamics of Violence in Central Africa* (2009) and an edited volume, *Forgotten Genocides* (2011). He served as a regional advisor on governance and democracy with USAID from 1992 to 1998 in Abidjan and Accra, and has been a visiting lecturer at the University of California at Berkeley, Brown University, Concordia (Montreal), as well as at the universities of Bordeaux, Antwerp, Copenhagen, and Helsinki. He is currently working on a short history of violence in the Congo, Rwanda, and Burundi.

DOMINIC LIEVEN is Senior Research Fellow at Trinity College, Cambridge (from 2011) and a Fellow of the British Academy (from 2001). Previously he was a professor at LSE. He graduated from Christ's College, Cambridge in 1973, was a Kennedy Scholar at Harvard, served in the British Foreign Office and did his doctorate at the School of Slavonic and East European Studies under the supervision of Professor Hugh Seton-Watson in 1975–78. His main publications are *Russia and the Origins of the First World War* (1983), *Russia's Rulers under the Old*

Regime (1988), *Aristocracy in Europe 1815–1914* (1992), *Nicholas II* (1993), *Empire: The Russian Empire and Its Rivals* (2001), and *Russia against Napoleon* (2009).

SINIŠA MALEŠEVIĆ is Professor and Head of the School of Sociology at the University College, Dublin. He is also Member of the Royal Irish Academy. His recent books include *The Sociology of War and Violence* (Cambridge University Press, 2010, Croatian translation 2011), *Identity as Ideology* (2006), *The Sociology of Ethnicity* (2004, Serbian translation 2009, Persian translation 2011), *Ideology, Legitimacy and the New State: Yugoslavia, Serbia and Croatia* (2002, Serbian translation 2005), and the co-edited volume *Ernest Gellner and Contemporary Social Thought* (Cambridge University Press, 2007). He is currently finishing a book on nation-states and nationalisms.

MICHAEL MANN is Distinguished Professor of Sociology at UCLA. His major publication project is *The Sources of Social Power:* vol. I *A History of Power from the Beginning to AD 1760* (1988); vol. II *The Rise of Classes and Nation-States, 1760–1914* (1993); vol. III *Global Empires and Revolution, 1890–1945* (2012); and vol. IV *Globalizations, 1945–2011* (in press), all published by Cambridge University Press. The German version of his book *Incoherent Empire* (2003) won the Friedrich Ebert Foundation prize for the best book on politics published in Germany in 2003. He has published two more books with Cambridge University Press: *Fascists* (2004) and *The Dark Side of Democracy: Explaining Ethnic Cleansing* (2005). His books have been translated into German, French, Spanish, Italian, Greek, Turkish, Chinese, Korean, and Japanese.

BENJAMIN MILLER is Professor of International Relations at the School of Political Sciences, University of Haifa, where he is Head of the International MA Program in Peace and Conflict Management. He is also the President of the Israeli Association for International Studies. Among his publications are: *When Opponents Cooperate: Great Power Conflict and Collaboration in World Politics* (2nd edn., 2002) and *States, Nations and Great Powers: The Sources of Regional War and Peace* (Cambridge University Press, 2007). He has also published numerous articles on international relations theory and international and regional security. Miller's current project focuses on explaining changes in US grand strategy since World War II. Miller received a Ph.D. from the University of California at Berkeley and he was a research fellow at Harvard University, MIT, Princeton University and McGill University.

He has taught at Duke University, the Hebrew University of Jerusalem, and the University of Colorado, Boulder.

STEPHEN M. SAIDEMAN holds the Paterson Chair in International Affairs at Carleton University's Norman Paterson School of International Affairs. In addition to his books, *The Ties That Divide: Ethnic Politics, Foreign Policy and International Conflict* and *For Kin or Country: Xenophobia, Nationalism and War* (with R. William Ayres) and *Intra-State Conflict, Governments and Security* (with Marie-Joelle Zahar), he has published articles and book chapters on the international relations and comparative politics of nationalism, ethnic conflict, and civil war. Professor Saideman spent 2001–2 on the US Joint Staff working in the Strategic Planning and Policy Directorate in the Central and East European Division as part of a Council on Foreign Relations International Affairs Fellowship. Saideman is now completing a book on NATO's experience in Afghanistan while continuing his work on the international relations of ethnic conflict by focusing on the dynamics of diasporas.

GUSTAVO SILVA CANO is a Juris Doctor candidate at the University of Pennsylvania Law School. He holds a BA from the Woodrow Wilson School of Public and International Affairs, Princeton University.

ANDREAS WIMMER is Hughes-Rogers Professor of Sociology and Faculty Associate in Politics at Princeton University. His research aims to understand the dynamics of nation-state formation, ethnic boundary making and political conflict from a comparative perspective. He has pursued these themes across the disciplinary fields of sociology, political science, and social anthropology and amateured in various methodological and analytical strategies, from fieldwork to quantitative cross-national analysis. His latest books are *Waves of War: Nationalism, State-Formation and Ethnic Exclusion in the Modern World* (Cambridge University Press, 2012) and *Ethnic Boundary Making: Institutions, Power, Networks* (2012).

Introduction
Wars and nationalisms

John A. Hall and Siniša Malešević

There is almost certainly a consensus in the general public that national-ism causes war. In an immediate sense this is, as both Michael Mann and Siniša Malešević point out in their contributions, quite wrong: wars had been fought for thousands of years before the advent of nationalism. Still, it is easy to see why nationalism is seen as likely to cause war once it gains salience in the historical record. If nationalism insists that one live with members of one's nation in a state free from alien rule, then avenues to violence open up immediately. Members of the nation left outside the state should be brought in and untrustworthy elements within expelled, with secession from imperial rule being all but mandatory. Europe's hideous twentieth century makes it only too easy to recognize these forces, all capable of leading to organized brutality. And at a more general level is it not simply the case that there is a link between the viciousness of modern war and the emergence of nationalism? Data on the causes of war in modern times collected by Kalevi Holsti and by Andreas Wimmer (whose contribution to this whole field, as we shall see, has been very great) certainly seem to show that the institutional change from empire to nation-state does a great deal to explain the incidence of war (Holsti 1991; Wimmer and Min 2006, 2009).

The essays in this volume, written by historians as well as social scientists, evaluate this claim and its corollaries, adding necessary com-plexities and seeking to specify mechanisms at work in different historical and geographical contexts. The purpose of this introduction is to specify the state of play within an intellectual field of great moral and political importance – one that is currently at the center of attention in social studies as a whole. That this specification involves commenting on the contributions of the participants of the volume is no accident; their chapters were solicited precisely to exemplify the condition of current scholarship, and thereby to crystallize understanding so as to set the agenda for future research.

1

The intellectual background

Traditional debates on the relationship between wars and nationalisms have generally focused on the question of causal direction. Is the proliferation of nationalist doctrines likely to cause war or is it the experience of warfare itself that leads to the development and expansion of nationalist feelings among the wider population? The rudimentary form of this debate was already present in late nineteenth- and early twentieth-century social science. The "naturalists" saw inherent cultural and biological differences as the principal generators of war and violence. In contrast, the "situationists" identified specific violent social and historical contexts as crucial in fostering strong national identities. At the turn of the century the quasi Darwinian and Lamarckian views that emphasized the inevitability of "race struggle" (Kidd 1893), innately competing "syngenic ethnocentrisms" (Gumplowicz 1899), and the "pugnacious instincts" of the culturally diverse groups (McDougal 1915) clearly had the upper hand. The general assumption was that both nationalism and war are natural phenomena that could be traced back to time immemorial. More specifically the naturalists were adamant that, unless they are carefully checked, the strong nationalist feelings are bound to lead towards organized violence sooner or later.

Nevertheless, by the early to mid twentieth century and especially after the carnage of the Second World War, the naturalist interpretations lost much of their support and credibility. Since the early studies of Sumner (1906), Simmel 1955[1908], Mauss 1990[1922], and Coser (1956), researchers have shifted attention towards the integrative qualities of external threat, concentrating in particular on the ways in which conflict situations change group dynamics. Rather than seeing groups as generators of violent conflicts the focus moved towards seeing conflict as a social device for transforming the patterns of collective solidarity. For Sumner (1906: 12) external conflict was likely to lead towards internal homogenization: "the exigencies of war with outsiders are what makes peace inside." In the aftermath of the Second World War the situationist paradigm became dominant and most social scientists were inclined to interpret the sentiments of intensive national solidarity through the prism of external threat and prolonged inter-group violence. Nevertheless, until the mid 1960s and 1970s there was little attempt to explain the origin and potency of nationalism; most scholars made no distinction between relatively universal psychological processes such as in-group favoritism or ethnocentrism and the historically specific phenomenon that is nationalism. It is only with the pioneering theories of Elie Kedourie (1960), Hans Kohn (1967), and most of all Ernest Gellner (1964) that nationalism became a subject of serious scholarship. Rather than assuming that national identities are given and primordial, these new approaches emphasized the historical novelty, geographical contingency and sociological necessity of national identifications in modernity. Gellner in particular formulated an original account that identified nationalism and economic growth as the two central pillars of state legitimacy in the modern age. Instead of looking at psychology or biology the analytical gaze shifted to historical sociology; nationalism makes sense only where there is an elective affinity between the demands of an industrialized economy and cultural homogeneity. Nationalism can flourish, it was claimed, when it is reinforced by expanding educational systems, standardized high cultures, increasing literacy rates, and the centralization of administrative power. By the mid 1980s and 1990s nationalism studies became a distinct research field producing a plethora of diverse theories of nationalism, variously focusing on the role of economic (Hechter 1999; Laitin 2007; Nairn 1977), cultural (Armstrong 1982; Hutchinson 2000; Smith 1986) or political factors (Breuilly 1993; Hall 1995; Mann 1995; Tilly 1990).

In a similar vein the study of war has moved away from its traditional focus on strategy, logistics, security, and leadership towards historically and sociologically nuanced analyses of the complex relationships between warfare and society. War has been reconceptualized less as an omnipresent and inevitable natural force and more as a historically specific and contingent social and political institution. Building on advances in archeology and anthropology the new approaches emphasized the relative novelty of warfare and its growth in parallel with state development. For most of recorded history, human beings have lived as simple gatherers and scavengers who generally did not engage in violent conflicts, making warfare a novel development of only the last ten thousand years. More specifically the growth of protracted wars had to wait another seven thousand years: the expansion of warfare intensified only with the development of the first civilizations – Mesopotamia, ancient Egypt, the Indus Valley and ancient China (Ferrill 1985; Fry 2007; Otterbein 2004; Reid 1976).

In this field Raymon Aron's (1958, 1966) pioneering work was decisive not only in bringing together sociology and international relations but also in providing a new analytical framework to explore the impact of warfare on social development. What Gellner had done for the study of nations and nationalism was replicated by Aron for the sociological study of war. Rather than treating the institution of warfare as an aberration that periodically interferes in the normal growth of social orders, as traditionally viewed by mainstream social science, Aron interpreted war as an integral component of social development. More specifically, Aron insisted that profound internal social changes can never be explained by focusing only on internal societal dynamics: rather, external geopolitical contexts often shape internal development. As the international order lacks the monopoly on the legitimate use of violence that characterizes sovereign states, the use of force remains normal. Under such historical conditions no peace is permanent and all pacified arrangements remain dependent on the interaction of states. In other words, the absence of warfare cannot be explained through reference to some internal developments such as economic growth, lack of class polarization, shared cultural values, or civilizational achievements. Instead it is geopolitical stability, regularly characterized by the dominance of powerful states, that often determines the direction of internal social development.

While Gellner and Aron have revolutionized the study of nationalism and war respectively, they did not devote much attention to the study of their relationship. It is only recently that scholars have been able to draw on these pioneering ideas to explore the impact of warfare on nationalism and vice versa. Historians and historical sociologists (Mann 1988, 1993, 2005; Posen 1993; Tilly 1985, 1990) have begun to link the rise and spread of nationalism to the geopolitical competition of states. Tilly (1985), Mann (1993), and Posen (1993) interpret the increase in national homogenization as a historical outcome of military and geopolitical rivalry of state rulers. In this view, military and technological innovations in pre-modern Europe intensified warfare while also making it more expensive. To finance wars, rulers had to mobilize domestic financial support and military participation, and as a consequence were forced to make citizenship rights and national attachments much more inclusive. The direct effect of these policies was the greater fiscal coordination, better administrative organization and tighter territorial centralization of modern nation-states. These institutional changes helped dissolve old aristocratic hierarchies, paving the way for much greater social integration and eventually for the appearance of nationally cohesive populations. Nevertheless, arms proliferation and the general increase in military capabilities of some states often act not as a deterrent but as a threat to their neighbors. Rather than soothing animosities, militarization encourages further militarization, thus creating permanent "security dilemmas" (Posen 1993). It is these geopolitically induced state insecurities that foster and maintain nationalist homogenization. Therefore, nationalism not only emerges as a direct corollary of state competition, but its proliferation and intensity remain tied to the historical contingencies of geopolitical situations. In a nutshell, for Mann, Posen and Tilly strong national identities were created in war through military means, and as such national cohesion remains first and foremost a potent military asset.

These historically grounded analyses have provoked an ongoing debate, with some scholars finding this realist approach too materialist, and others seeing it as not materialist enough. The culturalist approaches of Anthony Smith (1999, 2003) and John Hutchinson (2005, 2007) argue that to explain the impact of war on the rise of nationalist sentiments one needs to take seriously shared cultural understandings and especially collective myths, memories and symbols, most of which are linked to specific wars. For Smith and Hutchinson, war experience is decisive for the development of national consciousness as wars polarize distinct populations, strengthen stereotypical divides and enhance national self-perceptions. However, what really matters for Smith and Hutchinson is how particular wars are collectively remembered and commemorated. In this perspective nationalism entails celebration and collective remembrance of past wars which are interpreted through the prism of collective sacrifice. The monuments, cenotaphs and war memorials dedicated to the "glorious dead" lionize the war heroism of past soldiers in order to set the boundaries of normative obligation to present and future generations. In this context, for Smith and Hutchinson a nation is first and foremost a "sacred communion of citizens" and nationalism is a form of "surrogate political religion" (Smith 2010: 38). Wars are crucial for nationalism as their tragic experience creates shared collective meanings that bind diverse citizenry into a single nation. In the modern, secular context war memorials in particular emerge as potent collective symbols that define nations as moral communities. In this view nationalism is grounded in shared myths and memories of past wars as they provide a moral compass but also a sense of collective immortality where one's nation is seen as a replacement for, or a supplement to, a deity.

An alternative strand of criticism has emerged from a revitalized evolutionary theory insisting on the biological foundations of both war and nationalism. These contemporary sociobiological approaches are generally dismissive of earlier nineteenth-century naturalism, seeing it as oscillating between metaphysics and racialism and lacking sound empirical foundations. These new approaches aim to ground analyses in extensive empirical research drawing on recent developments in genetics and zoology, with a view to explaining both nationalism and warfare as an upshot of inherent group solidarity. For sociobiologists (Gat 2006; Ridley 1997; Van der Dennen 1995; Van Hooff 1990) the link between warfare and nationalism is to be found in the same evolutionary processes: the organism's proclivity towards self-reproduction. In this view both nationalism and war are social mechanisms through which genes are able to continue their biological existence. The central point is that when an organism cannot procreate directly it will do so indirectly, favoring kin over non-kin and close kin over distant kin. Hence war is understood to be an optimal means for acquiring scarce resources, territory, and a limited number of potential mates: "the interconnected competition over resources and reproduction is the root cause of conflict and fighting in humans, as in all other animal species" (Gat 2006: 87). In a similar way nationalism is conceptualized as a form of extended kinship rooted in the genetic principle of "inclusive fitness." Accordingly sociobiologists make no distinction between ethnocentrism and nationalism, arguing that such in-group sentiments "can be expected to arise whenever variance in inherited physical [and cultural] appearance is greater between groups than within groups" (Van den Berge 1995: 365). And the existence of strong ethno-national identities is understood to be one of the principal causes of warfare.

While the emergence of influential culturalist and biological approaches has made the debate on the relationship between war and nationalism lively, the intrinsic explanatory weaknesses of these two approaches have narrowed the scope of the debate. For one thing, both perspectives overemphasize the link between nationalism and violence: whereas evolutionary theorists wrongly assume that all violent action has group-based/biological underpinnings, the culturalists exaggerate the role of commemorations in maintaining the longterm intensity of nationalist solidarity (Malešević 2010: 182–90, 2011: 145–51). Instead of being an inevitable feature of culturally/ biologically different groups, recent studies show that nationalist violence remains historically unusual, as most political conflicts are still settled by non-violent means (Brubaker and Laitin 1998; Laitin 2007). Laitin shows that even in Africa, normally viewed as the epicenter of ethnic conflicts, nationalism and wars, "the percentage of neighbouring ethnic groups that experienced violent communal incidents was infinitesimal – for any randomly chosen but neighbouring pair of ethnic groups, on average only five in ten thousand had a recorded violent conflict in any year" (2007: 4–5). Further, the culturalist view does not devote much attention to the manipulative role played by the various social actors in creating and maintaining the ritualistic practices associated with the commemorations of past wars. Rather than being a spontaneous process initiated by the nationalist public, most ritualistic commemorations, war memorials and other remembrance events regularly entail prolonged organizational and ideological work, which is often the exclusive prerogative of the state and para-state agencies. Then the culturalist approach assumption that nationalist identification with past wars is automatic is belied by research showing that nationalist ideologies tend to spread unevenly among different social strata and different regions. All nationalisms wax and wane and they are unlikely to operate as a uniform and synchronized set of collective feelings. And even when individuals embrace nationalist rhetoric it is far from certain that this is not done for other, non-national, reasons (Kalyvas 2006). The simple fact, evidenced in most political crises and wars, that political leaders keep making repeated calls for national unity testifies to the fragility of social cohesion at the macro level. Rather than being a self-evident, automatic and habitual popular response under conditions of external threat, national solidarity is difficult to create and even more difficult to sustain.

This book aims to go beyond the existing debates by looking at the role of other social factors that have contributed towards the closer links between nationalism and warfare in modernity. Instead of focusing solely on the biological, cultural, economic, and political sources of this relationship, most chapters in the book chart a complex picture where the development of nationalism and warfare often goes hand in hand with broader historical and social transformations. Hence the authors explore the impact of imperial legacies, education, welfare regimes, bureaucracy, revolutions, the spread of popular ideologies, geopolitical changes, state breakdown, and other historical factors that have made the connection between war and nationalism much more apparent. Particular attention is paid to a central area of debate, namely that concerning the character of nationalism – not least as this remains an area of intense disagreement for many scholars. In a nutshell, the relation of nationalism to war has changed at various points in the historical record, thereby ruling out some of the simpler sentiments with which we began. But before discussing categories and the way in which they worked both in the era of the world wars and in the contemporary world, let us begin by considering a rather more discrete issue: one that allows rather clear conclusions to be reached.

Fighting for the nation?

It is often maintained that the emergence of nationalism changed the character of war, intensifying it as the people fought harder to extend or, more likely, to protect their nation. The image that best captures this is surely that of the French soldiers who apparently cried "Vive la nation" when counterattacking at the battle of Valmy in 1792. At a theoretical level, the issue was best laid out by Clausewitz, who in his teenage years had been part of the Prussian armies defeated by

Napoleon. Reflecting on this many years later he noted in his great *On War* (1976) that the emergence of the nationalist principle had changed the character of fighting:

a force appeared that beggared all imagination. Suddenly war again became the business of the people – a people of thirty millions, all of whom considered themselves to be citizens ... The people became a participant in war; instead of governments and armies as heretofore, the full weight of the nation was thrown into the balance. The resources and efforts now available for use surpassed all conventional limits: nothing now impeded the vigor with which war could be waged. (Clausewitz 1976: 591–92)

The claim is then that fighting for one's own nation is likely to increase the level of conflict simply because the level of commitment is likely to be greater than it ever had been for mercenary armies.

There is a mass of evidence suggesting skepticism about this claim. Randall Collins (and Michael Mann) claim that the actual experience of combat induces terror and hence great inefficiency in terms of fighting ability (c.f. Bourke 2000; Collins 2008; Grossman 1996). But there is a counterbalancing factor. Soldiers may well not care about large abstractions such as the nation, but they do care a very great deal about their immediate fellows, not least as their behavior might ensure their own survival. Collins claims that this is now well understood by the leaders of the armed forces of the United States, insisting as a consequence that its fighting capacity has improved markedly in recent years. There is a final point of great importance. Collins does not deny that wars have become more deadly, but he wishes to explain it in alternative terms. What matters in his view most of all is the increased kill capacity of modern weaponry.

This skepticism seems to be wholly justified – which is not to say that there have not been some exceptions in the historical record as a whole. Dominic Lieven (2010) notes that old-regime Russia was able to defeat Napoleon, although this does not lead him to dismiss Clausewitz out of hand. For he has in mind the fact that Confederate forces in the American Civil War fought long and hard, with high levels of participation, even though bereft of much logistical support (Lieven 2000). Still more important was the loyalty shown to Hitler by the Wehrmacht, which fought powerfully, literally to the bitter end. Nevertheless, as the pioneering study of Shils and Janowitz (1948) demonstrated, this stubborn resistance had more to do with the micro-group solidarity of platoons and loyalty to one's comrades and less with the Nazi doctrine itself.

A more general point needs to be added so as to place Collins's general point within a broader historical context, which thereby does a little to dilute its force. Richard Lachmann's contribution does not deny the difficulties of actual combat. But he does note that modern states have the capacity to conscript very large numbers. It may be that the fighting efficiency of such conscripts was poor, but the ability of modern states, acting in the name of the nation, to send millions into the meat grinder of world war nonetheless increased its magnitude of conflict. And Lachmann insists on a further point. Conscription warfare has a decided, but not universal, link to the spread of welfare provision, with preparedness to die resulting in leaders being forced to talk, as did Lloyd George, of creating a land fit for heroes. So at this point there is support for the contention, discussed below, that war did something to enhance national unity. Beyond this, there is an interesting ambivalence about Lachmann's position. On the one hand, he applauds the unwillingness of modern Americans to die in war (although one might note that resistance to war has been a staple of the history of the United States), but his progressive leanings push him hard in exactly the opposite direction. Conscription war has been an avenue of social mobility for African-Americans. Will professionalized high-tech war diminish that and so remove the chance for a future Colin Powell to emerge? And there are two further considerations to be borne in mind. First, the latest military revolution may yet change the central relationship between war and nationalism by making the means of destruction so specialized and high-tech as to have no impact on civilian life, albeit to this point one notes how very "normal" has been the increase of nationalist reaction whenever invading troops, as in Iraq, come to be seen as "occupiers." Further, the ways in which wars end will always have a powerful impact of their own. A key finding of the recent work of Michael Mann, for instance, is that the military industrial complex that became so powerful in the United States after 1945 has played a significant role in *diminishing* rather than increasing welfare provision – that is, in turning the United States away from the radicalism of the New Deal years to a much more conservative set of social arrangements (Mann 2012).

Variable categories

If categories should never be used uncritically, this is particularly so when dealing with this intellectual field. This is immediately obvious when considering the nature of war. The normal practice amongst social scientists is to define war as a conflict which leads to one thousand battle deaths. One problem here is that the First and Second World Wars were of a different order of magnitude, the first in part a very great interstate war, the second the most massive of all inter-imperial conflicts. Both wars altered the terms on which other states operated, the first causing revolutions that changed world politics, the second creating a division of the world that has but recently ended. A moment's reflection makes one turn to a crucial question. There have always been wars in the European multipolar sphere. Might it not simply be that nationalism is the language now used to articulate state competition, rather than an autonomous force? And there is of course a second general point to be made about war, justifying the use of the plural in the title used. Since 1945 few classical interstate wars have taken place. But organized violence has certainly continued, very often in the form of civil wars. There is a large literature spanning several disciplines which insists on the utter novelty of such conflicts. For example Kaldor (2001, 2007), Bauman (2001, 2002), Munkler (2004), and Duffield (2001) have argued that the late twentieth and early twenty-first centuries are characterized by a profoundly differ-ent type of war in which nationalism plays no significant role. These "new wars" are held to have a different organizing structure. Instead of the conventional militaries fighting on the battlefields most "new wars" are intra-state, asymmetric, low-intensity conflicts that target civilians. These violent conflicts tend to be dependent on external funding, making use of strategies that focus on the control of population rather than territory. Such conflicts are often fought by warlords in possession of private armies or criminal gangs, who employ guerrilla and terrorist tactics, rather than conscripts or professional militaries. Kaldor (2001) argues that these "new wars" are a direct product of globalized capital-ism, which allegedly has weakened the power of states to control their territorial and economic sovereignty. In this context nationalism is understood to be insignificant as the new lines of polarization are con-ceptualized in economic terms. Traditional ideological and territorial cleavages have been "supplanted by an emerging cleavage between ... cosmopolitanism, based on inclusive, universalist multicultural values, and the politics of particularist identities" (2001: 6). In a similar vein Bauman explicitly rules out nationalism: "nation-building coupled with patriotic mobilization has ceased to be the principal instrument of social integration and states' self-assertion" (2002: 84). But these judgments have little empirical backing. As several influential empirical studies (Kalyvas 2001; Lacina and Gleditsch 2005; Melander et al. 2007; New-man 2004; Sollenberg 2007) have demonstrated, the contemporary civil wars show more similarity than difference with civil wars of the previous two centuries. The ratio of civilian and military deaths has been largely stable with some oscillation around the 50/50 percent axis. The levels of atrocity, the reliance on guerrilla tactics and the prevalence of warlordism have not significantly increased. There is also little concrete evidence that globalization is the direct cause of these violent conflicts. Most important for this book, the relationship between warfare and nationalism also seems stable, as in most instances the stakes involve nationalism – that is, conflict as to which group should own the state (Hall [in press]; Kalyvas 2001, 2006; Malešević 2010; Wimmer and Minn 2006, 2009).[1]

This last point implies changes in historical time. This is certainly true of a further complexity concerning the nature of war, highlighted in Siniša Malešević's contribution. The popular view with which we started suggests that nationalism causes war. But lurking in the background is an alternative view present in social science. Charles Tilly (1990) gained fame and reputation as the result of his claim that "states make war, and war makes states." Might not the same be true of the relations between nationalism and war? There is no need to deny the occasions on which nationalism in one way or another initiates conflict to also accept that the causality involved can be reversed – that shared struggle in war can create feelings of cultural unity, as we have already seen when noting the assertions so powerfully made by Lachmann. Certainly Max Weber believed this. But time enters here: Tillyesque concerns may have worked best in the European past, Michael Mann's contribution insists, when the issue facing states was geopolitical survival rather than the capitalist pressures that surround them today within a world in which interstate war has lost salience due to the presence of nuclear weapons. Further, the mechanism identified by Tilly may have no bearing on the social world in which many contemporary civil wars take place. The states of much of the world since the collapse of Europe's overseas empires do not often engage in interstate war. This explains their thinness: that is, the lack of infrastructural reach which, if it existed, might create a sense of shared identity. A warning needs to be issued at this point, namely that one should resist voices suggesting that war in the South should be given a chance (Herbst 2004; Luttwak 1999). This is facile given the destructive power of Kalashnikovs and the ability to buy them "thanks" to funds provided from external sources, and utterly horrible to boot.

This brings us to a second general area of complexity: that of the current condition of the theory of nationalism. The essential point is that nationalism, like war, is best seen in plural rather than singular terms. As with religion, there are varieties of nationalist experience. What is at issue is not the definition of nationalism per se. Here a unitary view is possible, namely that the national community should look after its own affairs in

---

[1] The data set of Wimmer and Min (2006) may not work well for the world wars, if one pays attention not just to battle deaths but to the ability to wage war. In contrast, their data on civil wars since 1945 looks to be veridical.

order that it can survive and prosper. However, that general principle can find expression in different forms, two of which deserve special attention.

Ernest Gellner's *Nations and Nationalism* (1983) represents in its essence the most striking and severe version of the first form. This great modern *philosophe* was wont to claim that one should assimilate or get one's own state given that the only remaining alternative was to be killed (Hall 2010). Hence his definition of nationalism differed from that just given, stressing the need for each state to have a single culture, and each culture to have its own state. This view is represented in this book, almost as a presupposition, in the contribution by Benny Miller. He stresses that war is likely whenever there is an imbalance in the "state to nation" ratio: that is, whenever the correspondence described by Gellner is lacking (cf. Miller 2007). We will see in just a moment that this general viewpoint has been challenged, in our view successfully, but this is not to say even for a moment that it is without veridical application. It is always important to remember that none of the multinational empires and composite monarchies present in nineteenth-century Europe was able to turn itself into some form of more liberal multinational polity; all collapsed, all were replaced by nation-states. Europe since 1945 has been a zone of peace in part because the national question has been solved for the vast majority of states, largely through ethnic cleansing and mass murder. We will see in a moment that we can at least hope that this moment of nationalism was historically bounded, rather than being a permanent necessity in human affairs. But it would be as well to realize that the desire to nationally homogenize a particular territory is likely to remain a possibility, a permanent temptation for some nationalizing leaders.

The alternative view stresses the very varied arrangements which have allowed different ethnicities and nations to live together in peace. The key principle here is very clear, and it is best expressed in terms of Hirschman's *Exit, Voice and Loyalty* (1970). When a nation is denied voice – that is, when it is faced by a state denying it cultural rights and political representation – secessionist exit becomes attractive, or even necessary. The contribution by James Hughes describes in detail the way in which arbitrary discrimination leads to increased nationalist militancy. Allowing voice, in contrast, can produce loyalty, thereby undermining secessionist drives. Matthew Lange's text powerfully supports this position. It is as well to note that there is a technical point here, of great importance for those who wish to calculate the consequences of ethnic fractionalization. Bluntly, a strong distinction needs to be drawn between nominal and politically charged ethnicity – the latter resulting most often from the discrimination and exclusion noted in the last paragraph. An initial attempt to produce an index of politically charged – and so politically relevant – ethnic divisions was made for some African states by Posner (2005). Extraordinary efforts by Wimmer, Cederman and Min (2009) have created an index describing ethnicity and political life for the whole world in the period after World War II. This data set powerfully records various types of political inclusion and partnership, as well as discrimination. The end result is clear: the nationalist principle can be honored by the provision of cultural rights and political representation within a larger polity, for all that exclusion and discrimination lead to conflict and secession.

It is worth noting an interesting range of opinion amongst theorists who think in the alternative terms just noted. At one end stand thinkers seeking an open political system so that complete assimilation can take place; at the other end are those privileging, at times for normative reasons as much as on grounds of political necessity, the deep diversity of a self-maintaining nation within some larger political frame. If the important work of David Laitin stands at the assimilationist end of this spectrum, middling positions are provided by Donald Horowitz and also Wimmer, who both seek reasonable accommodations, whilst the works of Brendan O'Leary and of Alfred Stepan, Juan Linz, and Yogendra Yadav recommend the greatest degree of pluralism (Horowitz 1985; Laitin 2007; O'Leary 2005; O'Leary and McGarry 2005; Stepan, Linz and Yadav 2011; Wimmer 2002). These are interesting and important differences, and they most certainly matter in terms of practical policy proposals. But let us put the differences to one side so as to ask a basic question about this approach as a whole. How seriously should we take it?

An initial problem is best approached by remembering Bertrand Russell's attack on the social contract theory proposed by Rousseau. The idea that a set of venal and corrupt individuals would choose to make a contract turning them into virtuous citizens was ridiculous, indeed pathetic. A contract favoring civic virtue would only be made by those already virtuous! The point remains true for all contract theory, including that of John Rawls – which moves so quickly from an abstract original position to illicitly populating his subjects with the characteristic social values of the denizens of Cambridge, Massachusetts. The relevance for the alternative view of nationalism outlined here is particularly apparent in Wimmer's (2011) analysis of Switzerland. It turns out that the Swiss had many transethnic institutions and a vibrant civil society before the civil war that took place in the middle of the nineteenth century. So ethnicity had not been politicized, making it possible thereafter not to begin to politicize it, so as to create a multiethnic nation-state instead, albeit one based on cantons, which each tend toward homogeneity rather than plurality. A similar point must be made about Matthew

Lange's chapter. Discrimination most certainly led to violence in Sri Lanka and inclusion to the containment of hostility and the bearable dissatisfaction of Canadian politics; but the latter case depended upon the presence of a prior rich institutional portfolio.

But more can be said on this point. It is important, for one thing, to remember that ethnicity is by no means a simple matter. John Darwin reminds us of this by recalling the imperial ethnicities of the British Empire. Such imperial ethnicities existed elsewhere: for instance, firmly amongst soldiers, socialists and those of Jewish background in the Austro-Hungarian monarchy. This points to an equally important consideration, namely that of the presence of multiple and at times complementary identities. It is entirely possible to feel Canadian and Quebecois, Catalan and Spanish, and Tamil and Indian. Empirical work establishing this has been undertaken by Stepan, Linz and Yadav (2011), and it lies behind their belief that one can actually *craft* what they term state-nations – that is, that it is possible to get beyond the impasse identified by Russell. Independent India may have benefited to some extent from an institutional legacy that included a shared nationalist struggle, a powerful army and a competent bureaucracy. Nonetheless, many institutions had to be built, first to include different linguistic groups and then to encourage the Tamils of Tamil Nadu to pull back from their secessionist claims.

Two cautionary notes are in order as we turn away from this topic. The first concerns the need for varied types of data. The survey data of Stepan, Linz, and Yadav (2011) concern the general population, in itself a huge achievement. But one needs also to remember the category of John Darwin, namely that of an elite prepared to identify with the project of the larger state. Peoples can be relatively passive, however plural their identities may be, and their loyalties may be manipulable. The presence of elite unity, aware of the attractions, both in terms of career and commitment, of working for a larger political entity than their immediate nation can have independent force. Second, a cautionary word is needed about the notion of crafting. Perhaps the most dangerous misuse of a phrase of recent social science has been that of "imagined communities" (Anderson 1991): it has led to a dreadfully illicit idealism and voluntarism, taking for granted that we can imagine what we will whenever we wish. One would not want a similar fate to befall the notion of crafting. In this context one can usefully note Matthew Lange's demonstration of the ways in which education can enhance the possibilities for ethnic violence (Lange 2012). When a large, newly educated subaltern group finds that key top professions are monopolized by a minority ethnicity, great difficulties inevitably ensue. Such difficulties can be managed. But one should remember that there was an essential element of truth to Gellner's theory of nationalism, namely that the entry of the people into politics involves what is best termed social and political dynamite. Crafting is possible, but one should never imagine that it is easy.

Imperialism as the perversion of nationalism

But let us turn systematically to the era of the world wars – that is, to the key conflicts that altered the course of human history – because it is here that connections between nationalism and war may well be found. What *exactly* are the mechanisms, if any, linking nationalism and war? We can begin by noting something of a tension in the work of Wimmer. His first major intervention in this whole area suggests, especially when read carelessly, a smooth and almost inevitable move from empire to nation-state, the implication being that empire is a thing of the past whose downfall was engineered by rising nationalism (Wimmer and Min 2006). But his slightly later and more detailed empirical findings about the rise of nation-states in the modern world mandate a revision of this view. In fact, nation-states seem to have been created on the back of defeat in war (Wimmer and Feinstein 2010). The key consideration is simple: namely, that weakness brought on by defeat in war makes it impossible for empires to continue to cage nations seeking to escape. A classic instance of this was of course that of the earliest wave of nationalism in Latin America: freedom was obtained in largest part because the metropolitan state was at war with Napoleon. Realization of this point does not, however, close off debate, especially as it applies to Europe at the height of its hegemony in the nineteenth and early twentieth centuries. What were the origins of the two world wars? Did nationalism have some role in starting those wars, or did it merely benefit from their consequences? It may be useful to say immediately that behind the complexities to be noted stands a clear finding: of some causal relationship in 1914 and of, as it were, a total connection in 1939.

It is as well to begin with some cautionary points. First, one can usefully remember the skepticism shown by Gellner towards the view – his own! – that nationalism was an ever more implacable force as the nineteenth century developed. Nationalism was certainly present amongst Denmark's National Liberal Party in the middle of the century, and its aggressive stance towards the German minority played some part both in the civil war of 1848 and in the wars with Germany over Schleswig and Holstein.[2] The key point here, made by Siniša Malešević,

---

[2] Holsti's data set allows for several causes to a single war, whereas Wimmer's data set classifies each war in terms of a single factor. The war of 1864 is classified by Holsti as

is that one should not read nationalism too easily back into the past. There is the world of difference between riots, protests, and mere grumbles, supported by odd social groups, and a genuine broadly based nationalist movement seeking to allow the people as a whole to enter onto the political stage. His chapter on the Balkans emphasizes the importance of this point. For one thing, it makes clear that wars are not always caused by nationalism, and that conflict can undermine rather than help state building. For another, he does not deny that there can be a connection between nationalism and war, albeit he stresses the nationalism of intellectuals, high-ranking officers, and top civil servants, rather than of peasants, but he insists that this is only possible once long-term secular processes of state building and normative consolidation have taken place – categories utilized in a subtle way later in this volume by Bill Kissane.[3]

We can advance the general argument most clearly through the second point. It is dangerous and mistaken to see empires as necessarily doomed, archaic structures without relevance for modern times. This is far too simple. To possess large territory was held to give strength, making empires eminently modern: indeed, the leading edge of power. But there is considerable complexity here. Many European nation-states had been empires, in the sense that they had expanded from a core to incorporate diverse territories, and they then sought to establish overseas empires of their own. Some of the tensions involved here were pointed out in the brilliant opening pages of John Hobson's classic *Imperialism: A Study*:

The novelty of the recent Imperialism regarded as a policy consists chiefly in its adoption by several nations. The notion of a number of competing empires is essentially modern. The root idea of empire in the ancient and medieval world was that of a federation of States, under a hegemony, covering in general terms the entire or recognized world, such as was held by Rome ... Thus empire was identified with internationalism, though not always based on a conception of equality of nations ... the triumph of nationalism seems to have crushed the rising hope of internationalism. Yet it would appear that there is no essential antagonism between them. A true strong internationalism in form or spirit would rather imply the existence of powerful self-respecting nationalities which

---

being interstate and nationalist, by Wimmer merely as interstate. Wimmer may be wrong on this occasion. But he is right to classify the wars of Italian unification as interstate rather than, as is often believed, not least by Holsti, as nationalist.

[3] One can highlight the nature of Malešević's contribution by describing it as a defense that Ernest Gellner (who supervised his early work) lacked. A standard criticism of *Nations and Nationalism* was that it failed to explain nationalist movements that occurred before industrialization. Gellner offered various ways to explain this. Malešević's point is that he need not have done so, given that early nineteenth-century anti-Ottoman social movements had almost nothing to do with nationalism (see Malešević 2012).

seek union on the basis of common national needs and interests … Nationalism is a plain highway to internationalism, and if it manifests divergence we may well suspect a perversion of its nature and its purpose. Such a perversion is Imperialism, in which nations trespassing beyond the limits of facile assimilation transform the wholesome stimulative rivalry of varied national types into the cut-throat struggle of competing empires. (Hobson 1902: 6–7, 8)

But the situation was still more complex, filled with even more tensions (Kumar 2010). Logic and experience seemed to suggest that power could be increased by nationalizing one's empire, increasing force through coherence. Differently put, empires sought to become nation-states.

This is the world, social scientists and historians ought to know, of Max Weber: a member of the Naval League believing that Germany needed a place in the sun and a nationalist famously worried that an excess of Poles in East Prussia would diminish the power of the state. What this amounts to is a marriage between nationalism and imperialism, in which state strength seemed to depend upon the sharing of a culture and the possession of secure sources of supply and protected markets. This raises two analytic questions. First, is it the case that inter-imperial rivalries led to the disasters of twentieth-century Europe, as Lenin suggested when adopting Hobson's analysis and giving it his own Marxist twist? Just as important, second, is another matter that was clearly on Hobson's mind when he suggested that "imperialism is an artificial stimulation of nationalism in peoples too foreign to be absorbed and too compact to be permanently crushed" (1902: 10). This interesting statement calls for comment. Assimilation had indeed taken place in the states of the European heartland, over long periods of time, where state building predated national consciousness. Once the national principle emerged, however, complexities arose. Attempts at forcible assimilation might succeed when a dominant ethnicity was present, but they might well lead to resistance – likely to be successful when a *Staatsvolk* was absent. This is a very important point. It suggests that the actions of a radical state elite might so politicize a nation as to encourage it to think of exit. Differently put, it might not be the emergence of national awareness per se that led to war but rather the way in which homogenizing policies led politicized nations to become agents of historical change. Let us remember that there was and is, at least in principle, the alternative to total assimilation already discussed: namely, the granting of cultural rights within an open political system might give sufficient voice to create enough loyalty to make exit an unattractive option. It is very important to realize that these dilemmas were faced by the great powers at home as well as abroad – which is to say that imperialism remained present in the core as much as in the periphery

(Lieven 2000). If the Russians could ensure that the Ukrainians were but "little Russians," then they were the dominant group in the empire, with the chance of making a nation-state, but with little or no chance of assimilating the Poles. In contrast, there were not enough German ethnics and German-speakers to imagine nationalizing the Austrian lands, making relatively liberal rule logically necessary – albeit the logic was not fully accepted in Vienna. The logic of integration would of course have been well known to Hobson: it was the idea of Home Rule. The blunt point already made about the Great Powers is that none managed to decompress successfully, either at home or abroad: that is, to retain their multinational character whilst moving to some sort of liberal system. The question that arises here is simple: were modern empires doomed from the start because of the presence of the national principle, as might seem to be the case given the brevity of their existence, at least in comparison to that of Rome and China?

We can begin by looking at overseas empires. What always mattered most to the Great Powers was their security within the European heartland, and, more particularly, the determination not to let matters get so out of hand again that anything like the strains and stresses of the revolutionary and Napoleonic period could be repeated (Darwin 2007). It was this background condition that made it relatively easy to settle imperial disputes, especially over the partition of Africa. After all, imperial possessions, pace Marxist understandings, paid little (with the exception of India, which mattered enormously for the empire, as it allowed Britain to use Indian surpluses to balance the books, and to pay for a good deal of imperial defense). The balance within Europe is the factor that allowed Britain to gain a huge empire in the first place; equally, geopolitical factors do most to explain its longevity. French resentments were never likely to lead to war given the increasing power of Germany, whilst Germany itself for long did not wish to increase French and Russian power at the expense of Britain since that would weaken its own position (Kennedy 1983). Besides, the British Empire was, until the interwar period, open to trade from its rivals. In summary, imperial disputes before 1914 were always kept within bounds; they certainly did not actually cause the onset of disaster. Furthermore, the empires were a little more solidary, a little less at risk than hindsight suggests. Darwin's particular contribution, as noted, is to remind us of the presence of imperial ethnicities: that is, of groups loyal to the empire more than to any nation-state. This was certainly true in Canada, where all but the Québecois were really "Brits" overseas, members of a common Britannic nationalism. It was equally true of Austro-Hungary where, as noted, a core of Jews, army officers, and socialists resisted national appeals.

The presence of a measure of liberalism in both cases certainly mattered, although Lieven's contribution makes it clear that sheer timing ruled out the possibility of consolidating a shared Britannic identity. Further, the desire for inclusion was present in places where historical developments have made us imagine it to have been impossible: notably in British India before 1914, where the hope was for Dominion status equivalent to that given to Canada and Australia. And one can go further. The imperial power had the capacity to manage the threat of secessionist nationalism in an entirely different way: to divide and rule by playing different national claims off against each other, as the British did to great effect in India in the interwar years. Most important of all, of course, is the simple fact that the metropolitan states benefited during the world wars from huge numbers of loyal troops from their overseas territories.

Still, there is no denying that it was literally the trigger pulled by Gavrilo Princip that occasioned the onset of war in 1914. Furthermore, there was pressure in the key German case from middle-class "statist" intellectuals, proud of Germany's success and keen for their country to take a more prominent place in the world (Mann 1993: Chapter 21). Nonetheless, both Darwin and Mann make a strong case for seeing the origins of the First World War in entirely traditional terms. "The July Crisis revealed that the Achilles heel of Europe's global primacy was the underdevelopment of the European states system" (Darwin 2007: 373). There will never be full agreement as to the origins of the First World War, and it is certainly the case that there were multiple causes and significant conjunctural elements: the most important, perhaps, being the inability of Germany to act "rationally" because its court lacked the ability to calculate (Mann 1993: Chapter 21). Nevertheless, the chapters in this volume by Lieven, and by Hiers and Wimmer make the alternative case, stressing that the marriage of nationalism and empire played a vital role. The stiff note sent to Serbia by Vienna had as background a state fearful of losing its prestige, fearful of not being able to compete as a world state with its rivals, the most powerful of which did possess overseas territories. With hindsight we can see that the survival of the Habsburg monarchy in the face of the national question would have been best assured by peace and retrenchment. But that was not the nature of its rule, nor that of its immediate rivals. Status and prestige, so present in courts populated by officer corps immaculately turned out in white uniforms, was the very *raison d'être* of existence, and it was the need to maintain size and coherence in a world of intense geopolitical competition that played some role in the lack of flexibility of Europe's state system at the turn of the century. Lieven helps us understand this world. In the background was the fear that losing territory might lead to the sort of supine condition into which the Ottomans had fallen. The mutiny at the Curragh is best seen, Lieven suggests, in this light: less as the desire to prevent the Protestants in the north of Ireland from being ruled by Catholics than the determination, in the highest quarters, that the empire should be prevented from dissolving. It is important to underline the causal pathway here. It was the high level of geopolitical competition that stands behind the homogenizing policies of the great powers that then led to the politicization of their nations: a politicization that allowed the nations to occupy the vacuum consequent on great-power defeat in war.

It is worth highlighting three different mechanisms linking nationalism to war that have been noted to this point. The first simply says that the emergence of the nationalist idea doomed empires. The difficulty here is that there were not many cases before 1914 in which the desire for independence had led to war, although the actions of the Magyars more or less qualifies in this regard. Nonetheless, the general point of view can be maintained by saying that nationalism would have triumphed in the long run, possibly without the incidence of war, with the defeat of empires in the First World War then being seen as merely accelerating an inevitability. The second stresses the pressure brought by newly mobile middle-class elites who wanted their states to act more powerfully in the interest of the nation. The third position stresses the actions of traditional elites, who sought to homogenize their territories, thereby politicizing their nations. It is very noticeable in this regard that no Czech nationalist leader sought independence before 1914, not least as the granting of cultural rights had done much to satisfy national feeling. But the desire of Emperor Karl to "germanify" the empire after all changed matters, finally convincing Masaryk to go for independence. All of this suggests that much more research is needed, joining to the quantitative analysis pioneered by Wimmer historical reconstructions of particular nationalist movements and tracing the processes by which they gained independence.

The complexities just noted stand in marked contrast to the situation leading to the Second World War. Industry applied to war, together with the need of a conscription war to have grand aims ("a war to end all wars," "a war for democracy," the promise of "a land fit for heroes"), meant that conflict escalated by 1918 so as to make war savagely destructive and so no longer a rational policy for the states concerned. Mann may well be right to stress, as had Collins, the role played by the industrialization of war, thereby suggesting that nationalist fervor mattered little. Albeit, more research is needed here as well, given that the war aims of the Great Powers, once they became clear, certainly had implications for nationalism. State collapse and revolution followed, both making it impossible to create a sustainable geopolitical settlement when war ended, not least given the emergence of complete and competing ideological visions of the world. These conditions further played their part in the onset of the Great Depression, and the consequent increasing salience of the politics of economic autarchy (Darwin 2007: 417). It was in these circumstances that the marriage of nationalism and imperialism was firmly cemented. The ultimate perversions of nationalism were the empires envisaged by Germany and Japan in which the extermination of difference would allow the extension of a single race (Mazower 2008). Most scholars would accept Mann's claim that Hitler's national imperialism caused the Second World War, and accept his view of it as less a traditional interstate war than a huge inter-imperial conflict.

Of course, the Second World War ended European empires. Japanese victories had removed the aura surrounding occidental power, with the British Empire effectively doomed once it lost the Indian army. Anti-imperial militancy then made empire too expensive to maintain, especially as European states slowly discovered that they could prosper without overseas territorial possessions. The crucial argument was made with characteristic lucidity by Raymond Aron (1958). If metropolitan France wished to live up to its promise to make real citizens of the inhabitants of all its imperial possessions – that is, blessed by high standards of education, health and welfare – it would have to face a decline in its own living standards. It was not surprising to see that Paris let Algeria go so as to enjoy the standard of living to which it had become accustomed. Decolonization then took some time, with resistance from France being particularly obvious. But it was inevitable, not least as the two great superpowers favored ending the great European empires.

Post-war and beyond

What then of the world that was left behind? It is best to distinguish between two stages. During the Cold War the two superpowers fomented proxy wars, many of which involved nationalist claims (Westad 2005). Nonetheless, these Great Powers were fundamentally interested in stability, so that realism rather than the desire for further national self-determination governed their actions. Conditions have now changed: the world polity houses one Great Power with imperial pretensions, with both the nation-state principle and capitalism now fully globalized. In these circumstances what can be said about the relationships between nationalism and war?

A first point is simple. Many states in the modern world are but empty shells, within which much violence can take place in order that the national principle may be fulfilled. Centeno has made this point about Latin America in previous work (2002), and he does so again in this volume. The norm of non-intervention within the internal affairs of other states has now become a general cornerstone of the world polity. What has emerged in consequence are quasi-states, that is, states whose existence depends more upon international recognition than upon their own functional capacities for ruling their territories (Jackson 1990). This norm was not imposed by the advanced world on late-developing countries. To the contrary, the norm was adopted and maintained by the South, not least the Organization of African States, which went so far as being prepared to condemn one of its own members, Julius Nyerere, for his part in bringing down the hideous regime of Idi Amin in Uganda. Such visceral attachment to the norm is fully comprehensible. Many African states have boundaries drawn up by colonial powers caring so little about pre-existing social groupings that their straight lines went through them. The absolute artificiality of boundaries places a premium on maintaining them. As every state is artificial, rectification or simplification would surely lead to generalized disaster. But Lemarchand's description of the horrors of the Congo shows just how destructive is the alternative: civil war aided and abetted by outside interference.

But one should not surrender to pessimism. The most recent statistics show a diminution in the number of civil wars (Harbom and Wallensteen 2005; Lacina and Gleditsch 2005; Melander et al. 2007). Bill Kissane makes this point in his interesting comparison of the Irish Republic and Finland. And one can add something to his account of the former. At the back of the Easter Accord stands an agreement between London and Dublin: a determination to rule out irredentism on the one hand and a preparedness to let territory go on the other. This is to say that the desire for size at all costs is, as already noted, no longer present. The marriage between nationalism and imperialism is now over, at least in much of Europe, if not yet in Russia. And Kissane's chapter is an example of the possibility of political design and crafting. State-nations may yet come into their own in the contemporary world (Laitin 2007; Stepan, Linz and Yadav 2011). Political loyalty in combination with the accommodation of ethnic, religious and linguistic difference seems to allow India to work. Albeit, a part of that success is of course itself conjectural, due to shared nationalist struggle and the inheritance of a powerful army and pervasive bureaucracy. The previous argument makes clear that there is a key background condition at work here, namely the relative diminution in the intensity of geopolitical conflict. States can afford to be less unitary, to embrace federal and consociational arrangements, only when they are not continually engaged in warfare.

All the same, optimism should not turn romantic. Stephen Saideman's contribution shows that the downplaying of irredentism is in part xenophobic: small homogeneous states sometimes want to let external minorities go because they do not want to import strangers and so gain a new nationalities problem of their own. A rather similar force can now be discovered in Europe where those bereft of skills allowing them to swim inside the community as a whole seem ever more closely linked to nativist nationalisms. Then there are other worries. Obviously, some civil wars are so visceral as to make accommodation all but impossible. And there is a more particular worry. Eyre Crowe's famous "Memorandum of the Present State of British Relations with France and Germany" handed in to the Foreign Secretary Earl Grey on New Year's Day 1907 warned that Germany would expand "so England must expect that Germany will surely seek to diminish the power of any rivals, to enhance her own by extending her dominion, to hinder the co-operation of other States, and ultimately to break up and supplant the British Empire." This view was opposed by Thomas Sanderson in a "Memorandum" of 21 February 1907 in which he saw Germany as "a helpful, though somewhat exacting friend," adding that "it is altogether contrary to reason that Germany would wish to quarrel with us" (Gooch and Temperley 1928: 410, 420, 430–31). The moral of this story is simple. Germany did not have to take the path of aggression, but did so, in part for nationalist reasons. One of the questions of our age is that of the future course of China. Prosperity has come to China within the current rules of the world polity. But there are social forces within China itself, especially the newly educated, who want, as much as did the statist intellectuals of Wilhelmine Germany, more aggressive policies – a place in the sun commensurate with power and achievement. The history of Great Power relations in an age of nationalism may well not have ended.

Conclusion

The argument has been that the strongest links between nationalism and war resulted from great states being convinced that they needed coherence and size. Insofar as that is no longer the case, it is at least possible that great states will manage their nations with tolerance rather than command. This is not to underestimate the horrors caused by civil wars that involve the nationalist principle. But even these suggest that the age of empire is over. The fact that there are no obvious empires left to fall suggests further that there will be no new wave of nation-state creation, to match those in Latin America in the early nineteenth century, in

Europe after the two worlds wars and again after 1989, and in much of the world as the result of post-war decolonization.

But we should end on a note of caution. The imperial pretensions of the United States remain in place, and no alternative system for the world polity is in sight. For no state, certainly not the European Union or China, is as yet prepared to knock the United States off its perch – an action anyway harder to imagine in a world in which warfare has been changed by the invention of nuclear weapons. And might there not be something to the thought with which Lieven finishes his contribution to this book: if real ecological crisis hits us, is it not possible that size will once again become attractive?

REFERENCES

Anderson, B. 1991. *Imagined Communities: Reflections on the Origins and Spread of Nationalism*. London: Verso.

Armstrong, J. 1982. *Nations before Nationalism*. Chapel Hill: University of North Carolina Press.

Aron, R. 1958. *War and Industrial Society*. Oxford University Press.

1966. *Peace and War: A Theory of International Relations*. Garden City, NY: Doubleday.

Bauman, Z. 2001. "Wars of the Globalisation Era." *European Journal of Social Theory* 4(1): 11–28.

2002. "Reconnaissance Wars of the Planetary Frontierland." *Theory, Culture and Society* 19(4): 81–90.

Bourke, J. 2000. *An Intimate History of Killing*. London: Granta.

Breuilly, J. 1993. *Nationalism and the State*. Manchester University Press.

Brubaker, R. and D. Laitin. 1998. "Ethnic and Nationalist Violence." *Annual Review of Sociology* 24: 423–52.

Centeno, M.A. 2002. *Blood and Debt: War and the Nation-State in Latin America*. Pittsburgh: Pennsylvania State University Press.

Clausewitz, C. 1976. *On War*. Princeton University Press.

Collins, R. 2008. *Violence: A Micro-Sociological Theory*. Princeton University Press.

Coser, L.A. 1956. *The Functions of Social Conflict*. New York: Free Press.

Darwin, J. 2007. *After Tamerlane: The Rise and Fall of Global Empires, 1400–2000*. London: Penguin.

Duffield, M. 2001. *Global Governance and the New Wars: The Merger of Development and Security*. London: Zed Books.

Ferrill, A. 1985. *The Origins of War: From the Stone Age to Alexander the Great*. London: Thames & Hudson.

Fry, D.S. 2007. *Beyond War: The Human Potential for Peace*. Oxford University Press.

Gat, A. 2006. *War in Human Civilization*. Oxford University Press.

Gellner, E. 1964. *Thought and Change*. London: Weidenfeld and Nicolson.

1983. *Nations and Nationalism*. Oxford: Blackwell.

Gooch, G.P. and H. Temperley (eds.). 1928. *British Documents on the Origins of the War 1898–1914*. London: HMSO.

Grossman, D. 1996. *On Killing: The Psychological Cost of Learning to Kill in War and Society*. Boston: Little, Brown.

Gumplowicz, L. 1899. *The Outlines of Sociology*. Philadelphia: American Academy of Political and Social Science.

Hall, J.A. 1995. "Nationalisms: Classified and Explained." Pp. 8–33 in *Notions of Nationalism*, edited by S. Periwal. Budapest: Central European University Press.

2010. *Ernest Gellner: An Intellectual Biography*. London: Verso.

In press. *The Importance of Being Civil*. Princeton University Press.

Harbom, L. and P. Wallensteen. 2005. "Armed Conflict and Its International Dimensions 1946–2004." *Journal of Peace Research* 42(5): 623–35.

Hechter, M. 1999. *Internal Colonialism: The Celtic Fringe in British National Development, 1536–1966*. London: Routledge.

Herbst, J. 2004. "Let Them Fail: State Failure in Theory and Practice: Implications for Policy." Pp. 302–18 in *When States Fail: Causes and Consequences*, edited by R. Rotberg. Princeton University Press.

Hirschman, A. 1970. *Exit, Voice and Loyalty: Responses to Decline in Firms, Organizations, and States*. Cambridge, MA: Harvard University Press.

Hobson, J.A. 1902. *Imperialism: A Study*. London: James Nisbet.

Holsti, K. 1991. *Peace and War: Armed Conflicts and International Order, 1648–1989*. Cambridge University Press.

Horowitz, D. 1985. *Ethnic Groups in Conflict*. Berkeley, CA: University of California Press.

Hutchinson, J. 2000. "Ethnicity and Modern Nations." *Ethnic and Racial Studies* 23(4): 651–69.

2005. *Nations as Zones of Conflict*. London: Sage.

2007. "Warfare, Remembrance and National Identity." Pp. 42–54 in *Nationalism and Ethnosymbolism: History, Culture and Ethnicity in the Formation of Nations*, edited by A. Leoussi and S. Crosby. Edinburgh University Press.

Jackson, R.H. 1990. *Quasi-States: Sovereignty, International Relations and the Third World*. Cambridge University Press.

Kaldor, M. 2001. *New and Old Wars: Organised Violence in a Global Era*. Cambridge: Polity Press.

2007. "Oil and Conflict: the Case of Nagorno Karabakh." Pp. 157–83 in *Oil Wars*, edited by M. Kaldor, T. Karl, and Y. Said. London: Pluto.

Kalyvas, S. 2001. "'New' and 'Old' Civil Wars: A Valid Distinction?" *World Politics* 54: 99–118.

2006. *The Logic of Violence in Civil War*. Cambridge University Press.

Kedourie, E. 1960. *Nationalism*. London: Hutchinson.

Kennedy, P. 1983. "Why Did the British Empire Last So Long?" Pp. 197–218 in *Strategy and Diplomacy 1870–1945*, edited by P. Kennedy. London: George Allen and Unwin.

Kidd, B. 1893. *Social Evolution*. London: Macmillan.

Kohn, H. 1967. *The Idea of Nationalism*. New York: Collier-Macmillan.

Kumar, K. 2010. "Nation-states as Empires, Empires as Nation-states: Two Principles, One Practice?" *Theory and Society* 39(2): 119–43.

Lacina, B. and N.P. Gleditsch. 2005. "Monitoring Trends in Global Combat: A New Dataset of Battle Deaths." *European Journal of Population* 21(2–3): 145–66.

Laitin, D.D. 2007. *Nations, States and Violence*. Oxford University Press.

Lange, M. 2012. *Educations in Ethnic Violence*. New York: Cambridge University Press.

Lieven, D. 2000. *Empire: The Russian Empire and Its Rivals*. London: John Murray.
  2010. *Russia against Napoleon: The True Story of the Campaigns of War and Peace*. New York: Viking.

Luttwak, E. 1999. "Give War a Chance." *Foreign Affairs* 78(4): 36–44.

Malešević, S. 2010. *The Sociology of War and Violence*. Cambridge University Press.
  2011. "Nationalism, War and Social Cohesion." *Ethnic and Racial Studies* 34(1): 142–61.
  2012. "Wars that Make States and Wars that Make Nations: Organised Violence, Nationalism and State Formation in the Balkans." *Archives européennes de sociologie/European Journal of Sociology* 53(1): 31-63.

Mann M. 1988. *States, War and Capitalism: Studies in Political Sociology*. Oxford: Blackwell.
  1993. *The Sources of Social Power. Vol. II The Rise of Classes and Nation-States*. New York: Cambridge University Press.
  1995. "A Political Theory of Nationalism and Its Excesses." Pp. 44–64 in *Notions of Nationalism*, edited by S. Periwal. Budapest: Central European Press.
  2005. *The Dark Side of Democracy: Explaining Ethnic Cleansing*. Cambridge University Press.
  2012. *The Sources of Social Power: Vol. III Global Empires and Revolution, 1890–1945*. New York: Cambridge University Press.

Mauss, M. 1990 [1922]. *The Gift: Forms and Functions of Exchange in Archaic Societies*. London: Routledge.

Mazower, M. 2008. *Hitler's Empire: How the Nazis Ruled Europe*. New York: Penguin Press.

McDougall, W. 1915. *An Introduction to Social Psychology*. London: Methuen.

Melander, E., M.Oberg, and J. Hall. 2007. "The 'New Wars' Debate Revisited: An Empirical Evaluation of the Atrociousness of 'New Wars'." *Uppsala Peace Research Papers* 9: 1–42.

Miller, B. 2007. *States, Nations and the Great Powers: The Sources of Regional War and Peace*. Cambridge University Press.

Munkler, H. 2004. *The New Wars*. Cambridge: Polity.

Nairn, T. 1977. *The Breakup of Britain: Crisis and Neo-Nationalism*. London: Verso.

Newman, E. 2004. "The 'New Wars' Debate: A Historical Perspective is Needed." *Security Dialogue* 35(2): 173–89.

O'Leary, B. 2005. "Debating Consociational Politics." Pp. 3–42 in *From Power Sharing to Democracy; Post-conflict Institutions in Ethnically Divided Societies*, edited by S. Noel. Montreal; Kingston: McGill-Queen's Press.

O'Leary, B. and J. McGarry. 2005. "Federalism as a Method of Ethnic Conflict Resolution." Pp. 263–95 in *From Power Sharing to Democracy: Post-conflict Institutions in Ethnically Divided Societies*, edited by S. Noel. Montreal; Kingston: McGill-Queen's Press.

Otterbein, K.F. 2004. *How War Began*. College Station: Texas A&M University Press.

Posen, B. 1993. "Nationalism, the Mass Army, and Military Power." *International Security* 18(2): 80–124.

Posner, D.N. 2005. *Institutions and Ethnic Conflict in Africa*. New York: Cambridge University Press.

Reid, W. 1976. *Arms through the Ages*. New York: Harper and Row.

Ridley, M. 1997. *The Origins of Virtue: Human Instincts and the Evolution of Cooperation*. New York: Viking.

Sanderson, T. 1938. "Memorandum." In *British Documents on the Origins of the War 1898–1914*, edited by G.P. Gooch and H. Temperley. London: Stationery Office.

Shils, E. and M. Janowitz. 1948. "Cohesion and Disintegration in the Wehrmacht in World War II." *Public Opinion Quarterly* 12: 280–315.

Simmel, G. 1955 [1908]. *Conflict and the Web of Group Affiliations*. Glencoe: Free Press.

Smith, A.D. 1986. *Ethnic Origins of Nations*. Oxford: Blackwell.
  1999. *Myths and Memories of the Nations*. Oxford University Press.
  2003. *Chosen Peoples: Sacred Sources of National Identity*. Oxford University Press.
  2010. *Nationalism*. Cambridge: Polity.

Sollenberg, M. 2007. "From Bullets to Ballots: Using the People as Arbitrators to Settle Civil Wars." Pp. 178–204 in *Governance, Resources and Civil Conflict*, edited by Magnus Öberg and Strom Kaare. London: Routledge.

Stepan, A., J. Linz, and Y. Yadav. 2011. *Crafting State-Nations: India and Other Multinational Democracies*. Baltimore: Johns Hopkins University Press.

Sumner, W.G. 1906. *Folkways*. Boston: Ginn.

Tilly, C. 1985. "War Making and State Making as Organized Crime." Pp. 169–87 in *Bringing the State Back In*, edited by P. Evans. D. Rueschemeyer, and T. Skocpol. Cambridge University Press.
  1990. *Coercion, Capital and European States: AD 990–1990*. Oxford: Blackwell.

Van den Berghe, P. 1995. "Does Race Matter?" *Nations and Nationalism* 1(3): 357–68.

Van der Dennen, J. 1995. *The Origin of War*. Groningen: Origin Press.

Van Hooff, J. 1990. "Intergroup Competition and Conflict in Animals and Man." Pp. 23–54 in *Sociobiology and Conflict: Evolutionary Perspectives on Competition, Cooperation, Violence and Warfare*, edited by J. van der Dennen and V. Falger. New York: Chapman and Hall.

Westad, O.A. 2005. *The Global Cold War: Third World Interventions and the Making of Our Times*. Cambridge University Press.

Wimmer, A. 2002. *Nationalist Exclusion and Ethnic Conflicts: Shadows of Modernity*. Cambridge University Press.
  2011. "A Swiss Anomaly? A Relational Account of Boundary Making." *Nations and Nationalism* 17(4): 718–37.

Wimmer, A. and Y. Feinstein. 2010. "The Rise of the Nation-State across the World, 1816–2001." *American Sociological Review* 75(5): 764–90.

Wimmer, A. and B. Min. 2006. "From Empire to Nation-State: Explaining Wars in the Modern World, 1816–2001." *American Sociological Review* 71(6): 867–97.

2009. "The Location and Purpose of Wars Around the World: A New Global Dataset, 1816–2001." *International Interactions* 35(4): 390–417.

Wimmer, A., L.E. Cederman, and B. Min. 2009. "Ethnic Politics and Armed Conflict: A Configurational Analysis of a New Global Data Set." *American Sociological Review* 74(2): 316–37.

Part 1

Fighting for the nation?

1 Does nationalist sentiment increase fighting efficacy?

A skeptical view from the sociology of violence

Randall Collins

There is a belief among historians that the era of modern nationalism also promoted more violent wars, as in the *levée en masse* of the French revolutionary armies and the World War I binge of national bloodletting. Nationalism generated patriotic sentiment and more equal and merito-cratic military participation; hence the era of mass conscription (and sometimes enthusiastic volunteer) armies replaced the era of more limited battles carried out by aristocrats and mercenaries. The dark side of this nationalist fervor has been exposed repeatedly since the early twentieth century via ethnic cleansing and genocide.

The problem with this argument is that it fails to parcel out all the processes that affect fighting efficacy. Several major changes in military organization, technology, and tactics happened in the period overlapping with modern nationalism. I will argue that it was these changes that eventually made fighting more lethal, and that nationalism had at best an indirect effect, and more on the mobilization of soldiers to be killed than on their ability to kill others.

The baseline for all analysis of military behavior is that armies throughout most of history have operated at a low level of efficacy (for data and sources see Collins 2008). By this I mean that, putting all value judgments aside, a large proportion of soldiers engaged in combat fail to use their weapons, and most of those who do manage to wield swords and spears, or shoot arrows or guns, do so inaccurately; most blows and shots miss and do little damage. The heroism of warriors in combat has always been vastly exaggerated, and the reality obscured in mythology. Tribal warriors made a lot of noise, but only a few rushed forward from the safety of their own turf for a brief incursion into the enemy's, flinging an ill-directed missile, and quickly retreating. Such battles were ritual displays that usually came to an end when there was a single serious casualty, postponed to another time by mutual consent. Most damage in tribal war (and in the era of medieval clan vendettas as well) was done not by confronting the enemy but by ambushing isolated and temporarily outnumbered victims (Spierenburg 2008).

The phalanx style of warfare of ancient Greeks and Romans produced longer pitched battles, but their tight battle formations operated chiefly to march troops in an orderly group to the point of confrontation, and to some extent kept them from running away when fighting started. In battles described in detail by ancient historians (Xenophon, Julius Caesar, Plutarch, Appian), attacks were made with ferocious battle cries. In most cases a battle was won because one side lost its nerve and ran away before the other side reached them. Rapid retreat often saved their lives, unless the victors had cavalry who could chase them down and kill them from behind.[1] When well-disciplined phalanxes on both sides fought each other, the battle was usually a shoving match; only the front line could do any damage as long as the formation held up, and at close quarters their weapons had little room for lethal action. The phalanx with greater physical momentum had a greater chance of pushing the other back, and conceivably breaking its line. Hence ancient soldiers placed great emphasis on the advantage of seizing the heights and attacking downhill, and ancient historians describe situations in which an army was unnerved by seeing its enemy on the heights above it, and easily thrown into panic retreat before contact was made.[2] Thus ancient war, even where troops were held together by tight social organization on the battlefield, hinged largely on dramatic threats to break up and panic the opponent before actual physical damage was done.[3]

---

[1] Xenophon describes many battles (*c.* 400 BC) in which the Greek phalanx withstood assaults from less firmly disciplined Persian troops, or routed them merely by advancing in formation, but the battle ended with few casualties inflicted because the Greeks lacked cavalry to follow up.

[2] A complication is that very well-disciplined troops, chiefly Roman legions when faced with undisciplined barbarian armies, were capable of maintaining formation even when being attacked downhill. Both Greek and Roman soldiers were very aware of the value of their disciplined formation. The Romans in particular were skilled at building defensive walls and ditches, even in the midst of being attacked; thus they almost always won the battle of nerves – the battle of emotional dominance – when their opponents lacked their own level of organizational solidarity. When Roman legions fought each other in civil wars, the outcome was often a standoff, or a siege of rival engineering works. Exceptional battles between Roman troops could produce large casualties, where both sides had a high level of organization to sustain complex battle tactics.

[3] Ancient armies frequently had auxiliary troops of archers and stone-slingers, but these missiles were on the whole no more effective than crude long-distance weapons of the early gunpowder era. A disciplined phalanx of heavy troops – i.e. bearing heavy armor and shields – could withstand long-distance attacks, although it might not be able to catch the enemy to reciprocate the violence. The phalanx was always the decisive organizational core.

In the era of modern firearms, frontline performance continued to be largely ineffective. From their invention around 1500 until the late 1800s muskets, rifles and other individually operated guns were accurate only out to about one hundred yards; but even at shorter distances firing was wild and largely inaccurate and a large proportion of soldiers did not manage to fire their guns consistently. The basic problem was what I have called confrontational tension/fear (CT/F): the pattern of all face-to-face violence, where human confrontation raises emotional stress to such a level that fighters become clumsy, and are either paralyzed or wildly incompetent in using their weapons. In combat of all kinds, the height of courage is usually just to keep oneself from running away. Small-scale gang fights today, which resemble the undisciplined troop formations of earlier times, thus mainly have the pattern of loud bluster, brief encounters of wild firing, and rapid retreat.

Military technology over the centuries has become more lethal, in principle. Rifles have become accurate out to hundreds of meters, and automatic weapons have raised the sheer volume of firepower and have thus increased the rate of casualties inflicted, although the ratio of number of bullets per casualty has jumped vastly upwards – i.e. machine guns are not fired more accurately but make up for it by firing more and raising the level of random hits. Nevertheless, sociological studies in World War II and the Korean War found that only about 15–25 percent of frontline troops were regularly firing their guns at the enemy (Marshall 1947; further references and analysis in Collins 2008); most were near-paralyzed by CT/F. This was well into the era of full-scale nationalism; it was precisely the national, mass-conscript armies that looked the worst from the perspective of combat competence.

The key developments that made combat more effective, in the military sense, were in the realm of social organization. The first of these was the development of troop discipline through marching in formation. These paradeground armies not only inculcated some degree of group consciousness,[4] but were also designed to move troops around the battlefield while keeping their cohesion, and, by practice of drill, to make soldiers fire their guns en masse in a steady rhythm of firing and reloading. In practice, however, paradeground formations had trouble keeping up a steady fire, often shooting wildly and then breaking down into sporadic firing and uncoordinated participation. On the whole, these marching formations were most successful in keeping soldiers in place, keeping them from running away, and thus making them better targets

---

[4] The point is stressed by McNeill 1995, but he exaggerates the value of this innovation, since he fails to see the persistence of CT/F.

for enemy fire, especially long-distance artillery. This social innovation was better at enabling soldiers to stand and be killed than to kill others.

A second type of social innovation was the bayonet charge. As Anthony King (2007) has argued, troops under the stress of prolonged combat tend to lose morale, especially if they lose initiative and are pushed back by the enemy. Historically, one way of restoring emotional energy was to take the offensive, and to do so in a fashion that coordinated soldiers' bodies in a collective outburst of mutual entrainment: rushing at the enemy with fixed bayonets was more a way of keeping up one's own morale than of harming the enemy. In effect, it was a return to pre-firepower weapons, fighting with spears rather than guns. The bayonet charge was a way of remedying CT/F and the tendency for troops to fail to fire or to fire inaccurately; if fine motor coordination failed, the strategy was to put bodies into gross motion in order to get them in the faces of the enemy so that the latter felt more CT/F than the attackers. But it combined the main social technique of pre-modern fighting, the noise and intimidation of frenzied attack, with the discipline of modern organization. In the event, bayonet charges rarely led to so-called hand-to-hand combat, because the enemy faced with a bayonet charge that succeeded in getting close to them would usually break and run. Thus bayonet charges (notable in the US Civil War and World War I) were largely modes of counterattack. In the large combat formations of those wars involving tens of thousands of troops, commanders held troops in reserve, and sent them into action when assault had broken part of the front. Often this was successful in restoring the front line, in a pattern of reciprocal flows of attack (when the defense was emotionally overwhelmed and retreated) and counterattack (when the enemy advance lost momentum to a more coherent force advancing from deeper in defensive territory, and thus tended to flee back towards its starting point).[5] As in ancient warfare, battle among disciplined troops capable of keeping up some degree of formation in combat was largely a matter of imposing momentum on the enemy, scaring him into giving ground and losing social organization.[6] But in the more complex armies of modern war, generals took account of the tendency for parts of the army to break down, and sought to remedy this by designating reserve

[5] The crucial point at the battle of Gettysburg, where Union troops counterattacked with a bayonet charge against the Confederate attempt to turn the line at Little Round Top, was of this character.

[6] *Scaring* is not entirely the right word. The process was more like imposing momentum in the way that an athletic team imposes its momentum on its opponent – a phase of the game when one side is energized, well-coordinated, taking the initiative, while the other becomes sluggish, uncoordinated and ill-performing.

troops for counterattacks. Ancient battles tended to have one simple swing of momentum; modern battles might have many.

Historically, bayonet charges were most prominent in the era of nationalism. Does this mean that only troops motivated by national feelings could use them? I think it is a coincidence in time. The key social feature is the technique of warfare itself – the micro-interactional pattern of the soldiers with their fellows while carrying out a bayonet charge – rather than whatever national feelings there are in the background. As we know from sociological studies of troops in World War II, ideologies of whatever sort were rarely important for the motivation of frontline troops in any of the contending armies. Soldiers were mostly cynical about abstract rhetorics and fought largely out of feelings of loyalty to their immediate comrades (Holmes 1985; Stouffer et al. 1949). This plays into a third social innovation of modern warfare. The technique of moving troops on the battlefield by large parade-ground marching formations was becoming notably unsuccessful by the time of World War I; machine guns used by defensive troops inflicted heavy casualties on mass assaults, even when they relaxed strict paradeground order in crossing no-man's-land. By the end of the third year of war, late 1917, it was apparent that full-scale assaults were largely suicidal. All armies more or less simultaneously hit upon a solution: to break up formations into small groups specially trained to infiltrate trenches (Biddle 2004: 83–89; Gudmundsson 1989). In the German army, these were called *Stosstruppen*: shock troops. The veteran Ernst Jünger, in his book that became famous in Germany in 1920, *In Stahlgewittern* (In the Storm of Steel; 1920/2003), describes how these troops regarded themselves as elite, superseding even the traditional ranking of officers over enlisted men. The small-group tactics of men given local initiative did indeed succeed in breaking up the static lines of trench warfare, and in 1918 the Western front became more fluid again; but since both sides adopted the technique, the result was continued heavy casualties and the war's end through attrition. The *Stosstruppen* did indeed have high morale, but what motivated them was not national identity per se. They were an elite within the national army, not simply those who were most patriotic.

The name morphed into *Sturm Abteilung* (Storm Division), which was later appropriated by the Nazi militia. As Stefan Klusemann (2010) has shown, the Nazis were not simply one manifestation of nationalism among many. That was so, but precisely because there were so many nationalist movements in the post-war period, the Nazis had to innovate to stand out from the others, to attract attention and recruit more members by generating more emotional momentum, and one of their devices was to seize on the high-prestige identity of group formations inside the World War I army.

At the height of nationalist mobilization in modern history – World War II – all the devices of modern nationalism were operating full bore: propaganda, recruitment, and the total mobilization of populations on the home front for war support. There was also an explicit ideological sector of self-reflexive nationalism, so that some troops were explicitly called Nationalists.[7] But when we look at the organization of combat itself, we find that armies on the whole relied on other devices for motivating troops to perform in violent confrontation, such as the German army's technique of trying to keep small groups of friends together through their military experience (Shils and Janowitz 1948; for a controversial critique, see Bartov 1991). Less planned versions of this tended to happen as well in the Western armies, while the Communist armies used techniques of parallel hierarchy for surveillance and threat. Nazi troop formations additionally built up the status of elite divisions (the SS) within the military. Nationalism was more the rhetoric of politicians and the home front, while soldiers in combat were motivated and manipulated by small-group loyalties, coercion, or honorific elite standing inside the military itself.

I have been arguing, then, that the era of nationalism paralleled the era of modern warfare, but that the latter derived its effectiveness through innovating largely on the small-group level, away from overarching ideologies. In the latter half of the twentieth century in most Western countries a reaction against nationalism set in; this happened especially with the period of decolonization and domestic civil rights movements with their ideology of promoting ethnic subgroup identities and rejecting assimilation to a national identity. The Vietnam War was probably the most demoralized war fought by the US, in part because it happened at the height of domestic racial struggles, which also took place within the

[7] Among other reasons, to distinguish themselves pointedly from internationalist brands of ideology, notably communism, socialism, and to an extent, democracy. Peculiarly, the various nationalist movements tended to be international allies among themselves, showing that they were not simply localist or ethno/cultural-particularists. We thus need to distinguish among different brands of nationalism: (a) a naive, unreflective group identity (not necessarily primordial, but promoted ideologically during periods of state unification, monopolization of force, and state penetration into society); (b) ideologically reflexive nationalism, which sees itself on a more abstract level as a type of ideology combating other ideologies that it considers to be undermining the virtues of local solidarity. Paradoxically, the success of this ideological appeal tends to undermine or at least complicate its layer of naive nationalism. As Klusemann (2010) shows, the militant ideologically reflexive nationalists competed with naive nationalists for recruits and prominence in the political attention space.

military itself. But the US military also created a rotation policy for its troops that directly negated the lesson of World War II that troops fought especially out of loyalty to their buddies. Instead, every soldier was assigned for one year in the combat zone, giving soldiers an individual orientation and destroying group cohesion. Soldiers would commonly ask each other, "What's your number?," meaning "How many days do you have left before you rotate out?" (Gibson 1986). Both micro-interactional structures and national ideology were undermined at the same time.

I have been placing emphasis on frontline infantry troops, since this is where the problem of CT/F is strongest, and the innovations in social organization that I have discussed were solutions above all for infantry fighting morale. Another long-term trend is technological, but it also plays into the social interactions of combat. CT/F exists at the most human level of confrontation: where fighters can see their enemies as human beings. Thus another solution to CT/F has been to improve the technology of fighting at a distance. Artillery is as old as infantry guns. But the earliest cannon were clumsy and inaccurate; they could be used most effectively to demolish fortresses, thereby bringing an end to medieval warfare with castles and sieges of walled towns. Thus the early effect of artillery was to produce more infantry battles out in the open. Artillery became more mobile (when horse-drawn) and more accurate, and proved to be quite lethal against paradeground infantry formations. At the same time, infantry reduced the traditionally elite cavalry to a minor factor, since horses could not stand up to concentrated fire. But the real success of artillery lay in the fact that it solved the problem of CT/F, at least for its own gunners. They fired from so far away from the enemy – by the early nineteenth century at distances up to a mile – that they could no longer see the men they were killing. Artillery service was not regarded as very heroic, probably for the very reason of firing at an impersonal distance, but the success of Napoleon's armies was due above all to his appreciation of rapid deployment of light, mobile artillery around a battlefield. In effect, the French realized that paradeground infantry formations were chiefly a way to move large numbers of troops into combat, and to keep them from running away, but that flexible use of artillery caused most of the casualties and broke down enemy organization. I would not particularly stress Napoleon as an individual in bringing about this style of combat; the fact that he was an artillery officer implies that it was this combat branch that was coming to the fore.

The nationalism of the French Revolution and its *levée en masse* coincided with a technical development in the organization of combat, but examined more closely, it appears that it was "Napoleonic" organizational innovations that made the French armies so effective. Nationalism was more a phenomenon of the home front, affecting combat because it produced much larger armies, allowing French generals to carry out lengthy wars on far-flung battlefields, and to absorb large casualties with strategic confidence of replacing them. By the time the Revolutionary/ Napoleonic Wars had gone on for twenty years, French opponents had developed a number of tactical and organizational innovations of their own such as the guerrilla tactics avoiding pitched combat in Spain, and the Russian strategy of avoiding battle and relying on French logistics attrition; by the time of Waterloo, English and Prussian armies had caught up with and surpassed the French in staff organization and logistical support, as well as the effective use of mobile artillery (Black 2010).

Technical innovation in the military was most important when it also facilitated social innovation. The long-term trend has been towards more and more distant combat. By World War I, siege guns on land, and naval guns offshore or in naval battles, had ranges of up to ten miles and carried enormous explosive power. These gunners did not suffer from CT/F, and although their guns were not terribly accurate, the sheer volume of firepower laid on over a period of time could cause considerable destruction. In this sense, warfare – as killing power, and also as power to demoralize an enemy into defeat – became more efficient. There is also an aspect in which successful military innovations tend to cancel each other out; what one side develops to its proven advantage soon becomes imitated by rival armies. Just as *Stosstruppen* were adopted on all sides to end the impasse of trench warfare, long-distance artillery was similarly imitated. Imitation of the most effective combat techniques (both material and social) means that opponents tend to neutralize each other's advantages; wars become prolonged contests of mutual attrition. Hence modern-era wars have tended to become longer and more costly, both in lives and materiel. This has an indirect effect upon nationalism, since wars demand more resources extracted from the social base. In this respect, I am inclined to emphasize the reverse pathway: innovations in military technique (social/material) increase political pressure for national mobilization.

There are some further feedback loops from military innovations to the ideology of war, especially on the home front. Air power is the epitome of long-distance fighting, thus it solves the problem of CT/F for the fighters, and allows both a more heroic side of war to reemerge, and more devastating involvement of civilians, who become military targets. Take the heroic side first. Air power began as flying surveillance, and quickly became flying artillery. But since air power can be used as defense against air power,[8] World War I soon invented the aerial combat or "dogfight." This was romanticized into duels in the sky (although in fact fighters flew in larger formations and got much of their success from coordinated tactics). Fighter pilots became the military specialty with the highest morale and the greatest public adulation. The high morale came from low levels of CT/F – avoiding the gruelling life of the front line, while flying home to base in the rear area after every successful mission. Scoring systems were devised to count the number of aerial kills, giving ranks as "aces," and sports-like record-keeping contests over who was the highest-scoring ace. The jaunty, death-defying fighter pilot became publicized as the chief hero of modern wars, especially in World Wars I and II. Here again military technique, interacting with the social conditions of combat, allowed certain military specialties to be singled out and presented to the civilian population as idealized representations of the nation at war. The adulation of pilots was prominent in most belligerent nations, including Germany, France, England, the US, Russia, and Japan.

The downfall of this heroizing of the fighter pilot came about because of the shift to the era of asymmetrical wars. From the Korean War onwards most wars were fought between armies of vastly different technological capacity. US and UK fighter jets were so superior to Russian (and sometimes French) jets used in Korea, Vietnam, and the Gulf Wars that the system of aces went into abeyance. By the latter wars, there were too few enemy planes willing to risk combat for victorious pilots to build up sufficiently high scores. The trend was also abetted by long-distance electronic control of targeting, so that individual pilots had less autonomy; by the 1990s, fighter jets were used mainly as flying artillery, an unglamorous task of impersonal destruction at long distance.

Turn now to civilian involvement. One might argue that the twentieth-century trend towards the mass bombing of civilian targets was the result of the intensified nationalism of that period. But it has a technical rationale, as the emphasis of modern war turned to destroying enemy logistics and economic base. Bombing economic targets makes large numbers of civilians victims of war, and in that sense makes war more literally a war on the nation. There may be a feedback loop here, such that civilians subjected to such attack adopt a more stridently nationalistic attitude towards enemies and call for retaliation in kind; this loop played itself out in German attacks on Britain in World War II, which in

---

[8] It isn't clear that aerial combat is the best defense against aircraft attack; anti-aircraft ground fire itself accounts for some portion of EAD (enemy aircraft destroyed), at levels of effectiveness that have changed considerably over the last one hundred years.

turn fuelled the fire-bombing of German cities. Consciousness of the European experience probably increased the motivation for the US to use atomic bombs against Japan (among many other motivations). But it is not clear that nationalism is the fundamental starting point of this loop; military techniques, following their own momentum, brought about actions that at least temporarily exacerbated nationalist hatreds. But on the whole the aftermath of the civilian bombing tactics of World War II was a revulsion against this kind of nationalist excess, and surprisingly rapid reconciliation between the peoples of the once-belligerent nations.

To bring the survey up to the present, the trend of war-making in the post-Vietnam era has been the advance of two kinds of techniques: on one hand, a shift towards the even greater depersonalization of combat by long-distance technologies, and, on the other, the increasing use of local, small-group social techniques for generating combat morale. Both increase the efficiency of fighting, while reducing reliance on nationalism, perhaps to a minimum.

Particularly in the most advanced militaries (the US and UK), the trend has been towards high-tech weapons systems that integrate many components in delivering firepower to the target. Surveillance is carried out by satellites, aircraft, and increasingly by drones whose operators may be thousands of kilometers from the battlefield. GPS coordinates, infra-red sensors, laser tagging of targets, as well as computer analysis of aerial photos and video feed, divide the labor between those who seek the targets and those who physically service the weapons; many humans and machines cooperate before frontline troops fire a weapon that actually kills someone. Computer connections, radios, and cell phones make each combat vehicle or weapons platform (in current parlance) part of a large web of communications links. Whether this increases the efficacy of combat depends on one's criteria; the system combining long-distance sensors, information analysis, command-and-control, and execution on the battlefield may result in the misidentification of enemy targets and hitting civilians (or ostensible civilians, given the tendency to hide in civilian areas and disguise). If battle criteria are expanded to include the "hearts and minds" of a potentially hostile population, high levels of efficacy are elusive. By more old-fashioned criteria (eg. those of World War II), high-tech warfare is capable of causing a great deal of damage to personnel and materiel. Among other reasons, high-tech computer-linked combat diffuses authority and makes most weapons into group-operated weapons, and this is the type of fighting that has always had the highest firing rate, where social support overcomes CT/F.

But my chief analytical question is whether high-tech combat efficacy is correlated with nationalism. The answer is no. In today's military the predominant atmosphere is professionalism, or at least bureaucratic routine. For the great majority of combat participants, fighting is at a distance from enemies who have no human character and impose little self-sacrifice; no ideological fervor is called for.

This is similarly the case with the motivational techniques used in contemporary military training and in daily life in a war zone. The US military is one of the few organizations that have paid serious attention to social science findings. Low firing rates among World War II infantry were recognized and met by training reforms that emphasized realistic combat situations rather than artificial target practice on the firing range, and that relied on the technology of high-volume automatic weapons. Modern soldiers are taught to lay down a heavy fire rather than to aim. Small-group cohesion is now given great emphasis. Rigid lines of authority from higher officers have been largely deemphasized in favor of initiative by low-ranking officers on the spot, and combat operations are designed and enacted in a spirit embodying the principles of inter-action rituals (King 2006). All of this means that the modern military is more emotionally and morally self-sufficient than the mass conscript armies of the early and mid twentieth century. Soldiers in today's all-volunteer army might be viewed as mercenaries, insofar as they take on the work of fighting for wages rather than for ideology or through compulsion, but military organization has done quite a good job at motivating them. Besides techniques of small-group solidarity and the dispersion of authority, many frontline combat soldiers are given elite status through the proliferation of specialized troops: Marines, Navy SEALS, Special Forces, Rangers, Delta Force, etc. This is not to say that troops in today's high-tech military are totally lacking in patriotic/nationalist rhetoric (or indeed in some degree of cynicism and burnout), but nationalist ideology per se appears to be a negligible component in what makes them fight.

The bottom line is that today's high-tech armies have much higher fighting efficacy than any previous army historically. On a man-for-man basis, the delivered firepower of today's military is orders of magnitude higher than it was sixty years ago. The Western troops that fought in the 1991 Gulf War and subsequent wars are probably the least nationalist troops that the US or England has had since the eighteenth century, and arguably they are the best fighters.

One question that dangles is whether nationalism has affected the performance of the guerrilla-style armies of recent times. Such armies have fought against Western high-tech armies in asymmetrical wars. They have also fought against each other in symmetrical low-tech wars (such as many wars in Africa up through the Libyan Civil War), and these are the armies of contemporary ethnic cleansing. Is nationalism important either for mobilizing them, or for their performance in combat? There are two sub-questions: are Iraqi insurgents, Afghani Taliban, and similar guerrilla fighters motivated to join because of nationalist sentiments? And are such sentiments important in whatever fighting success they have?

Impressionistically, it appears that guerrilla armies have been recruited for many different reasons and ideologies. Religious justifications vary from the Lord's Resistance Army in Central Africa (with its horrific techniques for coercing child soldiers) to the pan-Islamism of Al-Qaeda. Nationalism is one rhetorical strand among others. As to their fighting efficacy, something like nationalism (or another idealistic ideology) may be important in resistance wars against Western high-tech armies. Here the insurgents operate without airpower, armor, and long-distance firing and command-and-control systems. This means that they must have a very different motivational and organizational system than the professionalized Western armies. I suspect that small-group loyalties are crucial, as is perennially the case. But the nature of an asymmetrical war fought against an occupying enemy army has one advantage to the defender: it needs only hold out sufficiently long, intermittently doing continuous small-scale damage to the invader's logistics and isolated outposts, until the political will to maintain the invasion dwindles.

Hypothetically, nationalism could provide the motivating ideology to hold out for a long period of time; empirically we just don't know if this is true. The key factor might be that the small-scale victories of guerrilla resistance support small-group morale enough so that the movement sustains itself over time.

In conclusion, there is little evidence that nationalism makes troops fight better. The main problem of combat is overcoming confrontational tension/fear. Nationalism, like all other ideologies, simply ignores the problem, and covers it up in practice by rhetoric and mystification. Troops motivated chiefly by nationalism and unsupported by workable techniques of combat performance tend to lose their nationalist fervor fairly soon (probably within a year) and to become cynical or alienated. It is not surprising that the peak level of non-firing in combat was found in the bureaucratic armies of World War II, at the peak of mass democratic nationalism. On the contrary, it has been those armies that emphasized small-group coordination and morale, and other techniques of social support and prestige within the military, that have been the most effective fighters – effective at killing and destroying, at any rate.

But nationalism may well have played an indirect role in making some nation-states win wars. It is one thing to recruit troops, another thing to get them into effective action on the battlefield. Something like nationalism or patriotism was important in motivating large numbers of volunteer troops in the US Civil War of 1861–65 (on the Confederate side as well, although this was a suddenly constructed nationalism), and idealistic appeals of the nation-state were at the center of the mass recruiting drives of World War I, and to an extent in World War II. On the whole, national appeals created the huge armies capable of winning by years of attrition. Given the relatively ineffective performance of such troops in combat, nationalism made it easier to be killed than to kill others – easier to lose than to win in combat. But given enough troops mobilized from the nation, sheer numbers would tell. Nationalism has lost many battles but won some massive wars.

REFERENCES

Bartov, O. 1991. *Hitler's Army*. New York: Oxford University Press.
Biddle, S. 2004. *Military Power. Explaining Victory and Defeat in Modern Battle*. Princeton University Press.
Black, J. 2010. *The Battle of Waterloo: A New History*. London: Icon Books.
Collins, R. 2008. *Violence: A Micro-Sociological Theory*. Princeton University Press.
Gibson, J.W. 1986. *The Perfect War: Technowar in Vietnam*. New York: Atlantic Monthly Press.
Gudmundsson, B. 1989. *Stormtroop Tactics: Innovation in the German Army, 1914-1918*. New York: Praeger.
Holmes, R. 1985. *Acts of War: The Behavior of Men in Battle*. New York: Free Press.
Jünger, E. 1920/2003. *In Stahlgewittern* [*In the Storm of Steel*]. London: Allen Lane.
King, A. 2006. "The Word of Command: Communication and Cohesion in the Military." *Armed Forces and Society* 32(4): 493–512.
  2007. "The Existence of Group Cohesion in the Armed Forces: A Response to Guy Siebold." *Armed Forces and Society* 33(4): 638–45.
Klusemann, S. 2010. "After State Breakdown: Dynamics of Multi-party Conflict, Violence, and Paramilitary Mobilization in Russia 1904–1920, Germany 1918–1934, and Japan 1853–1877." Ph.D. dissertation, University of Pennsylvania.
Marshall, S.L.A. 1947. *Men Against Fire. The Problem of Battle Command*. Norman: University of Oklahoma Press.
McNeill, W.H. 1995. *Keeping Together in Time: Dance and Drill in Human History*. Cambridge, MA: Harvard University Press.
Shils, E. and M. Janowitz. 1948. "Cohesion and Disintegration in the Wehrmacht in World War II." *Public Opinion Quarterly* 12(2): 280–315.
Spierenburg, P. 2008. *A History of Murder: Personal Violence in Europe from the Middle Ages to the Present*. Cambridge: Polity Press.
Stouffer, S.A., A.A. Lumsdaine, M.H. Lumsdaine, R.M. Williams Jr., M.B. Smith, I.L. Janis, S.A. Star, and L.S. Cottrell Jr. 1949. *The American Soldier: Vol. II Combat and Its Aftermath*. Princeton University Press.

2   Mercenary, citizen, victim
The rise and fall of conscription in the West

Richard Lachmann

States take risks when they arm troops and ask them to fight, kill, and die on their behalf. Most obviously, soldiers hold weapons that they could turn on their employers. There is a long literature on when and why soldiers mount coups, but that is not my concern here. Instead, I want to examine how states incur moral, political, and financial obligations when they hire, draft, or recruit troops to fight wars and how those obligations affect states' capacities to fight wars.

My focus is restricted to "Western" polities. Rulers in medieval and early modern Europe relied primarily upon mercenaries and upon aristocrats and their armed retainers. Rulers were limited in the length and intensity of commitment they could demand from either sort of fighter. The relationship between soldier and state was fundamentally transformed when and where states were able to impose conscription or convince citizens to volunteer. Beginning with the revolutionary United States and France, states offered draftees and volunteers a growing array of political and social rights. The transformation of subjects into citizens gave states access to armies of unprecedented size, endurance, and commitment, and made possible the bloodbaths of the nineteenth and twentieth centuries, from the Napoleonic Wars to the American Civil War, to the world wars (Rhodes 1988). The first part of this chapter is devoted to explaining the process and consequences of the transition from mercenary to civilian armies.

Recently, European and American citizens have been increasingly less willing to serve in the military or to endure casualties. The aversion to risking the lives of draftee and volunteer citizens, and resulting reliance on tactics that magnify civilian casualties in the countries where the US and its allies fight wars, has been labelled the "new Western way of war" (Shaw 2005). That description begs the questions of why Western citizens and their governments became adverse to casualties, and how low-casualty warfare has affected, and been affected by, understandings of citizens' rights and obligations. I seek to answer those questions in the latter part of this chapter.

Mercenaries: war without obligation

Medieval European rulers who wanted to expand their militaries beyond kin- and community-based corps of fighters, and reduce their reliance on aristocrats and their armed retainers, had to rely upon mercenaries. Of course, rulers could hire mercenaries only when they had money. Our understanding of states and wars has been shaped by the fiscal-military model, developed most clearly by Charles Tilly (1990). From that perspective, rulers slowly and unevenly developed the capacity to appropriate resources from subjects, which could be used to pay for armed forces. Armies, in turn, were used to acquire new territories that yielded additional revenues and to intimidate subjects within existing territories to turn over more of their possessions to the ruler.

Tilly's model is helpful in accounting for the era in which rulers relied on mercenaries for most of their fighting forces. Mercenaries, by definition, were fungible. They fought for whomever paid them. A ruler's lack of money led to less energetic fighting (if the mercenaries thought they might be paid in the future), or outright desertion (if they abandoned hope of ever getting paid), or looting of the deadbeat ruler's civilian population (either as a way to get the ruler to pay his arrears, or as a way to recover some money on their way home or to join another army). In a world of mercenaries, the side with the most money usually won the war. The military skill of the commanders could make a difference, especially if the balance of forces was close, but wars were usually not determined by single battles, and as a result combatants with more resources were likely to prevail over the course of wars lasting years.

The problem with this model is not in its assumptions about mercenaries' fungibility and the negligible long-term effect of temporary differences in soldiers' technical skills and commanders' strategic intelligence. The focus on money also puts military technology in its proper place, since, with rare exceptions, innovations in weaponry were quickly copied by any polity with the resources to pay for them. Rather, the fiscal-military model fails to acknowledge or explain how little of a ruler's nominal revenues were actually available to hire and equip fighters. Much, often most, tax revenue was lost to corruption and self-dealing by tax collectors, and to the officials charged with spending it on men and weapons. Corruption often showed up first in a lack of food for soldiers, which led to mass desertions (Parrott 1995). That is why there is so little relation between the size of a state's budget and its ability to conquer territories within Europe or colonies in the rest of the world. The richest power of each era (Spain from the 1560s to the 1600s and France from the 1630s to 1789) did not add territories during most of its years of fiscal supremacy, and the powers that accumulated territories (the Netherlands and then Britain) as often as not had smaller budgets than rivals who failed to add to their holdings or lost lands to poorer powers (Lachmann 2009).

Rulers attempted to supplement mercenaries with aristocrats' armed retainers and with local militias, but the loyalty and effectiveness of such forces were generally less than those of hired fighters. Aristocrats' soldiers were loyal to their patrons and fought only under their command. Aristocrats could, and often did, withdraw their men from battle if they disagreed with the king's war aims or if the ruler failed to entice them with favors to remain in the war. The cost of such favors reduced rulers' long-term ability to pay for mercenaries in future wars and thus, in the absence of significant territorial gains, which rarely happened, such favors were counterproductive. In any case, aristocrats retained command of their men and often failed to coordinate their plans with those of the king or his generals, and therefore their troops were of limited strategic value even when they fought alongside the king's mercenaries. Similarly, local militias, who were unpaid, did not travel far from the home towns they were willing to defend and usually were under the control of aristocrats (Mjoset and Van Holde 2002: 10). They could hamper invading armies, but rarely were significant in the outcome of wars.

Aristocrats' unreliability, frequent desertion by unpaid mercenaries and by militias, and the unprofessional leadership of noble officers "made Old Regime warfare profoundly indecisive. At the strategic level, limited aims – 'a few colonies or provinces' – did not warrant great risks" (Knox 2001: 61). In any case, few polities ever had the resources to mount wars that could keep enough troops in the field for long enough to achieve great objectives; hence permanent changes in European political boundaries were rare and usually minor once small polities were consolidated within European states by the seventeenth century.

To be sure, early modern European wars were more lethal than medieval campaigns, which often were mounted to capture rival kings and nobles to be held for ransom (Rogers 1995). However, it is a mistake to exaggerate the ubiquity of a "Western way of war" which Hanson (1989) claims was developed by the ancient Greeks, and which Rogers (1995) dates to the Hundred Years War. Yes, ancient Greek armies were mainly infantry, and their goal was to kill the enemy rather than take territory by maneuver. However, battles were short (Hanson shows that the heavy armor worn by the Greeks, which minimized casualties, also exhausted their wearers in a few hours), and the citizen soldiers returned to their farms or cities, literally at the end of the day. Medieval soldiers travelled further, but their battles too were short and the survivors often then returned home to fight again months or years later.

Long, high-intensity, and high-casualty wars, with decisive outcomes, required a large and steady supply of troops and a permanent officer corps with the professionalism to train their men to mount disciplined infantry and cavalry charges (Lynn 2001; Rogers 1995). Effective officers were expensive, since they had to be paid salaries and kept provisioned over their entire careers, but even wealthy rulers often lacked the political leverage to remove the dilettante aristocrats who commanded the mercenaries, as well as their own armed men, in early modern European armies and navies. Aristocrats were replaced, or induced to become serious professionals, only when and where rulers were able to challenge nobles' political control over military commands or to buy out or abolish venal military officers.

States made slow and uneven progress in purging and professionalizing officer corps. Rulers enjoyed limited success in prying control over "state" revenues from the tax farmers, venal officials, and local elites who siphoned off the funds those rulers needed to hire large armies and keep them in the field. Only Britain, and Prussia to a lesser extent, made significant progress in reforming their militaries in the eighteenth century. Yet the modest military successes of those polities (and Britain's defeat by American revolutionaries) should make us wary of assuming that a military revolution would have occurred in the absence of conscription (Murray and Knox 2001).

Conscription and the origins of citizenship

Conscription upended the relationship between fiscal capacity and military outcomes. For the first time, states were able to enlist armed men beyond their fiscal capacity and without appealing to local elites. Such a radical innovation, which was so destabilizing of existing elite power and privilege, was at first possible only in revolutionary polities, beginning with the United States and France. Here old elites were fatally weakened and revolutionary leaders, who themselves were in mortal danger from counter-revolutionaries, saw the draft as the most powerful way to elicit loyalty by giving the masses a stake in the state's survival, making them citizens with individual and uniform political rights as well as military obligations. The officers in the new, revolutionary American and French armies accepted the new, professional ethos, either because they had not been officers in the old-regime militaries and therefore had no privileges to lose, or because they had been low-level officers and any old regime sinecures they enjoyed were outweighed by what they received from their positions as professional officers in the new military.

Subjects became citizens and identified themselves as full members of national states primarily through military service. For most Europeans, their first significant interaction with government officials from beyond their localities came when they were drafted into the military. In addition to training for war, recruits and draftees were taught the national language, which became the working language of the armed forces, and often were given lessons in the civics and history of the state they served.

Service in a national army brought soldiers together with men from elsewhere in the polity, creating intense feelings of membership in a collectivity, the "sense of a deep, horizontal comradeship" that Benedict Anderson (1983: 7) writes about, which extended far beyond the lineages, occupational groups, religious communities, and localities that were the limits of almost all humans' feelings of solidarity until the American and French revolutions. "Citizen conscription ... help[ed] consolidate a politically mass-mobilizing regime ... by rendering all citizens formally equal ... by integrating them and their state into a single polity ... by politicizing them, their relations to one another, and to the state" (Kestnbaum 2002: 131).

Conscription, created by revolutionary governments in the United States and France as a desperate move to stave off defeat and the annihilation of their young regimes, transformed the strategy and dynamics of war. Conscription allowed armies to be replenished even after enduring massive casualties, making possible a strategy of total war first developed by Napoleon (Bell 2007), which vanquished states practicing older forms of warfare and dependent on aristocratic fighters and mercenaries.

Conscription transformed war in all its aspects, sparking organizational, ideological, and technological changes that combined to create a "military revolution." Eighteenth-century innovations in military technology and the use of drills to train soldiers were limited in their effectiveness by mercenaries' frequent desertion and the inability to control aristocratic officers who had the political autonomy to defy their supposed commanders and who held to "old-fashioned" notions of "courage and muscular prowess" in personal combat (McNeill 1982: 172) that led them to eschew the use of technologies and tactics that would allow for decisive outcomes with massive casualties.

The high levels of desertion prevalent in aristocratic and mercenary militaries fell off dramatically in conscript armies. Soldiers' loyalty was the product of a mix of factors that varied from polity to polity and over time: ideological fervor clearly was a powerful factor in the American,

French and later revolutionary armies, even if such fervor lessened over time and was not a significant factor in motivating conscripts who fought for ordinary regimes. Nationalist desires for vengeance and retribution motivated the soldiers of countries that had been attacked. For example, US soldiers in World War II were animated mainly by the thought of taking vengeance for the sneak attack on Pearl Harbor rather than by revulsion at vaguely understood fascist ideology or the, then, largely unknown Nazi genocide (Dower 2010). However, the main factor that kept conscripts from deserting was the enhanced legal and organizational capacities of the mass armed forces commanded by professional officers. Draftees were legally required to serve in a way that mercenaries and aristocrats and their retainers were not. Armies developed and employed police powers to enforce those legal obligations by catching and punishing deserters, often by execution.

As armed forces developed organizational and logistical capacities, and commanded budgets that allowed them to place large armies in combat far from home, conscripts were essentially marooned in war, unable to return home unless the war ended. This created a new set of loyalties and motivations among soldiers that, ultimately, was more resonant and powerful than ideology or nationalism. As one American private in World War II wrote: "[I] wondered a bit about what the guys with me thought they were fighting for, twenty-year-olds mostly from the Mid-West, never crossed the ocean before … If we killed we could go on living. Whatever we were fighting for seemed irrelevant" (quoted in Fussel 1989: 140). Another American soldier added: "It took me darn a whole war to figure what I was fighting for … It was the other guys. Your outfit, the guys in your company, but especially your platoon" (quoted in Fussell 1989: 140).

Militaries quickly figured out that instilling identity among and loyalty to the platoon and company was as important a part of basic training as teaching actual military techniques. Total war fed upon itself. If soldiers were trapped in a war until victory, they fought harder than if they were close enough to home, or supervised loosely enough, to slacken their effort or desert when the going got tough. Desertion in conscript armies is common only at point of defeat; it is the final unravelling of a losing combatant and merely quickens an inevitable outcome.

Conscription changed the qualities armies valued in their officers as well as in ordinary troops. Greater control over draftees, combined with their greater commitment, made it worthwhile and feasible for armies to invest time and resources into training troops. Aristocratic officers lacked the skills, desire, and work ethic to carry out intensive basic training for masses of recruits. Only those militaries that were able to eliminate or sideline dilettante aristocrats from the officer corps were able to create the organizational space and time in which professional officers could develop programs to properly train conscripts and volunteers whose military skills then quickly eclipsed those of supposedly professional mercenary and knightly fighters (Knox 2001).

Aristocrats emigrated or were purged from the French military during the Revolution, allowing them to be replaced with non-commissioned officers and soldiers who were committed to revolutionary politics and to new modes of warfare within unified hierarchical command. In any case, the new French officers lacked the noble titles or political power to resist orders from the top (McNeill 1982: Chapter 6). In Britain, reform of the officer corps remained incomplete throughout the nineteenth century. Numerous officers got their positions through patronage, profited from their offices, and sold their positions upon retirement (Harries-Jenkins 1977). This had a deleterious effect on the fighting prowess and morale of British troops, who like their twenty-first-century American counterparts, seemed to do best when turning their overwhelming advantage in firepower upon non-Western adversaries. The British navy, by contrast, reformed its officer corps in the eighteenth century (Baugh 1999), but then its mission was far more vital to British imperial domination, and so the self-serving antics of well-born officers were potentially more damaging and less tolerated by Parliament and the government. Naval officers were also more likely to be stationed far from home for much longer periods of time than army officers and therefore had a harder time maintaining and mobilizing political allies to override their commanders' orders in the field.

The old European regimes adopted reforms slowly and unevenly because the institution of conscription and the professionalization of the officer corps subverted aristocratic privileges. Thus, military reform was a struggle between an old ruling class with the capacity to protect its control over, and often ownership of, military offices, and reformist state elites who initially were far weaker than the entrenched interests they challenged. Reformers succeeded as much as they did for two reasons. First, defeat or the threat of defeat brought some aristocrats around to the need for reform. It did so because, beginning with Napoleon, defeat meant not just the loss of bits of territory and colonies, but destruction of the old regime and loss of all aristocratic privileges under foreign occupation. Second, and far more important, reformers gained access to alternative military and political resources through conscription. By drafting men and promoting officers from the ranks, reformers created new allies that challenged, counterbalanced, or overwhelmed aristocratic resistance to military reform in Europe.

The advantages of conscript over aristocrat and mercenary armies became evident to a widening set of military reformers and rulers over the course of the nineteenth century, most often through observing or experiencing defeat (Knox 2001). Prussia instituted the draft in 1814 and phased out the use of volunteer militias, as did both the Confederacy and the Union during the American Civil War, and Japan in 1872, providing the basis for the latter's twentieth-century imperial expansion (Jansen 2000; Mjoset and Van Holde 2002: 29–45). Britain, which took advantage of its wealth to pay its large pool of impoverished proletarians to serve in the military, was the last major power to adopt conscription, which it did only in 1916 after much of its volunteer force was wiped out in boneheaded assaults on German trenches (Fussell 1975).

Citizens with benefits

States rewarded the service and sacrifice of their draftees, or were compelled by soldiers and their families to pay for it after wars, with memorials for the dead and civil rights and social benefits for veterans and their families. Even if troops were animated to fight and persevere in battle for their comrades in platoon and company, they also saw themselves as soldiers for their country and expected to be recognized as such by their government and fellow citizens.

Conscription transformed the ways in which states memorialized war dead. War monuments, in the era of mercenaries and aristocrats, continued the ancient tradition of honoring generals' victories rather than the sacrifices of common soldiers. The Arc de Triomphe traces the evolution of war commemoration. It was originally designed, following the model of imperial Roman triumphal arches, to mark Napoleon's victory at Austerlitz in 1806, and only generals' names were carved on it. After World War I it became the site for the Tomb of the Unknown Soldier (Mosse 1990: 94–95, 99), which in France and in all other countries with such tombs, symbolizes the nation's commitment to honor every one of its war dead.

Soldiers' value to the nation was marked by increasingly strenuous and comprehensive efforts to find and recover the bodies of the dead and to place them in cemeteries. Dead soldiers have been recognized in stages, with the first major effort by any nation being that of the US during and after the Civil War. The Civil War began an American tradition, quickly imitated by many countries in the world, of accepting a national obligation to recover and recognize the body of each citizen who died for the nation. Before then, casualties were known to their families and communities but often were unknown and unacknowledged by the nation. Even families were not always certain if a loved one who had left home had gone to war, or if his failure to return meant that he had died in war or just preferred to make a new life elsewhere.

The United States, which pioneered conscription, has also been the innovator and the nation most committed to recovering and commemorating war dead. The Federal government in the 1867 National Cemeteries Act, the first such legislation in the world, took responsibility for identifying and properly burying each of the Union dead as an obligation to both its citizen-soldiers and their grieving families. The rituals of identification and burial individualized the dead at the same time as they became "a collective that represented something more and something different from the many thousands of individual deaths that it comprised … The reburial movement created a constituency of the slain, insistent in both its existence and its silence, men whose very absence from American life made them a presence that could not be ignored" (Faust 2008: 249). In other words, the Civil War dead were identified individually so that their families could take solace from the link, which their burial in military cemeteries symbolized, between their deaths and the great national cause.

The practice of identifying the dead and burying them in military cemeteries became standard in all Western militaries. This commitment was exemplified by the effort to recover bodies on the battlefield, even at the risk of the lives of other soldiers. The admonition to never let "a fallen comrade fall into the hands of the enemy" has become de facto policy in all branches of the US military. It has been fetishized in the ever more elaborate and expensive efforts to identify the remains of US troops from past wars, especially in Vietnam, with teams from the US Defence Department tracking down rumors, meeting with Vietnamese bounty hunters, and sending bone fragments back to America for DNA tests.

Bodies are recovered not just to honor the dead, but in the belief that the proper burial of remains will comfort the families of the dead. Cemeteries were seen in the nineteenth century as the proper sites for familial mourning that should and would continue until the dead soldiers and their relatives were reunited in heaven (Faust 2008: 137–70). In the late twentieth century, as psychological theories about stages of grief have modified, if not supplanted religious notions, the recovery and burial of soldiers' bodies came to be seen as essential for families' "closure." In both periods, governments, along with artists and journalists, sought to spare families and the broader citizenry the gory details of injuries and fatalities. The bodies of soldiers were sanitized in paintings; even photographs were posed to look like paintings, with blood and visible wounds hidden, although the photos soldiers took for themselves and often shared with families were realistic (Mosse 1990: 128–33, 149–51).

Soldiers, through service and especially in death, were acknowledged as truly equal citizens. "The cemetery at Gettysburg was arranged so every grave was of equal importance; William Saunders' design, like Lincoln's speech, affirmed that every dead soldier mattered equally regardless of rank or station. This was a dramatic departure from the privileging of rank and station that prevailed" in all earlier wars (Faust 2008: 100). Jews and Catholics were regarded and buried as equals with Protestants in the Civil War. Recognition of equality came later in other countries. British soldiers were arrayed in battle by order of seniority, and military cemeteries were segregated by class, throughout World War I. Only at the end of the war did the Imperial War Graves Commission bury the dead of all classes together in the British cemeteries in France (Fussell 1975: 197). The French and German governments also constructed cemeteries in which their dead were buried together and without regard for rank at the end of World War I (Mosse 1990: 80–93). As in the United States after the Civil War, the victors were buried in government-funded cemeteries, while the defeated Germans and Austrians, like US Confederates, were buried by private organizations, which like the Confederate burial societies became forces for revanchist politics.

Citizens' equality was also recognized by the progressive abolition of provisions allowing those with money to buy out their military service obligations, and by the use of merit promotion to fill the officer corps at ever higher ranks (Mjoset and Van Holde 2002: 10). The inability of the rich and privileged to avoid service, and publicized instances of public officials, nobles, and the wealthy killed in war, emphasized that equality, even if in reality well-placed young men could avoid service or maneuver to secure positions safely away from the front lines (as the well-publicized cases of George W. Bush, Bill Clinton, Dan Quayle, Ronald Reagan, and Lyndon Johnson illustrate). Similarly, well-known generals from modest backgrounds, Napoleon most famously, served to highlight the notion that national militaries were open to all and relied on the entire nation's talent to achieve victory.

Cemeteries and military burial rituals emphasized the dead soldiers' contributions to their nation. The uniformity of the graves, the restrictions on what could be carved on the graves, and the placement of large monuments in the cemeteries that honored and described the war, all conveyed the message that the most, indeed the only, significant fact about each soldier's life worthy of memory was their service and sacrifice in war. Soldiers were memorialized as individuals because they had died for their nation.

Recognition of the dead also allowed the sacrifices of their families to be acknowledged. Mothers in particular came to be seen as having contributed to the nation by giving birth to and raising sons who then fought and died in war (Gullace 2002). Widows of Civil War dead were given military pensions (Skocpol 1992), another American practice that was adopted elsewhere.

It is difficult to disentangle veterans' demands for voting rights and social benefits from broader class-based movements, and such an analysis is beyond the scope of this chapter. Veterans' benefits, like old age pensions, medical care, subsidized mortgages and university education, were tangible signs of a nation's respect for soldiers' service and sacrifice. As those benefits were extended to the general population (as was the case with voting rights after World War I and many social programs in the 1950s and 1960s), soldiers no longer stood out as special objects of public largesse, and military service lost some of its allure.

The decline of conscription: the end of a two-century era

Conscription was militarily so valuable because it gave armed forces access to huge numbers of soldiers who could be sacrificed on the battlefield, and who were more willing to die and to kill than aristocrats and mercenaries had been in earlier eras. States' capacities to convince or compel their citizens to risk their lives, or even to give a few years of service, for their country have declined dramatically in Europe and the United States since World War II (and might be in decline in much of the rest of the world as well).

Commitment to military service has fallen at the most basic level: countries first moved in recent decades to reduce the length of military service and offer more exemptions to students and conscientious objectors, and then abolished the draft entirely. The status of conscientious objectors has changed dramatically in Europe, from World War I Britain – when men who didn't serve were publicly humiliated by women who pinned white feathers on them, fired by employers, and stripped by Parliament of the right to vote at war's end (Gullace 2002) – to the late twentieth century – when beginning in the 1970s the Universal Declaration of Human Rights was reinterpreted to encompass conscientious objection and Amnesty International adopted imprisoned conscientious objectors as Prisoners of Conscience. The draft was abolished entirely in Britain in 1960, in Australia and New Zealand in 1972, in the US in 1973, in Belgium in 1994, in France and the Netherlands in 1996, and in much of the rest of Western Europe and most of the former Soviet bloc in the first decades of the twenty-first century. Russia is in the process of abolishing its draft (Mjoset and Van Holde 2002: 77–91). While Israel still has universal service (and is the only country in the world ever to draft women), "30 percent of Israeli eighteen year-olds did not serve at all or did not complete their service" in the early 1990s – a sharp rise from the near universal service of previous decades (Ben-Eliezer 2003: 19).

The European and American abolition of the draft is a rejection both of the sense that young men should be obligated to devote time to national service and also of the belief that nations face threats that deserve to be countered at the cost of their citizens' lives. How can we explain such a dramatic change? Why did the era of conscription end a mere two centuries after it began? The most common explanation is that

Western medical science not only ensures longer life, but, through the use of sophisticated pharmaceutics and artificial body parts, also promises an enjoyable longer life. Those advances will make it ever harder to ask a small minority of our citizens to lose their lives to ensure longer and better ones for the rest of us. Most twenty-first-century Westerners do not see death on their streets. They do not butcher the animals they eat. And they do not lose a large minority of their children to disease and hunger before the age of twelve. (Hanson 2010: 242)

DeWinter (2007) argues that "[t]oday's parents often have no more than two children, some may have only one son. His life is so precious that it has come to seem unbearable for him to be killed in battle." As a result, Western nations practice "risk-transfer war" in which the cardinal rule is to minimize one's own casualties even if it increases civilian casualties in the foreign lands where Western nations fight (Shaw 2005).

Hanson, DeWinter, and Shaw are careful not to see the Western concern for life as essential or eternal, in the manner of the US commander in Vietnam, William Westmorland, who was recorded in the film *Hearts and Minds* notoriously saying, "The Oriental doesn't put the same high price on life as does a Westerner. Life is plentiful. Life is cheap in the Orient." Hanson reminds us that the two World Wars fought mainly by the now risk-adverse Western powers were the bloodiest in human history. He contends that in the wake of future attacks on the US, "Western pieties about the moral limitations of Western arms [would] dissipate when wars are no longer seen as optional, but are deemed existential" (Hanson 2010: 245). DeWinter (2007) attributes Western pacifism to the decline in the birthrate and cites Gunnar Heinsohn, who "predicts that the birthrate in Arab and other Islamic countries will drop in the coming decades and then these nations will in turn settle down."

The relationship between birth rate and pacifism that DeWinter posits did not hold in those Western countries, most notably Germany, where the 1930s baby bust was accompanied by militarism (Mosse 1990: 159–200).

Conversely, China has not fought a war since its 1979 invasion of Vietnam, the same year that it instituted the one-child policy. Perhaps Giovanni Arrighi (2007) is correct in saying that China has decided on a national strategy that, building on its pre-modern form of regional hegemony, does not seek to achieve dominance with military means. Perhaps China remains too intimidated by the US to undertake any military action beyond its borders, although that did not dissuade it in 1950–51 or in 1979; nor does it dissuade Russia even today. For China, as for any major power, there are interests that could be advanced with military force. More likely, the now thirty-year absence of military involvement reflects a judgment by the Chinese leadership of how their population would react to significant wartime casualties, a reaction that would probably be intensified by the large proportion of only children who would die in such a conflict. Only sons have been exempt from military service in many countries throughout the history of conscription, and only surviving brothers of siblings who died in war were excused from the draft or allowed to leave military service after their siblings were killed. (That latter privilege is the basis for the plot of the film *Saving Private Ryan.*)

Iran provides a good test of DeWinter's theory. Iran's Islamic government encouraged a high birth rate during its war with Iraq (as Mao did in China in anticipation of a nuclear war with either the US or the Soviet Union) and then reinstated family planning programs in 1989, a year after the end of the war. Since then, Iran's birthrate has experienced one of the fastest declines in the world and is now below replacement level. Iran's current foreign policy is a sort of regional Nixon Doctrine, relying upon surrogates it finances and supports diplomatically to bring military pressure to its enemies, while keeping its own troops out of harm's way. We will see if Iran's avoidance of war continues.

Krishan Kumar (2003) sees Britain's empire as the source of an "imperial nationalism" that motivated Britons of all classes to identify with the nation and fight for it in war. Yet, the two moments of massive enlistment by Britons were against France in the Napoleonic Wars and Germany in World War I. The former was animated primarily by Protestant identity (Colley 1992), and the latter by exaggerated stories of German atrocities (Fussell 1975) and by nationalism that was focused much more on military competition among states within Europe than on their efforts at colonial conquest. Even if imperialism played as big a role in British identity as Kumar argues, the demise of imperialism can't account for the turn away from conscription in so many non-imperialist European countries. As for the US, depending on how one defines imperialism, it either never was an imperial power or it still is one, decades after the end of the draft.

Other authors argue that support for military service, and the fatalities that come with it, declines when nations lose wars, or, in the case of the United States, when it fails to achieve its military objectives quickly and painlessly. Defeats (such as those suffered by the Central Powers in World War I, the Axis in World War II, the US in Vietnam, the Argentines in the Malvinas/Falklands War, and the Soviets in Afghanistan) were often followed by greater civilian control over the military, an end to conscription, or massive cuts in the military budget. The question is whether such post-defeat anti-militarism is permanent or if it can be reversed. The pacifism that followed World War I dissipated in Germany and Russia almost immediately after their World War I defeats, while the winners remained anti-militarist until they were pulled into World War II. George H.W. Bush was convinced at the end of the 100-hour Gulf War, in which 148 US troops died, that, "[b]y God, we've kicked the Vietnam syndrome once and for all!" (Herring 1991: 104). The reality, as shown in the public reaction to casualties in Afghanistan and Iraq, was more complex, as I will discuss below.

Hanson contends that "American restlessness and mobility," which helped the US achieve victories in the world wars against less innovative enemies, "have also meant that political pressure can quickly mount against wars that get bogged down with high casualties and little progress" (2010: 147). In other words, America has an "excessively short time horizon" (Ferguson 2004: 13). Hanson's argument is supported by analyses of poll numbers (Feaver and Gelpi 2004; Gelpi, Feaver, and Reifler 2009) that suggest that the public tolerates high casualties as long as they perceive the US to be winning the war. For example, once defeat or stalemate became likely following Chinese intervention in Korea, Tet in Vietnam, or the rise of anarchic violence and civil war in Somalia and Iraq, the public turned against those wars. Conversely, "when military operations were perceived as successful, presidents appeared to receive an increase in support as casualties increased … [but] presidents did not receive this boost if the operation was considered unsuccessful" (Feaver and Gelpi 2004: 141–42).

Feaver and his colleagues do demonstrate that support for wars rises and falls with the perceived success of combat operations and that the general public, as well as civilian and military elites, calibrate the casualties they find acceptable to the importance of the military objective. However, their model does not address the long-term decline in tolerance for casualties or in the general public's willingness to risk their own lives for such objectives through the draft. Feaver et al. might be correct that the US public is still not totally adverse to any war deaths, but the number of casualties deemed acceptable is far fewer than for wars in past decades. Feaver and Gelpi (2004: 114–21) report on a 1999 survey that raises various hypothetical situations, and find that the median response of the "mass public" (i.e. civilians not currently in the military or in elite civilian government positions) is that one hundred deaths would be an acceptable cost to defend Taiwan or to intervene to bring democracy to the Congo, while five hundred deaths were acceptable to remove WMDs from Iraq. These responses are greater than zero but far smaller than the number of casualties in Vietnam or Korea before the public turned against those wars, and far smaller than would be needed to achieve those objectives, or than turned out to be needed to prosecute the Afghan and Iraq wars.

The low numbers of casualties that Americans polled in 1999 were willing to tolerate for any foreign policy objective may stem from the tenuousness of the link they saw between Taiwan or Iraq and the security of the United States, just as Western Europeans had trouble seeing how the Balkans mattered to them. Many Americans were convinced of the need to fight in Afghanistan and Iraq after 9/11, so Hanson may be right that future threats could increase Americans' or Europeans' willingness to fight and die abroad. However, the Bush and Obama administrations have had a far harder time convincing Americans to tolerate a few thousand casualties for those wars than their predecessors did in winning support for the sacrifice of tens of thousands in Korea or Vietnam. Clearly, the calculus of lives for security has turned decisively against extended wars with high casualties.

The rapid decline in the number of casualties that Americans, and Europeans even more, are willing to tolerate in order to achieve what they consider important foreign policy or humanitarian objectives goes beyond conscripts' self-interested opposition to being killed or maimed in war. Americans and Europeans are also unwilling to tolerate the deaths of fellow citizens who volunteer for military service. Indeed, Nixon's cynical calculation that opposition to the Vietnam War would end if he stopped sending draftees there proved wrong, as did the Bush presidents' view that Americans wouldn't care if volunteers died in the Persian Gulf or Afghanistan.

Opposition by Americans and Europeans to casualties among their fellow citizens in the military should not be mistaken for pacifism. Americans and Europeans remain willing to tolerate high numbers of deaths among foreign civilians as part of a strategy that minimizes deaths in their own countries' forces. Shaw (2005) is correct that Western countries no longer engage in the mass targeting of civilians, as they did during World War II, but he notes that they destroy infrastructure, even though such "collateral damage" leads to numerous civilian deaths. Such deaths, on the rare occasions when they are covered in the US media, are presented as accidental. Far more attention is given to the technological feats of "smart" weapons, which are presented as highly expensive, good-faith efforts by the US to minimize civilian casualties.

While Hanson believes that "the antiwar movement has become more sophisticated than in the days of Vietnam" (2010: 231) and Paul Joseph (2007) argues that militarism is undermined by multiculturalism, which makes it hard to stigmatize enemies abroad, in fact Americans pay less attention to the Afghans and Iraqis killed by their government than they did to the Vietnamese who died in their war. The most famous and searing images from the Vietnam War were the ones of the naked little girl covered with napalm running down the road and of the Vietcong prisoner as he was about to be executed by the Saigon police chief. The coverage by US journalists of American atrocities in Vietnam was unique in the history of war reporting in the US and indeed rare in world history. In most American and European wars, atrocities committed by one's own soldiers went unreported. Instead, governments encouraged or compelled journalists to publish stories and photos of atrocities, real and imagined, committed by the enemy both to encourage citizens to fight and to justify any attacks by their own government on the soldiers and civilians of enemy nations (Dower 1986; Fussell 1989; Roeder 1993).

Americans have been embarrassed by the photos from Abu Ghraib, but they have easily turned away from the few pictures they have seen of Iraqis or Afghans killed by their government's weapons (as opposed to the pictures of Afghan women mutilated by the Taliban that are splashed on the covers of newspapers and magazines). The demonstrations in the US against the Iraq war have focused on the American lives that will be lost rather than the far heavier cost to the Iraqis. Perhaps that focus reflects lessons that anti-war activists have learned from the politics of the Vietnam War (or from distortions of the actual relations between anti-war activists and American soldiers who fought in Vietnam [Lembke 1998]), but it is a strategy that accurately reflects most Americans' single-minded focus on the lives of their fellow citizens.

From sacrifice to safety: soldiers' lives in the twentieth century

The high value placed upon citizen soldiers' lives is the culmination of a centuries-long interaction between states' growing capacities to demand military service, along with taxes and numerous other resources and behaviors from its subjects, and those subjects' abilities to constitute themselves as citizens with civil, electoral, and social rights.

Soldiers also received benefits special to their status. The recovery and proper burial and honoring of their dead bodies became a sacred obligation of the state. Prisoners of war were accorded special status. Rules of war, formalized in the Geneva Conventions, gave as much attention to the proper treatment of prisoners of war as to the safety of non-combatants. In practice POWs were often better protected by warring states than were each other's civilians. Americans' revulsion at the Bataan Death March, which later was prosecuted as a war crime, and the seating of German prisoners of war at Southern lunch counters closed to black Americans in uniform, are both signs of the importance that Americans gave to this obligation.

POWs became a political issue during the Vietnam War as pro-war politicians in the US used them to sustain support for the war and to falsely assert that anti-war activists were unconcerned with the prisoners. George McGovern, in one of his few witticisms, mocked this by saying, "You'd think we fought the Vietnam War to get our prisoners back." The concern with POWs had the unintended effect of deepening Americans' empathy for soldiers' human suffering and that of their families, and led them to be seen as victims as well as heroes, ultimately weakening support for Vietnam and any other war that put American soldiers in harm's way. The POW "issue" is a rare case of a right-wing strategy that boomeranged.

This line of thinking continues with the image of the yellow ribbon, which Americans first wore to express their concern for the hostages (government employees rather than soldiers) held in Iran in 1979–81. Any geopolitical meaning to the hostages' ordeal was submerged in the drama of the 52 individuals held in Teheran. The yellow ribbon has since become a symbol of concern for any Americans in danger abroad. Yellow ribbons were tied to trees, attached to cars and trucks, and worn on shirts during the Gulf and Iraq wars.

The use of yellow ribbons to express concern for soldiers sent into combat by their own government suggests a surely unintended equivalence between the Iranian radicals who held the hostages in Iran and the US government that sent troops to the Gulf and Iraq. The crucial point, for those who display the yellow ribbons, is that Americans are in danger: the ribbons express above all else a desire that the individual soldiers return home safely from Iraq as the hostages did from Iran. Yet, if the American public's desire is merely for its soldiers' safety rather than for victory, then each casualty is seen as an unjustifiable loss.

The more human and individuated each soldier appears, the more important it is to protect his/her life. War coverage has changed dramatically in the United States, and in Europe and Israel as well, since the 1960s. During the Vietnam War, most of the coverage was on the outcomes of battles rather than on casualties. Indeed, even the weekly reports of war deaths, announced on the three TV networks' evening news shows, was understood, at least until Tet, as a measure of the war's progress more than of its human costs. Public reaction was strongest in the rare weeks when US deaths exceeded those of the South Vietnamese.

The *New York Times*'s coverage of the Vietnam War is a good measure of the stoical view of casualties that still prevailed in that era. Of the 5,910 articles the *New York Times* published on the war from 1965 through 1975, only 2,117 include any mention of Americans killed. Only 774 American dead were named in those articles, in a war in which 58,267 died. Biographical information was included about 23 soldiers, and photos of 23. There are only four references to the reactions of the families of the dead and only two articles mention the suffering of injured American soldiers. Two other articles discuss the funerals or burials of the dead.[1] This restrained coverage is far different from that of the *New York Times* or any other media outlet during the Afghan and Iraq wars, which contain frequent lists of the names, ages, and home towns of Americans killed, and numerous stories on grieving relatives, funerals, and the struggles of injured or psychologically traumatized soldiers.

The Vietnam War Memorial has become the template for how Americans think about their war dead. Indeed, the Memorial has displaced Arlington Cemetery, the Tomb of the Unknown Soldier, and all other sites as the most visited memorial in the US. In so doing it has altered the relationship between the individual and the nation. Unlike the dead citizen-soldiers of all previous American wars, whose worth and sacrifice, and those of their families, were ratified by their connection to and subsumption in a national cause, the Vietnam War dead are just dead individuals whose lives are given meaning only in the memories and suffering of their families and friends. In contrast to every previous war memorial, the Vietnam War Memorial makes "no symbolic reference to the cause or country for which they died, [and instead] immediately highlights the individual. But, once it has been determined that the

[1] These data were collected as part of a project I am undertaking with Mishel Filisha, Ian Sheinheit and Jing Li, graduate students in the Department of Sociology at the University at Albany, State University of New York.

individual will overshadow cause and country, the task of constructing that individual becomes the primary concern" (Wagner-Pacifici and Schwartz 1991: 400).

Certainly many relatives remember the Vietnam War dead as patriots; the most common souvenir left at the memorial is the American flag, but the focus on grieving survivors in retrospective coverage of Vietnam and of all subsequent wars downplays the solace of patriotism. This is seen in Jim Sheeler's *Final Salute* (2008), a book-length elaboration of his Pulitzer prize-winning series of articles for the *Rocky Mountain News*. Sheeler follows "casualty assistance calls officers" (CACOs), the men who knock on doors to inform the "next of kin" that their relative has died in Iraq. Tellingly, this personal form of communication was adopted only toward the end of the Vietnam War (Sheeler 2008: 39); before that, families were informed by letter. The timing of this change suggests that the Defense Department lost confidence that relatives would accept their soldier's death as the tragic fulfillment of patriotic duty. Nor have they recovered that confidence since. Indeed, the *Casualty Assistance Calls Officer Student Guide* advises CACOs to "avoid phrases or platitudes that might appear to diminish the importance of the loss … Pointing out positive factors such as bravery or service may be comforting later, but are usually not helpful at this time" (Commander … 2008: 2–11). There is no other mention of patriotism, service or duty in the guide, which is otherwise filled with advice on how to cope with grief and arrange funerals, and offers a summary of survivors' benefits.

The United States is not alone in this new way of regarding war dead. In Israel, newspapers were banned by law from publishing the names of the dead and injured during wartime. At the end of the 1967 and 1973 wars, newspapers published lists of casualties without biographical articles. The focus was on the collective achievements and sacrifices of the Israeli military. Beginning with the First Lebanon War, Israeli newspapers began to break the law (in part because, as the war dragged on, knowledge of casualties spread throughout Israel through informal means and the stated purpose of the law, to keep war information secret, was undermined). Articles increasingly focused on the grief of family and friends rather than the soldiers' contributions to the war effort. It became newspapers' standard practice to mark each casualty with detailed biographies and photographs.[2] Beginning in the 1990s, funerals for dead soldiers became "more individualistic and emotional" and parents began to sue in court for the right to replace the "standard

---

[2] These conclusions are based on data Ayala Gat, a graduate student in the Department of Sociology at Albany, collected on Israeli newspapers' coverage of casualties.

uniform text on the gravestones of fallen soldiers … [with a] personal formulation decided by the family" (Ben-Eliezer 2003: 30, 31).

Russia, the third Western country that has fought more than one war since the 1960s, has undergone a more limited transformation. There has been little governmental recognition for veterans and fatalities of the Afghan and Chechen wars (Oushakine 2009). Media coverage of both the Afghan and Chechen wars gave little attention to the suffering and deaths of Soviet/Russian troops. The Afghan War was presented in a positive light by the still-censored Soviet press. Russian journalists were only episodically critical of the Chechen War, and their negative reports focused on atrocities committed by Russia against Chechen civilians, not on the Russian troops, who remained anonymous in those stories (Koltsova 2006; Mickiewicz 1999). Instead families, led by mothers, have organized memorial services, created museums and monuments, printed books that presented the biographies of their dead sons (Oushakine 2009), and, like mothers after the US Civil War (Faust 2008: 61–101), travelled to battlefields to recover their sons' remains.

Russian mothers established Committees of Soldiers' Mothers that took direct action to save their sons' lives by supporting draft evasion and travelling to military bases where they pulled their sons from the army and took them home. They also forced the Duma to pass legislation in 1997 granting a general amnesty to all draft evaders (Caiazza 2002; Oushakine 2009: 202–58). That law and the mothers' disruption of conscription provided the impetus for the current transition to an all-volunteer Russian army. Similarly, Israeli parents' interference in their children's military assignments, as well as their complaints about per-ceived inadequacies in Israeli Defence Force (IDF) efforts to guard soldiers' safety, led the then Chief of Staff Ehud Barak "to exempt large numbers of young people from compulsory service … under the rubric 'not useful'" and to try to identify young people eager to serve in combat positions (and parents willing to support that decision) by "sending pre-draft young men a list of service options in which [the IDF] marketed itself and especially the combat corps" (Ben-Eliezer 2004: 55, 57).

This research could and should be extended. It would be worthwhile to conduct a similar study of British and Australian newspapers since their soldiers participated in US wars as part of those nations' status as little brothers to the US hegemon. Such a study could also be extended beyond media depictions to official recognitions of soldiers. Have the criteria for awarding war medals shifted? In the past, most medals were given for brave actions that allowed soldiers to kill the enemy. Are medals now given for actions designed to protect fellow soldiers more than for ones that will further battlefield victories?

Wars in the post-conscription era

How will states fight wars in the absence of conscription, and while under pressure from their publics to minimize casualties among the volunteers who serve in their armed forces? Shaw (2005) contends that technological innovations in precision bombing make possible a "new Western way of war," devoted to "force protection." Because the troops who operate high-tech weapons are so much more expensive to train than were legions of draftees, militaries have a financial reason to preserve their soldiers' lives. However, no economic calculus can justify the expenditure of $1 billion or even $100 million on a plane that will reduce the pilot's chances of being killed to near zero.

Shaw is mistaken to see the shift to casualty minimization as a result of possibilities opened by autonomous technological innovation. Nor can we credit military contractors; they always lobby for the development of super-expensive, technologically innovative weapons on which they realize the highest profit margins and the longest and largest contracts. The US has invested heavily in new military technology since the Cold War, and that technology only became focused on protecting troops, as opposed to gaining an edge over the Soviet Union, since the 1970s. Israel and NATO made the same shift in recent decades.

New weapons are developed at the behest and expense of militaries and are responses to strategic challenges rather than the other way around. The hugely expensive weapons designed to minimize casualties are developed and manufactured in response to specific and detailed demands by the US and other militaries. Those demands were responses to the new understandings and evaluations of military casualties we traced earlier in this article.

The imperative to minimize casualties has strategic as well as weapon procurement costs. While the US has maintained its indirect (imperial) control of much of the world with no casualties in most places and few in most others, some tasks can be accomplished only by putting forces at risk. Most famously, Osama bin Laden and his henchmen were able to escape Tora Bora because the Bush administration was unwilling to risk American lives. The Obama administration's strategy in Afghanistan and NATO's intervention in Libya are also limited by the need to minimize casualties. The US and Europeans failed to intervene to limit the Rwandan genocide because of an accurate assessment that the publics in those countries would not tolerate any deaths in their armed forces for that purpose. The list could go on and on.

Casualty avoidance is also at odds with the objectives of recent American military interventions, which seek to "win hearts and minds," rather than defeat or annihilate enemies. Such interventions require intensive interactions between invading troops and civilians in the countries the US is seeking to transform, a point that is central to the doctrine presented in the US Army's 2006 "counterinsurgency" manual, written under David Petraeus's supervision. Such interactions expose foreign troops to risk. If, instead, the US and other Western armies rely upon high-tech weapons such as drones, that minimize their casualties, they are more likely to antagonize rather than win over the local population.

Israel, for the moment, seems to have devised a strategy that allows it to keep much of the West Bank, and to protect both Israel proper and the West Bank settlers from attack, at minimal risk to Israeli soldiers. The wall (or more accurately walls, since there are barriers between settlements and the rest of the West Bank as well as along Israel's internationally recognized border), combined with the exercise of massive retaliation against Gaza, the West Bank, and Lebanon for attacks on Israel or Israelis, have reduced Israeli civilian casualties to almost zero in recent years.

Yet if the PLO, Hezbollah, Hamas, or any Arab state were to devise a strategy, or were willing to pay the price in casualties and destruction in order to counter Israel's reliance on technology and the wall(s), it is not at all clear if or how Israel could respond. The saga of Gilad Shalit, held by Hamas for five years after it kidnapped him in 2006, shows how resistant Israel is to casualties. Shalit became the focus of repeated demonstrations and mobilization. Polls show a majority of Israelis were willing to pay "any price" (Hasson 2009), including the release of hundreds of Palestinians considered by Israel to be terrorists, in exchange for Shalit's return.

What will states do when they cannot achieve their objectives with the minimal number of casualties they are willing to endure? In this, as in other realms, China may be a harbinger. States may continue to waste money on weapons and troops designed for wars they will never fight (China's invasion of Taiwan; US defense of Taiwan, South Korea, Germany, Texas, etc.), even as they tailor their foreign policies to pursue objectives that can be realized without military intervention. If wars in the era of mercenaries were fought with "limited aims" (Knox 2001: 61, quoted above), and conscription made possible total wars that led to total victories and unconditional surrenders followed by geopolitical transformations, the new era of low tolerance for casualties will lead to a different sort of warfare. Where Western nations can achieve their aims with asymmetrical warfare, inflicting casualties on enemies at thirty thousand feet, they will continue to do so. Where they can use technology to block terror and other attacks, they will do so. Indeed, so-called homeland security has been the fastest-rising (in most countries the only increasing) category of military spending in the first decade of the twenty-first century. The real question is what Western nations, above all the US, will do about goals that cannot be realized with few or no casualties. So far the US has been able to use its non-military power and high-tech weapons to secure oil and other vital resources without having to risk its own soldiers' lives. If American troops were needed it is unclear how many casualties the US government could get the public to endure in order to prevent or end an oil shortage. The capacity for self-delusion led to past interventions, such as by George W. Bush in Iraq and Afghanistan, in the hopes of quick victories, but the lack of success in both instances makes it highly unlikely that the US will send ground troops anywhere else in the foreseeable future, and certainly the US failures are object lessons and warning for any other Western state with similar ambitions. Russia's two wars in Chechnya suggest that Russia still has a higher toleration for casualties than the US. However, Russia has narrowed its objectives in Chechnya just as the US did in Iraq and Afghanistan.[3]

Of course there still are states and non-state actors including warlords, militias, al-Qaeda and other local and transnational affinity groups, that are capable of finding and mobilizing soldiers who are willing to die, and whose families and neighbors will not intervene to keep them out of war. So far, such warmongers mainly fight among themselves; the dominant form of warfare in the late twentieth and the twenty-first century is the civil war (Hironaka 2005). No state has launched an attack on the US or any other Western state in decades. Israel was last attacked by another state in 1973. There is no plausible circumstance in the foreseeable future where a state would take the risk of attacking the US or any other Western state, including Israel.

When non-state actors launch attacks on Western nations they are usually deflected or inflict limited casualties. Pre-emptive wars, such as that of the US in Iraq, are ineffective at preventing future attacks. Retaliatory attacks by Israel, and to a lesser degree by Russia, have been effective at preventing further attacks. However, the most effective strategy is to invest in homeland security (or to have a non-obnoxious foreign policy combined with no immigration: Sweden, lauded by Osama bin Laden for the former, fell

---

[3] Indeed, the Status of Forces Agreement Bush signed with Iraq in 2008 was in essence a treaty of unconditional surrender, requiring the US to abandon its most cherished goals for the invasion. The agreement prohibits the US forces in Iraq from attacking any other country and requires the US to abandon the permanent bases it built as staging grounds for such attacks. While Bush, no doubt, expected the Iraq government to waive those restrictions at a later date, the Obama administration, at least as of 2011, has made no effort to block the final pullout. The US also abandoned its ambition to privatize the Iraqi oil industry.

victim to a bombing in 2010 at the hands of an Iraqi immigrant). Obviously, much internal security money is wasted, and there is substantial variation in its effectiveness – with Israel at the top end of effectiveness. Even within countries there is variation. In the US the New York City Police Department is highly effective, while the Federal Homeland Security Department has a reputation for buffoonishness. Yet the paucity of attacks indicates that internal security agencies are capable of learning and refining their methods. The feared follow-ups to 9/11 never happened.

Perhaps, as Hanson (2010: 245–46) predicts, spectacular terrorist attacks (or a desperate oil shortage) in Western countries will lead to a revival of militarism and a willingness to tolerate high casualties in pursuit of security or revenge. It is not impossible, though unlikely, that non-state actors will get hold of nuclear weapons or find some other way of inflicting massive casualties that would be enough to reverse the intolerance of military casualties that has become the norm in Western countries in recent decades.

Most likely, casualty aversion will continue and deepen. Europe lost its colonial empires for many reasons, but in the absence of any willingness to fight wars, the minor role EU nations play individually and collectively in world geopolitics is unlikely to grow. Russia is unlikely to fight a third Chechen war or to be willing to lose thousands of lives holding other peripheral, non-Russian border regions. As long as Russia can continue to keep strongmen in power in Chechnya and other such republics with modest losses of Russian troops (along with massive death tolls among the targeted populations), it will continue to do so. Once that strategy is no longer viable, the Russian Federation will shrink. The Gilad Shalit saga indicates that Israel will not pay much of a price in lives to hold the Occupied Territories, although a core of fanatical settlers may fight on their own once Israel adjusts its borders.

Finally, US hegemony, especially as that nation declines relatively if not absolutely in almost all non-military realms, is unlikely to survive the current aversion to casualties and fetishization of prisoners of war and of the dead. The costs of hegemony, for the US and far more for the rest of the world, have been extremely high. We should rejoice that Americans are no longer willing to pay them.

REFERENCES

Anderson, B. 1983. *Imagined Communities: Reflections on the Origin and Spread of Nationalism*. London: Verso.
Arrighi, G. 2007. *Adam Smith in Beijing: Lineages of the Twenty-First Century*. London: Verso.

Baugh, D. 1999. "The Eighteenth Century Navy as a National Institution, 1690–1815." Pp. 120–60 in *The Oxford Illustrated History of the Royal Navy*, edited by J.R. Hill. Oxford University Press.

Bell, D. 2007. *The First Total War: Napoleon's Europe and the Birth of Warfare As We Know It*. Boston: Houghton Mifflin.

Ben-Eliezer, U. 2003. "The New Social Sources for Both Peace and War in Israel." *Israel Studies Forum* 18(2): 7–41.

2004. "Post-Modern Armies and the Question of Peace and War: The Israeli Defense Forces in the 'New Times'." *International Journal of Middle East Studies* 36(1): 49–70.

Caiazza, A. 2002. *Mothers and Soldiers; Gender, Citizenship, and Civil Society in Contemporary Russia*. New York: Routledge.

Colley, L. 1992. *Britons: Forging the Nation, 1707–1837*. New Haven: Yale University Press.

Commander, Navy Region, Mid-Atlantic, Casualty Assistance Calls/Funeral Honors Support Regional Program Manager. 2008. *Casualty Assistant Calls Officer Student Guide*. Accessed at: www.docstoc.com/docs/3432735/CASUALTY-ASSISTANCE-CALLS-OFFICER-STUDENT-GUIDE-Provided-by-COMMANDER-NAVY.

De Winter, L. 2007. "My Only Son." *Wall Street Journal*, 8 June.

Dower, J. 1986. *War Without Mercy: Race and Power in the Pacific War*. New York: Pantheon.

2010. *Cultures of War: Pearl Harbor/Hiroshima/ 9–11/ Iraq*. New York: Norton.

Faust, D.G. 2008. *This Republic of Suffering: Death and the American Civil War*. New York: Knopf.

Feaver, P. and C. Gelpi. 2004. *Choosing Your Battles: American Civil–Military Relations and the Use of Force*. Princeton University Press.

Ferguson, N. 2004. *Colossus: The Rise and Fall of the American Empire*. New York: Penguin.

Fussell, P. 1975. *The Great War and Modern Memory*. New York: Oxford University Press.

1989. *Wartime: Understanding and Behavior in the Second World War*. New York: Oxford University Press.

Gelpi, C., P. Feaver, and J. Reifler. 2009. *Paying the Human Costs of War: American Public Opinion and Casualties in Military Conflicts*. Princeton University Press.

Gullace, N. 2002. *The Blood of Our Sons: Men, Women, and the Renegotiation of British Citizenship during the Great War*. New York: Palgrave.

Hanson, V.D. 1989. *The Western Way of War: Infantry Battle In Classical Greece*. New York: Knopf.

2010. *The Father of Us All: War and History, Ancient and Modern*. New York: Bloomsbury.

Harries-Jenkins, G. 1977. *The Army in Victorian Society*. London: Routledge & Kegan Paul.

Hasson, G. 2009. "Poll Shows Israelis Ready to Pay 'Any Price' for Shalit." *Haaretz*, 23 December.

Herring, G. 1991. "America and Vietnam: The Unending War." *Foreign Affairs* 70(5): 104–19.

Hironaka, A. 2005. *Neverending Wars: The International Community, Weak States, and the Perpetuation of Civil War*. Cambridge, MA: Harvard University Press.

Jansen, M. 2000. *The Making of Modern Japan*. Cambridge, MA: Harvard University Press.

Joseph, P. 2007. *Are Americans Becoming More Peaceful?* Boulder, CO: Paradigm.

Kestnbaum, M. 2002. "Citizen-Soldiers, National Service and the Mass Army: The Birth of Conscription in Revolutionary Europe and North America." Pp. 117–44 in *The Comparative Study of Conscription in the Armed Forces*, edited by Mjoset and Van Holde. Amsterdam: JAI.

Knox, M. 2001. "Mass Politics and Nationalism as Military Revolution: The French Revolution and After." Pp. 57–73 in *The Dynamics of Military Revolution, 1300–2050*, edited by M. Knox and W. Murray. Cambridge University Press.

Koltsova, O. 2006. *News Media and Power in Russia*. London: Routledge.

Kumar, K. 2003. *The Making of English National Identity*. Cambridge University Press.

Lachmann, R. 2009. "Greed and Contingency: State Fiscal Crises and Imperial Failure in Early Modern Europe," *American Journal of Sociology* 115(1): 39–73.

Lembke, J. 1998. *The Spitting Image: Myth, Memory, and the Legacy of Vietnam*. New York: NYU Press.

Lynn, J. 2001. "The Western Army in Seventeenth-century France." Pp. 35–56 in *The Dynamics of Military Revolution, 1300–2050*, edited by M. Knox and W. Murray. Cambridge University Press.

McNeill, W. 1982. *The Pursuit of Power: Technology, Armed Force, and Society since AD 1000*. University of Chicago Press.

Mickiewicz, E. 1999. *Changing Channels: Television and the Struggle for Power in Russia*. Durham, NC: Duke University Press.

Mjoset, L. and S. Van Holde. 2002. "Killing for the State Dying for the Nation: An Introductory Essay on the Life Cycle of Conscription into Europe's Armed Forces." Pp. 3–94 in *The Comparative Study of Conscription in the Armed Forces*, edited by L. Mjoset and S. Van Holde. Amsterdam: JAI.

Mosse, G.L. 1990. *Fallen Soldiers: Reshaping the Memory of the World Wars*. New York: Oxford University Press.

Murray, W. and M. Knox. 2001. "Thinking about Revolutions in Warfare." Pp. 1–14 in *The Dynamics of Military Revolution, 1300–2050* edited by M. Knox and W. Murray. Cambridge University Press.

Oushakine, S. 2009. *The Patriotism of Despair: Nation, War and Loss in Russia*. Ithaca, NY: Cornell University Press.

Parrott, D. 1995. "Strategy and Tactics in the Thirty Years' War: The Military Revolution." Pp. 227–51 in *The Military Revolution Debate: Readings on the Military Transformation of Early Modern Europe*, edited by C.J. Rogers. Boulder, CO: Westview.

Rhodes, R. 1988. "Man-made Death: A Neglected Mortality." *Journal of the American Medical Association* 260(5): 686–87.

Roeder, G. 1993. *The Censored War: American Visual Experience During World War Two*. New Haven: Yale University Press.

Rogers, C.J. 1995. "The Military Revolution, 1560–1660." Pp. 1–10 in *The Military Revolution Debate: Readings on the Military Transformation of Early Modern Europe*, edited by C.J. Rogers. Boulder, CO: Westview.

Shaw, M. 2005. *The New Western Way of War: Risk-Transfer War and Its Crisis in Iraq*. Cambridge: Polity.

Sheeler, J. 2008. *Final Salute: A Story of Unfinished Lives*. New York: Penguin.

Skocpol, T. 1992. *Protecting Soldiers and Mothers: The Political Origins of Social Policy in the United States*. Cambridge, MA: Harvard University Press.

Tilly, C. 1990. *Coercion, Capital, and European States*. Oxford: Blackwell.

Wagner-Pacifici, R. and B. Schwartz. 1991. "The Vietnam Veterans Memorial: Commemorating a Difficult Past." *American Journal of Sociology* 97(2): 376–420.

Part 2

The varieties of nationalist experience

3 The state-to-nation balance and war

Benjamin Miller

How can we best explain the high war-propensity of certain states, especially if it persists over long periods of time, beyond the tenure of specific leaders? A related question is why is the danger of war concentrated in some specific locales such as China–Taiwan, Korea (and earlier also in Vietnam), Kashmir, the border area between Afghanistan and Pakistan, Turkey–Greece–Cyprus, Israel–Palestine–Lebanon–Syria, Iran–Bahrain/Iraq–Kuwait, the Balkans, and the Caucusus – while the danger of war almost doesn't exist in other places? Is it because of factors related to the global or regional balance of capabilities, the type of domestic regimes, or are there perhaps alternative causal factors?

I argue that the key for explaining variations in the war-propensity of states is their state-to-nation balance. This balance is composed of three major components: (1) The extent of success in state building, that is, state capacity or the level of stateness; (2) The level of internal national congruence; (3) The extent of external national congruence. Two key factors – demography and history – influence the likelihood that the national incongruence will be translated to nationalist challenges to the status quo.

Some of the key manifestations of the nationalist dissatisfaction with the status quo include: "illegitimate states," pan-national movements, irredentist-revisionist states, failed states, and "illegitimate nations." Internal incongruence and state weakness lead to challenges of incoherence manifested by "nations without states," failed states, "states without nations," and stateless refugees. External incongruence and state strength lead to revisionist challenges manifested by pan-national movements of unification or irredentist claims to territories held by other states on the grounds of national affiliation of the population or national-historic rights on the territory.

More specifically, variations in the extent of stateness and national congruence determine the level and the type of large-scale violence by producing different categories of states with regard to their war-proneness.

Strong but nationally incongruent states generate irredentist/revisionist policies. State strength and national congruence lead to a status quo orientation. Low levels of stateness and national incongruence bring about civil wars, transborder violence and foreign intervention. Weak but nationally congruent states produce the "frontier state" with boundary and territorial wars, but also with a high likelihood of the evolution of a status quo orientation over time. In sum, while not each case of a state-to-nation imbalance produces war, the underlying context of most wars nowadays, and in recent periods as well, is related to at least one of the manifestations of such an imbalance.

The phenomenon to be explained: state war-proneness

Typology of state war-propensity

The conflict literature usually advances some dichotomous distinctions regarding the key types of state war-propensity, even if it may also introduce various degrees of this typology. Yet, such dichotomies tend to lose some important nuances, especially with respect to types of war-proneness in regional wars. While there is a large literature on global/systemic/general wars, since most wars take place among neighbors it is important to try to understand the proneness of states also to this kind of war.

A common distinction in the literature with respect to war-proneness is between revisionist and status-quo states (Buzan 1991: Chapter 8; Kupchan 1998; Schweller 1994, 1996: 98–99, 1998: 22–24, 84–89; Wolfers 1962: 18–19, 96–97, 125–26).[1] This is a useful distinction also with regard to war-propensity on the regional level, but there are additionally important categories of war-propensity that are especially useful on this level and are not captured by the revisionist/status-quo state dichotomy. While revisionism and status quo present opposite foreign policy orientations, especially regarding war initiation, they are not exhaustive of the types of states prone to be engaged in regional wars. There are other important classes of states that produce war-proneness even if they do not make a deliberate choice to engage or not to engage in revisionism and related warfare. One such type of state provides an arena for civil wars, which frequently also trigger neighbors' intervention. The second such type is engaged in boundary/territorial warfare in neighborhoods where boundaries are not marked clearly and are not agreed upon by the parties.

---

[1] On aspiring revisionist regional powers in the post-Cold War era, see Job 1997: 187.

Thus, we get a fourfold classification of state war-proneness:

1. *The revisionist state*: a state that is dissatisfied with the current international order and is willing to incur high costs by using force to change the territorial status quo or the regime of other states.[2] Thus, the state's risk-taking propensity is high: it is risking great losses for the sake of great gains, which may include territorial gains, ideological gains (regime change), or enhancing its prestige and getting a "place at the table" (Schweller 1998: 21).
2. *The status-quo state*: a state that is satisfied with the current order and is willing to use force only to defend it and not to change the current distribution of rewards in the system.
3. *The incoherent or "failed" state*: a state that is prone to civil/ethnic wars and also to foreign intervention in these wars.[3]
4. *The "frontier" state*: a state that is located in a neighborhood where boundaries are unclear or disputed, and thus is prone to boundary and territorial wars.

The state-to-nation imbalance: an underlying cause of war-proneness

In order to go to war, regional states need both the motivation and the capabilities to do so. The great powers affect the capabilities of the local states and thus affect the emergence and duration of regional cold war and cold peace (Miller 2007). Yet, it is the state-to-nation imbalance that provides the basic motivation for war and therefore makes certain states more war-prone than others (see more specifically on this point below).[4]

The state-to-nation balance has two distinctive dimensions. While in practice there might be some interrelationships between the two dimensions, for analytical purposes it is useful to make a distinction between them. The first dimension refers to state strength or capacity. This is the "hard" element of state building. The second refers to the extent of congruence or compatibility between political boundaries and national identifications in a certain region. This is the "soft" component of nation building.

---

[2] In a recent work, Davidson (2002: 125–26) defines revisionism as a preference for changing the international "distribution of goods" – including, but not limited to territory, and a willingness to incur costs in pursuing that preference. See also Legro 2005: 10.
[3] To underline the need for these additional categories, I would point out that states that I would place in this category, at least in certain periods, include some of those which Maoz (2004: 118) places in the "pacifist" category: Haiti, Dominican Republic, Liberia, Afghanistan, Nepal, Panama, Burma, and Sri Lanka.
[4] For related discussions, see Mayall 1990 and Van Evera 1995: 257.

The extent of state strength (or the success of state building)

This variable refers to the institutions and resources available to states for governing the polity.[5] Weak states lack effective institutions and resources to implement their policies and to fulfill key functions. Most notably, they lack an effective control over the means of violence in their sovereign territory and an effective law enforcement system. Thus they face great difficulties in maintaining law and order and providing security in their territory. This, in turn, severely handicaps the economic activity in the state. These states are unable to raise sufficient revenues and to collect enough taxes to be able to maintain an effective bureaucracy and provide even elementary socioeconomic and other vital services to the population (mail delivery, regular water supply, road network, electricity, education, health care, etc.). Strong states control the means of violence in their sovereign territory and possess an effective set of institutions. Tilly (1975) focuses on the ability of the state to coerce, control and extract resources as the key to state making. Thus state strength or capacity can be measured by the ability of the state to mobilize manpower for military service and to extract financial resources (notably by taxation) from their societies (Gause 1992: 457). Another useful measure is the development of a communications and transportation infrastructure indicated, for example, (especially in the nineteenth and early twentieth centuries) by total railroad mileage (Centeno 2002: 110) or railroad density per 1,000 sq. km.[6]

The degree of congruence (or extent of success of nation building)

This variable refers to the extent of congruence between the state's political boundaries and the national aspirations and identities of the people in the state. The extent of national congruence must, however, also incorporate the state's contiguous neighborhood, namely, the extent to which the current political boundaries of the state and its adjacent neighbors reflect the national affiliations of the main groups in these states and their aspirations to establish states and/or to revise existing

---

[5] On state building, see Ayoob 1995, Migdal 1988, and Tilly 1975. See also Rotberg 2003: Chapter 1.

[6] While Tilly's indicators might roughly parallel Mann's "despotic power," the transportation measurement might roughly indicate Mann's "infrastructural power" (1993: 58–61). Despotic power refers to the power of state authorities over civil society; infrastructural power is the institutional capacity of the state to penetrate the territory and carry out decisions effectively. See also the indicators in Rotberg 2003 (esp. pp. 4–22), and Fearon and Laitin (2003: 80).

boundaries.[7] High congruence means that there is compatibility between the state and its contiguous neighbors (as entities administering certain territories) and the national sentiments of the peoples in these states (that is, their aspirations to live as national communities in their own states).[8] In other words, there is a strong acceptance and identification of the people in the neighborhood with the existing states and their territorial boundaries.

There are two primary senses in which a state's geopolitical and national boundaries may be *incongruent* in relation to the ethno-national criterion of one state per one nation:

1. A single geopolitical entity may contain numerous national groups. This is the internal dimension of incongruence.[9]
2. A single national group may reside in more than one geopolitical entity. This is the external dimension of incongruence.

The sources of the state-to-nation balance

Three forces reinforce the balance between states and nations: ethnic coherence or homogeneity,[10] civic nationalism (mainly resulting either from state-initiated nationalism or immigrant societies),[11] and strong states. The more dominant any one of these forces is, the greater the state-to-nation balance. In sum, state weakness is one dimension of the

---

[7] This section draws especially on Van Evera 1995. See also Brown 1993; Buzan 1991; Cederman 1997; Holsti 1996; Kupchan 1995; Hoffmann 1998; Mayall 1990.

[8] On the definition of state and nation, see Connor 1994: 90–117 and especially Barrington 1997: 712–16, who emphasizes "the belief in the right to territorial self-determination for the group" as a central part of the definition of a "nation," which is central for distinguishing nations from other collectivities. While many groups (including ethnic groups) hold common myths, values, and symbols, nations are unified by a sense of purpose: controlling the territory that the members of the group believe to be theirs. Thus, nations need not even be based on a certain ethnic identity: civic nations share cultural features but are generally multiethnic in their makeup. "Nationalism" is the active pursuit of control by a national group over the territory that it defines as its homeland. Thus, every nationalist movement involves the setting of territorial boundaries (Barrington 1997: 714), and national conflicts must involve disputes over territory to be truly "national." Key works on nationalism include Anderson (1991), Gellner (1983), Hobsbawm (1990), and Smith (1986) (cited, for example, in Suny, 1999/2000: 145).

[9] Woodwell (2004: 206), who relies on various datasets, uses the figure of 3 percent of a population. Welsh (1993: 45) uses the figure of 5 percent of the state's population as a threshold beyond which the state is not ethnically homogeneous.

[10] Most states are, however, multi-ethnic. Connor (1994) refers to 12 percent of states as ethnically homogeneous.

[11] Civic nationalism refers to an inclusive membership in the nation according to territory/citizenship. On the distinction between ethnic and civic nationalism see Smith 2000. For a useful overview, see Kupchan 1995: Chapter 1.

state-to-nation imbalance.[12] The other dimension is national incongruence. A state suffers from it when ethnic nationalism (rather than civic nationalism) is the dominant political affiliation in that state and there is a low congruence between the state and the ethno-national affiliations of the population either within the state or outside it. A state-to-nation incongruence, as will be elaborated below, leads to a nationalist dissatisfaction with the status quo.

Explaining variance: demography and history

There might, however, be variations in the translation of the state-to-nation incongruence to nationalist challenges to the regional status quo. Two key factors – demography and history – affect the likelihood that this incongruence will be translated into nationalist challenges to the existing states-system. The first factor is demography or, more precisely, the geographical spread of the ethno-national groups in the region. The second factor is the history of the state and the nation in the region: which preceded which, and especially whether some ethno-national groups lost the dominance they once held of the territories they settle now or in adjacent areas.

Demography

The first sense of incongruence – one state with a number of ethno-national groups – is more likely to lead to secessionist challenges under the following two conditions:

1. The more concentrated that ethnic majorities are in the region, the higher the number of attempts at secession. Concentrated majorities of ethnic groups (i.e., the members of the group residing almost exclusively in a single region of the state) are more likely to risk violence to gain independence than ethnic groups with other kinds of settlement patterns such as urbanites, dispersed minorities and even concentrated minorities. The settlement patterns of ethnic groups in the region thus affect the likelihood of attempts at secession.
2. The state is more likely to oppose such endeavors violently if it is a multinational state that fears a precedent-setting by the secession of one ethnic group that would trigger secessionist attempts by other ethno-national groups in its territory.[13]

---

[12] For an extended discussion of the sources of the state-to-nation balance, see Miller 2007: Chapter 3.
[13] See Toft 2002/3: 86–96 on the importance of precedent-setting logic. See also Walter (2003).

Thus, the combination of 1 and 2, that is, the presence of multi-national states with concentrated ethno-national majorities in a number of regions is likely to lead to violence, as in Chechnya, whereas the bi-national nature of Czechoslovakia eliminated the fears that following the secession of Slovakia there would have been other such attempts. At the same time, the dispersal of the Tatars across Russia led to peace in contrast to the civil war that erupted between Chechnya and Russia (Toft 2002/3: 104–14).

The second sense of incongruence, of a single ethnic nation residing in a number of regional states, poses revisionist challenges if at least in one of these states there is an ethnic majority of this group. It is more likely that such a majority, rather than minority groups, can mobilize the state's resources for its nationalist agenda. External incongruence is also magnified in proportion to the extent of the transborder spread of the national groups in the region: the greater the spread, the greater the imbalance. That is, a spread of a single ethnic nation into five neighboring states creates a greater imbalance in the whole region than spread into two states, which might create conflict only between these two states (even though this conflict might also have regional repercussions).

Thus, the spread of ethnic Germans in numerous states could be used by Prussia to pursue the wars of German unification in 1863–71 (Williams 2001: Chapter 3). Although under vastly different circumstances, Egypt's leader, Nasser, tried to use the Pan-Arabist card in order to unify Arabs spread among almost twenty Arab states. The Pan-Arabist agenda contributed to great instability in the Middle East, especially during the 1950s and 1960s, including the Arab–Israeli wars of 1948–49, 1956, and 1967, and low-intensity conflicts between and after these wars (Miller 2007: Chapter 4).

History – specifically, the history of state formation and of national independence

If the state preceded the nation, it is more likely that there will be a state-to-nation congruence. Vice versa, if ethnic nationalism preceded the state, incongruence is more likely. The state preceded the nation notably in the case of Western Europe, where nationalism was initiated by the state (Cederman 1997: 142; Tilly 1990), and in the case of the immigrant societies in the New World (Walzer 1997: 30–35). In Eastern Europe, the Balkans and the Middle East, however, ethnic nationalism had emerged before the states-system was created following the collapse of the multi-national Ottoman and Habsburg empires. Because many of the new states' boundaries did not coincide with the pre-existing ethnic nations, this has led to a mismatch between states and nations in these regions.

Nationalist challenges are more likely by national groups who lost the control they once held of territories in the region, especially if these territories are identified with a past golden age of national glory. These territories become major expressions of the nation's identity, both past and present (for detailed case studies in Central and Eastern Europe, see White 2000). The problem is, however, that due to changing boundaries and ethnic demographics over the years, in many cases there are competing nationalist claims based on "history" vis-à-vis the same territory. Moreover, these claims might clash with present ethnic distributions. The Land of Israel for the Zionists and Kosovo for the Serbs are good examples. Thus, the Palestinians constitute a clear-cut ethno-national majority in the West Bank, which is historically the important part of the Land of Israel for the Jews, and the Muslim Albanians are the ethnic majority in Kosovo, while the Serbs constitute the minority.

Finally, the translation of a state-to-nation incongruence into violence is influenced by the history of violence among the competing ethno-national groups. The less credible the connection between past nationalist violence and present threats, the lower the likelihood of the eruption of violence and vice versa. Such a variation might, for example, explain the more peaceful outcome in the case of the ethnic Hungarian minorities in Romania and Slovakia in contrast to the intense violence among the ethno-national groups in the Yugoslav case in the 1990s (Brubaker 1998: 282–83; Csergo and Goldgeier 2004).

The leaders of these challenges (state leaders or non-state leaders of nationalist groups) might truly believe in these nationalist causes or manipulate them for their own power purposes because of the popular appeal of these ideas. They will not be able, however, to manipulate these forces unless there are some popular forces and movements in the region who subscribe to these beliefs and are committed to act to advance them. Such forces are going to be stronger the greater the mismatch between the state boundaries and the nations in the region on the grounds of pre-existing ethnic-national affiliation of the population or national-historic rights to the territory.

Political manifestations of ethno-nationalist dissatisfaction with the regional status quo

Key manifestations of the state-to-nation imbalance include the intensity and level of the presence of each of the following five nationalist challenges in the region: "illegitimate states," pan-national movements, irredentist-revisionist states, incoherent or "failed" states, and "illegitimate nations." Knowing the figures for each of these components in a certain region does not allow us to predict the precise likelihood of war. Yet, this knowledge enables us to compare the level of war-proneness of different regions. In addition, changes in such figures in a certain region over time allow us to assess the rising or declining likelihood of armed conflict in the region. In general, the greater the presence of these five nationalist challenges in the region, the higher the imbalance.

More specifically, nationalist challenges can be divided into two types: domestic challenges from within states and interstate challenges. Internal incongruence, based on demography and history and reinforced by state weakness, produces the domestic challenges of incoherence, most notably the threat of *secession*. External incongruence, based on demography and history and reinforced by state strength, generates revisionist challenges, most notably *pan-national unification* and *irredentism*.[14]

Internal incongruence and state weakness lead to challenges of incoherence

1. Nations without states ("illegitimate nations") or "too few states" in the region refers to ethno-national groups aspiring for *secession* from the existing states. Too few states are said to be present when there are dissatisfied stateless national groups in the region who claim their right of national self-determination, and especially demand to secede and establish their own state. The propensity for such claims will increase if the dominant national groups in the existing regional states are intolerant of the political, socioeconomic and cultural rights of ethnic minorities. Examples of such dominant groups include the Sunnis in Iraq (until the US invasion of 2003), the Alawites in Syria (Hinnebusch 2003), the Sinhalese in Sri Lanka, the Thais in Thailand, and the Turks in Turkey (Ayoob 1995: 38).[15] Such intolerance and ethnic-based discrimination tend to increase the quest of oppressed ethnic groups to have their own independent states.[16]

---

[14] On secession and irredenta, see Carment and James 1997; Chazan 1991; Horowitz 1985: Chapter 6; 1991; Mayall 1990: 57–63; Weiner 1971.

[15] On the exclusionary policies of dominant ethno-national groups in the political, military, and economic domains, see Weiner 1987: 35–36, 40–41.

[16] Buzan (1991: Chapter 2) distinguishes between two types of multinational states: imperial and federal states. In the federal state no single nation dominates (as in Switzerland, Canada, and Belgium), whereas the imperial state uses coercion to impose the control of one nation over others (as in Austria-Hungary or the Soviet Union). As multinational states, both types of states are potentially vulnerable to nationalist pressures to secede. In the case of the imperial state, its stability depends on the ability of the dominant nation to maintain its control as a strong state. The federal state constitutes, however, a middle category between deeply divided and well-integrated

This domestic challenge to the existing regional states undermines their coherence. Examples of quests for national self-determination include the Kurds in Iraq and Turkey, the Tamils in Sri Lanka, the Chechnyans in Russia, the Kashmiris in India (in addition to the irredentist claim of Pakistan vis-à-vis Muslim Kashmir), Nigeria and the attempt of Biafra to secede from it in 1967–70, the Philippines and the Moros, Burma and the Karen, and, at least until 2005, Indonesia and the Ache province, among many other cases. Leading successful attempts of secession are Bangladesh from Pakistan (1971), Northern Cyprus from Cyprus (1974), Eritrea from Ethiopia (1993) and, more recently, East Timor from Indonesia (2002) and Kosovo from Serbia (2008).[17]

2. Weak or "failed" states. These are states that lack a monopoly over the means of violence in their sovereign territory. An effective set of institutions is missing. These states are unable to extract sufficient military and economic resources from their societies to suppress ethno-nationalist/separatist challenges. Numerous African states belong to this category, as well as Afghanistan and some post-Soviet and post-Yugoslav republics, and other poor and fragile Third World states in Central America, Asia and the Middle East.[18]

3. "States without nations." These are states that failed to build political communities that identify with their states as reflecting their political sentiments and aspirations and who accept their territorial identity. Many Third World countries mentioned in the previous category also fit here. Yet states that are relatively strong in their domestic coercive capabilities, such as the Soviet Union and Yugoslavia before their breakdown and potentially also some Arab states such as Iraq and Syria, might also belong here.

societies (Horowitz 1994: 37). Although ethnic groups have strongly held political aspirations and interact as groups, several favorable conditions have moderated the effects of ethnic conflict, among them the emergence of ethnic issues late in relation to other cleavages and to the development of parties, so that party politics is not a perfect reflection of ethnic conflict. Among these states are Switzerland, Canada, and Belgium: all, significantly, federations. These are also called consociational (Switzerland, and Belgium) or semiconsociational (Canada) democracies: a power-sharing arrangement among ethnic groups (Lijphart 1977; Walzer 1997). In deeply divided societies, such as Northern Ireland and Sri Lanka, the moderating conditions are absent. This issue is also discussed in Miller 2007: Chapter 8 and Conclusions.

[17] For a comprehensive list of secessionist attempts, see Gurr 2000. For a list of all secessionist and irredentist crises, 1945–88, see Carment and James 1997: 215–18.

[18] For a useful index of the failed states and an updated and comprehensive ranking of 60 failed countries, see *Foreign Policy* July–August 2008. See also the discussion and references in Miller 2007: Chapter 2.

4. Stateless refugees who claim the right of return to their previous homes. They continue to see their previous place of residence as their national homeland from which they were unjustly evicted by force or which they had to leave under dire circumstances such as war. These refugees are not integrated to an alternative political community in the state in which they currently reside and continue to see their stay there as temporary. This applies, for example, to various victims of ethnic cleansing in the recent wars in Yugoslavia during the 1990s, such as Bosnians, Croats, Serbs and the Kosovar Muslims, in addition to the Palestinians.[19]

External incongruence and state strength lead to revisionist challenges

When the second condition of external or transborder incongruence is present, one could expect challenges to the territorial integrity of other states, which include pan-national movements of unification or irredentist-revisionist claims to territories held by other states on the grounds of national affiliation of the population or national-historic rights on the territory.

More specifically, there are three patterns of transborder incongruence.[20]

1. *Majority–Majority*: the presence of two or more states with a shared *ethnic majority* raises the likelihood of attempts at *national unification* led by revisionist states.
2. *Majority–Minority*: the presence of a state with an ethnic majority and neighbor(s) with the same ethnic minority increases the likelihood of attempts at *irredentism* by the former state vis-à-vis the territories populated by the minority.[21]
3. *Minority–Minority*: a shared ethnic minority among contiguous states might result in a status-quo orientation of these states.

Shared majority leads to conflicts derived from competing claims to leadership of the ethnic nation made by the elites of each state (Woodwell 2004: 200), and to attempts at national unification, including by coercion, based on the claim that there are "too many states" in relation to the number of nations. The non-revisionist states are likely to resist coercive unification by the revisionist state. Supra/pan-national forces

---

[19] On the demand for the right of return of the Palestinian refugees, see Miller 2007: Chapter 4.
[20] See also Woodwell 2004.
[21] On other types of relations in this triangle, see Brubaker 1996.

(such as Pan-Germanism, Pan-Arabism or Pan-Slavism) challenge the legitimacy of existing states in the region and call for their unification because they all belong to the same ethnic nation. Such movements are especially dangerous to the existing regional order if they are championed by strong revisionist states.

The presence of such revisionist forces generates the "illegitimate state": a state whose right to exist is challenged by its revisionist neighbors because in their eyes either the state's population does not constitute a distinctive nation that deserves a state of its own, or its territory should belong to a neighboring nation on historical grounds. Examples include the illegitimacy of Taiwan in the eyes of China, South Vietnam in the eyes of North Vietnam, South Korea in the eyes of North Korea, Northern Ireland as part of the United Kingdom from the viewpoint of the Irish national movement, individual Italian and German states in the eyes of Italian and German nationalists in the nineteenth century, and individual Arab states in the eyes of Arab nationalists – specifically in different periods Kuwait (challenged by Iraq), Lebanon (challenged by Syria), Jordan, and Israel.[22]

The likelihood of the emergence of pan-national forces and illegitimate states increases when the division of a single ethnic nation into a number of states was done by force through a military conquest by a rival regional state (supporting a competing national movement) or imposed by imperial powers.

In the case of the majority–minority pattern of transborder incongruence, the "irredentist-revisionist state" claims territories held by other states on the grounds of national affiliation of the population or national-historic rights to the territory. Irredentist conflicts include the Arab/Palestinian–Israeli conflict, and the conflicts between Iran and Iraq over the Shatt-al-Arab, Afghanistan and Pakistan over Pakistan's North-West Frontier Province, Ethiopia and Somalia over the Ogaden, Pakistan and India over Kashmir, Serbia with Croatia and Bosnia in the 1990s, and the post-Soviet conflict between Armenia and Azerbaijan on Nagorno-Karabach.[23]

The "irredentist-revisionist state" culminates in "the Greater State" ("Greater Germany," "Greater Syria," "Greater Israel," "Greater Serbia," etc.). The expansionist efforts of this type of state are likely to be opposed by the neighbors and thus lead to conflict. Because of the importance states attribute to their territorial integrity, such conflicts can

---

[22] The Middle Eastern cases are discussed at length in Miller 2007: Chapter 4.
[23] For a list of all irredentist (and also secessionist) crises, 1945–88, see Carment and James 1997: 215–18.

escalate to violence. The likelihood of irredentism increases if political boundaries in the region cross ethnic nations so that a sizable portion of the ethnic nation is beyond the boundaries of the state that claims to represent this group or is dominated by it. Ethnic alliances – cases in which a majority group in one state is a minority group in a neighboring state – increase the likelihood of international conflict (Moore and Davis 1998) where the co-ethnics in one state (the majority group) are propelled by feelings of solidarity with their ethnic kin in a proximate state (the minority). As a result, the state hosting the transborder minority feels threatened by the majority state.[24] Likewise this transborder minority, feeling greater chances of success due to this solidarity, is more likely to be emboldened and to attempt (or be subverted to) an armed rebellion. Such situations may lead to intended or unintended escalation.

Similarly, irredentism is more likely to emerge if there are territories beyond the boundaries of the state to which there has been persistent and intense historical attachment as the homeland of the nation, where it was born and had glorified accomplishments (Smith 2000: 67–68). The key point for our purposes is not whether this is an objective historical account or whether it is based on national myths. What matters is that large groups of people believe in such a historical attachment and are ready to fight for it, although it is probably also based on some historical facts.

The international opposition to coercive changes of boundaries in the post-1945 era has, however, led to a growing support of secession of the ethnic kin as a partial substitute for irredentism (Chazan 1991; Saideman 2001; Woodwell 2004: 201).[25] Moreover, the transborder minority itself might prefer secession to irredentism due to the political interests of its leadership or the unattractiveness of the putative irredentist state because of its authoritarian regime, economic backwardness, or low prestige (Horowitz 1991: 16–18).

A subset of irredentism refers to *settlers*, that is, a nationalist group that resides beyond the state boundaries and advocates, with the support of irredentist groups back home, the annexation to the homeland of the territories they settle. This advocacy is in many cases against the wishes of at least a large share of the residents in these territories who are from a

---

[24] For a recent empirical study that shows a significant increase in dyadic conflict when two states share an ethnic group and an ethnic majority exists in at least one of the states, see Woodwell 2004.

[25] For examples of states that preferred to support a secession of their ethnic kin rather than irredentism because of realpolitik considerations, see Horowitz 1991: 15. But at least some of these cases can be explained based on the minority–minority pattern discussed below.

Antecedent conditions	>	Independent variables	>	Manifestations	>	Outcomes
Demography and history	>	The state-to-nation congruence	>	Nationalist challenges	>	Hot war

Figure 3.1 The causal chain between incongruence and violence

different ethno-national group and thus oppose this annexation. Illustrations include the Germans in Eastern Europe, the Protestants in Northern Ireland, and the French settlers in Algiers, in addition to the post-1967 Jewish settlers in the occupied Palestinian territories, and ethnic Arabs in the Kurdish part of Iraq.

At any rate, the minority–minority pattern of transborder incongruence makes it easier for states to act based on realpolitik calculations because they are less constrained by domestic/nationalist considerations related to a certain ethnic majority. On the one hand, states might take advantage of a restive minority in a neighboring state and support the minority in order to weaken that state. For example, Iran supported the Kurdish insurgency against the Iraqi government in the early 1970s. On the other hand, the domestic/emotional commitment of a state to an ethnic minority is much weaker than to a group that is the majority in the state, and thus an irredentist orientation is unlikely. Moreover, neighboring states might occasionally cooperate in suppressing common minorities that challenge their territorial integrity and pose a problem to regional stability. Thus, Iraq and Iran, and also Turkey in some periods, collaborated against the quest of the Kurdish minorities in their countries for self-determination, which threatened the territorial integrity of all of them.

Figure 3.1 presents the causal relations between incongruence and violence. It especially underlines the role of demography and history as antecedent conditions that affect the impact that the independent variable is likely to have on producing nationalist challenges to the status quo and, thus, on the likelihood of violence.

The state-to-nation imbalance and the war-propensity of states

The state-to-nation imbalance affects both the motivation for the resort to violence and the opportunity to do so. National incongruence affects the level of motivation by incorporating substantive issues of war such as territory, boundaries, state creation, and state building. External incongruence, in particular, affects motivations for interstate war related to nationalist revisionist ideologies such as wars of national unification and irredentism. Thus, the state-to-nation imbalance provides an explanation for many of the territorial conflicts among states. The extent of domestic incongruence affects the motivation for civil wars and for wars of secession.

The degree of state strength, for its part, exercises major effects both on the capacity of states to wage international wars and on the opportunities to initiate civil wars and for external intervention in the territory of the state. Accordingly, we get four combinations of types of states and types of violent conflicts in which they tend to be involved, if at all.

Types of states and their war-propensity

Table 3.1 shows the combined effect of the two dimensions of the state-to-nation balance on state war-proneness. This combined effect produces four distinctive types of states with regard to their war-proneness. Each one of these types of states has, in turn, distinctive effects on the types of wars in the region. Thus, the question of war and peace in a given region depends on the relative prevalence of each of these types of states in the

Table 3.1 *The effects of the extent of the state-to-nation congruence and of state strength on state and regional war-proneness*

	Congruence	Incongruence
Strong states	**Status-quo states** peaceful conflict resolution: states in post-World War II Western Europe; 20th-century Argentina and Brazil (and other states, especially in the Southern Cone of South America)	**Revisionist states** and nationalist unification; (pan-national movements) wars of aggression and diversionary wars: Prussia and the wars of German unification (pan-Germanism); Post-1949 China–Taiwan; North Korea vis-à-vis South Korea; Pakistan and India's Kashmir; "Greater Serbia"; pre-2003 Iraq and also "Greater Syria" (and pan-Arabism)
Weak states	**"The frontier state"** Boundary/territorial wars: 19th-century Argentina and Brazil (and many other states in South America)	Civil war and Intervention in **Incoherent/"failed" states** – separatism; security dilemma: post-Cold War former Soviet republics; Bosnia; Congo; Somalia; Sudan and many other African states; Afghanistan; Lebanon; Yemen; the Palestinian Authority; post-2003 Iraq

region. At any rate, the production of four distinctive types of states by the two dimensions of the state-to-nation balance – state strength and national congruence – shows that these two dimensions are generally independent of each other even if there might be some relations between them in certain cases. Thus, the production of the four types demonstrates the utility of the distinction between the two dimensions for explanatory purposes.

In cell no. 1 relatively strong states, which are nationally incongruent, pursue revisionist policies based on the "too many states" logic. There is a widespread national feeling, even if also manipulated by leaders for their own political agenda, that the nation is artificially and arbitrarily divided into a number of states. In this nationalist view, the nation should unify into a single state, which would reflect the national aspirations and sentiments of the single unified nation. For this "noble" purpose of national unification, the strongest state of that nation should not hesitate to use force.

A related variant is the "Greater State," claiming territories beyond its boundaries based on the national identity of the people or historical rights. To the extent that the revisionist state has internal incongruence, in addition to the external incongruence, its leadership has domestic incentives to behave aggressively and embark on diversionary wars according to the scapegoat theory. Leaders are likely to believe that wars with external enemies will strengthen their state and lead to national unity and solidarity, thus reducing challenges to their leadership, and strengthen their hold over power. The policies of, for example, Greater Serbia, Greater Iraq, and Greater Syria illustrate this type of state. This kind of state will be able to pursue such irredentist policies only so long as it maintains the monopoly over the means of violence in its territory, is able to mobilize relatively large armies and to raise considerable revenues from taxing its populations, and is able to ensure that overall state institutions function effectively. If state institutions become much weaker and cease to function effectively, the state's internal incongruence might lead to large-scale violence among the rival ethno-national groups in the state, and then these states might move to cell no. 2 of the failed states.[26]

In cell no. 2, incoherent or "failed states" are the combined product of weak states in which there is also a low level of citizen identification with the state and with its territorial identity as reflecting their national identity and aspirations. In other words, there are strong aspirations for secession; at any rate, the transborder ties with members of the same ethnic group residing in neighboring states are stronger than the affiliation with the citizens of their own state, who belong to a different ethnic

---

[26] This is what happened, for example, to post-2003 Iraq.

group. The weakness of incoherent states is permissive of the violent actions of revisionist groups and encourages other groups trying to defend themselves. Such moves trigger a cycle of escalation that the weak state is unable to contain because it is unable to defeat or bribe the insurgents (Byman and Van Evera 1998). Incoherent states may also bring about challenges to the regional order even though they are militarily and domestically weak (vis-à-vis their own societies). In this case, one should expect the eruption of civil/ethnic wars within these states, which also create temptations for their neighbors to intervene in these conflicts because of either security fears or a quest for profit. Afghanistan and Somalia are good examples of this type of state.

In cell no. 3, the combination of congruence and weakness of the state brings about the "frontier state," which is not fragmented ethnically and nationally, but also does not fully control its territory, and has boundaries that are not clearly demarcated. Regions populated by weak states with state-to-nation congruence, as in cell 3, are still prone to regional wars, although they might have the potential for peaceful conflict resolution at a later stage if state building succeeds through the strengthening of the regional states. As long as these states are weak, there is a high likelihood of territorial and boundary wars because the states' control over their territory is incomplete and the boundaries are not fully fixed, agreed upon or clearly drawn. As a result, there are numerous boundary disputes. A good example is nineteenth-century South America until the relative strengthening of the regional states starting in the 1880s.

In contrast, as in cell no. 4, the combined effect of congruence and strong states results in a much lower likelihood of resort to violence. As a result of state-to-nation congruence, states have less motivation to resort to violence and have fewer quarrels with their neighbors. They will tend to be status-quo states without ambitions of territorial expansion. Thus, mutual fears and the security dilemma are likely to decline. As strong states, they are also able not only to negotiate peaceful agreements with regional states, but also to maintain their commitments and to guarantee stable peace. Thus, both wars of profit and wars of insecurity will be less likely, as will be diversionary wars. Twentieth-century South America is a good example of the emergence of a dominant status-quo orientation in strong and congruent states (mainly Argentina and Brazil).

Conclusions and implications

Ethno-national conflict is a much more important source of regional conflict and violence than what the major streams of IR theory, notably realism and liberalism, would lead us to expect (Miller 2007: Chapter 1).

This is because issues of nationalism and ethnicity tend to be less divisible than material issues. Nations derive their identities to a large degree from particular places and territories, and the control of these is often essential to maintaining a healthy sense of national identity (Toft 2003; White 2000: 10). Thus, state-to-nation issues arouse strong emotions and passionate ideological commitments that make pragmatic compromise and bargaining more difficult.[27] As a result, domestic politics plays an especially powerful role in constraining the maneuvering room of political leaders on these issues. Strong commitment of domestic constituencies to ethnicity and nationalism generates pressures on and incentives for state leaders to maintain hard-line positions and even to go to war.[28] Because of the strong passions and domestic incentives produced by a state-to-nation imbalance, such an imbalance is likely to challenge the conventional realist logic of balance of power theory and deterrence. Highly motivated actors might initiate violence even if they are weaker in the overall balance of power.

With regard to liberalism, it is true that democracy, with power-sharing or federal arrangements, may mitigate the state-to-nation problem. Yet, under a state-to-nation imbalance, democratization can also aggravate the problem, at least initially (see Miller 2007, Ch. 8; for a related argument see Mansfield and Snyder 2005) or the state-to-nation imbalance may make it harder to establish democracy in the first place (Horowitz 1994).

The extent of the state-to-nation imbalance explains variations in war-propensity among different regions. The model proposed here is able to explain empirical variations among different regions such as the high war-proneness of the regions with high state-to-nation imbalance and strong ethno-national sentiments such as the Middle East, the Balkans, South Asia, and East Asia in contrast to the peacefulness of regions with relatively low state-to-nation imbalances and strong civic nationalism such as South America during most of the twentieth century and post-1945 Western Europe.[29] The model can also account for the evolution of warm peace in South America during the twentieth century due to

---

[27] On the role of emotions in ethnic conflict, see Peterson 2002.
[28] For studies which show that ethnic/national claims are major sources of territorial conflicts, see Carment 1993; Carment and James 1997; Holsti 1991 (esp. pp. 140–42, 144–45, 214–16, 274–78, 280, 308); Huth 1996: 108–12; Luard 1986: 421–47 (esp. 442–47); Mandel 1980; White 2000; Woodwell 2004.
[29] Although German unification continued to pose a challenge to stability until 1990, systemic factors outside the purview of the model – bipolarity and MAD (Mutually Assured Destruction) – stabilized the relations between the two parts of Europe during the Cold War. The expulsion of the ethnic Germans from Eastern Europe after 1945 has, however, reduced German irredentism toward this region.

relatively effective state building in the strongest states in the region. This process helped to create a state-to-nation balance in conjunction with the national congruence in the region (based on civic nationalism in immigrant societies and marginalization of the indigenous population).

The state-to-nation imbalance and issues related to it explain a substantial number of regional wars in the past two hundred years or so – surely not all of them, but more than most other explanatory factors. The theoretical model presented here is relevant for explaining different levels of conflict in different time periods and regions. Thus, the theory's purview is not limited to conflicts of the Cold War era (such as the Arab–Israeli wars or issues related to German unification) or even of the post-Cold War period (such as the wars in the former Yugoslavia and former Soviet Union). It extends equally well to major earlier conflicts like the wars of German unification in the nineteenth century and the Balkan Wars that preceded World War I. Similarly, the theory is relevant for explaining the French–German nationalist rivalry over Alsace-Lorraine.

The model can also explain the concentration of key crises in the contemporary international system such as the East Asian conflicts between China and Taiwan and in Korea. Both of these cases involve demands for ethno-national unification based on the claim that there are "too many states" in relation to the number of nations, as was earlier the case with the war in Vietnam. The Indo-Pakistan conflict is another case of state-to-nation conflict revolving around Pakistan's irredentist demands vis-à-vis India's Kashmir.

Variations in the components of the state-to-nation imbalance explain different types of regional wars, for example, strong states which are externally incongruent tend to be revisionist, while internally incongruent weak states are more likely to face secessionist challenges and civil wars. Shared ethnic majority is more likely to lead to conflicts over unification, while majority–minority in adjacent states may result in attempts at irredentism.

War must not erupt necessarily in every case in which there is a state-to-nation imbalance, but such an imbalance is potentially de-stabilizing and it is conducive to manipulations by leaders and states that are acting in their own power interests.

The state-to-nation imbalance is an *underlying* cause of regional wars. It makes certain regions more prone to wars than others due both to the emergence of substantive issues of conflict (territories and boundaries) and to the enhancement of the security dilemma and power rivalries in the region (that is, the search for power and profit by expansionist revisionist states) under the conditions of state-to-nation imbalance.

These power and security factors highlighted by the realist school are the *proximate* causes of specific regional wars.[30] The balance of power, the offense/defense balance, and security fears determine when the basic regional predisposition for war will lead to actual wars; in other words, they provide the opportunity rather than the basic motivation for war.[31] Namely, without their presence the underlying state-to-nation problems may not be translated into a specific war, but in the absence of a high degree of state-to-nation imbalance, power drives and security fears are less likely to take place and to lead to a resort to large-scale violence among neighbors.

The eruption of war partly depends on the regional balance of power, although the systemic environment is very important for the management of state-to-nation conflicts: Great Power disengagement and especially competition aggravate the problem, while Great Power hegemony and cooperation mitigate it.[32] The global factors on their own can at best bring about cold peace. Warm peace is also independent of the continuing stabilizing engagement of external powers in the region. Yet the domestic–regional prerequisites for warm peace, especially successful state and nation building or democratization leading to liberal compatibility, are very demanding and hard to reach in many regions. For this reason, Great Power hegemony or concert can be critical in advancing peaceful regional settlements (Kolodziej and Zartman 1996), even if only cold ones, in regions in which there are intractable state-to-nation conflicts that the regional actors have a hard time resolving on their own without external assistance. Indeed, the inclusion of systemic factors can allow the model to account for the transitions within regions such as the emergence of cold peace in the Middle East in the post-Cold War era and in the Balkans during the Cold War. It can also account for the environment under which a shift toward warm peace was made possible in Western Europe in the post-1945 era and in Eastern Europe in the post-Cold War period (Miller 2007). Yet the warming of the regional peace and its maintenance eventually depend on the regional parties and the way they resolve or transcend the state-to-nation issues.

Finally, the present framework helps to overcome the divide between domestic/civil and international conflicts by focusing on the state-to-nation balance in different parts of the world as affecting the hot

---

[30] On the distinction between underlying and proximate causes of war, see Lebow 1981; Van Evera 1995; Vasquez 1993: 293–97.

[31] For recent works on the offense/defense balance and the security dilemma, see Glaser 1997; Glaser and Kaufmann 1998; Van Evera 1998.

[32] For an elaborate discussion of the effects of the type of Great Power engagement on regional war and peace, see Miller 2007: chapters 2, 5, and 9).

outcomes of hot war and warm peace. Nevertheless, the cold outcomes of these conflicts are affected by variations in the type of great power engagement in these regions.

REFERENCES

Anderson, B. 1991. *Imagined Communities: Reflections on the Origins and Spread of Nationalism*. London: Verso.

Ayoob, M. 1995. *The Third World Security Predicament*. Boulder, CO: Lynne Rienner.

Barrington, L.W. 1997. "'Nation' and 'Nationalism': The Misuse of Key Concepts in Political Science." *PS: Political Science & Politics*. 30(4): 712–16.

Brown, M. (ed.). 1993. *Ethnic Conflict and International Security*. Princeton University Press.

Brubaker, R. 1996. *Nationalism Reframed: Nationhood and the National Question in the New Europe*. Cambridge University Press.

   1998. "Myths and Misconceptions in the Study of Nationalism." Pp. 272–306 in *The State of the Nation: Ernest Gellner and the Theory of Nationalism*, edited by John Hall. Cambridge University Press.

Buzan, B. 1991. *People, States and Fear: An Agenda for International Security Studies in the Post-Cold War Era*. Boulder, CO: Lynne Rienner.

Byman, D. and D. Van Evera. 1998. "Why They Fight: Hypotheses on the Causes of Contemporary Deadly Conflict." *Security Studies* 7(3): 1–50.

Carment, D. 1993. "The International Dimension of Ethnic Conflict." *Journal of Peace Research* 30(2): 137–50.

Carment, D. and P. James (eds.). 1997. *Wars in the Midst of Peace: The International Politics of Ethnic Conflict*. Pittsburgh, PA: University of Pittsburgh Press.

Cederman, L. 1997. *Emergent Actors in World Politics: How States and Nations Develop and Dissolve*. Princeton University Press.

Centeno, M.A. 2002. *Blood and Debt: War and the Nation-State in Latin America*. University Park: Pennsylvania State University Press.

Chazan, N. (ed.). 1991. *Irredentism and International Politics*. Boulder, CO: Lynne Rienner.

Connor, W. 1994. *Ethnonationalism: The Quest for Understanding*. Princeton University Press.

Csergo, Z. and J. Goldgeier. 2004. "Nationalist Strategies and European Integration." *Perspectives on Politics* 2(1): 21–37.

Davidson, J.W. 2002. "The Roots of Revisionism: Fascist Italy, 1922–39." *Security Studies* 11(4): 125–59.

Fearon, J. and D. Laitin. 2003. "Ethnicity, Insurgency, and Civil Wars." *APSR* 97(1): 75–90.

Gause, F.G. 1992. "Sovereignty, Statecraft, and Stability in the Middle East." *Journal of International Affairs* 45(2): 441–69.

Gellner, E. 1983. *Nations and Nationalism*. Oxford: Blackwell.

Glaser, C.L. 1997. "The Security Dilemma Revisited." *World Politics* 50(1): 171–201.

Glaser, C.L. and C. Kaufmann. 1998. "What is the Offense-Defense Balance and How Can We Measure It?" *International Security* 22(4): 44–82.

Gurr, T.R. 2000. *Peoples versus States*. Washington, DC: US Institute of Peace.

Hinnebusch, R. 2003. *The International Politics of the Middle East*. Manchester University Press.

Hobsbawm, E. 1990. *Nations and Nationalism since 1780: Programme, Myth, Reality*. Cambridge University Press.

Hoffmann, S. 1998. *World Disorders: Troubled Peace in the Post-Cold War Era*. Lanham, MA: Rowman & Littlefield.

Holsti, K.J. 1991. *Peace and War: Armed Conflicts and International Order 1648–1989*. Cambridge University Press.

    1996. *War, the State, and the State of War*. Cambridge University Press.

Horowitz, D.L. 1985. *Ethnic Groups in Conflict*. Berkeley: University of California Press.

    1991. "Irredentas and Secessions: Adjacent Phenomena, Neglected Connections." Pp. 9–22 in *Irredentism and International Politics*, edited by N. Chazan. Boulder, CO: Lynne Rienner.

    1994. "Democracy in Divided Societies." Pp. 35–55. in *Nationalism, Ethnic Conflict, and Democracy*, edited by L. Diamond and M.F. Plattner. Baltimore: Johns Hopkins University Press.

Huth, P. 1996. *Standing Your Guard: Territorial Disputes and International Conflict*. Ann Arbor: University of Michigan Press.

Job, B. 1997. "Matters of Multilateralism: Implications for Regional Conflict Management." Pp. 165–94 in *Regional Orders: Building Security in a New World*, edited by D.A. Lake and P.M. Morgan. University Park: Pennsylvania State University Press.

Kolodziej, E.A. and I.W. Zartman. 1996. "Coping with Conflict: A Global Approach." Pp. 3–34 in *Coping with Conflict after the Cold War*, edited by E.A. Kolodziej and R.E. Kanet. Baltimore, MD: Johns Hopkins University Press.

Kupchan, C.A. (ed.). 1995. *Nationalism and Nationalities in the New Europe*. Ithaca, NY: Cornell University Press.

    1998. "After Pax Americana: Benign Power, Regional Integration, and the Sources of a Stable Multipolarity." *International Security* 23(2): 40–79.

Lebow, R.N. 1981. *Between Peace and War: the Nature of International Crisis*. Baltimore, MD: Johns Hopkins University Press.

Legro, J. 2005. *Rethinking the World*. Ithaca, NY: Cornell University Press.

Lijphart, A. 1977. *Democracy in Plural Societies*. New Haven, CT: Yale University Press.

Luard, E. 1986. *War in International Society*. New Haven, CT: Yale University Press.

Mandel, R. 1980. "Roots of the Modern Interstate Border Dispute." *Journal of Conflict Resolution* 24(3): 427–54.

Mann, Michael. 1993. *The Sources of Social Power*. 3 vols. Vol. II: *The Rise of Classes and Nation-States, 1760–1914*. New York: Cambridge University Press.

Mansfield, E.D. and J. Snyder. 2005. *Electing to Fight: Why Emerging Democracies Go to War*. Cambridge, MA: MIT Press.

Maoz, Z. 2004. "Pacifism and Fightaholism in International Politics: A Structural History of National and Dyadic Conflict, 1816–1992." *International Studies Review* 6(4): 107–34.

Mayall, J. 1990. *Nationalism and International Society.* Cambridge University Press.

Miller, B. 2007. *States, Nations and the Great Powers: The Sources of Regional War and Peace.* Cambridge University Press.

Moore, W.H. and D.R. Davis. 1998. "Transnational Ethnic Ties and Foreign Policy." Pp. 89–103 in *The International Spread of Ethnic Conflict*, edited by D. Lake and D. Rothchild. Princeton University Press.

Peterson, R.D. 2002. *Understanding Ethnic Violence: Fear, Hatred, and Resentment in Twentieth-Century Eastern Europe.* Cambridge University Press.

Rotberg, R.I. (ed.). 2003. *State Failure and State Weakness in a Time of Terror.* Washington, DC: Brookings Institution Press.

Saideman, S.M. 2001. *The Ties that Divide: Ethnic Politics, Foreign Policy and International Conflict.* New York: Columbia University Press.

Schweller, R. 1994. "Bandwagoning for Profit: Bringing the Revisionist State Back In." *International Security* 19(1): 72–107.

1996. "Neorealism's Status Quo Bias: What Security Dilemma?" *Security Studies* 5(3): 90–121.

1998. *Deadly Imbalances: Tripolarity and Hitler's Strategy of World Conquest.* New York: Columbia University Press.

Smith, A. 1986. *The Ethnic Origins of Nations.* Oxford and New York: Blackwell.

2000. *The Nation in History.* Hanover, NH: University Press of New England.

Suny, R.G. 1999/2000. "Provisional Stabilities: The Politics of Identities in Post-Soviet Eurasia." *International Security* 24(3): 139–78.

Tilly, C. 1975. "Western State-making." Pp. 601–638 in *The Formation of National States in Western Europe*, edited by C. Tilly. Princeton University Press.

1990. *Coercion, Capital and European States: AD 990–1990.* Oxford: Blackwell.

Toft, M.D. 2002/3. "Indivisible Territory, Geographic Concentration, and Ethnic War." *Security Studies* 12(2): 82–119.

2003. *Geography of Ethnic Violence: Identity, Interests, and the Indivisibility of Territory.* Princeton University Press.

Van Evera, S. 1995. "Hypotheses on Nationalism and War." Pp. 251–85 in *Global Dangers – An International Security Reader*, edited by S.M. Lynn-Jones and S.E. Miller. Cambridge, MA: MIT Press.

1998. "Offense, Defense, and the Causes of War." *International Security* 22(4): 5–43.

Vasquez, John A. 1993. *The War Puzzle.* Cambridge University Press.

Walter, B.F. 2003. "Explaining the Intractability of Territorial Conflict." *International Studies Review* 5(4): 137–53.

Walzer, M. 1997. *On Toleration.* New Haven, CT: Yale University Press.

Weiner, M. 1971. "The Macedonian Syndrome: A Historical Model of International Relations and Political Development" *World Politics* 23: 665–83.

1987. "Political Change: Asia, Africa and the Middle East." Pp. 33–63 in *Understanding Political Development*, edited by M. Weiner and S.P. Huntington. Boston: Little, Brown.

Welsh, D. 1993. "Domestic Politics and Ethnic Conflict." Pp. 43–60 in *Ethnic Conflict and International Security*, edited by M. Brown. Princeton University Press.

White, G.W. 2000. *Nationalism and Territory*. Lanham, MD: Rowman and Littlefield.

Williams, K.P. 2001. *Despite Nationalist Conflicts: Theory and Practice of Maintaining World Peace*. Westport, CT: Praeger.

Wolfers, A. 1962. *Discord and Collaboration*. Baltimore, MD: Johns Hopkins University Press.

Woodwell, D. 2004. "Unwelcome Neighbors: Shared Ethnicity and International Conflict during the Cold War." *International Studies Quarterly* 48(1): 197–223.

4   State violence in the origins of nationalism

British counterinsurgency and the rebirth of Irish
nationalism, 1969–1972

James Hughes

Theories of nationalism concur that nationalism is a political idea that is
historically determined and structured over the *longue durée*, whether by
modernity and industrial order, or the power of the state, or beliefs about
ethnicity and culture. Nationalist political mobilizations are generally
held to be epiphenomena that, if not quite extraneous to the logic of
the metatheories, are considered to be much less important. When
Gellner synthesized his ideas about nationalism he employed literary,
botanical, and other metaphors to dismiss the idea that nationalism could
be an "old, latent, dormant force." Nationalism, according to Gellner,
was the political "crystallisation of units" that were suitable for the
conditions of industrial society. Most nationalisms, he argued, were
"determined slumberers" who refused to be awakened, indeed, they
went "meekly to their doom" in the dustheap of history (Gellner 1983:
47–49). In a famous statement, lifted from Sherlock Holmes (but which
is actually a reversal of Holmes's deductive thinking), he asserted that
most nationalisms do not project themselves violently:

> Nevertheless, the clue to the understanding of nationalism is its weakness at least
> as much as its strength. It was the dog who failed to bark who provided the vital
> clue for Sherlock Holmes. The numbers of potential nationalisms which failed to
> bark is far, far larger than those which did, though they have captured all our
> attention. (Gellner 1983: 43)

Gellner showed little interest in explaining the dynamics of national
and ethnic conflict, other than to attribute it partly to the agency of
"nationalist awakeners" and "human carriers," or to the lack of harmony
between political boundaries and high cultures (Gellner 1983: 48, 51).
We are left with a considerable puzzle as to why there might be a sudden
transformation of slumberers. What makes sleeping dogs rise and bark?
A closer attention to the interaction of agency and contingency is
required to give us a better purchase on an explanation for why the

nationalist "moment" occurs when it does, and why it becomes a powerful transformative political force when it does. For nationalist "moments" are nearly always crises of the state. Might some nationalisms, especially those that turn violent, be better analyzed within a context of interdependence, where one nationalism evokes or provokes another through a sequence of action and reaction, and where violence may be the catalyst? Linkages of this kind require us to focus on the micro foundations for a nationalist mobilization. I explore this thesis by examining the role of British nationalism and British state violence in sparking an awakening of Irish nationalism during the Northern Ireland "Troubles" that erupted in 1969 and became one of the deadliest and most protracted conflicts in Europe after World War II and before the civil wars of Yugoslavia (O'Leary and McGarry 1993).

Ideology and war in the Irish case

The importance of this conflict for scholars of nationalism resonates in two directions. First, the conflict is generally explained within a historical continuum of fractious relations between Britain and Ireland, unionist and nationalist, Catholic and Protestant. For the most part, the important literature on the conflict locates it within a macro-level historical explanation, with the main positions pivoting around glosses influenced by the metatheoretical structure/identity frames. The hegemonic British scholarly position on the conflict is that the nationalist element is confined to and is endogenous to Ireland, with the role of the British government being one of "umpire." It is a position born out of a Whiggish denial of any form of British nationalism. Any emphasis on long-run historical context and continuum, however, dances at the edge of a determinism and historicism that reduces all to the Irish "propensity for violence" as Townshend labelled it (1983: 1). Why did the political violence in Northern Ireland begin in 1969 and not earlier? Also, why did it so quickly escalate into an existential crisis for the Stormont regime, which was de facto abolished by the British government in 1972? Indeed, why did the Troubles so quickly become such a serious security crisis for the British state? What was it about the period 1969–72 that reinvigorated Irish nationalism, gave birth to the armed struggle of the Provisional Irish Republican Army (PIRA) and made it into one of the most formidable nationalist insurgent movements in the twentieth century?

It is generally accepted that the "shock" of concentrated violence in the early phase of the Northern Ireland conflict – the period 1969–72 – reverberated for the next two decades and from this period emerged a newly vibrant form of "physical force" Irish nationalism (see figures 4.1 and 4.2).

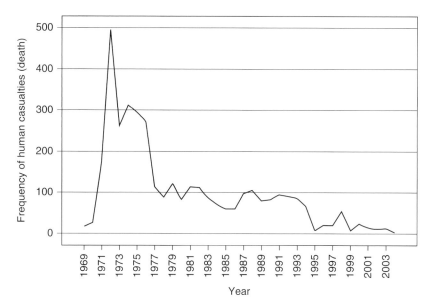

Figure 4.1 Conflict-related deaths by year in Northern Ireland, 1969–2003

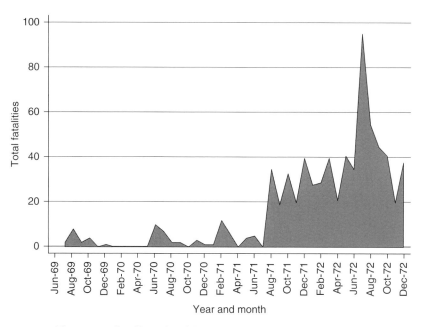

Figure 4.2 Conflict-related deaths by month in Northern Ireland, 1969–72

The scale of violence in terms of deaths and casualties tailed off quite dramatically from the mid 1970s, though the economic destructive power of the PIRA campaign peaked at the very end of the conflict in the first half of the 1990s when it inflicted a number of highly damaging bombing attacks on British cities. The polarization of positions between unionists and nationalists was only circumvented from the mid 1980s by bilateral British and Irish government agreements that were then steadily imposed in top-down fashion on the protagonists in Northern Ireland, and reinforced by external pressures from the USA and the EC/EU. The standard account holds that this process is what led to the "Belfast Agreement" of 1998.

Part of this standard account, from the very outset of the conflict, is that the British state acted as a "broker" (*The Times* 1969b: 7). Home Secretary James Callaghan's first major speech to the House of Commons on the British Army's deployment in August 1969 stated that the government's first objective was to "keep the peace between the communities" (House of Commons 1969: 48) (if not quite a neutral position given the British government's ongoing commitment to the partition of Ireland). The objective of the British military presence was, as the General Officer Commanding (GOC), Sir Ian Freeland put it, to "take a middle of the road line" between the antagonistic unionist and nationalist communities in Northern Ireland (McCreary 1970: 8). The army claims that it aimed at "separating" or "interposing" itself between the two communities and acting "even-handedly" (Ministry of Defence 2006: 2–4) until such times as a political accommodation could be reached. This benign gloss was promoted by successive generations of British politicians in a cross-party consensus on Northern Ireland, and was also popularized by the British media.[1] The "desired end-state" of military suppression of violence to allow a political process is the pivot for the British Army's own account of its role in the Troubles (Ministry of Defence 2006). However, while this report was framed as an exercise in "learning from mistakes," it is contradictory in that it shows a reluctance to account for the failures of "over-reaction" and a lack of sensitivity to the use of force, and also claims that successes rested on the army's culture of "restraint" (Ministry of Defence 2006: 8–15).

In contrast to this benign account I provide an explanation for radicalization that focuses on the violent British state security response in the period 1969–72, which was overwhelmingly directed against the Catholic community. One of the main lessons drawn by the British Army from its experience in Northern Ireland is the problem of "over-reaction" and

---

[1] See, for example, British newspaper cartoons from August 1969 at: http://cain.ulst.ac.uk/images/cartoons/douglas98.htm.

harshness, especially in the early phase. As *Operation Banner* puts it: "during the early 1970s … a desire to 'sort the Micks out' was often apparent" (Ministry of Defence 2006: 8–11). The British security response transformed what was, in essence, a peaceful democratic movement for reform and civil rights into a formidable nationalist cause championed by PIRA, itself only founded in early 1970. The resurgence of violent nationalism, both Irish republican and British unionist, was reflexively legitimized by a wholescale rediscovery and renewal of references to the historical progeny and continuity of the respective nationalisms. In sum, the reactive qualities in the emergence and relegitimization of the "physical force" tradition in Irish nationalism in this period leads me to the conclusion that this radical nationalism was not simply a product of internal war, but was also largely made in Britain – a product of British state violence. Moreover, this state violence was in character and form shaped by decades of British military experience in repressing anti-colonial movements, often nationalist.

The Stormont regime had existed for fifty years since the partition of Ireland, and had been consolidated on a sectarian basis around Protestant/unionist domination and discrimination against and exclusion of Catholics for at least 45 years. Although there were sporadic sectarian civil disorders during that period (at the state's birth in 1921–23 and again in the mid 1930s), the regime had never been seriously threatened. Irish nationalist political challenges to the Stormont regime were extremely weak throughout its existence, with the quasi-constitutional demoralized malaise of abstentionist politics dominating (i.e. Irish nationalists participated in elections but refused to take seats or recognize the legitimacy of Stormont or Westminster). However, that malaise seemed to be at a historical turning point in 1965–66, as the rapprochement between the Stormont government, under the moderate reformist unionist prime minister Terence O'Neill, and the pragmatic Irish government of Sean Lemass – both of which shared a technocratic focus – led to a shift away from abstentionism by the main nationalist parties in the North to a more fully engaged constitutional politics.

Secondly, the conflict in Northern Ireland surfaced one of the most enduring themes in Irish politics and the study of Irish nationalism, which for the previous generation had largely been peripheral – namely, the relative advantages and disadvantages, and the validity, of the "moral force" versus the "physical force" traditions in the struggle of Irish nationalists for independence from Britain. The only significant campaign by the violent nationalists of the IRA after partition (its so-called "border campaign" of 1955–62) turned out to be such a dismal failure and humiliation due to lack of popular support, in particular in the north of Ireland, that it set in motion a process of transformation of the IRA itself away from nationalism towards Marxism. The IRA's quasi-official historian, the American academic John Bowyer Bell, described the IRA as a "husk" and in the "doldrums" in the 1960s (Bell 1989: 336). A Belfast IRA leader later recalled that in 1961 the organization in the city had just 24 members and 2 guns (cited in Purdie 1990: 44). The 1960s saw a younger South-based IRA leadership abandoning "armed struggle" and embracing a Marxist social movement agenda. The new political direction was strongly shaped by Marxists from the Connolly Association in Britain. The 50th anniversary commemoration of the 1916 Rising in 1966 is notable not for a restatement of IRA adherence to the "physical force" tradition but for the intellectual rediscovery of the non-sectarian ethic of Irish republicanism, and a kind of intellectual republican chic – beginning with the foundation of the first of many Wolfe Tone Clubs in Trinity College Dublin. Under the influence of British and Irish communists, notably Roy Johnston, the IRA steadily supplanted much of its traditional nationalist ideology with a radical leftist agenda around the notion of "class struggle." While the overriding goal of a united Ireland remained the central ideological pillar, armed struggle against British rule was discarded in favor of a socialist revolutionary doctrine that emphasized cooperatives and engagement in social movements such as campaigns for better housing, land, and fishing rights. The new IRA program was for a "New Republic" based on "worker's unity," civil rights, justice and equality (Hanley and Millar 2009: 22–69; Kelley 1982: 86–90). Given the marginalization of the IRA in Irish political life in the 1950s and 1960s, and the embarrassment of its "border campaign," the debate was essentially resolved against the "physical force" tradition of nationalism in Ireland. The drift in the mid 1960s was for a convergence of Irish nationalists on both the Left and the Right towards forms of constitutional politics and engagement based on demands for civil rights, justice and equality in Northern Ireland, and looking to the Westminster government for redress.

Recent work by unionist historians on this period is incredibly lacking in nuance. For example, while it is generally recognized that the civil rights movement that emerged in Northern Ireland in the mid 1960s was not a creature of the IRA, the reactionary unionist position of the mid-to-late 1960s that the civil rights movement was, as the Stormont Minister for Home Affairs Bill Craig put it in 1968, a "Republican front" is also often echoed. Moreover, the descent into violent conflict is attributed to IRA manipulation of the civil rights movement. A recurrent unionist narrative is that a reformist Stormont regime was undermined by an IRA-republican-Catholic conspiracy which used the civil rights movement as a trojan horse; that the civil rights movement of the 1960s was an IRA "initiative"; that civil rights "agitation" "spiralled Ulster into the sectarian violence"; and that civil rights activists "sought to destroy tranquillity and generate violence" (English 2003: 82, 91, 96–98, 147). A major study of the student-led civil rights organization People's Democracy could not distinguish between the nationalist political symbolism and folk music culture of Catholics, who formed the bulk of the membership of the civil rights movement, and support for the IRA: "Much of the rhetoric, the imagery and the use of traditional music resembled that of Sinn Fein" (P. Arthur 1974: 112).

The IRA leadership was undoubtedly important in creating momentum behind a social movement for civil rights, and encouraged its members in the North to engage in it, but the establishment of what became the Northern Ireland Civil Rights Association (NICRA) in 1968 was not an IRA "initiative," and nor were the various direct actions, marches and street protests that NICRA undertook in 1968–69. NICRA was the product of a broad "coalition of forces," mainly liberal and leftist ideologically, but drawn from across the sectarian and class divide and with a common interest in reform. Republicans were just one element (Purdie 1990: 150–51). What unionists also fail to understand is that this republican element was an ideologically transformed IRA that had abandoned armed struggle for socialism, and potentially one that could be engaged in constitutional politics. The development of a civil rights movement was strongly influenced by the resonance of the Kennedy presidency in Ireland and the recent struggle for civil rights for blacks in the USA. As in the USA, the nationalist movement was a movement committed to the power of non-violent direct action and "moral force." There were obvious demonstration effects in the way that Catholics borrowed the tactics of the National Association for the Advancement of Colored People (NAACP) and Dr. Martin Luther King, whose protests had escalated in the spring of 1965. Television footage of the brutal police actions to stop the civil rights march on the Selma bridge in March 1965 seemed to Catholics to echo their experience in Northern Ireland. Banners and placards used in Catholic protests about housing and job discrimination made reference to the "Jim Crow" system and the black experience in Montgomery and Selma. NICRA marches, however, were often accompanied by nationalist bands playing Nationalist Party tunes. Some IRA members were among the stewards of marches and pickets, but according to Bell (1989: 357) their role was to contain the potential for violence. In contrast, leading leftist members of NICRA believed that the movement was being "wrecked" not by the IRA, but because it was being taken over by "moderate nationalists" in the North (specifically by leaders such as John Hume in Derry and Gerry Fitt in Belfast) who were intent on making it "a specifically Catholic movement" (McCann 1968: 4).

The violent conflict originated from the populist unionist reaction to the increasingly assertive Catholic demands for civil rights. The populist mobilization centered on Reverend Ian Paisley, and the revival of the Ulster Volunteer Force (UVF), an extremist unionist paramilitary group, as an armed force (Bruce 1989). Political symbolism was paramount in the jostling for political position that occurred in the 1960s in Northern Ireland. Two aspects, in particular, became a central feature of political mobilization. The first was the right to display the Irish flag, which was banned under Stormont legislation, even in Catholic areas. The second was the right to demonstrate, with Catholic protests being contained by police within "their own" areas and outside city centers, which were regarded as Protestant political spaces. Paisleyites undertook provocation marches and counterprotests as close to Catholic areas and marches as the police would permit. This protocol of civil rights protest and Paisley-ite counterprotest, with the Stormont police, the Royal Ulster Constabulary (RUC), taking sides by repressing the civil rights marchers, became routine in the course of 1967–69. One of the challenges posed by NICRA to the Stormont regime was that it was non-sectarian, but no matter how many Protestant liberals or Westminster MPs joined its protests, the RUC invariably treated them as nationalist protest marches to be confined to nationalist ghettos. The populist mobilization within unionism followed a classic outbidding trajectory, narrowing the political space for moderation and reform and all but destroying O'Neill's efforts to build an "opportunity state" for all. Paisleyism drove most shades of unionism into a paranoiac state of mind about an IRA "threat," in what *The Times* termed "Ulster's phobia about republican designs of annexation" (*The Times* 1969B: 7). What was fundamentally at stake was a revolutionary redistribution of power away from Protestants to the Catholic community, which would give the latter a stake in Northern Ireland. Crucially, the populist Unionists were intent on confrontational engagement with any Catholic political manifestation that seemed to overstep the line of containment that had been consolidated during decades of Protestant hegemony. The descent into violent disorder was provoked by the Paisleyite tactics of blockage and counterprotest. The most serious rioting for thirty years, the so-called Divis Street Riots in Belfast, was provoked in October 1964 during the general election campaign when the threat of a Paisley march forced the RUC to remove an Irish flag from a republican candidate's electoral office in the Falls Road. The first political murders were sectarian, conducted by the UVF against Catholics in May 1966 under the cover of a "declaration of war" against the IRA (Kelley 1982:

92–94). Paisleyism not only altered the decision calculus within union-ism, but also, by promoting police repression of civil rights protests, steadily alienated Catholics from the possibilities of constitutional engagement.

Confirmation that the IRA was a spent force militarily was evident throughout the events of summer 1969, when the local Stormont regime's capacity to govern disintegrated. Police repression of civil rights protests culminated in the so-called Battle of the Bogside in Derry in August, which saw the Catholic community offer large-scale resistance through rioting and the erection of barricades. The police attempted to quell the resistance by using CS gas, for the first time in the UK, and in massive quantities. The failure of the police to manage the rioting in Derry sparked a wave of anti-Catholic riots and pogroms in Belfast in which police and Protestant mobs cooperated. It was the beginning of what would become by 1972 the largest forced transfer and ethnic cleansing of civilian populations in Europe since World War II, with expert projections that a maximum of some 15,000 families of about 60,000 persons (overwhelmingly Catholics) were forced to move home between August 1969 and February 1973 (Darby 1974). The weakness of the IRA in 1969 brought a damning indictment from the Catholic street: "IRA: I ran away" was daubed on walls and pavements.

The failure of British governments to intervene in Northern Ireland until the place had reached a stage of ungovernability, even under Labour Party leaderships that had strong Irish Catholic constituencies in England and Scotland and were broadly sympathetic to civil rights and the reform of Stormont, is beyond the scope of this chapter. The procedural block on raising matters relating to Northern Ireland in the House of Commons was only lifted in October 1969. There is no doubting, however, the genuine sense of relief among Catholics at the British government's decision to deploy the British Army on August 14–15 to "restore law and order" by subordinating local policing and security to the British GOC, General Ian Freeland. Most accounts of the violence in Northern Ireland accept that there was a "honeymoon" between nationalist/Catholic communities and the British Army in the immediate aftermath of the British Army's intervention in August 1969. Testimonies of British soldiers gathered by Max Arthur and Ken Wharton provide much evidence for the positive relations between the British Army and Catholic communities in Belfast and Derry as Catholic communities greeted the soldiers as "liberators" from unionist repression (M. Arthur 1987; Wharton 2009, 2010). In the course of 1969 the Labour government had been raising the expectations of Catholics for reform by strengthening its "rights agenda," promising redress of the political and economic grievances of Catholics, and "full equality of treatment for all citizens" in the Downing Street Declaration of 18 August 1969 (*The Times* 1969a). The consensus dissipates over the question of what explains the breakdown of the "honeymoon," and the turn to a nationalist resurgence in the form of support for the PIRA insurgency – the shift from "cuppas and cakes to bullets and bombs" as one of Wharton's respondents put it (Wharton 2010: 28).

The counterinsurgency before the insurgency

There is a fair amount of consensus in the literature, supported by the data on deaths, injuries, shootings, explosions, and so forth, that there was a steady escalation of violence in the two years preceding 1972. That year is generally seen as a watershed given that it was the bloodiest year in the conflict and the one in which Stormont was "prorogued" and British direct rule was imposed. Accounts by contemporary British and Irish journalists – often astute observers of low-level dynamics – attributed the breakdown of the British Army/Catholic "honeymoon" to the army's over-reaction security response in late 1969–70 (see for example Bishop and Maillie 1987: 151). Similarly, recent work by psychologists on "what makes terrorists" has increasingly rejected personality disorders and focused on contextual pathways, concluding that the radicalization of the Catholic community in Northern Ireland and the growth of PIRA was the result of state excesses and the "ineptitude of the manner in which the state chose to subdue it" (Silke 2004: 242). This explanation is part of the standard account of the conflict, but it is unrefined. Some specific catalysts are usually identified, such as the April 1970 riot in the Catholic ghetto of Ballymurphy in west Belfast. Guardian journalist Simon Winchester observed: "If the bitter guerrilla war can be said to have its moment of violent birth at any one specific place, it was on a street corner on the Ballymurphy housing estate." He witnessed how the wholesale use of CS gas by the British Army had the "enormous power" to "weld a crowd together in common sympathy and common hatred for the men who gassed them" (Winchester 1974: 30–32). Many accounts see the Falls Road Curfew of early July 1970 as the turning point. Imposed by the British Army on a Catholic area of Belfast that had experienced the brunt of the interethnic rioting in summer 1969, the curfew involved several thousand troops, a major gun battle, and the firing of hundreds of CS gas canisters in a small, built-up residential area. For another British journalist, Peter Taylor (1998), this was the moment when "[u]nwittingly, the army had driven the community into the arms of the Provisional IRA." Gerry Adams (later allegedly a commander of

PIRA in Belfast) told Taylor that the curfew was a key event in both the expansion of PIRA and the legitimation of "physical force" (Taylor 1998: 81–83). Unionist academics, however, argue that the problem of spiralling violence was not caused by heavy-handed military tactics but, on the contrary, was the result of "softly-softly" British security policies that ignored unionist fears and allowed a resurgence of the IRA (Patterson 2008). This position reflects that of the Unionist political leadership in 1970, which pressured a reluctant army command to "sort out" Catholic "No Go" areas (Ministry of Defence 2006: 2–6).

The drift to nationalist violence in 1971 seems to be mainly explained as the result of a lack of strategic thinking by the British Army over how to manage security, tactical blunders, inappropriate military/policing crowd control technology, and the failure to speedily address Catholic grievances. However, I suggest that the moral endorsement from the Catholic community to legitimize the nationalist "armed struggle" was far from being as clear-cut or as determined by catalysts as either PIRA mythology or scholarly and journalistic accounts imply. Implicit in many accounts is the idea of a functional mismatch or capacity problem: soldiers were not policemen and could not adjust to the sensitivity required to win the support of communities. Some of the technology of policing, such as CS gas, was certainly crude and inexact in its collective throttling of Catholic communities.

What is generally overlooked in these accounts is that the British Army was historically a counterinsurgency army with a colonial mindset. It had been at the forefront of the British withdrawal from empire, which was frequently bloody. It had many recent decades of experience of attempting to manage colonial "civil disorder," though with a rather mixed record of success. Between 1945 and 1969 the British Army had engaged in some 53 deployments (most notably, Palestine in the late 1940s, Malaya from 1948 to the late 1950s, Kenya in the mid 1950s, Cyprus in the latter 1950s, Aden and Oman in the 1960s) that can be considered as colonial or counterrevolutionary wars, and only two (Suez and Korea) conventional wars. Consequently, the British Army's colonial mindset and counterinsurgency practices need to be brought into our explanation for the breakdown of the "honeymoon" with the Catholic community, the emergence of PIRA, and the revival of Irish nationalism.

Historically, the British Army, along with the French, was at the forefront of tactical and technological developments in waging "small wars," and what today is more generally termed "counterinsurgency." Colonial counterinsurgency, however, was practiced at some distance from the oversight of democratic governments in the UK, usually against non-white people, and well beyond the glare of independent investigative journalists. Northern Ireland's geographical proximity to Britain and Europe, and its accessibility to the mass media, would present a number of challenges for managing civil disorder there. Many of the senior commanders of the British Army that served in Northern Ireland in the critical period of 1970–72 and thereafter were leading practitioners of what we might term the "British model" of counterinsurgency. Most had seen extensive service in many of the key British counterinsurgency campaigns after World War II. A particularly significant figure in this regard was Brigadier Frank Kitson, who was to become Commander of British Land Forces in the early 1980s, but who exerted overall command of British forces in Belfast in early 1970 until his removal by Secretary of State William Whitelaw in April 1972. Kitson had a legendary reputation in the British Army as a "counterinsurgency warrior-intellectual" akin to that of General David Petraeus in the US military today. Kitson was a controversial figure. His name is not mentioned in one major study of the Northern Ireland conflict by a British military officer (Dewar 1985). In contrast, another senior British commander's memoir described him as an "incisive thinker and military theorist" who took a "robust" approach to counterinsurgency in Belfast, and claimed that "he was the sun around which the planets revolved … and very much set the tone for the operational style" (Jackson 2007: 54, 80–81). Kitson's role as an important change-agent in the evolution of the conflict in Northern Ireland has been recognized by other works, but they focus mostly on how his system was developed in the mid to late 1970s by the British Army in Northern Ireland, and less on his actual tour of duty in Belfast in 1970–72 (Faligot 1983; Newsinger 2002). The British Army strategy and tactics that were employed in this critical period were, by and large, those that he had formulated from years of lessons from the colonial "small wars."

In 1969 Brigadier Kitson obtained a visiting fellowship at University College Oxford to write what was to become a British Army manual for dealing with "low intensity operations" and subversion (Kitson 1971). The organizing idea underlying the book was how to deal with the threat of internal subversion within the UK, which was perceived to be most likely to emanate from communist "Moscow-directed" trade unionists. This thinking needs to be understood in the context of British politics of the late 1960s and early 1970s, when the issue of trade union militancy was seen by political elites as state threatening. Kitson merely drew on the lessons of his involvement in campaigns against Mau Mau nationalists in Kenya, and Chinese "communist terrorists" in Malaya, and elsewhere, to elaborate a plan of action for combined police and military operations against subversives in the UK.

Kitson's main contributions to counterinsurgency are in essence three-fold. First, he recognized the centrality of the population to the outcome of a colonial war or "Emergency." The priority of a government in an Emergency, he argued, should be "to retain or regain the allegiance of the population" (Kitson 1977: 59). The population-centric approach, and the importance of winning "hearts and minds" in counterinsurgency were a common lesson drawn by British, French and, later, US military theorists from the experience of colonial wars. Whereas the French and Americans tended to emphasize their failure to do so as a source of their defeat in Algeria and Vietnam, the British tended to view themselves as adept practitioners of counterinsurgency, given what they considered to be their successes in Kenya and Malaya. Recently, the American histor-ian Caroline Elkins's Pulitzer prize-winning study documented that sys-tematic brutality informed British policy and practice against the Mau Mau revolt, concluding that extreme coercion, not policies of "winning hearts and minds," characterized the counterinsurgency (Elkins 2005). At one level, Kitson was in many respects reiterating what other military thinkers, such as Thompson (1966), Trinquier (1964), and Vann (1965) had stated several years earlier. These were wars "for the people." However, whereas Thompson and Vann shared an emphasis on the need for combined political and social reforms with military/police operations, with the latter being highly discriminate in a way that did not alienate local communities, Kitson drew on his experience fighting the Mau Mau revolt and reworked Trinquier's philosophy that winning over popula-tions was mostly about "control." As Trinquier had put it: "*Control of the masses* through a tight organization … is the *master weapon* of modern warfare" (Trinquier 1964: 30). For Kitson, control of population was mostly about coercion: "conditions can be made reasonably uncomfort-able for the population as a whole in order to provide an incentive for a return to normal life and to act as a deterrent towards a resumption of the campaign" (Kitson 1971: 87).

Kitson had observed in his book, with regard to the classic Maoist formula, that the relationship between guerrillas and the supporting community was akin to that between fish and water: "If a fish has got to be destroyed it can be attacked directly by rod or net … But if rod and net cannot succeed by themselves it may be necessary to do something to the water" (Kitson 1971: 49). He followed Trinquier also in setting out a system of standard operating procedures by which counterinsurgency should be fought. Intelligence gathering was the key. He envisaged a "chain reaction system" whereby the accumulation of masses of "background intelligence" would generate "contact information," which would then allow the enemy to be killed or captured. Partly, this intelligence would come from the harsh interrogation of prisoners. Kitson also placed great store on "turning" terrorists through "carrot and stick" measures, and on creating what he called "countergangs" or "pseudogangs," which could infiltrate or deceive insurgents (Kitson 1960, 1977). For the most part, however, background information was to be gathered by classic colonial tactics of mass "screening" of populations (what the French army termed "ilôtage" in their "Urban Protection Apparatus" for Greater Algiers in 1957). Kitson's major innovation was to apply to counterinsurgency the card index and book record filing system (and later computers) that had been used for decades by intelligence services against subversives, only in an expanded form that was aimed not only at suspect individuals but at a comprehensive profiling of whole communities. He quoted with approval a journalist's comment that it was "making war with a filing cabinet" (Kitson 1977: 50). His third contribution was to propose the creation of a permanent "special unit" within the British Army to conduct counterinsurgency. This was a genuine foresight that he had originally proposed in the late 1950s, when "special forces" were in their infancy. Such units are today at the spearhead of counterinsurgencies.

Hardly had he finished his "low intensity operations" book than Kitson was in command in Belfast in January 1970 with a new testing ground to experiment with his theories. His arrival in Belfast set a new harsh tone for the army's role. Under Kitson, security practices that had been rather chaotically applied became standardized and routine. The key tactics were classic counterinsurgency techniques of cordon, screening, and search. In Belfast and other urban centers with large Catholic ghettos, this involved constant surveillance night and day by means of foot patrols, vehicle patrols, helicopters, electronic surveillance, mass house searches, and "stop and search" of individuals on a routine basis. Public space was securitized in new ways. The army established checkpoints on all major entry/exit points to the main Catholic areas (VCPs or vehicle checkpoints) and physically sealed off many roads and access points. Where necessary, main roads were widened to accommodate armored vehicles. Dozens of new military compounds were constructed for the swelling troop garrisons. By 1972 there were more than a dozen in north and west Belfast – often occupying what few open spaces or sports facilities existed. Army undercover operations were expanded under a Military Reconnaissance Force established by Kitson.

In previous counterinsurgencies British (and indeed French) tactics for dealing with the "water" had centered on mass arrests, concentration camps, collective punishments, and torture of prisoners to extract "humint" (human intelligence). Abuse of prisoners was reported in

Northern Ireland as early as 1970 from Palace Barracks (Kitson's HQ) in Belfast, but the famous case of the fourteen "guinea pigs" to whom the "five techniques" of interrogation/torture were applied came after internment was introduced in August 1971, later leading to a judgment against the UK at the European Court of Human Rights. Mass communal concentration camps or "protected villages" as employed in Kenya or Malaya were an impossibility in Northern Ireland for various reasons – the media glare being a most obvious one. However, as noted, communities could be contained in other ways. From early 1970, in addition to the routinization of the security measures outlined above, the British Army also started to develop its card index profiles of every Catholic family in north and west Belfast through everyday and systematic interrogation of each household. The securitization tactics were not applied to either Protestant areas or, indeed, middle-class areas with large Catholic populations. Over time, the British Army would develop a major systematic computerization of personal and vehicle records. The moderate SDLP leader Gerry Fitt would later declare of the Kitson tactics: "It's like something you'd find in the Soviet Union or South Africa – Big Brother is watching" (*Irish Times* 1977). The point that I wish to emphasize here is that the routinization by the British Army of communal control in north and west Belfast began at a time contemporaneous with Kitson's arrival, and when there was no insurgency.

From citizens to nationalists

What kinds of organizational responses occurred in Catholic communities in response to the violence of summer 1969? What kinds of bottom-up demands were being articulated in these communities? Here, my analysis is based on two sources: political pamphlets and other materials, mainly produced in west Belfast in 1969–72, and interviews with non-IRA participants in community-organized defense (known locally as "vigilantes"). What emerges from this grassroots approach is that Catholic communities were concerned overwhelmingly with rule-of-law issues and the aspiration for equality of citizenship, not with nationalist ideology. Indeed, as we shall discuss later, even PIRA struggled to break with the bottom-up rule-of-law approach emanating from what it saw as its natural heartlands of support: the Catholic communities in Belfast. In response to the interethnic violence of summer 1969, when the overwhelmingly Protestant local police (the RUC) had mobilized its reserve (all-Protestant) militia (the B Specials) and sided with Protestant mobs in attacking Catholic communities in Belfast, Catholic communities barricaded their areas and formed loosely organized community defense units (Insight Team, Sunday Times 1972). The spontaneous defense of what became known as barricaded "no-go areas" (no-go for the Stormont police forces) was subordinated to two main organizational forms: "citizens' defence committees" (CDCs) in which "community leaders" and moderate, respected members of the community often had prominent positions (a leading role was played by Paddy Devlin, a Stormont MP for the Northern Ireland Labour Party) and the Catholic Ex-Servicemen's Association (CESA) – Catholics who had formerly been in the British Army. In the months after August 1969 these were separate organizations, but with a significant membership overlap. CESA was valued because its members had military training, though by all accounts of my interviewees very few weapons were available to those manning barricades. The discredited IRA was at first only peripherally involved in the CDCs and CESA. The naming of the CDCs reflected their civic non-nationalist agenda – they were not "nationalist defence committees."

The "basic demands" of the CDCs in this period were wholly concerned with rule-of-law issues: policing (disbanding and disarming the B Specials, disarming and reorganizing the RUC), repeal of the draconian Special Powers Act (and releasing prisoners held without trial under its provisions), and the demand for the Westminster government to invoke Article 75 of the Government of Ireland Act (1920) to suspend the Stormont government, introduce direct rule, and push through reforms (*Barricades Bulletin* 1969a). As the CDC in Andersonstown in west Belfast put it: "It is time they [the British government] acted over Stormont's head. The people will accept nothing less" (*Barricades Bulletin* 1969b: 1). These demands were even more modest than those that were later recommended by the British government's own Cameron Report into the events of 1969 (Cameron 1969). Middle-ranking British Army officers (at the rank of Major) liaised closely, openly and regularly (weekly) with CDCs and CESA leaderships, often in meetings mediated by local priests. The content of the discussions was publicized in local pamphlets. The scale of the trust and communication between the British Army and local Catholic communities was such that soldiers could be invited into houses, attend Mass services unarmed, and drink in local pubs in these communities. In sum, there was general cooperation between the British Army and CDCs.

The tensions between Catholic communities in Belfast and Derry and the British Army deteriorated as the Kitsonian counterinsurgency tactics became standardized despite the absence of an insurgency. There was mutual cooperation over the removal of many barricades in late 1969. Catholics had their expectations of reform raised by the publication in October 1969 of the Hunt Report into policing, which recommended the disarmament of the RUC and the abolition of the B Special force and its replacement by a local non-sectarian militia, the Ulster Defence Regiment (UDR) (Hunt 1969). They were also reassured by the British government's appointment of Sir Arthur Young, an Englishman with a well-earned reputation for his efforts to reform security institutions and policing practice in British colonies (Kenya and Malaya), as head of the RUC. Catholic hopes waned, however, as time passed without the reforms being rigorously implemented. The RUC and B Specials/UDR were subordinated to British military command, as opposed to their being disarmed, demobilized, or reformed. Stormont's Unionist ministers sat on the joint political security committees, and pressured the British Army to use the emergency legislation and adopt harsh tactics. Unionist elites, with whom British commanders had more social and historical affinity, were relentlessly critical of the "softly-softly" approach towards the no-go areas, which they equated to British Army collaboration with the IRA (Hamill 1985: 23–24). Equally, they feared that the violent clashes in Protestant areas of Belfast between the army and the Protestant working class in October 1969 presaged a deeper breach within the unionist "family" and between it and the British state.

A new, harsher Kitsonian line in British Army tactics is evident in the first months of 1970. Wharton's works and the journalistic reports provide a host of ethnographic evidence of the breakdown of trust between Catholics and the army in early 1970. The infusion of violence into this relationship came spontaneously as a result of mass screening and house searching, beginning with small-scale rioting in Ballymurphy in west Belfast in January 1970. With great speed, a children's/teenagers' intifada erupted. This was not orchestrated by the IRA, but was spontaneous and spasmodic. However, it became an almost daily repertoire of stone throwing by schoolchildren, with more serious rioting involving petrol bombs being concentrated only in disturbances around the so-called "marching season" of Orange (unionist) parades in June and July. These youth riots in response to British Army tactics led to the first major escalation, in which the British Army commander, General Freeland, ordered that petrol bombers be shot on sight. The first time an alleged petrol bomber was shot dead by the British Army was in July 1970. The escalation was partly born out of a technological gap. Until August 1970, when so-called "rubber bullets" (baton rounds) and other riot gear became standard issue, the British Army had only limited responses to stone throwing. The usual response in the case of sustained stone throwing was CS gas, which was de facto a collective punishment in the confined residential areas of north and west Belfast. About ten thousand CS canisters and two and a half thousand gas grenades were used in

Northern Ireland in 1970 alone (Faligot 1983: 143). Securitization at the lowest tactical level – foot patrols led by corporals – is almost impossible to police by commanders, and not surprisingly it is at this level that we see much of the anecdotal evidence of abuse of Catholic teenagers in particular.

Other counterinsurgency experiences, including recent ones in Iraq and Afghanistan, suggest that there is a fundamental flaw in the capacity of the military to adopt tactics to win "hearts and minds" of communities. The Petraeus Doctrine emphasizes the importance of "cultural awareness as a force multiplier" and the role of "strategic corporals" and "strategic lieutenants" (Petraeus 2006). However, all the evidence from Northern Ireland and other campaigns demonstrates that it is precisely at the tactical level that military brutality and the alienation of communities occurs. Other low-level tactical errors in Northern Ireland included the deployment of Scottish battalions, generally viewed by both communities as sympathetic to the Ulster Protestants. The Scottish units played a pivotal role in some of the events seen as catalysts for the breakdown of the army–Catholic relationship, including the Ballymurphy riots of April 1970 and the Falls Road Curfew of July 1970. The electoral cycle in Britain, with a transition from a Labour to Conservative government, contributed to delays in formulating let alone delivering a policy for reform. The *Operation Banner* report admits the absence of strategic thinking in the British Army over how to manage the "civil disorder," and one of its subtexts is that the British Army lost the trust of Catholic communities through its tactical mistakes.

Data on the British Army's securitization policy in these early years is not readily available or easily disaggregated, but we do have reasonably reliable sources on some of its counterinsurgency activities. According to Hillyard (1988), there were around 75,000 arrests in 1971–86 (see Figure 4.3). One in every four Catholic men between the ages of 16 and 44 would have been arrested (or "lifted" in local parlance) at least once in the period 1971–86. The number of arrests does not automatically transfer into numbers of persons arrested. Hillyard reckons that many British Army detentions actually involved multiple persons, with only one quarter to half of those detained actually passed on to the RUC for formal arrest. Hillyard is unable to break this figure down by area, but we can reasonably assume that the arrests were concentrated in areas of violence – thus it is likely that the proportion of this group arrested in north and west Belfast would be much higher. We see a similar pattern for house searches. In 1971–86 the state security forces searched 338,803 houses. In theory this translates into 75 percent of all houses in Northern Ireland. Again, it would be a reasonable assumption that the searches

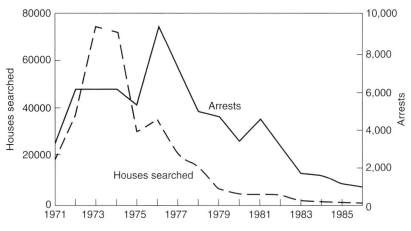

Source: Hillyard 1988: 199.

Figure 4.3 Conflict-related house searches and arrests in Northern Ireland, 1971–86

would have been concentrated on the 170,000 Catholic houses, and more specifically on those in areas such as north and west Belfast. This means that houses in these areas would have been subjected to multiple searches. It is clear from local pamphlets, local newspapers, and contemporary British journalism that the routinization of Kitson's system of cordoning, screening/interrogation, search and arrest (and the brutalization that often accompanied these tactics) severely strained the "honeymoon," especially given that the tactics were employed in a one-sided manner (Protestant communities not being subjected). For Hillyard, the British Army was, in practice, "treating the whole of the Catholic community as 'suspect'" (Hillyard 1998: 194–97). Allen Feldman refers to the state security practices against Catholics as the "collectivization of arrest" (Feldman 1991). That was the very point of the Kitson model of counterinsurgency.

The reinvention of Irish nationalism

The reassertion not of just the "physical force" tradition but of a new, vibrant form of Irish nationalism came out of a context of harsh British counterinsurgency tactics in the absence of insurgency. However, it is often mythologized by republicans as being born "out of the ashes of 1969" – the phoenix became a favored PIRA icon. PIRA vocabulary referred/refers to the new recruits that joined PIRA after summer 1969 as "69-ers" (among whom was Martin McGuinness, former PIRA chief of staff and current Deputy First Minister of the Northern Ireland Executive established after the Belfast Agreement of 1998). Alonso's interviews with republicans who enlisted as "volunteers" in the early years report a pattern of spontaneous recruitment based on spur-of-the-moment emotional reactions to events. Alonso, oddly, interpreted the recruitment as indicative of minds that were "captive" to nationalism (Alonso 2007: 67). But the evidence for an ideological impulse is not offered. For most it was a reaction to the defenceless realities of 1969 and the radicalization induced by the experience of street fighting in 1969–70, though some, such as Belfast PIRA leader Brendan Hughes, have traced their politicization to less insular and more global experiences and empathy with victims of injustice (Moloney 2010: 41). Some, such as Brighton bomber Patrick Magee, joined PIRA after personal experience of a British Army beating. Kelley reports a powerful explanation from one IRA volunteer interviewee: "No-one decided to join the Provos on an ideological basis in '70, '71, '72. They wanted a gun … Internment helped to change all that. It gave us time to think, to reflect, to argue, to develop some kind of political understanding" (1982: 157–58).

Belfast, and indeed Northern Ireland, had what Gerry Adams has termed "spinal Republican families" – including his own (Adams 2004: 5). These numbered only in the dozens. As we noted earlier the IRA was a "husk" in the late 1960s with a small and aged membership in Belfast. The violence in Derry and Belfast in summer 1969 irrevocably split the IRA. The split was formalized at an IRA convention in Dublin in December 1969, which saw the formation of PIRA, followed by a formal schism at the Sinn Féin Ard Fheis (Annual Conference) in January 1970. The principal cleavage had been evolving independently of developments in the North, and was between Marxists and anti-Marxists. Even on the eve of the summer of 1969 the Marxist leadership of the IRA and Sinn Féin were supportive of armed struggle elsewhere (such as Palestine) while attempting to transform the republican movement into a new progressive social movement. In the North its policy was to engage in the civil rights movement (*United Irishman* 1969).

This ideological divide was given a new urgency, intensity, and form by events in Northern Ireland. The Marxist/anti-Marxist schism was soon infused by a more traditional cleft between "physical force" and "moral force" philosophies. The "physical force" faction, namely those who wanted to organize an "armed struggle" in Northern Ireland, was overwhelmingly composed of the "spinal" republican families of the North, though they quickly accumulated support from other parts of Ireland and the USA. Adams (1986) has claimed that PIRA expansion only accelerated after the Falls Road Curfew in July 1970 (ironically, a British Army operation that targeted the Marxist-leaning Official IRA in the Falls area). He has also attributed the rise in nationalist sentiment among Catholics not to republican measures but to the politicization that came out of the brutal anti-Irish racist conduct by the British Army (Adams 1997: 126). A close reading of PIRA literature in the period 1970–72 reveals, however, that PIRA initially struggled to define its own version of republicanism. For the "honeymoon" between the army and Catholics placed a huge question mark over the viability and legitimacy of a return to "physical force" nationalism. A major challenge for PIRA in this early period of the conflict was how to break the link between the army and Catholics, widen its support base and communicate nationalist/ republican values to Catholic communities. But its direction toward an armed struggle against the "British presence" was not fixed.

PIRA capacity to engage in an armed conflict was in any event extremely weak, given the downgrading of the "physical force" currents amongst nationalist intellectuals over the previous decade. The first issues of PIRA's main newspaper, *Republican News*, published for the first time only in June 1970 and edited by a veteran of Belfast's "Old IRA," James Steele, sought to do two things ideologically. First, they sought to explain the founding rationale of PIRA. PIRA was distinguished from the "compromises," "communist aims," and "Red agents" that had infiltrated the IRA in the 1960s (a recurrent theme in *Republican News* in 1970–71). Secondly, they took the first steps towards an ideological capture of the heritage of the 1916 Rising, the War of Independence, and the United Irishmen. There were some crucial advantages to the Belfast locus of PIRA. Belfast and the northern conflict presented a vast array of Irish Republican topoi on which to draw in order to relegitimize the "physical force" tradition. The distinction between the two concepts was fuzzy in the history of Irish nationalism, with most episodes demonstrating an interrelationship between the two rather than a clear distinction (Curtis 1988).

Historically, both English and Irish nationalist positions on Ireland mirrored each other in that, as James Connolly had put it, the "governing power" should be taken "peaceably if possible, forcibly if necessary" (Connolly 1971[1916]: 28). The recent experience of Northern Irish Catholics seemed to confirm the necessity for "physical force" over "moral force." The non-violent civil rights movement had been met by the Stormont regime with police repression and demagogic populist mobilization – developments that seemed to confirm the infamous retort of the nineteenth-century nationalist John Mitchel that "moral force" was "humbug." Belfast held the Omphalos of Irish republicanism – McArt's Fort promontory – where Tone and his fellow United Irishmen (almost all northern Presbyterians) had taken an oath in June 1795 "never to desist" until they had "subverted the authority of England over Ireland." Throughout 1970–71, *Republican News* propagated profiles of the northern "Protestant patriots" who had been at the core of the United Irishmen leadership. Furthermore, the recovery of the historical memory of "physical force" nationalism extended to publishing songs and poems, and to identifying paraphernalia that came out of previous eras of armed struggle. Crucially, the no-go areas established in Catholic areas of Belfast after 1969 were ghetto spaces largely beyond the control of the state, which offered opportunities for unfettered nationalist agitprop and socialization. Indeed, it was the form of the British state's attempts to reassert control in 1970–71 that brought friction with those communities. Bean's sympathetic study of PIRA argues that the "resistance communities" that became the bedrock of its support in the early phase of the conflict were grounded in the "power of common local experiences in shaping a political outlook," and that PIRA was not a "mere reproduction of tradition" (Bean 2007: 54–56). In fact, the reproduction, reinvention, and romanticization of nationalist tradition was precisely the strategy followed by the founders of PIRA from early 1970. What is striking about this strategy, however, is how hesitant it was. Contrary to what unionist historians postulate, there was no grand PIRA strategy, and PIRA itself was only in embryonic form organizationally.

PIRA's ideological uncertainty over "physical force" is evident in the first three issues of *Republican News* in July–August 1970 (which includes the period in the immediate aftermath of the Falls Road Curfew). In Issue no. 1 there was a vague reference to the need to build up a "movement of resistance." Violent resistance, however, was only implicit at this stage (*Republican News* 1970a: 3). The "verbal struggle for Irish freedom" of the Official IRA was ridiculed. The reporting of PIRA leader Daithi O'Connell's speech at Bodenstown on June 14, 1970, wherein he had called for a British withdrawal, derided the "verbal struggle for Irish freedom" of the Official IRA and hinted at the prospect of armed resistance: "the more your troops impose their will, the nearer you bring the day of open confrontation" (*Republican News* 1970a: 7). Similar obliqueness of language on armed struggle is evident in Issue no. 2. There would be "no peace," the editor declared, until there was a "complete evacuation of England's armed occupation" (*Republican News* 1970b: 2). While from the outset there were consistent warnings to Catholics against "fraternization" with British forces, and constant spotlighting of British Army brutality in Catholic areas, the hesitancy of the PIRA approach to the Catholic community is evident in Issue no. 3 of *Republican News*, which observed that the Falls Road Curfew "must surely give them [the Catholic community] the necessary food for thought" (*Republican News*

1970c: 3–4). It is only in issue No. 4 in September 1970 that we see the first explicit references by PIRA to the need to "eject the invader," though the means are still not wholly transparent (*Republican News* 1970d: 1–6). This issue called for "training and discipline" and admonished those "with no real taste for the struggle ahead." It predicted "a gradual transition from the current, practical, defensive tactics of today to that of, not too distant, direct offensive confrontation with the forces of imperialism in Ireland." The goal was to make "matters so unpleasant" for the British that they would leave – but without details (*Republican News* 1970d: 1–6). The tentative approach to violence in PIRA's information war continued until early 1971. A cartoon showed a uniformed PIRA volunteer, unarmed, with outstretched hands, pleading "what price freedom?" (*Republican News* 1970e: 1). Equally, the Catholic ghettos were flooded with republican propaganda, pamphlets, and books as part of the reeducation strategy.

It was only in January–February 1971, that is to say one full year after its foundation, that PIRA offered an unequivocal statement of its commitment to violent resistance. Here, too, we find the insignia of the United Irishmen (the uncrowned harp) emblazoned for the first time on *Republican News*. In an op-ed titled "Our Policy," the PIRA leadership explicitly associated with and endorsed the "tradition of physical force resistance to British interference in Irish Affairs." The means to achieve this goal was a secret "Republican armed underground resistance movement" (*Republican News* 1971a: 8). Throughout the first half of 1971, even after its armed campaign had begun, the PIRA agitprop was still battling to get Catholics "off the fence." Much use was made of British Army brutality and tactics to justify the argument that there was "no other way" but armed resistance and "just retaliation" (*Republican News* 1971b: 12; 1971c: 5).

The PIRA information war to make the case for violent nationalism became much easier in the wake of the British Army's intensification of its counterinsurgency tactics in 1970–71, and in particular as the violence escalated in 1971–72. Yet even after a two-year experience of British Army counterinsurgency, including the critical turning points of the introduction of internment in August 1971 and Bloody Sunday, the shooting of unarmed civilian protesters by the British Army in Derry in January 1972, non-PIRA local activists in West Belfast CESA and other forums were lamenting the "inability of the state to function impartially" and the breakdown of the "British Army's traditional discipline," and appealing most of all for restraints on British Army "Kitsonian tactics" (*Andersonstown News* 1972a: 1–2; 1972b: 1). Meanwhile, we should observe that the pressure from above, from Kitson himself, was for non-restraint. Indeed, as reported in the memoirs of General Mike

Jackson, Kitson fumed at commanders whom he perceived to be too soft, such as Colonel Derek Wilford (leader of the paratroopers on Bloody Sunday) who Kitson debriefed and admonished because he "didn't go on and sort the whole bloody mess out" (Jackson 2007: 71). Apparently, Kitson opposed the introduction of internment, but it seems likely that this had more to do with its small scale and the incoherent and ineffectual manner in which it was prepared and conducted, for his writings are unequivocal in highlighting the advantages of the "massive use" of internment (Kitson 1977: 58–59).

Conclusion

Paddy Devlin, one of the most moderate political representatives of the Catholic community in this period, lamented that Kitson "probably did more than any other individual to sour relations between the Catholic community and the security forces" (1975: 119). The British Army itself now accepts that there was no insurgency in Northern Ireland in 1969–70 and that its own tactical malpractices were a contributing factor to the onset of the "Troubles." In the literature on the conflict, however, there remains a hegemonic position that the conflict can be located within a continuum of Irish nationalism, and the IRA's "physical force" tradition in particular. Catholic demands in the period 1969–72 were a continuation of those identified by the civil rights movement: appeals for equality of citizenship, for the rule of law, and for an interventionist, impartial and reformist British state. I have attempted to show that the nationalist impulses to the onset of the Troubles are caricatured in much of the scholarly literature. I have also drawn attention to the fulcrum years of 1969–71. In these early years of the conflict, support among Catholics for a nationalist armed struggle was largely nonexistent, and nationalist armed struggle was even regarded with uncertainty and ambivalence by the newly formed PIRA. In 1970–72, PIRA grappled with an information war to inculcate the values of "physical force" nationalism among Catholics. It was not that the British Army's "honeymoon" with Catholics dissolved as a result of its harsh response to episodic rioting in 1970–71, culminating in internment (the standard account), but rather that the working-class Catholic communities of Belfast and Derry, in particular, were alienated by a brutally systematic British counterinsurgency policy implemented under commanders and troops who were schooled in colonial and racial "small wars." It is a testament to the power of the nationalism constructed by Kitson's counterinsurgency that it fed a protracted conflict lasting a generation. Some dog, some bark.

REFERENCES

Adams, G. 1986. *The Politics of Irish Freedom*. Dingle: Brandon.
  1997. *Before the Dawn*. Mount Eagle: Brandon Press.
Alonso, R. 2007. *The IRA and Armed Struggle*. London: Routledge.
Andersonstown News. 1972a. 1(1) November 22–29: 1–2.
  1972b. 1(2) November 29 – December 6: 1.
Arthur, M. 1987. *Northern Ireland: Soldiers Talking*. London: Sidgwick and
  Jackson.
Arthur, P. 1974. *The People's Democracy, 1968–73*. Belfast: Blackstaff Press.
Barricades Bulletin. 1969a. No. 2.
  1969b. No. 3.
Bean, K. 2007. *The New Politics of Sinn Féin*. Liverpool University Press.
Bell, J.B. 1989. *The Secret Army: The IRA 1916–1979*. London: Poolbeg.
Bishop, P. and E. Mallie. 1987. *The Provisional IRA*. London: Corgi.
Bruce, S. 1989. *God Save Ulster! The Religion and Politics of Paisleyism*. Oxford
  University Press.
Cameron. 1969. *Disturbances in Northern Ireland. Report of the Commission
  appointed by the Governor of Northern Ireland Chairman: The Honourable Lord
  Cameron, D.S.C*. Belfast: HMSO. Accessed at: http://cain.ulst.ac.uk/hmso/
  cameron.htm.
Connolly, J. 1971 [1916]. *Socialism Made Easy*. Dublin: The Plough Book
  Service.
Curtis, L.P. Jr. 1988. "Moral and Physical Force: The Language of Violence in
  Irish Nationalism." *Journal of British Studies* 27(2): 150–89.
Darby, J. 1974. *Intimidation in Housing*. Research Paper. Belfast: Northern
  Ireland Community Relations Commission. Accessed at: http://cain.ulst.ac.
  uk/issues/housing/docs/nicrc.htm.
Devlin, P. 1975. *The Fall of the Northern Ireland Executive*. Belfast: Paddy Devlin.
Dewar, M. 1985. *The British Army in Northern Ireland*. London: Arms and
  Armour Press.
Elkins, C. 2005. *Imperial Reckoning: The Untold Story of Britain's Gulag in Kenya*.
  New York: Henry Holt.
English, R. 2003. *Armed Struggle: The History of the IRA*. London: Macmillan.
Faligot, R. 1983. *Britain's Military Strategy in Ireland: The Kitson Experiment*.
  London: Zed Press.
Feldman, A. 1991. *Formations of Violence: The Narrative of the Body and Political
  Terror in Northern Ireland*. University of Chicago Press.
Gellner, E. 1983. *Nations and Nationalism*. Oxford: Blackwell.
Hamill, D. 1985. *Pig in the Middle: The Army in Northern Ireland 1969–1984*.
  London: Methuen.
Hanley, B. and S. Millar. 2009. *The Lost Revolution: The Story of the Official IRA
  and the Workers' Party*. Dublin: Penguin.
Hillyard, P. 1988. "Political and Social Dimensions of Emergency Law in
  Northern Ireland." Pp. 191–212 in *Justice Under Fire: The Abuse of Civil
  Liberties in Northern Ireland*, edited by Anthony Jennings. London: Pluto
  Press.

House of Commons. 1969. *Hansard: Parliamentary Debates* 788 October 13: 48.

Hunt. 1969. *Report of the Advisory Committee on Police in Northern Ireland*. Belfast: HMSO. Accessed at: http://cain.ulst.ac.uk/hmso/hunt.htm.

Insight Team, Sunday Times. 1972. *Ulster*. London: Penguin.

Irish Times. 1977. "Fitt Objects to Computer." 13 April.

Jackson, M. 2007. *Soldier: An Autobiography*. London: Bantam.

Kelley, K. 1982. *The Longest War: Northern Ireland and the IRA*. Dingle: Brandon Press.

Kitson, F. 1960. *Gangs and Countergangs*. London: Barrie and Rockcliff.

1971. *Low Intensity Operations: Subversion, Insurgency and Peacekeeping*. London: Faber & Faber.

1977. *Bunch of Five*. London: Faber & Faber.

McCann, E. 1968. "Who's Wrecking Civil Rights." *Ramparts* 1(1): 4.

McCreary, A. 1970. "The General." *Belfast Telegraph*. 9 February: 8.

Ministry of Defence. 2006. *Operation Banner: An Analysis of Military Operations in Northern Ireland*. Army Code 71842: Prepared under the direction of the Chief of the General Staff. London.

Moloney, E. 2010. *Voices From the Grave: Two Men's War in Ireland*. London: Faber & Faber.

Newsinger, J. 2002. *British Counterinsurgency: From Palestine to Northern Ireland*. Houndmills: Palgrave Macmillan.

O'Leary, B. and J. McGarry. 1993. *The Politics of Antagonism: Understanding Northern Ireland*. London: Athlone Press.

Patterson, H. 2008. "The British State and the Rise of the IRA, 1969–71: The View from the Conway Hotel." *Irish Political Studies* 23: 491–511.

Petraeus, D. 2006. "Learning Counterinsurgency: Observations from Soldiering in Iraq." *Military Review*. January–February: 45–55.

Purdie, B. 1990. *Politics in the Streets. The Origins of the Civil Rights Movement in Northern Ireland*. Belfast: Blackstaff Press.

Republican News. 1970a. 1(1).

1970b. 1(2).

1970c. 1(3).

1970d. 1(4) September–October 1970.

1970e. 1(6) November–December 1970.

1971a. 1(8) January–February 1971.

1971b. 1(9) March 1971.

1971c. 1(11) May 1971.

Silke, A. 2004. "Fire of Iolaus: The Role of State Countermeasures in Causing Terrorism and What Needs to Be Done." Pp. 241–55 in *Root Causes of Terrorism: Myths, Reality and Ways Forward*, edited by T. Bjorgo. London: Routledge.

Taylor, P. 1998. *Provos: The IRA and Sinn Féin*. London: Bloomsbury.

The Times. 1969a. "Seven Point Declaration." 18 August: 1.

The Times. 1969b. "Editorial." 30 August: 7.

Thompson, R. 1966. *Defeating Communist Insurgency: Experiences in Malaya and Vietnam*. London: Chatto & Windus.

Townshend, C. 1983. *Political Violence in Ireland: Government and Resistance since 1848*. Oxford University Press.

Trinquier, R. 1964. *Modern Warfare: A French View of Counterinsurgency*. Trans. Daniel Lee. New York: Frederick A. Praeger.

United Irishman. 1969. 6 June.

Vann, J. P. 1965. *Harnessing the Revolution in South Vietnam*. Accessed at: smallwarsjournal.com/documents/bobandrews1.pdf.

Wharton, K. 2009. *Bullets, Bombs and Cups of Tea: Further Voices of the British Army in Northern Ireland, 1969–98*. Solihull: Helion.

Wharton, K. 2010. *Bloody Belfast: An Oral History of the British Army's War against the IRA*. Stroud: History Press.

Winchester, S. 1974. *In Holy Terror: Reporting the Ulster Troubles*. London: Faber & Faber.

5   When does nationalism turn violent?
A comparative analysis of Canada and Sri Lanka

Matthew Lange

Of all the civil wars that have erupted over the past half-century, a large number – but hardly all – involve nationalist movements pursuing greater autonomy. While the sheer number of ethno-nationalist civil wars offers evidence that nationalism can contribute to warfare, many countries with multiple and competing forms of nationalism are not afflicted by civil war and manage nationalist tensions in non-violent ways. Thus, nationalism appears linked to warfare but is neither necessary nor sufficient for it.

This chapter explores factors that help determine whether nationalist movements turn violent. It compares competing nationalist movements in Canada and Sri Lanka and considers why the former has been overwhelmingly peaceful while the latter has suffered a long and devastating civil war. The analysis suggests that nationalism promotes civil war by intensifying grievances and shaping incentives but that these effects depend on contextual factors. Most notably, nationalism has only limited motivational effect in environments with abundant resources and effective and non-discriminatory political institutions. Alternatively, it intensifies the grievances caused by economic scarcity and ineffective and discriminatory political institutions, increases incentives to eliminate nationalist rivals in environments with limited resources and ineffective and discriminatory political institutions, and thereby contributes to nationalist violence.

Theoretical approach: nationalism, grievances, interests, and elites

For this analysis, I draw on my recent work (Lange 2012) and employ a theoretical approach that considers how nationalism helps motivate people to act violently. It focuses on two mechanisms. The first is the competition mechanism. Through it, individuals act violently in order to eliminate competitors. It is a variant of the rational-choice mechanism, as individuals eliminate competitors because it is in their interests to do so. The second mechanism is emotive and promotes violence through frustration and aggression. Specifically, the frustration-aggression mechanism contributes to violence when individuals are unable to attain their expectations, as the latter sparks frustration and aggressive actions.

Individual-level incentives and personal grievances can both cause the competition and frustration-aggression mechanisms. That is, an individual might benefit personally from eliminating a rival, and an individual might become frustrated and act aggressively over personal grievances. Yet nationalism can also promote both mechanisms by causing individuals to perceive and pursue national interests and national grievances. For example, nationalism can cause individuals to pay attention to their community's share of resources and attempt to eliminate nationalist rivals in an attempt to increase their community's share of resources. Similarly, nationalism can cause individuals to become frustrated and aggressive over grievances that afflict their national community and can promote nationalist scapegoating when another community is viewed as the source of the grievance. While national interests and grievances can promote violence, both the competition and frustration-aggression mechanisms are logically most powerful when individual and national interests and grievances coincide.

Any number of factors can promote violence through the competition and frustration-aggression mechanisms. I pay particular attention to two. The first is the economy. Most notably, competition commonly occurs over economic resources. Moreover, nationalism commonly causes individuals to pay close attention to the overall economic well-being of their community, thereby promoting grievances and scapegoating during periods of economic hardship. The second is politics. Because political institutions are valuable resources, they can also spur competition. Moreover, and likely more important, politics can also be an influential source of grievances, thereby instigating the frustration-aggression mechanism. Most notably, state coercion, discriminatory policies, and non-responsive governments are common sources of powerful grievances.

The competition and frustration-aggression mechanisms have the potential to cause any number of individuals to act violently in pursuit of nationalism. In this chapter, I focus on how they affect the educated elites. Indeed, a common finding of Benedict Anderson, Ernest Gellner, Anthony Smith, and other scholars of nationalism is that nation building is a top-down affair dominated by educated individuals: literati write nationalist texts and popularize grievances, the educated consume these messages and organize movements, and the educational systems and other institutions help spread these ideas to the masses. Moreover, the social movement literature finds that educated elites possess the mobilizational resources to organize broad-based movements, be they nationalist or non-nationalist. The educated elites therefore offer a strategic research site for the study of nationalism's impact on violence, as the educated appear most greatly affected by it and, in turn, are the most influential mobilizers of violent nationalist movements.

Competing nationalisms and limited violence in Canada

From its very beginning and continuing to this day, the educated elites have dominated the Quebec nationalist movement. For example, several quantitative analyses of individuals who support the Parti Québécois (PQ), a provincial political party that is the main nationalist organization spearheading the separatist movement, show that the educated are greatly overrepresented among PQ supporters (Cuneo and Curtis 1974; Hamilton and Pinard 1976; McRoberts and Posgate 1980). Pinard and Kowalchuk (in press) provide the most thorough analysis to date and find that educated individuals have dominated party administration and been much more likely to vote for the PQ.

In line with the active involvement of the educated, the separatist movement only became a powerful force in Quebec after the educational system expanded dramatically and produced an increasingly large number of educated individuals. Per capita expenditure on education in constant dollars increased from a measly $3.85 in 1945 to $23.28 in 1960. By 1970, in turn, it had risen to $89.83, a level of per capita spending over 23 times greater than just twenty-five years earlier (Latouche 1974). The expansion of enrolment coincided with growing expenditure. The first area to expand was elementary education, and its student body grew by as much as 25 percent annually in the late 1940s (Behiels 1985: 152). A similar but slightly later expansion occurred in secondary education. In 1952, only 4 percent of Francophones of secondary-school age (13–20-year-olds) attended school (Behiels 1985: 168). Shortly thereafter, however, public secondary schools were constructed throughout the province, and private schools were subsidized (Behiels 1985: 170; Linteau et al. 1991: 245). Through these efforts, the secondary enrolment rate skyrocketed throughout the 1950s, increasing from only 4 percent in 1952 to 66 percent in 1961. The secondary enrolment rate continued to increase rapidly over the next decade, reaching 94 percent in 1971.

Education and educational expansion are linked to the separatist movement in different ways. For one, independence has often been more in the economic, political, and social interests of the educated. Public-sector provincial employees, for example, are among the strongest supporters of separatism because separatism is in their personal interests and because they believe that it is in the best interests of Quebec (Behiels 1985: 44; Breton 1964; Gagnon and Montcalm 1990: 68; Heintzman 1983: 39). Considering Quebec, the public sector has been very active in promoting state economic management in an effort to modernize Quebec and improve the economic position of Francophone Québécois. Moreover, public sector employees see independence as a means of giving themselves full control. Similarly, independence would place more power and resources at the hands of the public sector and would promote even further public sector expansion, thereby increasing the economic opportunities of educated Francophones (Breton 1964).

Other analyses find that the frustration of educated Francophones over limited economic opportunities contributed to the nationalist movement. Indeed, the opportunities of the Francophone population in business and the federal administration were quite limited until the 1950s and 1960s, and studies find that Anglophones held top positions and earned considerably more than Francophones. Based on data from the 1970 census, for example, Anglophone males earned between 11 and 25 percent more than Francophone males, and the earning differentials went up with education level, meaning that the educated Francophones experienced a greater gap in income than less-educated Francophones (Shapiro and Stelcner 1987: 98–100). Coinciding with these findings, a survey from 1970–71 found that among Francophone Québécois, perceptions of inequality increased significantly with education level: the educated were more likely to believe that linguistic inequalities were real and that Francophones faced disadvantages in the labor market. The data also showed that Francophones with more education were more likely to report having experienced discrimination in the workplace and were much more likely to say that something needed to be done to address linguistic-based inequality (Laczko 1987). Several qualitative analyses make similar arguments about the frustration of the educated and their support for the separatist movement (Clift 1982: 22; Gagnon and Montcalm 1990: 9; Guindon 1964: 155; McRoberts and Posgate 1980: 119–21).

The impediments to ethno-nationalist violence in Quebec

While interests and grievances appear to have pushed the educated to organize and support the Quebec separatist movement, the political and economic environment severely constrained grievances and reduced incentives for ethno-national militancy. In particular, the political and economic environment increased the costs of radicalism, diminished the benefits of radicalism, and helped to reduce frustration. As a result, the nationalist elites remained moderate and opposed militant action that would lead to ethno-nationalist violence.

Despite periods of economic slowdown, post-World War II Canada (including Quebec) has experienced steady economic growth, and it presently has among the highest living standards in the world: its United Nations Development Program (UNDP) Human Development Index was ranked fourth in the world in 2009. Besides general prosperity, the particularly advantaged economic position of the movement's main base of support – educated Francophones – has also suppressed movement radicalism. Education has been strongly and negatively related to unemployment, meaning that the educated are well *under*represented among the unemployed (Government of Quebec 2010). Even in 1982, a particularly difficult period of economic slowdown that affected the educated and less-educated alike, the unemployment rate of individuals in Quebec aged 25 and older with eight or fewer years of education was 13.6 percent, but this rate declined steadily and consistently to only 5.8 percent among individuals with university diplomas (Fortin 1984: 434).

The relatively deprived position of the Francophone community vis-à-vis the Anglophone community improved after World War II, and this is another factor that helps to explain the limited violence of the separatist movement. For instance, while significant earnings differentials existed between Francophone and Anglophone Québecois as late as 1970, these differentials had already improved considerably by that time and virtually disappeared by 1980. Even more, although educated Francophones were most affected by inequality in 1970, by 1991 the economic returns of education were actually greater among Francophones (Lian and Matthews 1998). Vaillancourt, Lemay, and Vaillancourt (2007: 10) also find that the percentage of firms owned by Francophones increased from 47 percent of the total in 1961 to 67 percent in 2003. Thus, not only has the economic situation of Francophones in Quebec improved in absolute terms, it has also improved greatly relative to Anglophones, and limited the radicalism of the nationalist movement by reducing both grievances and incentives for separatism. Along these lines, Stevenson (2006: 306) describes how the improved economic position of nationalists caused the movement to become increasingly moderate: "By the mid-1970s, Quebec nationalists were becoming older and more affluent than they had been during the Quiet Revolution, and they had more to lose than before from economic uncertainty, disorder, and violence."

The wavering support of university students for the Front de libération du Québec (FLQ) – a leftist revolutionary group that employed violent tactics in pursuit of Quebec independence – provides evidence in favor of this point. As demonstrated by membership and participation in demonstrations, university students strongly supported the FLQ before the federal government declared a state of emergency in reaction to the FLQ's kidnappings of two prominent officials (Pierre Laporte and James Cross). Yet once the Canadian government clamped down on students, student support dried up almost instantly. Bédard (1998: 187–88) points to two main reasons for their rapid disengagement. First, the eventual death of Pierre Laporte at the hands of his FLQ captors repulsed students, showing that they were unwilling to go to such lengths to gain independence and that their grievances were not powerful enough for them to support violent militantism. Second, continued support of the FLQ posed potential dangers to the students because the government was now arresting people associated with the FLQ. And, because students had great potential for mobility and risked it by joining a militant movement, all but a handful chose to disassociate themselves from it. Thus, government forces keeping surveillance over students shortly after the declaration of the War Measures Act concluded that student radicalism had disappeared: "Students are concerned now about their examinations and are not in the mood for extra curricular meetings" (Bédard 1998: 171).

Besides the general availability of resources and the improving economic situation of the Québécois, the case also suggests that effective democratic government limited ethno-nationalist violence in different ways. For one thing, the Canadian state, at all levels, used relatively limited coercion in dealing with the separatist movement and therefore did not spark violence through its own violent methods. Indeed, state violence against particular ethnic communities commonly instigates or intensifies ethnic violence, but the Canadian state showed great restraint in using physical violence against the separatist movement.

An example that highlights the limited use of violence most clearly is, somewhat ironically, the enactment of the War Measures Act by the Trudeau government in 1970 after the FLQ's kidnapping of Cross and Laporte. After the declaration, the Canadian military had a strong presence in Quebec, and 497 people were incarcerated (of whom 62 were eventually charged and 32 were refused bail). Although a coercive measure, the Act was only declared after the premier of Quebec and mayor of Montreal demanded it, showing how wary the federal government was of using coercion. Such measures did not instigate anti-state violence because the coercion was very limited. Indeed, nearly all of those detained were quickly released, the Act was only used temporarily, and the police and military did not beat or kill anyone. In other countries with less democratic and effective governments, states of emergency pose much greater risks of violence because of a greater willingness of the government to resort to violence as well as the government's more limited ability to maintain law and order and control police and soldiers on the ground during periods of crisis.

Besides very limited state violence, neither the Canadian government nor the Québecois provincial government has formally discriminated against Francophone Canadians in the post-World War II period, and this is a second way in which the political institutions limited nationalist violence. Several recent works have found that formal discrimination designates individuals as subordinate and outside the political community and is therefore an important source of grievance provoking nationalist violence. In Quebec, this lack of formal political discrimination therefore deterred violence. Even more, political reforms actually sought to increase the presence of Francophones in both the public and private sectors, a policy that further limited the willingness of individuals to resort to radicalism in pursuit of independence.

Finally, yet likely of greatest importance, political institutions have limited nationalist violence in Quebec by providing formal and effective political channels for disgruntled actors to address nationalist grievances. For example, the federal government has consistently attempted to accommodate Québecois nationalism by treating Quebec fairly (other provinces would say, giving Quebec an unfair advantage) with equalization payments, making a concerted effort to increase the place of French within the federal government, and allowing a separatist party to participate in the national parliament. More important, a federated system of government has allowed Francophone Québecois to control provincial politics and thereby implement policy to address ethno-national grievances. Bill 101, with its efforts to improve and protect the use of French in the public and private sectors as well as in public education, is a notable example. In this way, most Francophones desiring change have sought to do so peacefully through formal politics, not violence. As a consequence, the leaders of the separatist movement, although sympathizing with the FLQ, spoke out strongly and unequivocally over the organization's use of violence and sought change through peaceful means.

Competing nationalisms and civil war in Sri Lanka

Similar to the Quebec separatist movement, the Tamil separatist movement has also been an elite-driven affair. Unlike Quebec, however, young militant sections of the movement were not banished but were accepted by the more mainstream leaders. In fact, the older generation of nationalist leaders handed over the reigns to their younger and more militant counterparts, thereby instigating an ethno-nationalist civil war that began in 1983 and ended in 2009. A second key difference is that both sides of the nationalist conflict were mobilized, and the Tamil separatist movement only occurred after episodes of severe anti-Tamil violence.

At the heart of the violence in Sri Lanka are two competing ideas of nation: one Sinhalese and one Tamil. During the final three decades of the nineteenth century, the intelligentsia from the Sinhalese and Tamil communities began revival movements. The movements were spearheaded by highly educated literary figures who strove to increase the national consciousnesses of their respective ethnic communities. According to Farmer (1963: 52–53), the revivalist associations of both Sinhalese and Tamil communities "formed part of a reaction from complete submission to Westernization and hence an important ingredient in the movement towards nationalism and national independence. From the communal point of view, they served to perpetuate differences between Sinhalese and Tamil, between Buddhist and Hindu." Similarly, Tambiah (1996: 39) claims that they "heightened, made self-conscious, and deepened the communal and ethnic consciousness, solidarity, and exclusiveness" of Sinhalese and Tamil communities.

Among the Tamils, the revivalist intelligentsia championed Tamil literature and art and popularized the Saiva doctrines of Hinduism, thereby helping to create a "heightened cultural and linguistic consciousness" opposed to that of the Sinhalese (Tambiah 1986: 108). Arumuga Navalar (1822–79), the key figure among the Tamil–Hindu revival movement in Sri Lanka, viewed Tamil culture as severely threatened by colonialism and missionaries and actively preached the need for a Hindu revival. In pursuit of this goal, he ran a printing press, promoted the use of Tamil, and wrote poetry. His greatest concern, however, was with education, and he believed that "education was the indispensable instrument of religious recovery" (K.M. de Silva 2007: 147). The movement therefore played an important role in expanding education among Tamils and providing an education that imparted Tamil nationalism.

The Sinhalese revivalist movement began more than a generation after its Tamil counterpart. It too focused on the protection and strengthening of culture in the face of foreign interference. Anagarika Dharmapala (1864–1933) and Munidasa Cumaratunga (1887–1944) were two of the movement's most influential leaders. Dharmapala focused his energy on the revival of Buddhism and played an important role in constructing a Sinhalese–Buddhist identity that was opposed to Hindus and Muslims. He suggested that Sri Lanka had been unfairly taken from the Buddhists and declared the dire need for Sinhalese

Buddhists to reinstate their great culture before its demise. Cumaratunga lived a generation after Dharmapala and spent much of his life fighting to protect the Sinhala language rather than Buddhism. He claimed, "Language without dignity produces men and women without dignity. Men and women without dignity are as base as beasts and can be made to stoop to any meanness" (Dharmadasa 1972: 133–34). Cumaratunga's ideas and leadership were instrumental in the rise of the Hela movement, which sought to return Sinhalese culture to its past splendor by shunning Indian, colonial, and other alien influences. The movement's primary base of support was the Sinhalese intelligentsia, including monks and, especially, teachers (Dharmadasa 1992: 275; Jayawardena 2004; Tambiah 1996: 40–42). The movement helped "instill confidence and self-respect into the minds of the Sinhalese literati who hitherto had suffered from a sense of inferiority" and was "a landmark in the rise of Sinhalese language nationalism" (Dharmadasa 1972: 141, 1992: 281).

Besides playing an instrumental role in the construction and invigoration of oppositional ethno-nationalist identities, the educated also organized and orchestrated acts of nationalist violence. Most important, university students and young university graduates formed the core memberships of Tamil nationalist organizations that actively organized and orchestrated ethno-nationalist violence. Most notably, the LTTE, or Tamil Tigers, was dominated by disheartened and relatively educated youths (Thangarajah 2002: 185). Early on, its core membership was university students and graduates, and the LTTE grew out of dozens of student-based organizations, including the Tamil Students' Federation, the TUF Youth Organization (the youth organization of the dominant Tamil political party), the Unemployed Graduates Union (an organization of disgruntled university and secondary school graduates), and EROS (a student organization of Tamil university students studying in London) (Hellmann-Rajanayagam 1994: 176; Pfaffenberger 1990: 254–55). In this way, educated Tamil youth founded and directed the organizations that used violence to pursue Tamil communal interests, comprised most of the members of these organizations during the initial phase of separatist violence, and thereby played a vital role in instigating the separatist movement.

Notably, the Tamil separatist movement used violence largely in reaction to violence, as Sinhalese nationalism contributed to several episodes of anti-Tamil violence. And, similarly to the Tamil separatist movement, the educated dominated and actively participated in Sinhalese nationalist violence against Tamils. Public servants participated in violence in 1958, several Sinhalese doctors and lawyers attacked and drove out their Tamil counterparts during the ethnic violence of 1983, and several educated and unemployed individuals actively participated in the 1983 riots (Tambiah 1986: 52, 99; Vanniasingham 1988: 16). Most important, university students and young university graduates formed the core memberships of the People's Liberation Front (JVP), a Marxist and Sinhalese nationalist organization that played an important role in popularizing anti-Tamil sentiments, and that pressured the government to play hardball with the LTTE and pursue a strongly pro-Sinhalese agenda.

The determinants of ethno-nationalist violence in Sri Lanka

Although the Tamil nationalist movement had been non-violent until the late 1970s, it did not reject violence as a means of pursuing Tamil nationalist interests once violent Tamil organizations began to form. Instead, the older leadership grudgingly accepted violence and let the militant organizations usurp and radicalize the movement. And even before Tamil nationalists turned violent, Sinhalese nationalists had orchestrated several violent acts against Tamils, something Anglophones did not attempt in Canada. The different economic and political contexts of Sri Lanka are factors that help to explain these differences from Quebec.

Limited economic opportunities in Sri Lanka

Because many Sri Lankans pursued education as a means of advancement, a large number of educated individuals expected and believed that they had the legitimate right to climb the socioeconomic ladder. There was a general expectation that education would and should give access to white-collar jobs, which were relatively well paid, stable, and imparted considerable status in a country where the overwhelming majority were manual workers. In fact, teachers commonly preached the merits of white-collar employment and the demerits of manual labor, thereby increasing student aversion toward the latter (Hettige 1991: 61).

During the British colonial period, white-collar expectations were almost always met because of a shortage of educated individuals. As independence approached, the expectations of students increased even further, as Sri Lankans finally began to work their way up to the highest positions within the administration. Unfortunately for educated Sri Lankans, the combination of three factors severely restrained their mobility by the 1950s and especially, the 1970s. First, an education explosion in Sri Lanka created a very large pool of newly educated individuals in a relatively short period of time: the number of students enrolled in government and state-assisted schools was 360,000 in 1920, 800,000 in 1945, and 2.7 million in 1970 (Kearney, 1979: 59). Second, the overall size of the population grew rapidly. The total population aged 25 years of age and younger increased from 3.8 million in 1946 to 7.2 million in 1968 (K.M. de Silva 1986: 166–67). Finally, Sri Lanka experienced very limited economic growth during and after the education and population explosions. The country's per capita growth rate between 1950 and 1975 averaged less than 2 percent per year, expanding from $1,274 to only $1,901 (in constant 2005 US dollars) over the period (Heston et al. 2009).

Due to the convergence of all three factors, the market for white-collar employment was swamped with qualified applicants, and the mass of educated youth experienced a decrease in relative wages. Between 1963 and 1982, the earnings ratio of employed individuals with up to O-level education (eleven years) and employed university graduates declined from 1:3.6 to 1:1.3 (Peiris 1999: 186). Moreover, the educated with low-paying jobs were actually lucky, as many had a very difficult time finding any job whatsoever. Indeed, because of the scarcity of white-collar jobs and because so many educated individuals believed it was beneath them to accept manual work, the unemployment rate soared among the educated, making the country an "outstanding example of the global phenomenon of educated unemployment" (K.M. de Silva 1986: 167).

Figure 5.1 shows data on unemployment rates by education level and age group in 1969–70. It shows that unemployment was greater among the more educated for all age groups but that the youth were particularly hard hit. While the table shows that individuals who had passed their O-level exams after the eleventh year of schooling had much higher unemployment than those who had either not taken or failed the O-level exams, Kearney (1979: 74) finds that the unemployment rate was even higher for individuals who had thirteen or more years of education: it was 23 percent for individuals aged between 25 and 34 years with thirteen or more years of education versus only 17 percent for individuals in the same age group who had successfully completed their eleventh year of education. Notably, the set of individuals who successfully completed their eleventh year of education also includes people who completed thirteen or more years of education, suggesting that the difference in unemployment rates is even greater than these statistics suggest.

Although experts on ethno-national violence in Sri Lanka point to a number of causes for the phenomenon, it is commonly accepted that the employment problem among the educated youth was one of the most influential (Alles 1990; Attanayake 2001; Bandarage 1998;

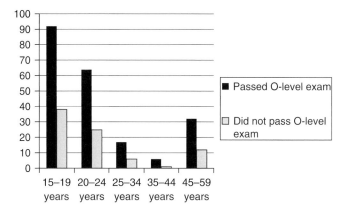

Source: Emmerij 1972: 487.

Figure 5.1. Unemployment rate by age and education in Sri Lanka, 1969–70

K.M. de Silva 1986; Hettige 1991; Jayawardena 2004; Kearney 1975, 1978; Manogaran 1987; Moore 1981; Pfaffenberger 1990, 1994; Senaratne 1997; Shastri 1994; Tambiah 1986). This line of argument suggests that the inability of the educated youth to find white-collar jobs caused anxiety, frustration, and anger, all of which increased their chances of acting violently. According to Kearney (1975: 737):

It is not difficult to imagine the consternation and despair of a youth who, after completing an education that had always in the past led to employment as a clerk or school-teacher, is advised to return to the mud of his father's paddy field. Even this prospect might not be open. The family plot may have been sold or given to his less-educated older brothers since his education was presumed to have removed him from dependence on agriculture. Population growth, in any case, had inexorably produced increasing pressure on the land, fragmentation of holdings, and landlessness.

Similarly, Wijesinghe (1969, 1973), a psychologist at a Sri Lankan university, described how the poor economic prospects of students caused extreme angst and promoted a dramatic increase in student violence. He also noted that this frustration-induced violence was directed against a variety of targets, including themselves.[1] The most common focuses of frustration and aggression, however, were the

---

[1] Similarly, Kearney and Miller (1985) find that frustration among the educated over limited mobility promoted high rates of suicide in Sri Lanka.

government and rival ethnic communities. This dual focus, in turn, contributed to a violent Tamil movement.

Educated Tamils despised the government because they held it accountable for discriminatory policy that restricted their mobility. As a consequence, they vented their frustration and aggression on the government in the form of a separatist movement (Balasingham 2004: 19–20; Bhasin 2004; K.M. de Silva 1986; Kearney 1979: 79; Manogaran 1987: 119; Pfaffenberger 1990, 1994; Phadnis 1984; Sahedevan and DeVotta 2006: 56; Shastri 1994; Wijesinghe 2004: 266). Indeed, the "most militant agitators for separatism were the educated unemployed" (K.M. de Silva 1986: 261–62). Demonstrating the link between the unmet expectations of educated Tamils and separatist violence most clearly is the fact that the separatist movement grew out of Tamil student associations and, most notably, the Unemployed Graduates' Union, a Tamil organization comprised of unemployed high school and university graduates (Pfaffenberger 1990: 254–55).

The Sinhala Only Act was the single most important discriminatory policy that caused educated Tamils to blame the government for their hardship and to focus their frustration and aggression on it. The Act made Sinhala the only official language of Sri Lanka, and all public servants were required to speak it, something that most educated Tamils could not do and that placed them at a fundamental disadvantage in an extremely competitive job market (Jayawardene and Jayawardene 1987: 162). In addition, the Act legitimized Sinhalese political dominance and discriminatory hiring practices. Thus, Tamils received only 1 thousand of the 140,000 jobs offered by the government in 1978, and the percentage of Tamil civil servants declined considerably between 1949 and 1981 (Samarasinghe 1984: 178; Tiruchelvam 1984: 186). The percentage of Tamils employed by the state in general clerical service, for example, declined from 40.7 percent in 1949 to only 5.4 percent between 1978 and 1981, and the Tamil share of professional and managerial posts plummeted from 60 and 30 percent, respectively, in 1956 to only 10 and 5 percent in 1979 (Samarasinghe 1984: 178; Thangarajah 2002: 175). Pfaffenberger (1994: 10), in turn, notes that limited employment opportunities intensified frustration and anger because unemployed Tamil males "could not marry, at least not respectably; they could not obtain lands because they could not marry; and, indeed in Jaffna's puritanical culture, they could not even find sexual partners."

Besides the government, educated Sinhalese and Tamils scapegoated one another for their grievances. Ethnic scapegoating was caused by the strength of ethnic identities, high levels of ethnic-based inequalities and discrimination, and extreme ethnic competition. Indeed, because of the salience of ethnicity and competition over scarce jobs, each community kept track of ethnic-based representation in elite jobs and education and felt aggrieved when their community was underrepresented or marginalized. In this way, individual grievances over unmet expectations pushed Sri Lankans to search for scapegoats, ethnic-based collective grievances caused people to blame rival ethnic communities for the general hardship faced by their community, and both individual and collective grievances promoted ethnically oriented frustration and aggression among the educated.

Frustration among educated and unemployed Sinhalese over unmet economic expectations also promoted anti-Tamil violence and contributed to both discriminatory policy and the Tamil separatist movement. In particular, the Sinhalese were also severely affected by the limited economic opportunities, and they commonly scapegoated Tamils for their plight because Tamils had historically held a disproportionate share of white-collar positions. Their attacks on Tamils, in turn, provided another powerful grievance and thereby helped fuel the separatist movement.

Even before the education explosion caused an enormous oversupply of educated labor, ethnic inequality and limited mobility caused educated Sinhalese elites to instigate violence against advantaged communities, including violence against Christians in 1883 and against Muslims in 1915 (Jayawardena 2004). In a similar fashion, it contributed to the first round of Sinhalese–Tamil violence shortly after independence (Jayawardena 2004: 71–73). During both periods, educated Sinhalese were at a heightened risk of perpetrating ethnic violence because of their greater sensitivity to ethnic inequalities, the latter of which directly affected their upward mobility. The shortage of white-collar jobs after independence, in turn, only intensified resentment and frustration over ethnic inequalities (K.M. de Silva 1986: 85). According to Tambiah (1986: 56), frustration over unemployment and resentment over the disproportionate share of white-collar jobs held by Tamils triggered "time and again the communal riots directed by the have-nots against a nominated 'enemy,' the Tamils, who have been stereotyped as privileged, and about whom the Sinhalese man on the street has been taught to say, 'We have already given them too much.'" The first JVP insurrection in 1971, in turn, pushed the government to implement more university admissions policies that benefited Sinhalese at the expense of Tamils. The case therefore shows how limited economic resources caused Sinhalese to scapegoat Tamils, and how the resulting anti-Tamil violence and policy helped to spark a violent separatist movement. In Canada, on the other hand, abundant resources limited both the scapegoating of Anglophones by Francophones over economic inequalities and the scapegoating of Francophones by Anglophones after the government of Quebec passed pro-Francophone policy that negatively affected Anglophones.

Ineffective political institutions: discrimination and incapacity

The previous section focused on economic factors that contributed to nationalist violence in Sri Lanka, but it also highlights how political factors interacted with the economy to create grievances. In particular, the political institutions discriminated against Tamils, did not allow them to effectively address their grievances through formal channels, and condoned communal violence against Tamils. This not only pushed Tamils to accept separatism as a means of preserving the Tamil community but also pushed them to accept violence as the only means of attaining independence.

Sri Lankan political institutions offered the Tamil community very little ability to pursue their interests. As a tiny minority, Tamils were at the mercy of the Sinhalese and were unable to push the Sinhalese-dominated governments to pursue Tamil interests when they were perceived as opposed to those of the numerically dominant Sinhalese. This was especially the case since large segments of the Sinhalese community blamed the Tamils for the limited economic opportunities available to Sinhalese. As a means of partially circumventing this problem, Tamil leaders demanded a federated system of government that would devolve more powers to the local level, a situation that would empower Tamils in those regions with high concentrations of Tamils. The central government, however, did not want either to lose power or to grant any sort of political autonomy to the Tamil community, causing demands for federalism to fall on deaf ears.

Even more than simply being unable to pursue their interests through formal political channels, Sri Lankan Tamils felt that governments openly oppressed them. As noted previously, the government implemented employment policy that benefited Sinhalese at the expense of Tamils, causing the latter to view the government as a means of oppression. A similar and equally consequential government policy that was perceived as flagrantly anti-Tamil was a university admissions policy that implemented quotas negatively affecting the number of Tamils accepted into university. And, because the playing field of education and mobility was no longer level, Tamil students were furious and decided to pursue their interests through a new method: by organizing a violent separatist movement (C.R. de Silva 1984a: 119; C.R. de Silva 1984b: 133; K.M. de Silva 1984: 100; Jayawardene and Jayawardene 1987: 159; Jayaweera 1990: 68;

Manogaran 1987: 127; Sabaratnam 2001: 218; Shastri 1994: 212–13; Tambiah 1986: 17; Wilson 2000: 103). Indeed, it is no coincidence that the period during which Tamil students organized the LTTE (1974–75) was also the period in which admissions policy most dramatically affected Tamil university admissions (Thangarajah 2002: 182). The admissions issue infuriated students and sparked the organization of the Tamil Students Movement as a means of protesting the policy, and it subsequently splintered into 35 different insurgency groups, many of which played an active role in the separatist movement (Gunaratna 1998: 106). K.M. De Silva (1986: 242) goes so far as to claim that no issue "did more in radicalizing the politics of the Tamil areas in the north" than university admissions. "Nothing has caused more frustration and bitterness among Tamil youth than this, for they regarded it as an iniquitous system deliberately devised to place obstacles before them" (K.M. De Silva 1986: 262).

More than simply implementing policy that advantaged Sinhalese at the expense of Tamils, the government was incapable and unwilling to suppress anti-Tamil violence. From the 1950s on, several bouts of communal violence occurred between Sinhalese and Tamils. Members of the Sinhalese community always instigated this violence, and Tamils suffered the most from its destruction. One reason for such destruction was that the police, who were overwhelmingly Sinhalese, commonly failed to step in to stop the attacks and even participated in them. Indeed, Tambiah (1996) describes how one government official actually gave information listing the addresses and ethnicity of registered voters to political thugs so that they could attack the homes of Tamils. Moreover, when the police and military waged campaigns against the LTTE and other separatist groups, they commonly used excessive violence that provoked further outrage among Tamils. For example, in retribution for LTTE killings of police officers, the military burnt the library housing the largest collection of Tamil literature, including a number of priceless artifacts and documents. This act caused many Tamils to see the government as trying to annihilate their cultural heritage.

Thus, unable to address their grievances through formal politics, facing discriminatory policy that impeded the advancement of Tamils, and suffering violence as the police looked on and participated, Tamil nationalist leaders had their backs against the wall and saw violence as their only option.

Comparison and conclusion

This chapter has analyzed separatist movements in Canada and Sri Lanka in order to explore potential factors that affect whether nationalist movements are peaceful or violent. While any number of factors can contribute to differences in violence, the analysis highlights two general factors that appear to have considerable influence: the availability of economic opportunities and the effectiveness of political institutions.

The Sri Lankan case study offers evidence that the lack of economic resources created frustration and aggression and fuelled nationalist violence in two ways. First, both Tamils and Sinhalese had very limited economic opportunities and attempted to eliminate ethnic competitors: Sinhalese by attacking Tamils and passing anti-Tamil policy, and Tamils by fighting for an independent Tamil state. Second, both Tamils and Sinhalese had ethno-nationalist grievances, with each blaming the other for the economic hardships. As a consequence, both communities scapegoated one another, thereby contributing to ethno-nationalist violence.

This situation contrasts starkly with Canada and the Quebec separatist movement. Here, economic opportunities were prevalent, especially among the Québecois educated elite. As a consequence, the nationalist elites saw less of a need to resort to violence and would have suffered potentially great economic costs had they resorted to violence. Similarly, the Anglophone community had considerable economic opportunities and, unlike the Sinhalese, did not have incentives to eliminate Québecois nationalists for their own economic benefit. Besides creating different incentives for violence, the more advantageous economic environment of Quebec also deterred violence by reducing grievances, as the separatist elites generally were not frustrated by an inability to find white-collar jobs. And, although they were frustrated by a glass ceiling in the private sector, they dominated the very large and expanding provincial public sector and could also see that the situation was improving rapidly. Thus, both the Tamil separatists and the Sinhalese nationalists had economic incentives in favor of violence in Sri Lanka, but both Francophone and Anglophone Québecois had incentives against it in Canada; economic difficulties caused great frustration among the Tamil separatists and Sinhalese nationalists but not among the Québecois separatists or Anglophone Canadians living in Quebec.

The political context also helps to explain variation in nationalist violence. Most notably, an effective and decentralized state and robust democracy allowed Québecois nationalists to pursue their interests and address grievances through formal political channels. Thus, peaceful methods were possible and allowed nationalist leaders to successfully implement policy protecting nationalist interests. Tamils, however, found themselves completely unable to address grievances and pursue communal interests because the state was used to pursue Sinhalese interests at the expense of Tamils. Even more, the Sri Lankan state proved unable and unwilling to stop violence against Tamils and actually

participated in it at times. This situation was affected by limited economic resources, as the JVP and other Sinhalese nationalist groups were
frustrated over their limited economic opportunities and pushed the
government to implement pro-Sinhalese and anti-Tamil policy. Overall,
the analysis therefore shows how the economic and political contexts
shape nationalist grievances and interests and thereby help to motivate
violence in some places but restrain it in others.

These findings strongly support those of Hiers and Wimmer in
Chapter 9 showing that grievances caused by political institutions and
discriminatory policy promote nationalist civil wars. They differ, however, in that Hiers and Wimmer downplay the importance of the economy, whereas I find that both politics and the economy are important
and that both interact. In particular, economic difficulties promoted both
anti-Tamil violence and anti-Tamil policy in the absence of discriminatory policy against Sinhalese (in fact, in the presence of strongly pro-
Sinhalese policy). This violence and policy in combination with the
limited economic opportunities of Tamils, in turn, provoked Tamil
separatist violence. In Canada, on the other hand, abundant economic
opportunities helped to limit the militancy of the separatist movement.
Even more, abundant resources helped to restrain an Anglophone backlash after the Quebec government implemented policy that benefited
Francophones at the expense of Anglophones.

REFERENCES

Alles, A.C. 1990. *The JVP: 1969–1989*. Colombo: Lake House Investments Ltd.
Attanayake, A. 2001. *Sri Lanka: Constitutionalism, Youth Protest and Political Violence*. Matera: Ajith Printers.
Balasingham, A. 2004. *War and Peace: Armed Struggle and Peace Efforts of Liberation Tigers*. Mitcham: Fairmax.
Bandarage, A. 1998. "College Degrees Bear Bitter Fruit in Sri Lanka." *Chronicle of Higher Education* 45(17): B8.
Bédard, É. 1998. *Chronique d'une Insurrection Appréhendée: La Crise d'Octobre et le Milieu Universitaire*. Saint-Laurent: Septentrion.
Behiels, M. 1985. *Prelude to Quebec's Quiet Revolution: Liberalism versus Neo-Nationalism, 1945–1960*. Montreal: McGill-Queen's University Press.
Bhasin, A.S. 2004. *India in Sri Lanka: Between Lion and Tiger*. Colombo: Vijitha Yapa Publications.
Breton, A. 1964. "The Economics of Nationalism." *Journal of Political Economy* 72(4): 76–86.
Clift, D. 1982. *Quebec Nationalism in Crisis*. Montreal: McGill-Queen's University Press.
Cuneo, C. and J. Curtis. 1974. "Quebec Separatism: An Analysis of Determinants within Social-Class Levels." *Canadian Review of Sociology* 11(1): 1–29.

de Silva, C.R. 1984a. "Sinhala–Tamil Ethnic Rivalry: The Background."
    Pp. 111–24 in *From Independence to Statehood: Managing Ethnic Conflict in
    Five African and Asian States*, edited by R. Goldmann and A.J. Wilson.
    London: Frances Pinter.
    1984b. "Sinhala–Tamil Relations and Education in Sri Lanka: The University
    Admissions Issue – The First Phase, 1971–7." Pp. 125–46 in *From
    Independence to Statehood: Managing Ethnic Conflict in Five African and Asian
    States*, edited by R. Goldmann and A.J. Wilson. London: Frances Pinter.
de Silva, K.M. 1984. "University Admissions and Ethnic Tension in Sri Lanka,
    1977–82." Pp. 97–110 in *From Independence to Statehood: Managing
    Ethnic Conflict in Five African and Asian States*, edited by R. Goldmann
    and A.J. Wilson. London: Frances Pinter.
    1986. *Managing Ethnic Tensions in Multi-Ethnic Societies: Sri Lanka 1880–1985*.
    New York: University Press of America.
    2007. *Sri Lanka's Troubled Inheritance*. Kandy: International Centre for Ethnic
    Studies.
Dharmadasa, K.N.O. 1972. "Language and Sinhalese Nationalism: The Career
    of Munidasa Cumaratunga." *Modern Ceylon Studies – A Journal of the Social
    Sciences* 3(2): 125–43.
    1992. *Language, Religion, and Ethnic Assertiveness – The Growth of Sinhalese
    Nationalism in Sri Lanka*. Ann Arbor: University of Michigan Press.
Farmer, B.H. 1963. *Ceylon: A Divided Nation*. London: Oxford University Press.
Fortin, P. 1984. "Le Chômage de Jeunes au Québec: Aggravation et
    Concentration, 1966–1982." *Industrial Relations* 39(3): 419–48.
Gagnon, A. and M.B. Montcalm. 1990. *Quebec Beyond the Quiet Revolution*.
    Toronto: Nelson Canada.
Government of Quebec. 2010. "The Labour Market: Integration of Graduates
    Into the Labour Market." Accessed at www.mels.gouv.qc.ca/STAT/indic01/
    indic01A/ia01603.pdf.
Guindon, H. 1964. "Social Unrest, Social Class, and Quebec's Bureaucratic
    Revolution." *Queen's Quarterly* 71: 150–62.
Gunaratna, R. 1998. *Sri Lanka's Ethnic Crisis and National Security*. Colombo:
    South Asian Network on Conflict Research.
Hamilton, R. and M. Pinard. 1976. "The Bases of Parti Quebecois Support in
    Recent Quebec Elections." *Canadian Journal of Political Science* 9(1): 3–26.
Heintzman, R. 1983. "The Political Culture of Quebec, 1840–1960." *Canadian
    Journal of Political Science* 16(1): 3–59.
Hellmann-Rajanayagam, D. 1994. "Tamils and the Meaning of History."
    Pp. 54–83 in *The Sri Lankan Tamils: Ethnicity and Identity*, edited by
    C. Manogaran and B. Pfaffenberger. Boulder, CO: Westview Press.
Heston, A., R. Summers, and B. Aten. 2009. *Penn World Table Version 6.3*.
    Center for International Comparisons of Production, Income and Prices.
    University of Pennsylvania.
Hettige, S.T. 1991. "Human Resources Development in Sri Lanka:
    A Sociological Perspective." *Sri Lanka Journal of Social Sciences* 14: 49–64.
Jayawardena, K. 2004. *Ethnic and Class Conflict in Sri Lanka: The Emergence of
    Sinhala-Buddhist Consciousness 1883–1983*. Colombo: Sanjiva Books.

Jayawardene, C.H.S. and H. Jayawardene. 1987. *Terror in Paradise: The Battle for Eelam.* Ottawa: Crimcare Publications.
Jayaweera, S. 1990. "Education and Socio-Economic Development." *Sri Lanka Journal of Social Sciences* 13: 47–72.
Kearney, R. 1975. "Educational Expansion and Political Volatility in Sri Lanka: The 1971 Insurrection." *Asian Survey* 15(9): 727–44.
    1978. "Language and the Rise of Tamil Separatism in Sri Lanka." *Asian Survey* 18(5): 521–34.
    1979. "Politics and Modernization." Pp. 57–81 in *Modern Sri Lanka: A Society in Transition*, edited by T. Fernando and R. Kearney. Syracuse, NY: Syracuse University Press.
Kearney, R. and B. Miller. 1985. "The Spiral of Suicide and Social Change in Sri Lanka." *Journal of Asian Studies* 45(1): 81–101.
Laczko, L. 1987. "Perceived Communal Inequalities in Quebec: A Multidimensional Analysis." *Canadian Journal of Sociology* 12(1/2): 83–110.
Lange, M. 2012. *Educations in Ethnic Violence.* New York: Cambridge University Press.
Latouche, D. 1974. "La Vrai Nature de … la Révolution Tranquille." *Canadian Journal of Political Science* 7(3): 525–36.
Lian, J. and D. Matthews. 1998. "Does the Vertical Mosaic Still Exist? Ethnicity and Income in Canada, 1991." *Canadian Review of Sociology and Anthropology* 35(4): 461–81.
Linteau, P., R. Durocher, J. Robert, and F. Ricard. 1991. *Quebec Since 1930.* Trans. R. Chodos and E. Garmaise. Toronto: James Lorimer & Co.
Manogaran, C. 1987. *Ethnic Conflict and Reconciliation in Sri Lanka.* Honolulu: University of Hawaii Press.
McRoberts, K. and D. Posgate. 1980. *Quebec: Social Change and Political Crisis.* Toronto: McClelland and Stewart.
Moore, M.P. 1981. "Unemployment of Educated Youth: A Problem for Whom?" *Marga Quarterly Journal* 6(2): 97–105.
Peiris, G. 1999. "Insurrection and Youth Unrest in Sri Lanka." Pp. 165–99 in *History and Politics: Millenial Perspectives. Essays in Honour of Kingsley de Silva*, edited by G. Peiris and S.W.R. de A. Samarasinghe. Colombo: Law and Society Trust.
Pfaffenberger, B. 1990. "Ethnic Conflict and Youth Insurgency in Sri Lanka: The Social Origins of Tamil Separatism." Pp. 241–58 in *Conflict and Peacemaking in Multiethnic Societies*, edited by J. Montvill. Toronto: Lexington Books.
    1994. "Introduction: The Sri Lankan Tamils." Pp. 1–27 in *The Sri Lankan Tamils: Ethnicity and Identity*, edited by C. Manogaran and B. Pfaffenberger. Boulder, CO: Westview Press.
Phadnis, U. 1984. *Ethnic Conflict in Sri Lanka – An Overview.* New Delhi: Ghandi Peace Foundation.
Pinard, M. and L. Kowalchuk. In press. "New Middle Class and Other Segments of Intellectuals, as Class Bases of the Quebec Movement: An Empirical Assessment." In M. Pinard and L. Kowalchuk (eds.) *The Quebec Independence Movement.* Montreal: McGill-Queen's University Press.

Sabaratnam, L. 2001. *Ethnic Attachments in Sri Lanka: Social Change and Cultural Continuity.* New York: Palgrave.

Sahedevan, P. and N. DeVotta. 2006. *Politics of Conflict and Peace in Sri Lanka.* New Delhi: Manak Publications.

Samarasinghe, S.W.R. de A. 1984. "Ethnic Representation in Central Government Employment and Sinhala–Tamil Relations in Sri Lanka: 1948–1981." Pp. 173–84 in *From Independence to Statehood: Managing Ethnic Conflict in Five African and Asian States,* edited by R. Goldmann and A.J. Wilson. London: Frances Pinter Publishers.

Senaratne, J.P. 1997. *Political Violence in Sri Lanka, 1977–1990: Riots, Insurrections, Counterinsurgencies, Foreign Intervention.* Amsterdam: VU University Press.

Shapiro, D.M. and M. Stelcner. 1987. "Earnings Disparities among Linguistic Groups in Quebec, 1970–1980." *Canadian Public Policy* 13(1): 97–104.

Shastri, A. 1994. "The Material Basis for Separatism: The Tamil Eelam Movement in Sri Lanka." Pp. 208–35 in *The Sri Lankan Tamils: Ethnicity and Identity,* edited by C. Manogaran and B. Pfaffenberger. Boulder, CO: Westview Press.

Stevenson, G. 2006. *Parallel Paths: The Development of Nationalism in Ireland and Quebec.* Montreal: McGill-Queen's University Press.

Tambiah, S.J. 1986. *Sri Lanka – Ethnic Fratricide and the Dismantling of Democracy.* University of Chicago Press.

1996. *Leveling Crowds: Ethnonationalist Conflicts and Collective Violence in South Asia.* Berkeley: University of California Press.

Thangarajah, C.Y. 2002. "Youth, Conflict and Social Transformation in Sri Lanka." Pp. 172–207 in *Sri Lankan Youth: Challenges and Responses,* edited by S.T. Hettige and M. Mayer. Colombo: Friedrich Ebert Stiftung.

Tiruchelvam, N. 1984. "Ethnicity and Resource Allocation." Pp. 85–195 in *From Independence to Statehood: Managing Ethnic Conflict in Five African and Asian States,* edited by R. Goldmann and A.J. Wilson. London: Frances Pinter.

Vaillancourt, F., D. Lemay, and L. Vaillancourt. 2007. *Laggards No More: The Changed Socioeconomic Status of Francophones in Quebec.* Toronto: C.D. Howe Institute, Backgrounder No. 103.

Vanniasingham, S. 1988. *Sri Lanka: The Conflict Within.* New Delhi: Lancer.

Wijesinghe, C.P. 1969. "Youth in Ceylon." Pp. 31–44 in *Youth: A Transcultural Psychiatric Approach,* edited by J. Masserman. New York: Grune and Stratton.

1973. "Youth Unrest and the Psychiatrist in Sri Lanka." *Australian and New Zealand Journal of Psychiatry* 7: 313–17.

2004. "Education Policy in Sri Lanka: The Failure of Good Intentions and Little Learning." Pp. 251–309 in *Protection of Minority Rights and Diversity,* edited by N. Wanasundera. Colombo: International Centre for Ethnic Studies.

Wilson, A.J. 2000. *Sri Lankan Tamil Nationalism: Its Origins and Development in the Nineteenth and Twentieth Centuries.* Vancouver: UBC Press.

Part 3

Empires and nation-states

6 Empire and ethnicity

John Darwin

Empire and ethnicity have been among the most powerful forces that have shaped the modern world. Yet, as I shall try to suggest, their highly ambivalent relationship has so far not been explored systematically – or, insofar as it has, with unsatisfactory results. This is a bold claim to make. Let us see first where the argument stands at the moment.

Where they have imagined the encounter between empire and ethnicity, historians and social scientists have typically seen it as overbearing, aggressive, or simply exploitative. Empire is usually perceived (despite much contrary evidence) as an administrative monolith, a leviathan that was capable of repressing all opposition (and certainly of suppressing any ethnic assertion) – until, that is, its own strength gave way. Faced with "indigenous" cultures and identities (the elements of ethnicity), empires in this view reacted in four ways. The first response was to subjugate: to destroy the capacity for autonomous political action or force it into channels and molds that imperial agents could control. That might mean the removal or crushing of "traditional" leaders and the confiscation of their wealth. It might mean the banning of external forms of identity, as the tartan was banned in the Scottish Highlands after 1746. It invariably meant the systematic disarming of a conquered community, rooting out the old status of arms and arms-bearing or restricting it tightly to a tiny favored minority. The second response followed quickly behind. The act of conquest required justification to opinion both at home (however narrow in practice the "political class") and abroad (to appease rivals enraged by successful predation). It was natural enough to disparage the conquered as barbarians or worse. Their "disorders" were a threat to the industrious and peaceful. Their customs affronted those of a higher morality. Their modes of production were stagnant and wasteful at best. Their religious beliefs were mere superstition. Their sole chance of

This is a revised and expanded version of the paper that was originally published in *Nations and Nationalism* 16(3), 383–401, in July 2010. We are grateful to Wiley/Blackwell for permission to reproduce this article in the present form.

progress, moral or material,[1] lay in a providential intervention to release them from the tyranny of their stationary state. Conquest was not a catastrophe, or even an accident, but the beginning of history. It was an act of enlightenment.

The third response was a retreat into pragmatism. All too often conquered populations ("ethnicities") proved resistant to the civilization and culture of the conquerors, or (a common variation) the conquerors themselves lacked the means or the nerve to impose them by force. Impatient of the difficulty and skeptical of the benefit, the conquering imperialists abandoned the effort, or confined it to those whose bureaucratic abilities as administrative scribes they could not do without. For the rest of the population their ambitions were comparatively modest. They needed a revenue to pay for their rule and also (usually) a garrison. And they insisted on *pax*: or, at worst, a localized disorder plausibly characterized as criminal, not political. To achieve these objectives, conquered populations needed to be fixed in "their" place, spatially just as much as politically. Migrants and nomads or those who practiced a swidden cultivation could no longer be suffered to roam over the landscape disturbing those in their path or (as the new rulers suspected) living by theft. Each group should have its "location," clearly marked on the map. Within settled societies, the same rule would apply in vertical terms. Social obligations should be fixed, social identities assigned, social power codified. The ruler should know whom to deal with and no change should occur without his consent.

Fourth, in support of this effort, the agents of empire invoked custom and practice since "time out of mind." They imagined or invented a timeless past and a "traditional" culture to which conquered peoples adhered. They portrayed their own political system as a "restoration" after the chaos and disorder that imperial intervention had ended. Caste in India and the tribe in Africa acquired at their hands a new and much less flexible meaning as the indelible markers of social and political status. Indeed, so strong was the presumption that caste and tribe were age-old forms of identity that imperial rulers felt entitled to fabricate them into existence where the record was lacking: in the popular phrase they "invented tradition" (Dirks 2001; Ranger 1983). The result was not to restore a "customary" past but to forge (in both senses of the word) a "neo-traditional" order, frozen in time and bent to the interests of thuggish local enforcers – rural elites whose real warrant to rule (and exploit) was the irresistible firepower of their imperial patrons.

[1] The annual reports of the British Government of India were grandly entitled "The Moral and Material Progress of India."

Hence the great irony of imperial purpose: the promise of "progress" – the "civilizing mission" – turned out in practice to mean the denial of change. Far from imposing their Western modernity on conquered communities, the rulers conscripted a bogus ethnicity to shore up their power. And though, in the last gasp of their imperium, they were willing to abandon their ethnic experiments in the search for new allies, the change came too late to save their successors from the damage inflicted by the ethnic divisions that their rule had entrenched. The evil that empires did thus lived on after them.

It would be hard to dispute all the items on this charge sheet. Nor should we try. But two points could be raised. The first has already been made by a growing number of scholars for whom the imperial "invention of tradition" seems too pat and simplistic (Spear 2003). Indeed, it seems to fly in the face of much that was known about colonial regimes. Two generations of research, much of it in local and provincial archives, had revised the old story of imperial "control." Histories of imperialism colored by self-interest or sentiment portrayed the men on the spot as titans in shorts, ruling their districts by sheer exertion of will. Justice was served. Crime and corruption fell on their knees. The poor were raised up, the malignant laid low. Free from the oppression of landlords and usurers, or tyrannical chiefs, subject peoples could become an industrious peasantry, shrewdly aware of how much they owed to their alien masters, shrewdly indifferent to the nationalist rhetoric of urban "extremists." Some, but not much, of this agreeable fable survived skeptical scrutiny. Its basic assumptions were demolished with merciless logic by the two wisest historians of modern imperialism. In a foundational essay, John Gallagher and Ronald Robinson showed that British imperialism (and by implication, most others as well) was forced to depend upon the self-interested help of those they described as "collaborative elites" (Gallagher and Robinson 1953). Lacking the means and the manpower to govern by force, the British almost invariably chose to seek out the local power-holders and offer a bargain. Emirs, sheikhs, pashas, chiefs, khans, and zemindars could stay in their place and rule their own roost, so long as they offered (and sanctioned) no challenge to imperial authority. Much of the detail was settled in the "durbar diplomacy" of division or district. As might be expected, it suited both sides to present the local regime as solidly loyal. The reality was often a tacit acceptance that the district official (often in post for less than two years) could do little to challenge the local "big men" and their patterns of clientage. Collecting the revenue and preventing disorder were burdens enough (Frykenberg 1965).

It was hard to see how this "limited raj," so cautious in dealing with local elites, could enjoy a free hand in making identities, let alone imposing its blueprint on resistant communities. It was always more likely that the encoding of custom and the ascribing of status were cooperative ventures. Their terms were bound to derive from well-placed informants with a great deal at stake. No doubt the authorized versions were drafted to help the loyal collaborator and shore up his claims. But they could hardly ignore the "local knowledge" of oral tradition or, in literate societies, the opinion of scholars and scribes. It followed from this that the forms of ethnic identity, whether tribal or caste-like, were the product not so much of Machiavellian repression as of pragmatic reciprocity. And as we shall see, the relations of empire and ethnicity were always deeply ambivalent. Ethnic allegiance might be disruptive and dangerous to imperial authority. But regularized and "re-formed" it could be put to very good use.

This last observation suggests a second and bolder revision. If empire and ethnicity were not polar opposites and if indigenous forms of ethnicity could be fashioned in concert with the agents of empire, perhaps empire itself could (under certain conditions) become the prime source of an *ethnic* identity. This is not to revive the dreary old claim that (some) European peoples (the British head the list of the usual suspects) owed their identity to feelings of racial superiority over non-white-skinned peoples. Still less to suggest that British society was "constituted by" empire (a bafflingly vacuous phrase). The argument here is that empire created distinctive kinds of ethnicity, not just by promoting a "tame" indigeneity, but by subsuming local sources of meaning in a new supra-local identity. This "imperial ethnicity" existed "at home" in the metropole, where it had to compete (in the British case) with other versions of English- or Britishness. But its real field of influence lay in the overseas empire. Here "British connection" (the contemporary phrase) served as the keystone of provincial identities and lent them some (though not all) of their ethnic characteristics. While the most striking examples can be seen in the migrant societies of the so-called "white dominions" (Canada, Australia, New Zealand, and – with some qualifications – South Africa), imperial ethnicities emerged among non-British and non-white peoples as well. We will see later what conditions first encouraged and then discredited this perhaps surprising phenomenon. And before we go very far we will need to consider what we mean by our two terms of art, "empire" and "ethnicity." It will help, first of all, to glance at Ernest Gellner's view of the matter.

Gellner was of course deeply interested in empire and ethnicity, although his view of both was to change quite sharply. In his best-known book, *Nations and Nationalism* (1983), he insisted that nationalism and the nation were artifacts of modernity. Indeed, their existence was necessary because an industrialized society required its population to share a common high culture. This was partly so that its individual members should be able to change their social roles easily (an essential condition of greater economic efficiency), partly to allow them to grasp the standardized concepts required by intense, high-speed, social communication (the key characteristic of "modern" societies). An ethnically based nationalism was thus a natural and legitimate means of escape from a dank pre-modernity into the sunny uplands of modernity – although its precise contribution was left studiously vague. Indeed, the whole transformation from agrarian to industrial society was little short of miraculous. "It is unlikely," said Gellner (in *Plough, Sword and Book*),

> that we shall ever know with precision the precise path by which we have escaped from the idiocy of rural life … The transformation was too profound and too contrary and indeed offensive to the established patterns of thought and values to be understood in advance. Had it been [so] … surely the threat it implied to most established interests would have led to a more determined attempt to thwart it. (Gellner 1988: 170)

But however it was reached, the contemporary pattern (in the 1980s) of centralized, culturally homogeneous states – "nation-states" – was the inescapable format of modern society, the only safe vehicle of progress.

"Empire," by contrast, was pre-modern and regressive. It was also coercive and violent. In Gellner's model, empire is conceived as *agraria*. *Agraria* was a patchwork of ethnic communities each with its own "low" culture, language and *terroir*, domineered over by a sword-bearing elite and its clerical sidekicks who jointly administered earthly and supernatural terror. Empire worked by maintaining the differences between its various ethnic "cells." The imperial elite preserved a monopoly over its single "high" culture and ensured that its lines of command and control should always run vertically (from ethnic unit to center) and remain in safe hands. It was easy to see that empire could not be compatible with any form of modernity. Nor, logically, could it survive the collapse of the economic, political, and cultural conditions that typified pre-modernity. Once the transition was necessary and unavoidable, and demanded the universalization of high culture (to secure literacy, mobility and swift adaptation), the cellular structure of empire became obsolete. An empire must become a nation or, more likely, dissolve into nation-bearing units.

We might hazard the guess that this historical vision drew much of its force from contemplating the history of Eastern and Central Europe, that graveyard of empires. But by the time he came to compose his last (posthumously published) book, *Language and Solitude: Wittgenstein, Malinowski and the Habsburg Dilemma* (1998), Gellner's perspective had shifted considerably. He was now much less certain that the ethnically based nation-state was the hallmark of modernity – or should be allowed to exist. If "the moral sovereignty of ethnic culture is nationalism's central principle" then a halt had to be called before it could do further damage. The nationalist vision of a closed and exclusive *Gemeinschaft* had turned into a nightmare of ethnic conflict and cleansing. The Eastern Europe of the 1990s had begun to resemble a bloodier version of its post-1918 incarnation. Gellner looked back with more than a touch of nostalgia to the Habsburg Empire, Robert Musil's *Kakania*. Under the Habsburgs (or so Gellner claimed), cultural autonomy had been able to flourish. But it had not been allowed, while the Habsburg monarchy lasted, to squeeze out the cosmopolitan culture that had turned nineteenth-century Vienna into one of the great centers of European thought. The Habsburgs had also protected their most cosmopolitan citizens, the Viennese Jews. The Habsburg version of empire had been the best of both worlds: it permitted the growth of ethnic high cultures but checked their Gadarene rush towards exclusion and conflict. What Gellner called the "only humane solution" to the problem of nationalism was the Habsburg Empire on a global scale. "Colonise simply everybody – i.e. deprive their political units of sovereignty – whilst allowing them absolute cultural freedom of expression." It was "obvious," he argued, that "such a programme is our only hope" (Gellner 1998: 144).

Of course, such a program is stymied by a tedious defect: it is impossible. It was, perhaps, Gellner's last tribute to one of his great intellectual heroes, Bronislaw Malinowski. *Nations and Nationalism* is in its own way a thoroughly Malinowskian text. What Gellner proclaimed as Malinowski's supreme insight – that history serves as a charter for contemporary practice – lies at its heart. Nations and nationalism might pretend to have existed since time out of mind, but they were really modern productions to meet modern needs. But Gellner now found another less fashionable side to Malinowski's worldview. Malinowski had been a vigorous champion of British "indirect rule": a form of colonial administration widely adopted in the years between the World Wars, especially in Africa. Indirect rule rejected the principle of governing colonies as if they were nations-to-be. It denied that the object of rule was to impose foreign culture and values upon subject peoples. Instead they should be encouraged to codify their customary laws and preserve the ethnic divisions that predated colonialism. Above all, they should be protected against the uncontrolled pressure of external influence – a task that required an Imperial Guardian for an indefinite time. Malinowski defended this program robustly. "Why not frankly state," he urged

that the only sound policy is that of racial and cultural preserves ... the steamroller of Western culture is undoubtedly levelling the cultures and societies of the world ... But against this universal levelling there is developing a strong reaction. (cited in Wells 1932: 678)

It was a view that drew a savage rebuke from the high priest of modernity, H.G. Wells. "This renewed fragmentation of mankind which Dr Malinowski seems to welcome," he wrote, "... is a relapse from cosmopolitanism to Polish patriotism, unworthy of the L.S.E" (Wells 1932: 678). What more damning indictment?

Wells, if Gellner is right, misunderstood Malinowski's intent. Although the evidence is somewhat opaque (Young 2004), Malinowski was far from being a Polish nationalist *pur sang*. He looked back instead to the wide cultural autonomy that the Poles had enjoyed in Habsburg Galicia (where in fact they enjoyed what might be called "master-race" status over the Ruthenian Slavs) (Steed 1913: 291–92). Politically and culturally, it was the ideal solution. It balanced the demand for a local high culture against the need for cultural openness and wider connections. For unlike Wittgenstein, Gellner's *bête noir*, Malinowski did not believe that culturally specific forms of language were all that humans could manage. They must also have access to, and were capable of deploying, a context-free language to express abstract thought, to engage in what Gellner calls the "rational-universal," and escape intellectual imprisonment in that cultural gulag the national *Gemeinschaft* (Gellner 1998: 148).

From this rapid traverse of Gellner's ideas we can glean three valuable points. First, the big claim he is making is that in any long view of world history the relations between empire on the one hand and ethnic solidarity on the other form an inescapable theme, and one unlikely to fade in the foreseeable future. Secondly, that as that mysterious dual personality Gellner-Malinowski insisted, some versions of empire were entirely compatible with ethnic autonomy in the cultural sphere, and much more accommodating (and acceptable) than the myths of nationalist freedom-fighting would have us believe. Thirdly, that in many (if not all) societies, the moment may come when the need for a common high culture becomes an urgent priority. When that time arrives, the local elite may have to choose from a limited repertoire of cultural "kit." As we will see later on, the demands of the "Gellnerian moment" could not always be met from strictly local resources. It was then that imperial ethnicity came into its own.

Before we go further, some definition of terms is required. The word "empire" is bedevilled with scholarly pedantry: defining and redefining it is an academic parlor game, and about as much use. A great deal of the difficulty comes from the common presumption that empires should be seen as spasmodic aberrations in the course of world history, impeding our progress towards universal nationhood or (to some hardy minds) the goal of world government. For the "aberration" school, empire is really a pathological condition: geopolitically, culturally, and even psychologically. The symptoms are shocking to our modern sensibility: racist ideology, sometimes brutal coercion, economic exploitation, roistering pageantry, and (a recent entry on the roster) "epistemic violence." Empire is an alien thing, another country, another world. But if we shake off our presentist blinkers and take a long view of world history, we might also see that empires have been among the commonest political forms, and that a nation-state system is the true aberration – underwritten (for the time being) by the peculiar geopolitical and ideological conditions of the post-1945 world. What I mean here is the *banal* form of empire, defined simply as a case where influence and authority (which shade into each other) overlap ethnic, linguistic, and ecological boundaries and where one ruler or polity seeks to draw other regions and states into his (its) geopolitical, economic, and cultural system through a set of functional, spatial and hierarchic arrangements. Lax as it is, this definition allows us to separate out the other common types of political unit: nation-states that claim (and may even possess) a common ethnic identity, city-states, small states too weak to engage in expansion, and federations whose constituent parts enjoy real political choice. It strips the meaning of empire back to the bare wood and throws overboard the distracting top-hamper of semantic distinctions. It has one more advantage. It reminds us that the building of empires was rarely the sole handiwork of delinquents and madmen. Empires arose (and may still arise) from the global maldistribution of all kinds of resources, including human capital and command over communications. To the British version of empire, we will turn in a moment.

What of ethnicity? Here I have leant very heavily on the admirably lucid discussion in Thomas Eriksen's *Ethnicity and Nationalism* (1993). What I take from this is really four points. First, although ethnicity is not to be thought of as the irresistible stamp placed on the individual by his or her *primordial* matrix (of place, language, religion, and descent or lineage), it is not freely chosen. Ethnicity is rooted in place and time, and in the customs, traditions, language, religion, and (perhaps fictive) descent that are held to derive from that place or time. The individual's options are limited, perhaps very closely. Secondly, as Eriksen says, ethnicity does not exist on its own: it appears only when the presence of an "alien" group is detected. Thirdly, ethnicity is always a work in progress: it is constantly remade to meet the needs of the moment. Fourthly, although ethnicity may be very "political," it is not primarily a state-based or state-seeking form of identity. Nationalism, which is – and which insists upon – an ethnically based state, should therefore be seen as a subset of ethnicity.

Helpful as this is, I want to supplement it with the valuable suggestion advanced by Patrick J. Geary in *The Myth of Nations* (2002). Geary reminds us that writers in the classical world drew a vital distinction between *gens* (ethnicity deriving from place, customs, language, descent, etc.) and *populus* (a community constituted by its acceptance of an allegiance and a law). A *gens* might be timeless, but a *populus* had its origins at a particular moment: it thus had a *history*. The Romans were a *populus*: they could trace their formation back to *Ab Urbe Condita*. They had a history, so they thought, unlike the barbarians around them. To this simple distinction, Geary adds something else very useful. The barbarian *gentes*, he says, in practice ignored this division. While they claimed an identity that was supposedly based on "ethnic" criteria, more often than not what had fused them together was allegiance (not origins) and law (not custom). The two sorts of identity could be deployed simultaneously and in mutual support (Geary 2002: 55 ff.). It was not just barbarians who discovered this trick. How smoothly and seamlessly it could be done (if only rhetorically) can be seen in the bombastic proclamation in which the first king of "Great Britain" announced the unity of his dual realm in 1604 under "one Imperiall Crowne." It was, he declared,

evident to sense that the Isle within itself hath almost none but imaginarie bounds of separation without, but one common limit or rather Gard of the Ocean Sea, making the whole a little world within it selfe, the Nations an Uniformitie of constitutions both of body and mind, especially in Martial prowesses, A Communitie of Language, the principall meanes of Civil Society, An unitie of Religion, the chiefest bond of heartie Union and the surest knot of lasting peace. What can be more express testimonie of God's authoritie … ? (Larkin and Hughes 1973: 95)

Here was a state in which the primary bond of allegiance was to be supercharged by real or imaginary "ethnic" characteristics.

Let us turn (at last) to the more particular history that this chapter addresses. The British Empire can hardly be thought of as a "typical" empire, but its extraordinary scale and diversity may allow us to see some of the different ways in which "imperial ethnicities" could arise. Its global functions, claims, and extent were of decisive importance in shaping its ethnic "encounter." First, its whole *raison d'être* lay in the constant shifting of peoples, goods and ideas between different parts of the world in ways that were likely to destabilize old ethnic identities and enforce adaptation. Secondly, because like all empires they required an ideological platform, the British were driven by the sheer scale of their interests to devise justifications that had a universal appeal. This too was to have an ethnic significance. Thirdly, partly because the scope of their power was so wide, escape from its grasp for long appeared futile. Its semi-ubiquity and (apparently) impregnable strength seemed to proclaim – as many of its subjects believed – its providential purpose and origin. Against its god-like prestige, ethnic *nationalist* movements seemed foredoomed to fail. Fourthly, in contrast to the empires envisaged in Gellner's scenario, the core of this empire was not an *agraria*, but the foremost *industria*. Here the processes of centralization, standardization and "high" cultural unification were well under way. From all this complexity, I want to suggest, issued three distinct kinds of "imperial ethnicity."

The first was at home. There, it has sometimes been argued, empire was the solvent of ethnic disunity. Empire as opportunity reconciled the Celtic periphery to an unequal union (or semi-union) with England. To Scots, Irish, and Welsh it was their empire too: the "English connection" was the price that they paid. Empire also brought "psychic" returns. Amid the shared "joy of ruling" the four British nations could forget their mutual resentments. If that wasn"t enough, they could join forces in disparaging the "Other" and reminding themselves of their collective achievements. In recent years, much of this has been challenged as merely "intuitive" history, as indeed some of it is (see Porter 2004; the best introduction is Kumar 2003). That empire was the *dominant* element in a modern British identity was always far-fetched, not least because those who proposed it displayed such a crude understanding of what "empire" actually meant. Nonetheless, there were ways in which empire evoked, or was used to invoke, what, following Eriksen, we might see as a distinctively ethnic dimension of Britishness.

The timing was not accidental. Although some of the strands that it drew on were already entrenched, imperial ethnicity in Britain was really a mid- to late-Victorian phenomenon. We might be tempted to trace its appearance to the convergence of pressures, both domestic and foreign. By the 1870s at the latest, there was a growing awareness that a modern "mass society" was coming into existence, indeed *must* come into existence. It was what we might call Britain's "Gellnerian moment." A common high culture with shared concepts and meanings had become an urgent priority. The need was most obvious in the political realm

whose key institutions were more aristocratic than popular. Following
the instinct that Geary describes, contemporaries understood that simple
allegiance would not be enough. It must be propped up by an "ethnic"
appeal. English (British) institutions must be "organically" linked to a
distinct habitat, history, everyday culture, and pattern of life if they were
to win the affections of the new urban masses. The task was made harder
(and also more urgent) by a second sensation. At almost the same
moment, Britain's place in the world drew anxious attention. It was not
only (or perhaps even chiefly) because new rivals emerged. What contemporaries noticed was that the world had become a "closed system" in
which no part of the globe was immune from the pressures and fears that
affected the others (see Darwin 2009: 66–68). If "splendid isolation" had
ever been possible, that moment had passed. The British had to live in a
world in which the vast archipelago of their possessions and interests,
looped around the globe like a necklace, was caught up in the web of
world politics. Their defense would require an ever-ready alertness.

What sharpened the edge of this geostrategic awareness was the
apparent conquest of distance. The spread of regular steamship travel
east of Suez, the rapid extension of undersea cables after $c.1870$, and
the steady expansion of railway construction outside Europe and North
America reinforced the perception that economically and politically, as
well as geostrategically, the old barriers of remoteness were rapidly
vanishing. For the British particularly, this emerging "new world" held
a threat and a promise. Holding their place would become more and
more strenuous. They were becoming more dependent on overseas
trade not only for markets but for their foodstuffs as well. The doctrine
of free trade as well as their huge vested interests ruled out a retreat to
protection or autarky. The risks of the nineteenth century's "semi-
globalization" could not be evaded. But there was also the promise.
In the "globe-wide world," Britain's "central" position (commercial
and maritime) and its far-flung communities of overseas British promised a huge dividend. Britain alone, remarked the historian Sir John
Robert Seeley, was a "world-state": the other great powers were
continent-bound (Seeley 1883: 293). Was the glass of empire half-full
or half-empty? Hence the curious ambivalence of the Late Victorians'
imperialism, at once anxious and boastful, euphoric and gloomy.

On those eager to summon an ethnic reinforcement to British identity,
this conjuncture exerted a critical influence. From mid century onwards,
and with more and more vehemence, the British were portrayed as a
colonizing people whose institutions, culture, and outlook had been
shaped above all by their migrant experience. John Richard Green wrote
the first popular history to reject the "high political" narrative of

Macaulay's *History of England*. In his *The Making of England* (1882), the colonizing theme is supreme. "With the landing of Hengist and his warband," he wrote, "English history begins ... From the hour when they set foot on the sands of Thanet we follow the story of Englishmen in the land they made their own" (Green 1882: 31). Britain had been molded to their colonizing design: "It was England that settled down on British soil" (Green 1882: 178). Green was not the first to describe the instinct of migration as heroic and nation-building. "The great purpose and interest of England in colonization is the multiplication of her race," declaimed Gladstone (Darwin 2009: 44). But he forged an obvious link between the increasingly dominant view that England's unique constitutional path was Anglo-Saxon in origin,[2] and the effects of what might be called a "settler" ethnicity. The idealized type of English individual was the free yeoman settler who demanded representative institutions. Adaptable and prag-matic, the settlers transformed and improved the lands "they made their own." In the year after Green's *Making* was published, Sir John Robert Seeley, Regius Professor of History at Cambridge, published his lectures on *The Expansion of England*. Seeley too insisted on migration as a central feature of the modern English/British community. "England will be wherever English people are found," he declared. The English (like most English people before the 1950s and 1960s, Seeley slipped smoothly between "English" and "British") were "one great homogeneous people, one in blood, language, religion and laws but dispersed over boundless space" (Seeley 1883: 159).

That Seeley (and Green) had touched a deep chord can be seen from the astonishing success of Seeley's outwardly dry, academic little book. In the course of three years it sold eighty thousand copies and it remained continuously in print until 1956 (see Wormell 1980). Its influence can be traced in the pronouncements of three generations of political leaders (of all political parties). Its most powerful message was that the British drew their modern identity not from one place in particular but from their diasporic experience as founders and settlers. Their key ethnic markers were imperial, not local. To an acute foreign observer some fifty years later, this imperial ethnicity seemed deeply entrenched. "England and the Empire are one," remarked Andre Siegfried in 1931, "and no such thing exists as an England conceived separately ... Because the British Empire has spread out over the entire world, English nationalism is based more on racial feelings than an attachment to the soil" (Siegfried 1931: 207). In his trumpet blast of patriotism in the worst year of the Second

---

[2] The great academic authority for this view was Stubbs's *Constitutional History of England*, published in three volumes 1873–78.

World War, the popular historian Arthur Bryant (then an influential columnist) denounced the false path of industrial squalor that had led Britain astray. "Canada, Australia, New Zealand and the Rhodesias," he intoned (South Africa has gone missing), "are the lifeline of the English future. There lies the appeal of the British people from the slums, the dole and the regimentation of the factory" (Bryant 1942: 336). The same vision of the Empire (now rechristened the "Commonwealth") as an extension of Britain persisted after the war. Lamenting the fall in the birth rate, the Royal Commission on Population stressed the importance "for the maintenance of the solidarity of the Commonwealth that the British contribution to further Dominions' migration should be substantial" (Royal Commission on Population 1949: 135).

Of course, the means of migration could not be ignored in the new ethnic story. In the late nineteenth century the idea of the British as an essentially *maritime* people was refurbished and popularized with impressive deliberateness. "A world-Venice with the sea for streets," had been Seeley's depiction of what he called "Greater Britain" (Seeley 1883: 283). His more florid contemporary, the historian and polemicist James Anthony Froude, an ardent supporter of redemptive "overseas Britains," extolled the maritime instinct that preserved the independence of Britain and on which its world power had been built. "After their own island, the sea is the natural home of Englishmen; the Norse blood is in us and we rove over the waters ... as eagerly as our ancestors. When we grow rich our chief delight is a yacht" (Froude 1886: 18) – a view Froude could personally vouch for. For the leading British geographer of the day, Halford Mackinder, it was Britain's island position, the strength of its tides, its marine-influenced climate, and its global centrality in the system of oceans, that had shaped its history and people most strongly. "It has been a special function of the insular people," he wrote in his geographical *magnum opus*, called significantly *Britain and the British Seas* (1902), "to convey to the outer lands what was best not merely in British but European civilisation" (Mackinder 1902: 358). And as Jan Rüger has brilliantly shown, a huge (and strikingly successful) effort was made by the Navy at much the same time to stamp Britain's maritime past and future on the popular mind (see Rüger 2007). The huge naval reviews in the Solent, with the symbolic seating of the monarch on her (or his) "ocean throne," and the naval displays in the Thames inspired a flood of "navalist" writing, adult and juvenile.[3] Some 4 million people saw the fleet in the Thames in 1909 (Rüger 2007: 50). None of this is to claim that these

---

[3] The now-forgotten novels of John F. Westerman catered to the juvenile market.

versions of imperial ethnicity exerted an unchallengeable sway over British public attitudes. They had to compete – or combine – with alternative versions that stressed urban, industrial, or rural locations as the shapers of British identity. Indeed, the curious pluralism of their ethnic markers (quite apart from those that derived from ideas of Scottishness, Welshness, or Irishness) may explain both the deep reluctance in British opinion to abandon the claim to be a "global" people with worldwide interests and influence, and also its tepid response once empire *did* end. All forms of ethnicity, as Eriksen argues, have to be nourished: they need a purpose and champions. Without those they die.

I have suggested already that imperial ethnicity was not just a phenomenon among the British "at home." Indeed, its most vocal exponents were found overseas in the empire of settlement, the so-called "white dominions." It is easy to forget that until the 1950s and 1960s, Canada, Australia, and New Zealand (South Africa, where Afrikaners formed a majority among whites, was the obvious exception) were thought of in Britain, and seen by themselves, as "British nations" or "British peoples." "Canada is a British Nation in North America," remarked the Canadian minister of defense, Brooke Claxton, on a wartime visit to Washington (Claxton 1943). "Australia is a British people, Australia is a British land," declared its (Labour) prime minister, John Curtin in 1944 (Day 1999: 543). Insistence on their "Britishness" and loyalty to British values was required of all politicians in Australia and New Zealand, except those with a death wish. Among the "English" in South Africa (as the English-speaking minority among whites styled themselves), political expediency demanded a certain discretion. But the "ethnic" pride that derived from being an imperial people reinforced the "race" pride of being white.

At one level, perhaps, the explanation is obvious. The majority populations in Canada, Australia, and New Zealand had arrived there as fragments of British society. They were bound to look homeward not least because so many arrived as advance parties, preparing the way for the "chain migration" of neighbors and family. Others came not intending to stay permanently (by some estimates around 40 percent of British emigrants returned home – perhaps to migrate somewhere else later) or made frequent return visits. But it might have been expected that the significance of being British-born would have declined over time, as a smaller proportion of the dominions' populations were new arrivals from home and local loyalty trumped the imperial tie. And up to a point that was true. But the twist in the tail was that being "British" was redefined as a "supra-local" not a geographical identity. Now Britain itself was one of the "Britains."

Why did this happen? A vital part of the answer is that, like the British at home, the overseas British experienced the "Gellnerian moment." By the late nineteenth century, there was a growing awareness that their self-governing states were so many lines on a map, the product of cession, seizure or treaty.[4] Their institutions were the gift of imperial authority; even their names were the labels stuck on them by colonial officials. But like other "modernizing" societies they now needed governments to wield more social and cultural power, and unofficial or voluntary bodies to enlighten local opinion. They needed, in short, to build a national community. And like Patrick Geary's barbarians, they grasped the necessity of reinforcing civic allegiance with something more visceral, even primordial. The strength of local divisions – the result of piecemeal foundations and the administrative convenience of British officialdom – made this all the more urgent.[5] These settler societies needed a historical charter, a usable myth of their origins.

But their options were few. None of them could claim to be original peoples, so indigenous roots were excluded as a source of identity. (In Canada, the existence of the French Canadian minority that had arrived a century and a half earlier was an additional embarrassment.) Nor had there been "fusion" with aboriginal "first peoples" – at least not in a form that could be clothed in the mantle of historical destiny. Nor could they take the American route and found their societies on the claim of popular sovereignty – as a people "made" by revolution. They were forced to turn back to their own British origins in search of primordial tradition. In much the same way, they instinctively drew on the huge ready-made inventory of social and cultural practices that Britain could offer to achieve the "instant" modernity that "progress" demanded. Last and not least, they were all too aware that their political institutions were fragile: beset by corruption, local "log-rolling," and class and race friction. What better protection than the patina of British antiquity, to be applied like a paint?

But the Britishness asserted in these settler societies was not deferential. It was selective and critical. "Imperial" Britishness did not aspire merely to replicate what existed "at home." Quite the reverse. It insisted that British ethnicity (although the word was not used) was energized by its encounter with the colonial environment, where virtuous attributes, long lost at home, could flourish anew. Thus overseas Britons in North America or the South Pacific became hardier and healthier. They were braced by the North (a Canadian trope [Zeller 1987: 266–67, 271]) or the test of the

---

[4] Canada by cession, Australia by seizure, New Zealand by treaty.
[5] Before 1867–73, "Canada" was seven separate colonies; before 1901, "Australia" was six.

Bush. They were forced to respond to the pioneer challenge, to become dynamic and enterprising. The fetters of class had been struck from their limbs. The relics of feudalism had no purchase there. Imperial Britishness was democratic, even populist. The Britons it made were "Better Britons," a much-improved version of the original model. The nations and peoples they made were British nations and peoples, but "sister nations" and "independent British nations." Far from deferring to the wisdom of Whitehall, they thought the London politicians pathologically lacking in spirit and courage, who would betray their interests for a mess of pottage – usually one cooked in the chanceries of Europe. Above all they saw empire – the British Empire – as a joint enterprise in which they should be partners.

The Imperial Britishness of the white settler colonies was thus a pure form of imperial ethnicity. Its primordial elements had been systematically imperialized. And although it was meant to assist in the building of nations, it was well understood that those nations would be British, they would remain part of the Empire, and that an unbreakable bond would tie them to Britain (see Darwin 2009: Chapter 4). But like the domestic variety, imperial ethnicity in the white dominions could not exist in a vacuum. When the geopolitical context that gave it its meaning began to unravel, it soon withered away. Intriguingly, what followed was not the emergence of new ethnic nationalisms – for precisely the reasons that applied a century ago. Instead, in Australia, New Zealand, and perhaps even in Canada, the sources of national identity have been hard to agree on. Ethnic complexity and indigenous claims have made the local past a poor warrant for a "nation-state" future.

However, the most intriguing, and perhaps most surprising, cases of imperial ethnicity occurred where indigenous (i.e. Asian or African) elites embraced a version of imperial identity and endowed it with moral and physical qualities. The best example here is that of the Indian nationalist leadership before 1914. Disparaged as "moderates" who demanded too little and accepted too much, their failure to extract more far-reaching concessions from a confident Raj is often contrasted with the Gandhian tactics of mass mobilization, civil disobedience, and ideological warfare deployed in the early 1920s, between 1930 and 1934, and in the Quit India movement of 1942. The early leaders of the Indian National Congress rejected mass agitation and the resort to violence. Far from demanding the Gandhian program of *purna swaraj* – a complete independence that would sever "British connection," they favored instead the form of self-government that the "white dominions" enjoyed: full internal self-rule but inside the ring-fence of empire. Great stress was laid on Indian loyalty to Britain and the "king-emperor," as the British monarch was styled in India. The object of the Indian National Congress, said its 1912 president, "was to create a nation whose citizens would be members of a world-wide empire … Our great aim is to make the British Government the National Government of the British Indian people" (Congress 1934: 58–59).

How was this to be done? The answer was: with British help. The Congress leaders constantly emphasized Britain's duty to practice the liberal principles on which the British prided themselves. But they also expected that the "providential" creation of the Raj would forge a new kind of Indian. England's mission, declared Surendranath Banerjea, for long the dominant figure in Bengal's nationalist politics, was to help "in the formation of a manly, energetic, self-reliant Indian character" (Palit 1891: 8). Indians who acquired these values and habits, key ingredients of a re-formed ethnicity, would be fitted to govern themselves. Indeed, they might even claim to be British. "May I be permitted to make an appeal," asked a much older Banerjea, by this time a member of the Viceroy's Legislative Council, "that we may all feel and realize, no matter whether we are Englishmen or Scotchmen or Irishmen or Indians, that we are Britishers, fellow citizens in a common empire" (Return 1913: 258). Banerjea might have been vehement, but his was not a lone view. Indians should be sent to finish their education in Britain, Motilal Nehru (father of the more famous Jawaharlal), told the Royal Commission on Public Services in India in 1913, "to acquire those characteristics which are essentially British" since the administration in India "must have a pronounced British tone and character and too much stress cannot be laid on Indians acquiring that character as a habit" (Kumar and Panigrahi 1982: 256, 258). He was as good as his word. Jawaharlal went to Harrow and from there to Cambridge.

Like their Canadian or Australian counterparts, these leaders of British India were acutely conscious of the need for a "Gellnerian" constitution that bound people and rulers together and of the inadequacy for that purpose of alien colonial rule. But they faced a not dissimilar dilemma. They thought India's resources for nationhood to be seriously lacking. Indeed, its primordial traditions of language, descent and religion they considered both divisive and dangerous. When the Maratha politician Bal Gangadar Tilak urged a "new politics" of mass mobilization around Hindu religiosity and Maratha tradition and proposed a conscious rejection of Western ideals, they rounded furiously on him and hurled him out of the Congress. They saw with more clarity than their "Gandhian" successors that invoking religious emotion and popular grievance might drive the British from India, but could hardly assist in building a unified nation. That nation must be built, they agreed, but from the top down, not the bottom up. The first task was to inject the prospective governing class with an imperial (really British) gene of moderation and "manliness." With this ethnic transfusion, they would be fitted to man the constitutional machinery through which the British had unified India. Round these British-built institutions, the new "British Indian" nation would gather: privileged, enfranchised and loyal, but free from the old "cellular" ties of lineage and clan, religion and caste, language and locality. Nothing could be further, we might notice in passing, from the Gandhian vision of *Hind Swaraj*, the (British-)suppressed manifesto of 1909: an India of self-sufficient "village-republics" that rejected the state, modern technology, codified laws, and the English language itself.

This Indian experiment in an elite imperial ethnicity was not unique. To other "anglo" elites, the enthusiastic embrace of British social values and habits, English language and literature and the Christian religion, was all of a piece with their hopes of reclaiming the state-building structures that the British had brought for their own national program. Like the leaders of Congress, the Krio elite in British West Africa, including the self-styled "Black English" of Sierra Leone, were all too aware that to make a West African nation out of diverse and recalcitrant elements would require British help, and could hardly be ventured outside the protective umbrella of imperial power. Their policy was "to preserve strictly and inviolate" their connection with the British Empire, declared the first National Congress of British West Africa in 1920 (Madden and Darwin 1994: 660). They would have to prove themselves fit to (self-)govern like "Englishmen," to persuade the British officials to part with their power. "I love this ideal of Imperial West Africa," declared one Krio patriot (Casely-Hayford 1903: 269). Like their counterparts in India, what they really resented was not "British connection" but the implicit denial by the bureaucratic garrison of British officials that they were not "British" enough to be accorded the rights of free-born Englishmen. A variant of this feeling could be found in South Africa, among mission-educated Xhosa and Mfengu (see Switzer 1993). British colonial rule in South Africa had made them British subjects and given them British rights, said the leaders of the African National Congress (founded 1912): "The natives are as fully British subjects as are all the members of the various races," declared its petition to King George V in 1914 (Karis et al. 1972: 129). "The ministers of Queen Victoria," said D.D.T. Jabavu (who taught Nelson Mandela), "made Britons of all civilized black men under the Union Jack" (Karis et al. 1972: 202). Pretoria was unmoved.

Thus far, the examples of imperial ethnicity have been drawn largely from the British Empire: reasons of space preclude an extended discussion of other cases and places. But there are good reasons to think that imperial ethnicity was a very widespread phenomenon, perhaps as ubiquitous as empire itself.

To sketch out a vast field, we might begin by observing that the relationship between empire and ethnicity spanned (and spans) a huge range of possibilities. At one extreme, the rulers of empires set out to merge their subject ethnicities into a common identity. We might want to argue that the most culturally unified of today's nation-states were typically forged in this mold. It was also the practice pursued with outstanding success in the south and southwest of China, as indigenous peoples were transformed into *min* – imperial subjects who adopted Han cultural practices (Faure 2006: 171–89). Those grand imperialists Lenin and Stalin dreamt of a similar future. Soviet "nationality" policy envisaged the progressive fusion of smaller ethnicities into larger "socialist nations" which would eventually combine with the "Soviet-Russian nation" in a single Soviet *narod* (Hirsch 2005: 316–17). In fact, few empires (including the Soviet) could follow this path or chose to do so. Most had to fall back on more hand-to-mouth methods, in which the indefinite survival of ethnic distinctions was taken for granted.

So at the other extreme, imperial rulers regulated their relations with both "inner barbarians" (those inside the imperial frontier) and "outer barbarians" by deploying "ethnic" criteria. The peoples they dealt with were assumed to enjoy a distinct way of life, or to occupy a distinct ecological niche. They had to be managed through their own ethnic hierarchies and in accordance with their customs. They were (as yet) unassimilable. Of course, as James C. Scott has argued, there was often a poor fit between the ethnic identities that outsiders imagined and those actually chosen by the peoples themselves. In Southeast Asia, at least, these were often a matter of tactics, opportunism, or "positionality" (Scott 2009: Chapter 7). The choice of ethnic identity reflected the chances available at a particular time: economic, political, or ecological.

However, "imperial ethnicity" in the sense used in this chapter was really a subset of the wider relationship between empire and ethnicity. It is perhaps best defined as the assertion or acceptance of an ethnic identity that promised (or seemed to) a privileged access to the resources and opportunities that an empire could offer. In principle, the scope for such ethnic opportunism was huge and the range of niche functions that empires required was almost equally wide. Here there is space to consider just three of the circumstances in which imperial ethnicity came to hold a significant place in the political systems of empires.

The first and most obvious arose from the need to preserve the solidarity of a conquering elite at the creation of empire. As long as they formed an embattled minority and faced continued resistance, strict ethnic loyalty might be the price of survival. But where the conquered society had a glamorous culture and offered ample inducements for outsiders to "go native," maintaining internal cohesion in the ruling elite was bound to be harder. It was precisely this problem that confronted Qing emperors in China once they had won the long-drawn-out struggle to impose their power in the south. The core of their military strength was their army of Manchu "bannermen," drawn, like the dynasty, from the frontier people living north of the Great Wall. Manchu generals and governors were the Qing emperors' "steel frame," keeping close watch on their Han Chinese officials for signs of rebellion. Under the Yongzheng emperor (1722–35) "banner education" was taken much more seriously and the deliberate cultivation of a Manchu identity became a matter of policy. "Study hard and learn well how to speak Manchu, how to shoot from a stance and from horseback, and how to handle a musket. Obey established customs and live frugally and economically" was one commander's advice (Elliott 2006: 47). Strenuous efforts were made to maintain the connection between ethnic Manchus and their banner affiliation by forms of "genealogical vetting." And in the late eighteenth century, documenting the history of the Manchus and their "manifest destiny" became a major academic activity. The "Researches on Manchu Origins" were meant by their compilers to remind all Manchus of their true ethnic identity and their duty to observe the old customs (Crossley 1999: 306). Indeed, up until the end of the Qing dynasty in 1911, Manchus were expected to preserve their language, to live separately from Han and avoid intermarriage.

A second variation occurred where the ruling power co-opted the aristocracy of its conquered provinces into the governing caste. The "Baltic barons" of the Romanov Empire – Brunnows, Budbergs, von Engelhardts, Lievens, Pahlens, von Uexkulls and Wrangels – retained their (Lutheran) religion and their (German) language. Dorpat University (in modern Estonia) was re-founded by Tsar Alexander I in 1802 as a German-language university (and remained as such until the 1890s). The Baltic barons looked back historically to the Teutonic Knights and enjoyed a monopoly of land ownership in Russia's Baltic provinces. But their special status as a privileged descent group in a sea of Slavs was bound up with their dynastic allegiance to the Romanov tsars and was cemented by service in the imperial army and bureaucracy (Hosking 1997: 160–62, 382–83; Lieven 1989: 32–35). A similar pattern can be seen at work in the Habsburg monarchy. There, dynastic fidelity was even more vital to imperial cohesion. In this multiethnic amalgam of conquest and inheritance, the monarch was forced to rely on a ruling elite recruited originally from all across Europe, including Germans, French, Italians, Spanish, Magyars, Czechs, Scots and Irish (the finance minister in 1808 was a Count O'Donnell). They formed a "caste of inter-related families battening on the Dynasty and its peoples" (Mickiewicz, quoted in Steed 1913: 205). In the late eighteenth century, perhaps to counter the rise of territorially based patriotisms, the Habsburgs began to promote an imperial "super-ethnicity." Apart from the "court nobility" – Schwarzenberg, Thun, Lobkowitz, Kinsky, Clam-Martinic, Andrassy, Pallavicini and Esterhazy, to name some of the grandest – its most vital adherents were found in the army and bureaucracy, the chief props of the dynasty. There, where loyal service was rewarded with a patent of nobil-ity (the sought-after "von"), the tradition of dynastic allegiance – being *Kaisertreu* – transcended old ethnic identities. The wearing of the Emperor's coat, remarked Wickham Steed in 1913, "has become to them a second nature and they are not only intensely 'black and yellow' (the imperial colours), but also what Emperor Francis II (1792–1835) called 'patriots for me'. In their camp is Austria" (Steed 1913: 62). It was precisely this outlook that was so brilliantly rendered in fiction in Joseph Roth's novel *The Radetsky March*. Its hero's father (the great-grandson of "illiterate Slovenian peasants") "had never wished to see his father's homeland. He was an Austrian, a servant and official of the Habsburgs, and his homeland was the Imperial Palace in Vienna" (Roth 1996: 125). Its most diplomatic expression was that of Wisniewski, the (ethnically Polish) ambassador to Italy. "'Are you Polish?' asked the Queen. 'Je suis Autrichien de Galicie' was Wisniewski's reply" (Bruckmüller 2006: 4).

A third variation can be seen in the recruitment of martial or service groups who were carefully endowed with a distinctive identity (or delib-erately adopted one) as a badge of allegiance to their imperial master. The most notorious case was that of the Cossacks. Cossack regiments – such as the Transbaikal, Amur, Ussuri, and Semirechia – were used by the tsars to maintain their control over the vast wastes of Siberia and rewarded with land. But the classical pattern of Cossack formation was that of the Don Cossacks. Originally a freebooting frontier society of very mixed ethnic origins (including Turks, Tatars, Greeks, and Circassians), by the late seventeenth century they were on their way to becoming a closed ethnic community whose privileged status in the Romanov Empire was earned by military service (Boeck 2009). Unlike ethnic Russians, with whom intermarriage was forbidden, they were exempt from taxation and serfdom. They received a grain subsidy. Before 1700, their distinctive red caps and colourful clothes had become an ethnic marker. In 1720 a census was held to register true Cossacks and exclude refugees from the serf population. "The Don Cossacks were not a captive nation annexed by an aggressive empire," argues a recent historian, "but a community created through the joint efforts of imperial officials and the residents of a closing frontier" (Boeck 2009: 245). We might be tempted to see a parallel case in the role of the Mamluks, the privileged slave-soldiers of the Ottoman and Iranian empires. By the eighteenth century, they were often recruited from Christian Georgians sold into captivity, and then converted to Islam. Their (remote) ethnic origins were meant to seclude them from political sympathy with the subject populations they were sent to rule over. That was the purpose behind sending Georgian Mamluks to Baghdad and Cairo as the Sultan's enforcers. In both cases, it seems, their loyalty was less than complete. But the ethnic solidarity created by exile and privilege was the key to their rule, whether in Egypt (Crecelius and Djaparidze 2002: 320–41; Hathaway 1995: 39–52) or Iraq (Cole and Momen 1986: 112–43; Niewenhuis 1982).

These ethnic groups (and many others besides) were formed and dissolved as economic, political, and geopolitical fortune dictated. But their key characteristic was to be artifacts of empire. They sought not a state of their own but a privileged place within a system of empire, for employment, preferment, or social advantage. Unlike the ethnicities created by empires to manage "lesser breeds," or those chosen deliberately to keep that state at bay – the pattern in "Zomia" – they were "insider" ethnicities that claimed equality or better with the "core" peoples of an empire (where they existed). But their very distinctiveness, and their salient connection with the imperial regime, exposed them to disaster when those empires collapsed or when dynastic allegiance was replaced by nationality as the prime political bond. Amid the wreckage of empires that still litters the globe we might see (if we look closely enough) the scattered bands of survivors who escaped from, or made peace with, the successor regimes into which so many empires dissolved.

From this brief overview of a vast terrain, any conclusions are bound to be speculative. We might venture three. First, that history was not kind to these "imperial ethnicities" and historians have largely ignored them. But revisiting them ought to remind us that we live in a world largely made by empires and among ethnic identities as often forged in collaboration with those empires as rallied against them. This was just as true of other empires as it was of the British. We will misunderstand both the imperial past and the post-imperial present if we fail to acknowledge the often intimate links between these two forms of allegiance.

A second conclusion that we might draw from the cases discussed here is how close a connection so often existed between ideas of ethnic identity and what we might call the constellation of geopolitical power.

Invoking ethnicity was a political act, and so was diffusing it (or trying to) among "target" communities. It was hardly surprising that ethnicity should be used to harness imperial power and exploit its resources as well as to resist it. There is no reason to think that future ethnicities will be different: perhaps a salutary thought in the age of geopolitical flux that opens in front of us. Finally, the sketch offered here confirms Eriksen's insight that ethnicity is both extraordinarily adaptable and perhaps also indispensable. It reinvents itself constantly and assumes different guises. What really matters, as Ernest Gellner insisted at the end of his life, are the checks and balances by which its influence is channelled and, if need be, contained. Empires come and go, but ethnicity, like the poor, is always with us.

REFERENCES

Boeck, B. 2009. *Imperial Boundaries: Cossack Communities and Empire-Building in the Age of Peter the Great*. Cambridge University Press.
Bruckmüller, W. 2006. "Was there a "Habsburg Society" in Austria-Hungary?" *Austrian History Yearbook* 37: 1–16.
Bryant, A. 1942. *English Saga 1840–1940*. London.
Casely-Hayford, J.E. 1903. *Gold Coast Native Institutions*. London: Sweet and Maxwell.
Claxton, B. 1943. *Brooke Claxton Mss. National Archives of Canada, MG 32 B-5, vol. 22*. Ottawa.
Cole, J.R.I. and M. Momen. 1986. "Mafia, Mob and Shiism in Iraq: the Rebellion of Ottoman Karbala 1824–1843." *Past and Present* 112: 112–43.
Congress Presidential Addresses. 1934. Madras.
Crecelius, D. and G. Djaparidze. 2002. "Relations of the Georgian Mamluks of Egypt with their Homeland in the Last Decades of the Eighteenth Century." *Journal of the Economic and Social History of the Orient* 45(3): 320–41.
Crossley, P.K. 1999. *A Translucent Mirror: History and Identity in Qing Imperial Ideology*. Berkeley and London: University of California Press.
Darwin, J. 2009. *The Empire Project: the Rise and Fall of the British World-System*. Cambridge University Press.
Day, D. 1999. *John Curtin: A Life*. Sydney: Harper Collins.
Dirks, N. 2001. *Castes of Mind*. Cambridge University Press.
Elliott, M.E. 2006. "Ethnicity in the Qing Eight Banners," Pp. 27–57 in *Empire at the Margins: Culture, Ethnicity and Frontier in Early Modern China*, edited by P.K. Crossley, H.F. Siu, and D.S. Sutton. Berkeley and London: University of California Press.
Eriksen, T. 1993. *Ethnicity and Nationalism*. London and New York: Pluto Press.
Faure, D. 2006. "The Yao Wars in the Mid-Ming and Their Impact on Yao Ethnicity." Pp. 171–89 in *Empire at the Margins: Culture, Ethnicity and Frontier in Early Modern China*, edited by P.K. Crossley, H.F. Siu, and D.S. Sutton. Berkeley and London: University of California Press.
Froude, J.A. 1886. *Oceana*. London: Biblio Bazaar.

Frykenberg, R. 1965. *Guntur District 1788–1848*. Oxford: Clarendon Press.

Gallagher, J. and R. Robinson. 1953. "The Imperialism of Free Trade." *Economic History Review* (2nd series) 6(1): 1–15.

Geary, P.J. 2002. *The Myth of Nations*. Princeton University Press.

Gellner, E. 1983. *Nations and Nationalism*. London: Blackwell.

  1988. *Plough, Sword and Book*. London: Collins Harvill.

  1998. *Language and Solitude: Wittgenstein, Malinowski and the Habsburg Dilemma*. Cambridge University Press.

Green, J.R. 1882 [2005]. *The Making of England*. London: Kessinger Publishing.

Hathaway, J. 1995. "The Military Household in Ottoman Egypt." *International Journal of Middle East Studies* 27(1): 39–52.

Hirsch, F. 2005. *Empire of Nations: Ethnographic Knowledge and the Making of the Soviet Union*. Ithaca, NY, and London: Cornell University Press.

Hosking, G. 1997. *Russia: People and Empire*. London: Harper Collins.

Karis, T.G., G.M. Carter, G.M. Gerhart, and S. Johns (eds.). 1972. *From Protest to Challenge: A Documentary History of African Politics in South Africa*. Stanford, CT: Hoover Institution Press.

Kumar, K. 2003. *The Making of English National Identity*. Cambridge University Press.

Kumar, R. and D.N. Panigrahi (eds). 1982. *Selected Works of Motilal Nehru*. 6 vols. Vol. I. *1899–1918*. Delhi: Vikas.

Larkin, J.F. and P.L. Hughes. 1973. *Stuart Royal Proclamations*. 2 vols. Oxford: Clarendon Press, Vol. 1, p. 95.

Lieven, D. 1989. *Russia's Rulers under the Old Regime*. New Haven and London: Yale University Press.

Mackinder, H. 1902. *Britain and the British Seas*. London: Clarendon Press.

Madden, F. and J. Darwin. 1994. *Select Documents in the Constitutional History of the British Empire and Commonwealth*. 8 vols. Vol. VIII: *The Dependent Empire 1900–1948*. Westport, CT: Greenwood Publishing Group.

Niewenhuis, T. 1982. *Politics and Society in Early Modern Iraq*. Amsterdam: Nijhoff Publishers.

Palit, R.C. 1891. *Speeches by Surendra Nath Banerjea 1876–1880*. Calcutta: Lahiri.

Porter, B. 2004. *The Absent-minded Imperialists: Empire, Society and Culture in Britain*. Oxford University Press.

Ranger, T.O. 1983. "The Invention of Authority in Colonial Africa." Pp. 211–62 in *The Invention of Tradition*, ed. by E. Hobsbawm and T.O. Ranger. Cambridge University Press.

"Return of Indian Financial Statement and Budget for 1913–14 and of the Proceedings of the Legislative Council of the Governor-General thereon." 1913. *British Parliamentary Papers 1913* (paper no. 130).

Roth, J. 1996[1932]. *The Radetsky March*. London: Everyman.

Royal Commission on Population. 1949. Report: Cmd 7695.

Rüger, J. 2007. *The Great Naval Game: Britain and Germany in the Age of Empire*. Cambridge University Press.

Scott, James C. 2009. *The Art of Not Being Governed: An Anarchist History of Upland Southeast Asia*. New Haven and London: Yale University Press.

Seeley, J.R. 1883. *The Expansion of England*. Boston, MA: Roberts Brothers.

Siegfried, A. 1931. *England's Crisis*. London: Harcourt, Brace and Co.

Spear, T. 2003. "Neo-traditionalism and the Limits of Invention in British Colonial Africa." *Journal of African History* 44(1): 3–27.

Steed, H.W. 1913. *The Habsburg Monarchy*. London: H. Fertig.

Switzer, L. 1993. *Power and Resistance in an African Society: The Ciskei Xhosa and the Making of South Africa*. Madison: University of Wisconsin Press.

Wells, H.G. 1932. *The Work, Wealth and Happiness of Mankind*. London: Heinemann.

Wormell, D. 1980. *Sir John Seeley and the Uses of History*. Cambridge University Press.

Young, M.W. 2004. *Malinowski: Odyssey of an Anthropologist*. London: University of Toronto Press.

Zeller, S. 1987. *Inventing Canada: Early Victorian Science and the Idea of a Transcontinental Nation*. University of Toronto Press.

7   The role of nationalism in the two world wars

Michael Mann

I here focus in some depth on the causal relationships between nationalism and the two world wars of the twentieth century, asking two main questions: did nationalism cause these wars and did these wars intensify nationalism? Nationalism is generally defined as an ideology embodying the feeling of belonging to a group united by common history and a combination of ethnic/religious/racial/linguistic identity, which is identified with a given territory, and entitled to its own state. There is nothing inherently aggressive about nationalism, though it becomes more aggressive if one's own national identity is linked to hatred of others' national identities. Most scholars of nationalism would not claim that a sense of national identity is ever total in the sense of displacing all other identities, but they do tend to argue that, whether overt or latent, nationalism has dominated modern warfare. It is highly likely that a war between countries in the age of nation-states will have the effect of increasing the aggressive component of nationalism, but I am more interested in the reverse relation: does nationalism cause war? Clearly nationalism has to take rather aggressive forms if it is to do this.

This question can be first addressed by asking whether nationalism and war have tended to rise and fall together, in roughly the same time and place. There seems to be general agreement that nationalism first became widespread in Europe at some point in the eighteenth or nineteenth centuries, became generally more aggressive at the beginning of the twentieth century, and then spread out to the world in both mild and aggressive forms. So I initially ask whether this corresponds in any way to the incidence of wars in Europe and then the world in the modern period.

Rough statistics of war are available in Europe for the period after 1494 as assembled by Levy (1983), and these can be compared to the incidence of wars involving China and other major Asian states. Much better statistics for the world as a whole from the period after 1816 come from the Correlates of War (COW) data set, which has been refined by various authors. This data set separates three types of war: civil war, interstate war, and extra-state (i.e. colonial) war fought by one state against a native group of combatants.

These varied data reveal that for over five hundred years (indeed, probably over the entire second millennium AD), Europe saw more wars than East Asia and probably more than all other continents. Europeans were from Mars (Gleditsch 2004; Lemke 2002). In contrast, East Asia saw a three-hundred-year period of peace between the 1590s and 1894, broken only by barbarian incursions into China and five fairly small two-state wars. During the preceding two hundred years China had been at war only once, with Vietnam. Japan saw peace for two centuries until the 1880s. In contrast, the European powers were involved in interstate wars in nearly 75 percent of the years between 1494 and 1975, and no 25-year period was entirely free of war in Europe (Levy 1983: 97). Gleditsch says that from 1816 to the 1950s Europeans contributed 68 percent of the world's interstate wars. However, serious COW undercounting of colonial wars means that the real figure was probably over 80 percent (see Mann 2012: Chapter 2).

There were two long-term changes in wars within Europe. They became steadily fewer but they also became more deadly, killing more people in aggregate absolute terms as well as per war. At the tail end of the period, in the first half of the twentieth century, civilians were also being killed in much larger numbers. There was then another sudden big shift after World War II. About 60 percent of all conflicts in the period 1816 to the 1940s were interstate wars, but this fell in the 1950s to 45 percent, in the 1970s to 26 percent, and by the 1990s to only 5 percent. Civil wars now became the main problem across the world. After 2001, only the United States and its most intimate allies have started interstate wars. The European nations had virtually stopped making any kind of war.

These trends do not support the notion of any close causal relationship at the macro level between war and nationalism. In Europe wars had been much more frequent in the pre-nationalism period. The growing lethality of war, especially for civilians, might seem to offer some support for a nationalist explanation, for masses of people in different states were killing each other, and it might be argued this was because they hated each other. Yet a plausible counterargument might be that the industrialized technology of modern war enabled mass killing, and when this was extended to performing effective naval blockades and aerial bombing, it slaughtered vastly more civilians too. I will investigate this later. But today Europeans barely make war any more and yet their competitive nationalism remains vigorous, for example in sports. Indeed, very few nations anywhere in the world still kill each other even though nationalism has now spread to the world. Peoples still kill each other in civil wars, but their combination of ethnic/religious/regional divides make this a very different version of nationalism to that often invoked to explain interstate wars.

So I conclude from this section that a limited nationalism/interstate war correlation *might* be found in the nineteenth and twentieth centuries when nationalism rose up and the lethality (though not the frequency) of interstate war increased, but not to the further past or to the present. Its reign was at most brief, if indeed it ever did reign. I will investigate this possibility by focusing on the two most lethal wars of the period, world wars I and II.

World War I

Many scholars say that nationalism was an important cause of World War I, but all that most of them seem to be saying is that the war was fought between nations or states. Of course, most of the populations participating in World War I already felt to some degree a sense of national identity. In most cases this reinforced the state, which had therefore become a nation-state. But three of the Great Powers – Austria-Hungary, Russia, and the Ottoman Empire – were multiethnic empires in which nationalism was now playing something of a disintegrating role. We must note a further complication. The Great Powers all had empires, and so nationalist identities were blended with imperial ones and, for all except Austria-Hungary and the Ottoman Empire, this added racial identities to the mix.

Yet any causal relationship running from nationalism to war is undercut by the fact that popular pressure was not responsible for starting the war. True, the first crisis of 1914 was precipitated by self-styled Serb nationalists assassinating the Austrian Archduke. But thereafter the downward slide to war involved tiny diplomatic and military elites with almost no popular participation in the process. The war started in the European high-diplomacy tradition with Great Powers going to war in support of small, threatened client states, in this case Serbia and Belgium, like most wars over the previous five hundred years, long before the emergence of nationalism. Three regimes were more aggressive than the others in the slide to war: Austria-Hungary, Germany, and Russia. But two of these three regimes, in Austria-Hungary and Russia, disliked and feared nationalism. In Germany, France and Britain, organized labor, peasants and the middle class were not generally warmongers, apart from that middle-class fraction centered on state employees which I labelled "nation-statist" in Volume II of *The Sources of Social Power*

(1993). Nor was the capitalist class. Capitalists were among those trying to prevent war. Nor was global imperialism responsible for war. Colonial disputes between the Great Powers were all settled by negotiation. The war started in Europe not the colonies (all this is evidenced in the final chapter of Mann 1993).

Revisionist historians (e.g. Gregory 2003; Mueller 2003; Verhey 2000) tell us that the nationalist and imperialist pressure groups that organized pro-war demonstrations during the slide to war were outnumbered by larger anti-war protests. This slide to war was perpetrated by political and military elites. Parliaments were sometimes addressed by ministers but not with frankness. Whole cabinets were not consulted, and indeed the British cabinet would have disintegrated had British policy been fully revealed to it. Of course it remains entirely normal that decisions on war and peace are not made through any process of consultation with the masses, which is a general weakness of the "nationalism causes war" argument. There are still very few pro-war demonstrations during contemporary slides to war. Rallies round the flag come after the war has started – and they don't last long.

However, once declared, the Great War, like almost all modern wars, was at first quite well supported across the classes and across most of the political spectrum (Audoin-Rouzeau and Becker 2002: Chapter 4; Strachan 2001: Chapter 2). The statesmen could lightly tug at the strings of national identities that were already established. In the second volume of *The Sources of Social Power* (1993) I argued that these national identities had been established by the gradual extension of power infra-structures across the territories of states. Economies, working conditions, health and education infrastructures, and military conscription were increasingly regulated nationally by the state. People were factually impli-cated in the nation-state as a circumscribed network of social interaction, segregated from others. They were organizationally caged.

This led to a fairly latent emotional sense of national identity encapsu-lated by Billig's (1995) term "banal nationalism," a secure national iden-tity based on what he calls the "flagging" in everyday life of symbols of national identity. The flag was not so much fervently waved as just hanging there on buildings, while language, cuisine, music, and supposedly dis-tinctive landscapes all evoked a sense of nationality. Billig says that this banal nationalism might become briefly "hot" during national crises, which in this context meant enthusiastic and confident support for the justice of the national cause, an optimistic view of the likely outcome of war, and a willingness to fight if asked to. However, in 1914 these sentiments were filtered through social structures that remained decidedly hierarchical. People deferred to local notables, women deferred to men, young men deferred to their elders and betters. These were half-citizens, half-subjects. So when asked to fight, they did so. There wasn't much fear expressed in the popular press or in street demonstrations after the war began. Isolated in their nation-states, individuals experienced a brief collective surge of popular enthusiasm, a rally around the flag, partly because people in all countries bizarrely thought this war would be easy as in the adventure stories all the young men had read. Thus in all countries they cheerfully, irrationally expected to win the war quickly. The troops left their homes in September and October shouting "Back by Christmas!" So this may have been a war precipitated by elites, but once begun it was fought, provisioned, and to some extent supported by the masses. How and why did they sustain war, and was it for nationalist reasons? I consider first the soldiers, then the civilians.

Why did the soldiers fight?

Why did they fight and why did they continue fighting, since they faced enormous risks in waging such a war? Were they aggressive nationalists? A mixture of discipline and enthusiasm began it. Trained reservists used to military discipline could promptly enlarge the professional armies. They were supplemented during the first year or two by volunteers, a product of initial war enthusiasm. 308,000 Germans had volunteered by the beginning of 1915, while at first the British, without many reservists, relied almost entirely on untrained volunteers, getting as many as they could handle: a remarkable 2.4 million in the first eighteen months of the war (Gregory 2003: 79–80). But then volunteering began to decline. Most countries had to introduce conscription in late 1914 or early 1915. Britain was the last to move to conscription, in 1916. No country had difficulty enforcing conscription and there was little draft evasion. Only a few minority populations, such as Irish Catholics and French-Canadians, seemed reluctant. Voluntary and compulsory enlistments were quite popular for five main reasons.

1. Young men were enveloped by a militaristic culture that depicted wars as normal, honorable, and heroic. The stories read by British schoolboys were about the glory of empire and navy, and the heroes with whom the reader could identify always survived, to be garlanded with glory. Some 41 percent of British boys belonged to organizations like the Boy Scouts or the Boys' Brigade. Britain, like Europe as a whole, was drilled. The "we" in these stories was clearly British, but there was more militarism than nationalism and British and French stories were also more racial than national, for the villains were more

often colonial natives than other Europeans. When the setting was a European conflict, the enemy was normally depicted as honorable. This imperial racism related poorly to the actual war, since most of the armies were multiracial. The nation fought alongside its natives, against the enemy nation and its natives. Obviously, there was some nationalism in this culture, and it was made more objectively aggressive in association with militarism. It generated enthusiasm for war, but it rarely preached national hatred within Europe.

2. Adventurous motives kicked in, in the form of desire for escape from the drudgery of mundane working-or middle-class life, and a quest for adventure among young males. Adventure was not envisaged as bringing death. This also contributed enthusiasm but it was not nationalism.

3. Recruits signed up thinking this was a legitimate war of self-defense. This is what the government and the media told them, and they had no alternative sources of information about foreigners. "Other countries had attacked us or were strangling us" (the German version), and "God was on our side." This was a war of "our civilization" against "their barbarism," obviously an aggressive form of nationalism, though it only appeared after the war had started, helped along by the publicity of enemy atrocities. Germans were enraged by the *francs-tireurs*, the French and Belgian guerrillas, and then by the British blockade that starved them. German atrocities in Belgium and northern France enraged the British and French. Though atrocities were exaggerated by soldiers' insecurities and by propaganda, some were real, as they had always been real in European wars.

4. Recruitment was local. British and French and German volunteers signed on in local units, most famously in the British Pals' battalions, and their commitment was to people they knew. They were honored and partly financed by their local community. To avoid being shamed in their community by refusing to enlist was also a motive, tinged with sexual fear. Peer group pressure to enlist emphasized the need to "be a man," especially in the eyes of women, some of whom in Britain held out yellow feathers in the streets to shirkers. This was local rather than national community attachment.

5. The steady pay was a factor at first, and it probably continued to be a factor among the poor, since the war soon brought full employment (Silbey 2005: 81, 123; Winter 1986: 29–33). This was not nationalist.

Though some of these motives were expressed in nationalist terms, their substance had been present among recruits to European armies over most of the previous millennium: a militaristic culture, barbaric enemies, local community pressures, masculinity, adventure, steady pay, and encouragement from social hierarchies. What the nation-state had mainly added was a centralized system of recruitment, training, and pay. The soldiers were not initially afraid, for they expected to win quickly. But once at the front their experience was not at all like the adventure stories. Death came raining down, rarely through heroic personal combat, mostly from long-range artillery fire. It was almost unbearable to cower down before it with largely unpredictable chances of dying. Officers were convinced that the experience shattered most of their men and that only about 10 percent had the offensive spirit to attack the enemy at all. Killing was hard to do, except for those manning artillery batteries (Bourke 1999: 73). The armies maintained their cohesion nonetheless. At the front, comradeship was reinforced by the intimacy of the soldiers' living conditions and their extreme shared experience and interdependence. A man on his own was a dead man; his unit was a support group, sometimes even a surrogate family. Again, comradeship and hierarchy were primary, the traditional dual organization dominating warfare.

Unfortunately, there was no systematic research on soldier motivations until the World War II *American Soldier* studies. Volume II of that project revealed that most American infantrymen said that their primary motivation during combat derived from the strong emotional ties that developed within the unit rather than any more general social commitment either to the army as a whole or to national ideology (Stouffer et al. 1949).[1] Nationalism was relatively unimportant. This was probably also the case in World War I, say Smith et al. (2003: 98–100), though they also detect a process of "nationalization" occurring among French troops during the war. Since local dialects blocked communication, common French trench slang appeared while army meals forced a common French diet on men whose prior cuisines had previously been highly regional. French soldiers imbibed more French national culture as the war progressed. This indicates war having an effect on national sentiment, not vice versa.

Of course, most soldiers did have a banal sense of national identity, seeing themselves as straightforwardly German, French, British, etc., though colonial troops did not, and they fought just as well. Anzacs discovered through their conflicts with martinet British officers that they were not after all British, though they were fighting for the British Empire

---

[1] This may not have been true of all World War II armies. Despite similar conclusions (influenced by the *American Soldier* research) of Shils and Janowitz (1948) on the German Wehrmacht, more recent research has suggested that large numbers of German soldiers were strongly motivated by Nazi ideology. The American data have not been challenged.

(and not directly for Australia or New Zealand, which were not threatened by Germany). The war was important for developing their distinct sense of national identity. Since almost all bought into the notion that this was a defensive war, national identities became patriotic defense, an appealing sentiment, though there were also allies to place in the nationalism cosmos. For the French and especially the British, this required a switch, as the traditional enemy had become the friend. Hastily German spy stories, such as John Buchan's famous *Thirty-Nine Steps* (1915), emerged, peopled by villainous Germans.

There has been some debate about French soldiers' perceptions of the war. Audoin-Rouzeau and Becker (2002: Chapter 5) argue that most French soldiers had come to believe that they fought in a just national cause, defending civilization against barbarism – a cause blessed by God. Other French historians doubt that ideological commitment was very relevant to soldiers' experiences in the trenches. Maurin (1982) suggests that by 1916 the *poilus* (the hairy ones, the infantry) had forgotten why they were fighting. They fought because they were told to and because this resonated amid the disciplining hierarchies to which they were accustomed: class, state, school, and Church. He shows how in the South local hierarchies of church and state, often at ideological logger-heads in peacetime, joined together in organizing highly festive local recruitment fairs (Maurin 1982: 599–637). Apart from the involvement of schools, what would have been different in earlier centuries? European countries were still very hierarchical. People did what they were told. They had internalized the fact that hierarchy and discipline were normal, natural. Now the hierarchy was nationally organized as well as reaching down into the village. Eugen Weber's classic *Peasants into Frenchman* (1976) charts for us the nineteenth-century development of this.

Smith et al. (2003: 101–12), on the other hand, detect French patriot-ism of a more grounded type (literally!) among the *poilus*. The *poilus* felt it was their job to expel the Boches from France and being mostly soil-tilling peasants, they appreciated that this required digging trenches every meter of the way. The defense of the soil of France was not an abstraction for them; it was their lifeblood. They also believed that they were defending their families and communities and, misled by vague promises from above, they hoped that they were creating for their children a New France. But this nationalism was expressed in surprisingly traditional culture. During quiet times at the front they carved and molded wood, metal, and other substances into figurines and bas-reliefs, conventional idioms rooted in pre-war conformities. Bullets and twisted metal became cruci-fixes and sculptures of the Sacred Heart, and landscapes and female nudes were painted exactly like those depicted in popular newspapers. The

French Napoleonic War soldiers imprisoned in Britain had left similar artifacts, which can be seen scattered through local museums in Britain.

British troops appear closer to Maurin's routinized authority model. Their defense of Britain was not so direct, for they were fighting abroad. Though most were fearful once at the front, they had a banal sense of being British, and this included patriotism, though alongside habituation to obeying their social superiors. They were deferential to officers provided the officers treated their own authority as normal and did not condescend to them (says Bond 2002). These were all still hierarchical societies, now buttressed by strict military discipline. Among the combatant Great Powers, Austro-Hungarian soldiers showed the weakest commitment to the regime. By 1917 the politically conscious among the minority nationalities knew they would be better off in defeat than in victory. Yet they fought almost to the end. It was difficult to do otherwise. The hierarchies were in place and people did what they were told because that was how the world worked.

Naturally soldiers' individual motivations varied. Most tried to keep their heads down, a few were super-patriots, a few viscerally hated the enemy, others developed respect for the enemy, some remained excited by high-octane, masculine adventure, some just liked killing people (Bourke 1999; Ferguson 1999: 357–66). Their post-war reluctance to talk about their war experiences involved consciousness that their own behavior, sometimes cruel, sometimes cowardly, most often prudent, had not been consistent with supposed warrior ideals. Scholars are divided on the question of human propensity for violence. Some believe that human beings dislike violence, especially killing, and are very poor at it (e.g. Collins 2008); others believe they adore it. But whatever might be natural human dispositions, human societies developed elaborate social organizations and legitimacy routines that made killing on a mass scale a whole lot easier (Malešević 2010), especially in traditionally warlike Europe.

At the front there was more resignation than enthusiasm. Death and injury were substantial risks. Over half of all French soldiers were wounded twice or more. Most men were numbed, intermittently terrified, and enduringly emotionally damaged. Alcohol and tobacco helped, psychiatric medicine did not. British and American doctors recognized shell shock, the French recognized *commotion* (concussion) or *obusite* (shellitis) (Audoin-Rouzeau and Becker 2002: 25), but the military and medical authorities often assumed that these were covers for shirking. In World War II, combat exhaustion was thought to render most American soldiers ineffective after 140 to 180 days, and one in ten American soldiers were hospitalized for mental disturbances. In the Great War, soldiers served continuously for much longer periods. Keegan (1978: 335; 1999: 331, 338, 348–50, 401) says that this war revealed a psychological threshold among soldiers above which they would not willingly engage in further offensives, and that all the main armies had reached this threshold by the summer of 1918, except for the recently arrived Americans, who were therefore able to decide the issue. Demonstrations of nationalism or patriotism seemed in bad taste in such an environment and were discouraged by the soldiers.

Most of the rural Bavarians studied by Ziemann (2007) served in fairly quiet zones. Their letters home revealed them as reluctant warriors, not nationalists, solidly in favor of peace from 1917 onwards. Class consciousness was strong, for they saw their officers as abusive, arrogant Prussians. They said they suffered harsh discipline, though this was alleviated by privileged leaves allowing them to return to their farms at times of seasonal pressure.

Survival actually required compliance with orders. Surrendering was dangerous because the enemy response was unpredictable. In the heat of battle, many who threw down their arms were killed by specialized "trench-cleaners" consumed with rage at the deaths of their friends, or fearful that escorting prisoners back through no-man's-land was too dangerous (Audoin-Rouzeau and Becker 2002: 40). Surrendering was safer in large numbers but this only happened at the end of the war. Russians were surrendering massively in 1917, and from August 1918 German surrenders on the Western front rose almost fourfold (Ferguson 1999: 131). Deserting was risky too, for you might be caught and summarily shot. The rate of French desertions was only 1 percent. It was higher in Italy and Russia but still not considered a serious problem by the high commands (Ferro 1972; Maurin 1982: 522; Wildman, 1980: 203–45). It was highest in the Ottoman armies, where the authorities lacked the infrastructures to catch deserters. Turkish, Kurdish, and Arab soldiers might melt away if they were stationed near their homes. But at the front, survival was seen as easier by staying within the command structure than by stepping outside of it. Frontline troops were better supplied with food, alcohol, and tobacco than were civilians. A secure material routine reinforced the sense of unit loyalty that developed across most armies. It was the only available protective environment, enveloping the soldier (Keegan 1978: 274–8, 314–17). It was a true cage (dwarfing the caging metaphor that I have long used for the nation-state!), in which the well-fed animals felt securer inside than outside, and from which they couldn't see outside. Maurin's French veterans say they knew virtually nothing of the overall conduct of the war beyond what they read in newspapers brought in from the rear (1982: 581–97). Middlebrook's

(1971) British veterans of the Somme saw only a few yards in each direction and their eyewitness accounts add up to chaos. New recruits at the front were better informed and also more nationalistic, since there was far more propaganda back home than at the front. The soldiers' communications and logistics were controlled by the chain of command. That, rather than an independent ideological commitment, is why most soldiers fought to the end.

In the British, German, Ottoman, and American armies there were almost no mutinies. There were big French mutinies in 1917 but the soldiers merely refused to fight until certain reforms were made. The incoming commander, General Pétain, made the reforms (and executed a few mutineers) and they resumed fighting. Just over three thousand British soldiers were sentenced to death for desertion, cowardice, mutiny, or other offences, though only 346 sentences were carried out. But this was more than the French total of executions and seven times the German figure, though the Italians shot more than twice this number (Ferguson 1999: 346). These were all small numbers given the size of the armies. After the battle of Caporetto, Italian soldiers fled in disarray before the advancing Austrians. But this was a military rout, the result of an incompetent command structure. As in France, the appointment of a more competent and caring commander solved the Italian problem.

We might expect that if nationalism were really important in the armies then those of the two losing multiethnic empires might be rent by divisive nationalisms. Ottoman soldiers endured two routs, the first when Enver Pasha led them too hastily into a frontal attack on Russian entrenched positions at the beginning of the war in 1914, the second at the hands of the British in September 1918 at Megiddo in Palestine. They were poorly led in both battles. In between times, despite enduring the worst conditions, they fought hard, earning the respect of their adversaries. Discipline dominated ethnicity in this multiethnic army. As the war progressed, the Austro-Hungarians' ability to resist the Russians weakened, and the Russian Revolution may have saved them from collapse. Yet weakness stemmed from poor organization and equipment. In common with Russia, the High Command had difficulty amidst primitive communications in fighting a two-front war and the officer corps was soon decimated. But even in regiments composed of national minorities – who by 1917 mostly wanted to leave the Dual Monarchy – there were only a few serious incidents, all of which occurred in the last months of the war, from May 1918 onwards, and on a smaller scale than the French mutinies (Zeman 1961: 140–6, 218–19; Rothenberg 1977: 78–84). The introduction of Prussian sergeant-majors then persuaded

Czechs, Ruthenes, Croats, and others to fight for the Habsburg overlord, even to the end (Stone 1975: 254–55, 262–63, 272–73).

In the Central Powers, once it became known that the high commands no longer wanted to prosecute the war, everything changed. Released from hierarchical organizational constraints, officers and men were free to make decisions. Would the logistical routine of moving supplies and men be continued tomorrow? Should the soldiers sit where they were, inactive and confined to barracks and positions? Was there any point in fighting, when surrender was imminent? They now discussed these questions openly. Most Austrian soldiers at this point decided to stop fighting. The German Revolution started when Kiel sailors refused to sail out against the British. But regiments varied: some obeyed orders, some mutinied, but most sat still. As long as army units were engaged in combat, the command structure only rarely allowed what we might imagine to be a mass of soldiers to communicate with one another. But once organization disintegrated in defeat, soldiers and workers rose up in revolt, showing that compliance and legitimacy had been less ideologically than organizationally based.

Their risings did not lead to successful revolutions (except in Russia), while some soldiers in the defeated countries plus Italy (with its flawed victory) had quite a different response. Enamored of the organizational combination of discipline and comradeship that had sustained them during the war, and angered by a defeat they blamed on civilians, leftists, and aliens in the nation (such as Jews), they founded post-war paramilitaries which developed into fascist parties, seizing power in Italy, Germany, Austria, and eventually Romania and Hungary too. For them, militarism and a nationalism involving intense hatred of foreign and domestic enemies were yoked tightly together, fuelling each other. They were to cause World War II.

The impact on civilians

World War I has often been called a total war, and it did mobilize most of the civilian population in the war effort. To what extent did the people support a war fought in their name? It is not possible to be exact about public opinion, since there were no national elections or opinion polls, but there was plenty of censorship. If discontent was expressed, the government suppressed it. The establishment was generally loyal, for most political parties and pressure groups supported the war. There was some early positive enthusiasm for war, especially among the middle and upper urban classes, but there was also anxiety and alarm. In Britain, letters to newspapers expressed varied sentiments: Welsh writers often lacked enthusiasm, while even many English correspondents said they would have preferred neutrality to war. They also expressed more hostility to Russia and Serbia than to Germany. The supposedly massive pro-war demonstration on the August 3rd bank holiday on the eve of war turns out to have been only between six thousand and ten thousand strong, in a London of almost seven million. War enthusiasm in Britain in August 1914 was just a myth (says Gregory 2003). Mueller (2003: 66) says that British and German people felt simultaneously fear and enthusiasm, panic and war-readiness. War was most commonly seen as a necessary evil, a part of the image of war as self-defense (Ferguson 1999: Chapter 7).

This was especially true of France's *Union Sacrée*, unity to defend the (sacred) nation. Becker (1985: 324) says its core was simply that France had been invaded and needed to be defended. True, this also gave the opportunity to take back Alsace and Lorraine, an issue dear to French nationalists. But on the other hand, French socialists declared that they were not fighting against the German people, only against its reactionary leaders and capitalist class. Becker (1977) examined French children's essays and found big regional differences and more support for the war in urban than in rural areas. Popular support grew as the war began. Then propaganda kicked in, mostly transmitted through the patriotic self-censorship of the editors and journalists themselves, writing of unbroken military success laced with heroism. Eventually, the French public learned to decode the real meaning of reports like "Our brave young lads are far from beaten. They laugh, joke and beg to be allowed back to the firing line" (in Becker 1985: 38). This meant a defeat. All these victorious battles, yet the front line seemed not to move! Almost everyone wanted peace, and leftists, strikers, and others often demanded it. But German leaders were not offering peace, and the one surviving element of the notion of a *Union Sacrée* was the idea that peace must not be bought at the price of defeat (Becker 1985: 325).

Many Germans later remembered August 1914 as a moment of intense national solidarity, the final accomplishment of German unification. Yet Verhey (2000; c.f. Ziemann 2007) shows this was a myth. There was in fact much government propaganda. Supporters of the war were given license to publicize their views, while dissenters were censored. A carnival atmosphere in German cities lasted about six weeks and then faded. Villages were less warlike, and workers and peasants were more pacific than the bourgeoisie and the educated. The real enthusiasts were young, middle-class urban males. The first string of victories brought some enthusiasm, visible through flag flying even in working-class city neighborhoods. But the war's stalemate then dissipated this. Germans

who still favored the war shifted from open demonstrations of enthusiasm to grim determination to just keep on going.

What benefits Germans expected from the war differed according to
class and politics. Conservatives hoped that the war would suppress class
struggle by bringing a patriotic rallying around the flag and the regime.
Liberals and socialists hoped the war would bring progressive benefits
to the people, especially once it was seen as total war involving major
sacrifice from the masses. German subjects would become citizens.
Likewise elsewhere: the French hoped for a New France, and the
British, a land fit for heroes. The right wing of the German Social
Democratic Party had no difficulty combining socialism and patriotism.
Its Center would have opposed the war had it not feared that this would
give the government grounds to suppress the party. Only the Left voiced
outright opposition, and arresting and sending Karl Liebknecht to the
front was enough to get other left deputies to vote for war credits. It was
difficult to oppose the war without embracing unpopular defeatism, since
the enemy was not seeking peace. Only in Russia, Italy, and the United
States did socialist groups stick by their principles and denounce the war.
Practical politics mixed with some patriotism generally triumphed over
principles. But if nation triumphed over class in 1914, as is often
asserted, class immediately hit back by demanding reforms as the price
of sacrifice.

Most people believed the claims of their leaders that they were fighting
in a just war. Few had international experience, which might have led to
alternative views. In that absence, defense of little Belgium or of democracy (Britain), or of the Republic (France), or of our rightful place in the
sun or of our spiritual idealism (Germany), or even of the monarchy
(Austria-Hungary) could initially justify much. Views of the enemy as
criminals, parasites, or a plague grew, encouraged by propaganda. The
French were seen as decadent, materialistic, and corrupt; Germans were
regimented and hostile to liberty; Britons were rapaciously capitalistic;
Russians were corrupt Asiatics living under despotism, with a primitive
religion. The Russian specter was especially useful in Germany since it
could rally round Catholics as well as Protestants, and liberals and
socialists as well as conservatives, while Britain's alliance with Russia
was seen as a betrayal of Western civilization (Hewitson 2004: Chapter 3;
Mueller 2003; Nolan 2005: 2–6, 47–8; Verhey 2000: 118, 131). Again,
however, this more aggressive nationalist rhetoric was the consequence,
not the cause of war.

Audoin-Rouzeau and Becker (2002: Chapter 5) note that in France
the war came to be seen as a crusade, a struggle between civilization and
barbarity, and the enemy was believed to be committing atrocities against

civilians: murders, rapes, mutilations and deportations. There were some racial stereotypes of the enemy. Some French troops claimed that Germans smelled bad and gave racial-science explanations. Some Germans denounced the racial treason of the British and French, for in Germany it was said that their non-white colonial troops in Europe were cannibals. Isabel Hull (2005) says that the German military had already devised an institutional culture of a war of annihilation – swift, ruthless, savage in destroying the enemy – to compensate for its lack of numbers and its two-front commitment. Yet the Russian and Balkan armies seem to have been equally terrible toward civilians, and all the armies raped women and shot prisoners.

The British naval blockade was in some ways the greatest atrocity, probably killing over half a million German and Austro-Hungarian civilians. The collapse of animal feed and fertilizer imports was particularly damaging, contributing to a fall in Germany's agricultural production of at least 40 percent (Offer 1989). From 1916, Berlin's mortality rates began to rise dramatically, generating an enduring demographic crisis absent from London and Paris, which saw only brief temporary crises: London in 1915, Paris in 1917 (Winter, 1999: Chapter 16). Blockading was a traditional British naval tactic in European war, not a feature of stronger nationalism.

In Germany rations got smaller and discontent greater. Police reports singled out working-class women as especially discontented, for they could not be easily sanctioned (by being sent to the front). They staged numerous demonstrations. Food shortages undercut attempts to get more women into the war industries, as did the conservative attitudes of German employers. What was the point of a low wage if there was nothing to buy with it? Better to put one's efforts into illegal means of getting food (Daniel 1997: 196). The result was a labor shortage as well as a food shortage. Swelling discontent also meant that the authorities felt forced to extend their propaganda and their surveillance. Discontent was not necessarily leftist. There were calls for a food dictator with the power to force internal enemies, such as farmers and merchants, into more patriotic behavior and there was little class solidarity between workers and peasants (Moeller 1986). Germans and Austrians both voiced anti-Semitic stereotypes of the food hoarder (Daniel 1997: 253; Davis 2000: 132–35).

More anti-regime solidarity existed among the urban populace. Many believed that profits were enormous, pursued to the detriment of the war effort. Rationing was introduced but was perceived as unfair when distribution systems broke down and black markets flourished (Feldman 1966: 63–64, 157, 469–70, 480–84). As war bit hard into living standards, some starved while others consumed conspicuously. The experience brought the living standards of urban workers and the lower middle classes closer together. Davis (2000: Chapter 3) reports much middle-class sympathy for the protests of poor women. Smith (2007) sees a growing nationalist vernacular: a populism emerging in opposition to the Wilhelmine regime, led by the middle class but then uniting Germans across class lines and shattering the status- and class-ridden world of the monarchy. This movement achieved its greatest successes with the establishment of the dictatorship of Hindenburg and Ludendorff in late 1916, which made the Kaiser irrelevant. Smith sees the revolution of November 1918 not as a disjuncture caused by a suddenly lost war, but as a steadier intensification of this rising nationalist vernacular, once again an effect of war.

To contain dissent, all combatants lodged greater coercive powers with employers, backed by ministries and military authorities suppressing dissent. Emergency measures restricted health and safety codes, especially for women and adolescents. Labor market and trade union freedoms were mostly suspended. In response, strike rates began to rise in the combatant countries during the last two years of war, though they were not rising as fast as in neutral countries like Norway, Sweden, and Spain. Though deprivation and post-war turbulence were linked, the timing of disturbances was weakly related to cost-of-living movements, and the revolutionary core proved to be relatively well-off industries such as metalworking (Cronin 1983: 30; Feldman 1977; Meaker 1974: 38–39). But co-opted leftist party and union leaders could no longer lead dissent. Some concessions were made to them to help bolster their authority over the workers, but class dissent had been organized out, and in response was slowly finding new shop-floor organization. Employers felt pressures to conciliate in the metalworking and ammunition industries, with labor shortages and a desperate need for production. In Britain, when Lloyd George tried to remedy labor shortages by bringing in unskilled dilutees into skilled jobs, he commented ruefully that the actual arrangements for the introduction of diluted labor had to be made separately in each workshop, by agreement with the skilled workers there. French unions were weaker and they were excluded from government/ employer negotiations until late in the war. Skilled men back from military service remained under military discipline and their employer could send them to the front for insubordination. That was also true in Russia. French conditions then improved as the socialist armaments minister Albert Thomas made collective bargaining compulsory and introduced minimum wages (Becker 1985: Chapter 17; Broue 2005: 53; Feldman 1966: 116–37, 373–85, 418–20; Gallie 1983: 232–34;

Godfrey 1987; Hasegawa 1981: 86–89; McLean 1983: 73–91, 120, 138; Pedersen 1993: Chapter 2, esp. 84–86; Smith et al. 2003). While shop stewards quietly extended their informal powers, union, socialist party, and government controls contained them. Class conflict was restrained by organizational controls more than by nationalism.

The war was formally nationalist, not one regime against another, but entire nations defending their security and values. Thus people hoped that popular sacrifice would be rewarded with more citizen rights afterwards. In Britain about 60 percent of men already had the vote, but in March 1917 all British men (but not women) were granted the vote. In Germany and Austria this was the first occasion on which Socialists had ever been consulted about major policy matters, and the Prussian class franchise was abolished in 1917 (though it remained in the other Länder, and the German Reichstag did not have full sovereign powers). In the economic realm rationing, minimum wages, and regulated prices seemed the prologue to social citizenship in Marshall's sense. The coming to power of Lloyd George and Clemenceau, and even the military dictatorship in Germany were implicit recognition of the shift. Austro-Hungarian nationalist movements assumed that they would receive more self-government after the war in return for their sacrifices. The British made definite promises to Arabs who revolted against the Ottoman Empire. They would get their own state if they joined British troops against the Ottomans. Many did so. Alas, perfidious Albion brought them into the British Empire. Colonial nationalists already in the British and French empires made the same assumptions, expecting self-government afterwards. They also were to be deceived. But popular expectations were raised, and this was dangerous for regimes especially if they could not win the war. The two Russian revolutions of February and October/November 1917 burst the dam and emboldened militants elsewhere. In January 1918 it appeared as if revolution might spread elsewhere in Europe. But there the divisions that had appeared in the war between leaders and militants made the revolutions abortive.

World War II

Nationalism played a much larger role in World War II, though it was rather particularistic. The immediate cause of World War II was Adolf Hitler. In World War I, miscalculations all round had produced a war of unintended consequences. This was different: though there were miscalculations and unintended consequences, one man, his Nazi movement, and his powerful country started the war, as Japanese military elites initiated the Asian war. Decisions were again set amidst general ideological predispositions, but in 1939 most Europeans, scarred by the Great War, were less militaristic than they had been in 1914.

But there were in fact two Europes. In one, fascism was taking militarized nationalism to new heights in a few countries. Nazism had also broadened imperial racism to include supposedly inferior races within Europe. Nazi aggression was fuelled by this new ideological blend to provoke war. In this sense nationalism of an especially extreme kind did cause this war in Europe, while a less extreme blend of nationalism, militarism, and imperialism came to power in Japan and provoked war in Asia. These are the most obvious nationalism-to-war causal chains I have found.

Yet the rest of Europe was in retreat from militarism and aggressive nationalism. Britain and France had been badly burned by the first war, and most people wanted to avoid another one at all cost. British leaders saw their country as a satiated power, controlling one fourth of the world's land surface, aware that its hold on empire was getting precarious. Imperial interests lay in peace and collective security to preserve what Britain already had. France was even more in favor of peace, on account of military weakness, greater political divisions, and the German threat. The Bolsheviks did not want war either since they were busy transforming the economy and decimating the Party and the High Command. The US was even more pacific and domestically obsessed. Mussolini was keen on war, but only against Africans. Europeans turned away from war until they realized that Hitler could not be stopped any other way. Before then, they scurried to avoid war. Even when they did face up to the possibility of war, each country hoped that another one would do the fighting. The only shared foreign policy was to spill the blood of others. Only Hitler was fully prepared to spill as much German blood as was necessary, and since he recognized the difference between himself and other leaders, it emboldened him. But even most Germans were queasy about war, so Gestapo agents reported. Hitler's aggressive foreign policy was popular precisely because he had got back the territories lost in 1918 by sheer bluff, without having to wage war. Once Britain and France declared war, most Germans wanted peace. But by now they had no organizational means of expressing dissent.

In the end British and French leaders were prepared to fight, though not before ideology – not of nations but of class – had intervened. They spurned the chance of an alliance with the Soviet Union, also threatened by Nazi aggression. We do not know if such an alliance would have deterred Hitler from war. Maybe it would have, but if he had nonetheless gone to war, this alliance might have defeated him in only a year or two, thus saving millions of lives, including those of most Jews and gypsies.

The biggest stumbling block to an alliance was ideological anti-communism. Political leaders in Britain and France did not want the Red Army to move westward. That could foment class revolution, they believed. A minority led by Churchill swallowed its ideological distaste on realist geopolitical grounds. It had long been British policy to support a balance of power in continental Europe. When Napoleon had managed to dominate most of Europe, Britain had allied with Russia in order to attack him from both sides. Again in World War I Britain had allied with Russia and France against Germany. Exactly the same logic was called for in World War II. Yet Chamberlain and Daladier and their foreign ministers did not accept it and they clung to power until after war was declared (du Réau 1993; Imlay 2003: 34). After the fall of the Popular Front in April 1938, the rightist French government needed the votes of fascist-leaning deputies. By now most of the Left in both countries favored war, but because of anti-fascism, not nationalism.

Chamberlain still had a parliamentary majority and much popular support. Britain and France were not betrayed by a handful of appeasers, for public opinion did not want war and the parliaments reflected that. This was not like World War I when elites alone had decided whether it would be war or peace. That was true in the dictatorships, but not in Britain or France, or in the United States where democracy also favored peace (though Roosevelt had almost zero influence on European developments). By the time of Munich, some change had occurred. An opinion poll showed British opinion to be fairly evenly divided over whether to aid the Czechs. But when Chamberlain returned from Munich waving his infamous bit of paper, declaring peace in our time, there was a surge of relief and he was greeted as a hero, the man who had averted war. After Hitler tore up the Munich agreement, Chamberlain's position was revealed to have been "illogical ... Incomprehensible, except in terms of ideologically motivated anti-communism, rooted in the fear that war might bring revolution" (Carley 1999: 181). Class ideology had triumphed over nationalism.

When the war came, Germany again had better, more lethal soldiers. A German infantryman consistently inflicted about 50 percent higher casualties than did either his British or his American counterpart. Was this due to greater nationalist commitment? As in the first war the Germans had a more mission-oriented command system giving more autonomy in combat to officers and NCOs so that they could move more flexibly and rapidly than their opponents. They also remained logistically leaner and more fighting-focused, with a higher proportion of combat troops over support and service troops (Dupuy 1977: 234–5; van Creveld 1982). Under fascism, German armies had also become more classless than most armies (yet perhaps not more than the US Army). Higher class or education did not get you promoted, authority and courage did. At a time of lagging militarism elsewhere, German young men had been under military discipline in the 1930s, both in the Hitler Youth and the paramilitary National Labor Service. Millions had been enrolled as volunteers in collective mobilizations, the *Volksgemeinschaft* (national community) in practice (Fritzsche 2008: 51). The Wehrmacht had then added a more rigorous and harsher operational training than that practiced in any other army, and a harsher punishment system for officers. The combination, as Fritz (1995) notes, generated a collective elitism, a sense of superiority won through greater commitment and sacrifice, and a sense of a *Frontgemeinschaft* (front community), which was the cutting edge of the *Volksgemeinschaft*. The soldiers were disproportionately members of the Nazi Party and their diaries and letters home idolized Hitler, remaining loyal to him to the end. Even after they were experiencing defeat and the Americans were experiencing victory, the American desertion rate remained several times higher than the German rate (van Creveld 1982: 116). The German soldiers' morale did reveal a higher national commitment, but of a novel, fascist kind. Indeed, soldiers' diaries and letters echoed Hitler's own boast after the seizure of Crete: the German soldier can do anything. So it is difficult here to separate out nationalist-rooted high morale from superiority in military organization, but both were present, reinforcing each other. For Japan also it is difficult to separate out the main causes of the Japanese soldier's resilience: a nationalistic culture emphasizing hierarchy and community, the growing militarization of the Japanese state through the 1930s, and the "Imperial Way" strategy adopted by the High Command, emphasizing *seishin*, spiritual mobilization, which could supposedly overcome the enemy's numerical and technological superiority. Japanese forces also perpetrated terrible atrocities, especially in China, as they had not in their war with Russia in 1905. In the meantime Japanese militarism had taken command of the state, and the disciplinary codes of the army had gotten much tougher. But the war also had a "nationalizing" effect on the population of China. Defined by Japanese soldiers as Chinese and racially inferior, and subjected to terrible atrocities, many now realized for the first time that they were indeed "Chinese" – again, nationalism was more an effect than a cause of war.

France crumbled quickly, largely as a consequence of Germany's better military organization and tactics. But thereafter this was compounded by a highly divided nation, most of whose leaders preferred to make a deal with Hitler and get a half-fascist puppet state to continuing the resistance. But Britain as an island nation could fight on. It also had high morale, especially after the Battle of Britain and when Churchill subordinated his own imperialism to populist defense of the nation. Most British people admired Churchill's defiant rhetoric and felt that he expressed their own sentiments. Despite grumbling and a high strike rate, they were prepared to sacrifice for ultimate victory. It was democracy against fascism, they believed. There was growing nationalism. Yet the Mass Observation diarists (the best insight into contemporary opinion) said that what Britain meant to them was "banal": a romantic view of the countryside and villages, the notion of gentle order, the easy tolerance and good humor of the people. There was little high-flown nationalist rhetoric or flag-waving patriotism (Mackay 2002: 253).

Churchill, experienced in World War I and fully aware of Britain's desperate situation, knew that class divisions could weaken the nation. He recognized the need to bring Labour and trade union leaders fully into the government. They made it clear that the price for popular sacrifice was progressive reform. Ernest Bevin, trade union leader and the new Foreign Secretary, inserted into Churchill's and Roosevelt's 1941 Placentia Bay Statement of War Aims a clause securing for all improved labor standards, economic advancement, and social security. Labour ministers were put in charge of most domestic policy (which Churchill considered less important), and this ensured that reforms would indeed happen. A Labour and a Liberal minister commissioned William Beveridge to produce his famous report envisaging a comprehensive cradle-to-grave welfare state. A Gallup poll revealed that 86 percent of respondents said it should be implemented. The Labour Party as well as a progressive Tory group endorsed it. Churchill did not, but was chastened by public opinion into voicing vaguely worded expressions of support. By 1943, polls showed that most people expected that eventual victory in the war would be followed by major improvements in their lives (Mackay 2002: Chapter 6). This was a nationalism embodying class compromise.

The Soviet Union and the United States were brought reluctantly into the war only when attacked by Germany and Japan. There was not much bellicose nationalism in either country. US opinion polls revealed a dislike of European militarism and a popular determination to keep out of Europe's wars. Roosevelt's attempts to manipulate the Atlantic theatre to get the US into the war earlier foundered on Congressional and popular pacific sentiment (Kershaw 2007). Stalin did then mobilize Russian nationalist sentiment for what he called the Great Patriotic War, and Russians fought astonishingly hard considering the losses and deprivations they suffered. American nationalism grew after 1941, though most American civilians actually benefited from the war and sacrificed almost nothing for which they might need rewarding. The troops obviously did sacrifice and they got their own welfare state afterwards in the GI Bill of Rights. There is no doubting the capacity of mass mobilization war to mobilize nationalism, but only German and Japanese nationalisms in their Nazi and militarist clothing had caused the greatest war ever.

The US and Britain are not generally credited with wartime atrocities. Yet devastating aerial bombing culminating in Hiroshima and Nagasaki (though the fire-bombing of Tokyo and Dresden caused more casualties) was inflicted at a distance, causing more civilian than military deaths. As with naval blockades in World War I, lethality came from improved technology more than from greater ferocity of intent, though revenge for earlier German bombings was an important motive for the British perpetrators, while racism directed against the Japanese was important among the Americans. But militaries have always used the highest level of technology available to them. The blame for these Anglo-American mass killings does not lie primarily with nationalism.

Conclusion

I have given a skeptical account of the commonly assumed relationship between nationalism and war. I found no overall correlation between the incidence of war and of nationalism in the modern period. I attribute the increased lethality of twentieth-century wars to technology rather than nationalism. I found that amid the causes of World War I, nationalism figured only in minor ways. The reverse causation loomed much larger. The war was (almost) a total war, mobilizing whole populations, and this increased nationalism during the war. Among the troops, however, this was subordinated to compliance with officers and comrades, which was traditional in well-trained armies, while nationalism never eliminated class or racial divisions. These exploded in the combatant great powers and in their colonies as the war ended.

World War II differed, since it was caused principally by the extreme nationalism of the two main aggressor regimes, in Germany and Japan. However, theirs was a distinct variety of nationalism, inflected with fascism and extreme militarism. Among their opponents, class-based anti-communism had overcome national solidarity in the run-up to war, making resistance to Hitler initially more difficult. Class ideologies helped bring France to defeat, while systematic class compromise allowed Britain to resist. The US and the USSR also showed great reluctance to go to war. When attacked, they also responded with more bellicose nationalism.

So, with the exception of Nazi Germany and militaristic Japan, the predominant causal relation was that war generated nationalism, not vice versa. This relationship was neither universal nor particularly strong, and nationalist war efforts needed the weakening of class ideologies through compromise. It is far more plausible to focus on civil wars as likely sites of nationalism, though of a rather different type (see Mann 2005).

REFERENCES

Audoin-Rouzeau, S. and A. Becker. 2002. *14–18: Understanding the Great War.* New York: Hill and Wang.

Becker, J. 1977. *1914: Comment les français sont entrés dans la guerre.* Paris: Presses de la Fondation nationale des sciences politiques.

1985. *The Great War and the French People.* Leamington Spa: Berg.

Billig, M. 1995. *Banal Nationalism.* London: Sage Publications.

Bond, B. 2002. *The Unquiet Western Front: Britain's Role in Literature and History.* New York: Cambridge University Press.

Bourke, J. 1999. *An Intimate History of Killing: Face-to-Face Killing in Twentieth-Century Warfare.* New York: Basic Books.

Broue, P. 2005. *The German Revolution, 1917–1923.* Leiden: Brill.

Carley, M.J. 1999. *1939: The Alliance That Never Was and the Coming of World War II.* Chicago: Ivan R. Dee.

Collins, R. 2008. *Violence: A Micro-Sociological Theory.* Princeton University Press.

Cronin, J. 1983. "Introduction." In *Work, Community and Power: The Experience of Labor in Europe and America, 1900–1925,* edited by J. Cronin and C. Sirianni. Philadelphia, PA: Temple University Press.

Daniel, U. 1997. *The War From Within: German Working-Class Women in the First World War.* Oxford and New York: Berg.

Davis, B. 2000. *Home Fires Burning: Food, Politics, and Everyday Life in World War I Berlin.* Chapel Hill: University of North Carolina Press.

Dupuy, T. 1977. *A Genius For War: the German Army and the General Staff, 1807–1945.* Englewood Cliffs, NJ: Prentice-Hall.

du Réau, E. 1993. *Edouard Daladier, 1884–1970.* Paris: Fayard.

Feldman, G. 1966. *Army, Industry, and Labor in Germany, 1914–1918.* Princeton University Press.

1977. *Iron and Steel in the German Inflation, 1916–1923.* Princeton University Press.

Ferguson, N. 1999. *The Pity of War: Explaining World War I.* New York: Basic Books.

Ferro, M. 1972. *The Russian Revolution of February 1917.* Englewood Cliffs, NJ: Prentice-Hall International.

Fritz, S. 1995. *Frontsoldaten: The German Soldier in World War II.* Lexington: University Press of Kentucky.

Fritzsche, P. 2008. *Life and Death in the Third Reich.* Cambridge, MA: Belknap Press.

Gallie, D. 1983. *Social Inequality and Class Radicalism in France and Britain.* Cambridge University Press.

Gleditsch, K. 2004. "A Revised List of Wars between and within Independent States, 1816–2002." *International Interactions* 30: 231–62.

Godfrey, J. 1987. *Capitalism at War: Industrial Policy and Bureaucracy in France, 1914–1918.* Leamington Spa: Berg.

Gregory, A. 2003. "British War Enthusiasm: A Reassessment." Chapter 3 in *Evidence, History and the Great War*, edited by Gail Braybon. Oxford: Berghahn.

Hasegawa, T. 1981. *The February Revolution.* Seattle: University of Washington Press.

Hewitson, M. 2004. *Germany and the Causes of the First World War.* Oxford and New York: Berg.

Hull, I. 2005. *Absolute Destruction: Military Culture and the Practices of War in Imperial Germany.* Ithaca, NY: Cornell University Press.

Imlay, T. 2003. *Facing the Second World War: Strategy, Politics, and Economics in Britain and France 1938–1940.* New York: Oxford University Press.

Keegan, J. 1978 *The Face of Battle.* Harmondsworth: Penguin.
  1999. *The First World War.* New York: Knopf.

Kershaw, I. 2007. *Fateful Choices: Ten Decisions That Changed the World 1940–1941.* London: Penguin Books.

Lemke, D. 2002. *Regions of War and Peace.* Cambridge University Press.

Levy, J.S. 1983. *War in the Modern Great Power System, 1495–1975.* Lexington, KY: University of Kentucky Press.

Mackay, R. 2002. *Half the Battle: Civilian Morale in Britain during the Second World War.* Manchester University Press.

Malešević, S. 2010. *The Sociology of War and Violence.* Cambridge University Press.

Mann, M. 1993. *The Sources of Social Power.* 4 vols. Vol. II *The Rise of Classes and Nation-States, 1760–1914.* New York: Cambridge University Press.
  2005. *The Dark Side of Democracy: Explaining Ethnic Cleansing.* New York: Cambridge University Press.
  2012. *The Sources of Social Power.* 4 vols. Vol. III *Global Empires and Revolution, 1890–1945.* Cambridge University Press.

Maurin, J. 1982. *Armée – Guerre – Societé: Soldats Languedociens, 1899–1919.* Paris: Sorbonne.

McLean, I. 1983. *The Legend of Red Clydeside.* Edinburgh: John Donald Publishers.

Meaker, G. 1974. *The Revolutionary Left in Spain 1914–1923.* Stanford University Press.

Middlebrook, M. 1971. *The First Day on the Somme, 1 July 1916.* New York: Norton.

Moeller, R. 1986. *German Peasants and Agrarian Politics, 1914–1924: The Rhineland and Westphalia.* Chapel Hill: University of North Carolina Press.

Mueller, S.O. 2003. *Die Nation als Waffe und als Vorstellung: Nationalismus in Deutschland und Grossbritannien in Ersten Weltkrieg.* Goettingen: Vandenhoek & Ruprecht.

Nolan, M. 2005. *The Inverted Mirror: Mythologizing the Enemy in France and Germany.* New York: Berghahn Books.

Offer, A. 1989. *The First World War: An Agrarian Interpretation.* Oxford: Clarendon Press.

Pedersen, S. 1993. *Family, Dependence and the Origins of the Welfare State: Britain and France, 1914–1945.* Cambridge University Press.

Rothenberg, G. 1977. "The Habsburg Army in the First World War: 1914–1918." Chapter 4 in *The Habsburg Empire in World War I*, edited by Robert Kann et al. Boulder, CO: East European Quarterly.

Shils, E. and M. Janowitz. 1948. "Cohesion and Disintegration in the Wehrmacht in World War II." *Public Opinion Quarterly* 12(2): 280–315.

Silbey, D. 2005. *The British Working Class and Enthusiasm for War, 1914–1916.* London and New York: Frank Cass.

Smith, J. 2007. *A People's War: Germany's Political Revolution, 1913–1918.* Lanham, MD: University Press of America.

Smith, L., S. Audoin-Rouzeau and A. Becker. 2003. *France and the Great War, 1914–1918.* Cambridge University Press.

Stone, N. 1975. *The Eastern Front, 1914–1918.* New York: Scribner.

Stouffer, S., E.A. Suchman, L.C. DeVinney, S.A. Star, and R.M. Williams Jr. 1949. *The American Soldier: Studies in Social Psychology in World War II: Combat and Its Aftermath.* Princeton University Press.

Strachan, H. 2001. *The First World War: To Arms.* New York: Oxford University Press.

van Creveld, M. 1982 *Fighting Power: German and US Army Performance, 1939–1945.* Westport, CT: Greenwood Press.

Verhey, J. 2000. *The Spirit of 1914: Militarism, Myth, and Mobilization in Germany.* New York: Cambridge University Press.

Weber, E. 1976. *Peasants into Frenchmen: The Modernization of Rural France, 1870–1914.* Stanford University Press.

Wildman, A. 1980. *The End of the Russian Imperial Army.* Princeton University Press.

Winter, J. 1986. *The Great War and the British People.* Cambridge, MA: Harvard University Press.

   1999. "Surviving the War: Life Expectation, Illness and Mortality Rates in Paris, London, and Berlin, 1914–1919." Pp. 487–524 in *Capital Cities at War: Paris, London, Berlin, 1914–1919*, edited by J. Winter and J.L. Robert. Cambridge University Press.

Zeman, Z. 1961. *The Break-Up of the Habsburg Empire, 1914–1918: A Study in National and Social Revolution.* London: Oxford University Press.

Ziemann, B. 2007. *War Experiences in Rural Germany, 1914–1923.* New York: Berg.

8   Empire, ethnicity and power

A comment

Dominic Lieven

This comment is partly rooted in reflections on two chapters written by John Darwin and Michael Mann for this collection. It uses their chapters as a springboard for thoughts about empire, ethnicity, and power in the modern age. John Darwin's paper is about ethnicity and empire. It argues that although ethnic consciousness is usually taken to be the enemy of empire it can actually be the opposite. He roots his argument in a discussion of British imperial ethnicity in the late nineteenth and twentieth centuries. Michael Mann's chapter looks at the role of nationalism in the causes and the outcomes of the two world wars of the twentieth century. He argues that nationalism's impact was less than is often assumed.

The two chapters by Darwin and Mann cover different but overlapping themes. What unites them is a concern for the impact of geopolitics and political identity on the twentieth-century competition between the great imperial powers. This is a vast and complex theme but some of its core elements are relatively simple. For a polity to survive it needs to meet the requirements of the era in which it lives and the society over which it rules. By 1900, the nation in one form or another seemed best able to meet the domestic requirements of most modern European societies. But in the world of international relations the future seemed to belong to empires of continental scale and resources. Much of twentieth-century history therefore witnessed efforts to square the circle by creating imperial nations and national empires. Though societies and the nature of global power have to some extent evolved over recent decades, many of the realities that underpinned these efforts to merge empire and nation are still very relevant.

The power of the nation rested in part in the ideas on which it was based. Some of these ideas dated back to concepts of popular sovereignty, citizenship, and civic equality underpinning the French Revolution.

The nation gave power, rights, and status to its citizens but it also demanded from them a conscious and self-sacrificing commitment to the polity that went well beyond what was normally expected by old-regime rulers, including the rulers of empire. The other main body of ideas underpinning the nation was initially of mostly Germanic origin. It stressed the role of language, ethnicity, and history in creating unique political communities that alone had the right and the power to hold the allegiance of their members. Scholars distinguish between Germanic "ethnic nationalism" and the "civic nationalism" of 1789, and in some respects rightly so. In reality, however, the two versions greatly over-lapped. Ethnic nationalists also rooted sovereignty in the people, albeit in a *Volk* which might not include everyone living on the state's territory. Moreover, few real-world civic nationalisms were not also in part ethnic. Who after all would ever be willing to die for the bloodless, purely civic nation? If the principles of 1789 may have been universal and civic, the people who embodied them in 1789 were very definitely French. The Revolution served for many of them as confirmation that France was indeed (as they had always known) "La Grande Nation," the leader both of Europe and of civilization. Napoleon's European empire was in part based on this conception.

As Ernest Gellner (with others) has always insisted, the nation was much more than the product of mere ideas. It was also the child of modernity. Mass literacy, urbanization, exposure to market forces, and the destruction of the cozy networks of "rural idiocy" fed into the need for a wider and more modern sense of community. In particular, as Darwin mentions, Gellner stressed the need for efficient modern soci-eties to share a common high culture. Politics also intruded. As modern-ity shredded traditional allegiances and encouraged liberal and socialist ideologies, the rulers of polities sought alternative sources of collective solidarity that would preserve their own interests and status. Modernity also meant the spread of the very unlovable bureaucratic state, whose encroachment on everyday lives was to some extent made more tolerable by the rhetoric of the nation as family writ large.

The strength of the national idea was also linked to the belief that it greatly enhanced the power of a polity and society, above all by mobiliz-ing the people in defense of the state. Though much of nineteenth-century European history was taken as proof of this belief, its origins lay in the 1790s and its greatest prophet was Clausewitz. He starkly contrasted aristocratic fun and games in the dynastic wars of the eighteenth century with the total, people's war launched by the French Revolution. Not merely did the Revolution unlock the community's full potential power, it also allowed war to be fought in a new fashion. Like the American minuteman, the Revolutionary light infantryman was an intelligent and committed citizen-in-arms. He could be trusted to operate independently and with initiative. Armies made up of such men could, so it was said, move and fight with more speed and flexibility than the untrustworthy hirelings and terrorized peasant conscripts of the Old Regime's armies.

In reality Clausewitz's vision of the wars of his era was exaggerated. If the *levée en masse* of 1793 was indeed to some extent the people in arms, in subsequent years France's armies were largely recruited and motivated by more traditional means. What mattered above all was numbers, for the Revolution removed the obstacles to mobilizing the resources of what was still potentially much the most powerful country in Europe. To an extent the Revolution allowed France to catch up with Frederick's Prussia, whose mobilizational capacity in the Seven Years War (in which one out of every ten Prussian subjects died) gives the lie to the idea that eighteenth-century warfare was sport of any kind. It remains true that in certain key respects Napoleon's army was the (much-improved) heir of the Revolutionary forces but the point to note is that in the end it was defeated by the European Old Regime. Clausewitz's Prussia was an Old Regime modified in some significant ways but Austria, Russia or even Britain were far less modified. The core of the coalition that defeated Napoleon on land in 1813–14 was Russia, whose army had successfully adapted many of the narrowly military advances in warfare that had occurred since 1793 without changing the foundations of the Russian Old Regime. Traditional religious and dynastic loyalties were core elements of what it meant to be Russian at that time, and these certainly motivated the tsar's soldiers. But so too did the traditional caste values of the officer corps and the enormous loyalty of the rank-and-file veterans to regiments that had become their lifelong home and fatherland. If properly trained, Russian conscripts in time could hold their own against any light infantrymen, as could the hard-bitten soldiers of Wellington's Light Division.

A key reason why Clausewitz retains his attraction for scholars is, however, that he was in many ways better at prophecy than at a balanced description of the wars of his own era. He spotted the chicken in the egg and understood just what a monstrous bird it might become. By 1900 Clausewitz's view of war looked very realistic and so too, therefore, did the crucial importance of nationalist commitment for military effectiveness. Wars would now be decided by huge armies comprised of civilians who had spent at most three years in the ranks, in most cases many years before they were recalled to the colors upon mobilization. Moreover, unlike in the Napoleonic era, they would no longer be fighting shoulder to shoulder with their comrades with an NCO behind every fifth man's back. Modern firearms dictated open-order tactics and required attacking infantry to cover a killing ground one kilometer or more in depth. Conscious of this challenge, generals and statesmen believed that only patriotic indoctrination could motivate an effective modern soldiery. The nation appeared to be the most effective school of patriotism.

A key problem was that the logic of power led in contradictory directions. In terms of international power, the future appeared to belong to empires of continental scale and resources. Very few ethno-national communities could even dream of expanding on this scale, but a couple could and even seemingly did. Alexis de Tocqueville had prophesied that the future would belong to continental-scale Russia and the USA. After the United States survived the Civil War this prophecy looked good. If some polities were of continental scale then maybe all who wished to remain in the first league must match them. Hence for European polities the geopolitical logic of colonial empire, which was their only hope of acquiring such scale and resources. Technological development played a crucial role in the argument for empire because it shrank distances and opened up continental interiors to development. This meant above all, but by no means exclusively, the railway. By the last third of the nineteenth century, Britain could no longer rely on monopolizing the Industrial Revolution, and her margin of power over rivals shrank. As other countries joined the scramble for empire there was additional good reason to stake out claims for the future by grabbing whatever "free" territory was still available. One fifth of the world's land surface changed hands between 1870 and 1913. Growing protectionist trends in the global economy strengthened the case for asserting sovereign control over territory. Moreover, one never knew what might lie beneath supposedly barren and empty lands.

This was a lesson the British learned in Southern Africa. Having earlier allowed the Boers to establish semi-independent republics in what appeared to be a wilderness, by the 1890s Britain confronted the fact that this wilderness had become the world's richest trove of gold and diamonds, and the inevitable core of Southern Africa's economy. This had serious political implications given the fact that Boers were a majority of the population of Britain's Cape Colony and that other powers (above all Germany) were becoming increasingly interested in Southern Africa. These realities go far towards explaining why Britain fought an expensive war in 1899–1902 to force the Boer republics back into the empire. One obvious lesson from these events was the need to plant your flag anywhere that might conceivably become useful. Another lesson, learned above all by Germany, was that British maritime hegemony allowed it to make mistakes and recover from them without seriously damaging its interests. So long as Britannia ruled the waves there was little any continental power could do to stop it imposing its will beyond Europe. The Germans had some reason for grievance. Having come late to the colonial table they had received pathetic trifles. Meanwhile between 1895 and 1907 in Africa, Persia, Manchuria, and the Philippines, countries that already possessed huge territories were gobbling even more and leaving Germany on the sidelines.

This was the geopolitical reality underlying British discussions of imperial ethnicity, the topic of John Darwin's chapter. In the late nineteenth and early twentieth century it was axiomatic for many imperially minded British observers that, to remain a great power, Britain had to create a national empire, rooted in a common Greater British White ethnic identity. Of course, the non-White empire would not be discarded, but it was accepted that it must always be ruled at arm's length from Britain. Eighteenth-century fears that metropolitan freedom would be undermined by Asiatic despotism played a role here. So too did unwillingness to share common citizenship with non-Whites. Merging with the British freedom-loving White communities overseas was, however, totally different and, in principle, acceptable. Consolidating this Greater British imperial identity and developing institutions to give it political weight became the life's work for a number of key figures in British politics.

They failed for many reasons. Timing was against them. When the White colonies were granted wide-ranging autonomy in the mid nineteenth century, distance made effective federal institutions barely an option. In any case in the mid nineteenth century Britain was supremely powerful and the White colonies were weak. London had no great need or incentive for all-imperial institution building. By the time the need became evident, colonial full self-government was entrenched and to claw back powers for London would be difficult. In addition, British and colonial economic interests by no means necessarily coincided. To attempt to keep the colonies as both markets for British industry and purveyors of raw materials would have invited the kind of conflicts that had led to the American Revolution of the 1770s. In any case Britain's exports went far beyond her White empire, and the British electorate was unwilling to pay a premium for colonial food imports. British dogma on parliamentary sovereignty was also not easily squared with any version of imperial federation. In the long run, fundamental geopolitical factors would also intrude. Any version of a Greater British Empire would still have to cede hegemony over the Western Hemisphere to the Americans and exercise global dominion in tandem with them. Moreover, and most basically, once Britain lost the margin gained by being the first industrial nation the British Isles became a perilously small core territory on which to base an empire scattered across the globe. Paul Rohrbach made this point about German metropolitan territory but it applied to Britain too.[1]

Awareness of these realities was a key factor in British politics and foreign policy before 1914. Historians have devoted much attention to nationalism's challenge to empire in early twentieth-century Europe. Their focus has been overwhelmingly on Eastern and Central Europe, however, not least because in this region the conflict between empire and nationalism is believed to have been one of the key causes of the outbreak of the First World War. But in the first half of 1914 the British Empire seemed in more immediate danger of collapsing than the Austrian one. This comment only sounds bizarre because the Irish crisis is generally seen as domestic rather than imperial. In one sense this was the case. It was extremely important for both British and Irish political development that what had been in many respects England's oldest colony was integrated into the United Kingdom in 1801.

Nevertheless the Irish crisis of 1911–14 was very much an imperial crisis too, and above all in the eyes of much of the British ruling elite and of the Conservative Party. A number of factors drove the Conservative leadership to take an extremely radical stance on Irish Home Rule, which included inciting (or at least condoning) armed resistance in Ulster and mutiny in the British Army's officer corps. Tactical calculations and party politics, as always, mattered. Anger at losing three elections in a row was probably increased by the fact that after the Liberal Unionist secession in the mid 1880s the great majority of the old ruling classes now backed the Conservatives. But what mattered above all was the fear that Home Rule in Ireland would be the beginning of the disintegration of the British Empire and therefore of Britain's global power. This insight was by no means necessarily wrong. When trying to understand why it was that hopes and fears about empire drove supposedly conservative German and Austrian elites into dangerously radical policies in July 1914, the comparison with the British elite's handling of the Irish issue is illuminating. What it illustrates above all is that for many Europeans, and especially elite Europeans, empire was the most important issue in international politics at that time.

Before 1914, London faced a crisis of empire both domestically and in Europe. The self-regulating European balance of power was crucial both to the security of the United Kingdom and to the maintenance of its

---

[1] Rohrbach's views are discussed in Fischer 1967.

empire. Among contemporary historians John Darwin is the outstanding exponent of this reality. Because the continental powers usually balanced each other and had a big vested interest in stopping the rise of any would-be hegemon, Britain did not need to invest enormous resources to defend its security in Europe. A coalition of continental powers against it was unlikely since these powers were rivals. Meanwhile no single power was likely to have the resources both to challenge British maritime supremacy and guard its own land frontiers. Unlike almost all their European counterparts, British young men were not conscripted. By the historical standards of empire, Britain played a very low price in terms of both blood and treasure for global hegemony between 1815 and 1914. That, in turn, made it easier for a small island both to run a global empire and to sustain the costs of democracy. The growing strength of Germany threatened the foundations of British global power but in the two decades before 1914 the British showed they had the economic resources, political will, and diplomatic skill to check Germany's advance. Unfortunately for all concerned, Germany refused to be checked.

By British standards the German polity established in 1871 was always a strange kind of empire. In the first place, unlike the United Kingdom, it actually called itself an empire (*Reich*). This title had little to do with notions of imperialism current in Victorian parlance or contemporary scholarship, however. As the ruler of a polity with three other royal houses (Bavaria, Saxony, and Württemberg) the King of Prussia had to be something more than merely royal. The word *empire* also established the new polity's credentials as heir to the tradition of the Holy Roman Empire. But this was explicitly stated to be not the feeble Reich of the last few centuries, but rather the realm of the medieval Hohenstaufens, which Prusso-German nationalists saw as a would-be German nation-state killed off in its adolescent promise by papal conspiracy. The whole point of Bismarck's Reich was indeed that it was a limited national empire, not the embodiment of some vision of Greater Germany spreading across much of Central Europe. As Bismarck well knew, the latter would stir up the resentment of the other great powers and would create a German polity with a Catholic majority that the Prussian king and elites could not hope to manage.

In time, however, "empire" began to take on connotations alien to Bismarck's initial thinking. In part this was out of deference to the spirit of an increasingly imperialist era, the same spirit that made Disraeli proclaim Queen Victoria as Empress of India and persuaded the Japanese to translate their monarch's title as "emperor." In the late Victorian era, to be an empire was to be virile and to have a future among the great peoples of the world. To fail in the game of empire was inter alia to delegitimize the metropolitan polity, as the Italians and Spanish discovered after disasters against assorted Ethiopians, Americans and Moroccans. It was in this context that Germany acquired a colonial empire, but the pathetic German colonies did little for Germany's status and nothing for her power.

In principle a much more alluring German Empire beckoned in Europe where even in 1871, 24 million German-speakers lived outside the borders of the new German Empire. Initially a purely diplomatic move, the 1879 Austro-German alliance can to some extent, in retrospect, be seen as a first shy step in the direction of a German Mitteleuropa. Just as the twentieth-century Anglo-American strategic alliance was buttressed by ethno-linguistic and ideological solidarity, so too in time was the alliance of Europe's Germanic powers. But before 1914 Germany's rulers were in no coherent sense planning to build an empire in Eastern Europe. Germany's booming capitalism had global, not regional, interests and perspectives. The Germany about which schoolchildren were taught lay within the Reich's borders. Only after the war began did clear, though actually often contradictory, thoughts emerge about Mitteleuropa or an empire in the East. The concrete plans based on these thoughts depended greatly on the ebb and flow of military operations. Not before Hitler's time were these thoughts turned into a single coherent imperialist program. He, of course, took the merger of ethnic and imperial identity to its logical extreme, though he added to it elements which were alien even to the most ruthless variant of pre-1914 imperialism.

All this bears directly on Michael Mann's chapter about nationalism and the origins of the two world wars. He argues that decisions for war were taken by tiny elites, with the masses and their sentiments barely counting. It is true that (as is usually the case) the key decisions were made by a handful of men, in Germany as elsewhere, in the summer of 1914. Moreover, in 1914 Germany was not a democracy. Those parties that stood for democracy but were largely excluded from power were certainly more peace-loving than the country's rulers or the political groups from which the latter drew support. Nevertheless, nationalism did have a mass base in Germany and, as wartime developments showed, even much of the leadership and following of the SPD (Sozialdemokratische Partei Deutschlands) was by no means entirely immune to its calls. As for the Reich's leaders, to varying degrees they used nationalism as a means to consolidate support for the regime. Bülow in particular made a successful foreign policy the core of his domestic political strategy. To an extent he sought to emulate eighteenth-century Britain where support for the newly united kingdom and its aristocratic rulers was enhanced by a brilliantly successful strategy of overseas colonial and commercial expansion. But there was more to German foreign policy than an attempt to manipulate domestic political interests. There was a strong sense in much of German society, and above all among German elites, that their polity deserved to play a leading role in the world, and it was widely assumed in this era that only empire offered this possibility. Nevertheless, in most cases conceptions of empire and *Weltpolitik* were incoherent. Frustration at the constraints placed on Germany by the European balance of power was not matched by a clear conception of how to break out of it. Moreover, among the handful of key decision-makers in July 1914 the sense that the world's future belonged to empire also had a distinctly pessimistic element to it. Part of their reason for choosing war in 1914 was the conviction that Germany had some chance of winning the inevitable struggle between empires now but none at all in a decade's time given the rapid growth of Russia's potentially overwhelming power.

Once the war began, the basic rules of European geopolitics kicked in. From the sixteenth century onwards it was always easier to build European empires beyond Europe than within it. That is why Europe's greatest empires tended to have their cores on the continent's periphery. Within Europe, expansion almost inevitably raised up against the potential hegemon a coalition of states whose military-fiscal systems had been honed by the constant competition between the European great powers. In these circumstances it was difficult but possible for a would-be European emperor to conquer the Carolingian core of Europe, in other words France, Germany, the Low Countries, and northern Italy. Even if he achieved this, the emperor then faced two formidable centers of power on Europe's periphery: one across the Channel in Britain and the other in the Great Russian heartland. These two peripheral power centers were likely to gang up against the heir of Charlemagne because his strength was a standing threat to their security and ambitions. To mobilize sufficient resources from Europe's Carolingian core to take on the British and Russians simultaneously was very difficult, not least because different types of power were needed. In the British case one required naval strength, in the Russian a military-logistical potential that would enable a European emperor to reach and hold the heartland of Russian power east and south of Moscow. Napoleon and Hitler both fell foul of this geopolitical conundrum.

Nevertheless, the challenge facing the would-be European emperor was very difficult but not in principle impossible. Russia and Britain might fail to gang up on him, out of foolishness, mistrust, or the desire to leave the burden of resisting Germany to others. This scenario happened in the 1930s, and Michael Mann is right to cite British distrust of Soviet communism as one of its causes. A second possibility was that the British and Russians might gang up on him and one or other might then be defeated, as happened to Russia in 1917.

In principle both in the 1900s and in the 1930s Russia had two options when faced by German power and expansionism. Either she could unite with France and Britain and hope thereby to deter German aggression, or she could seek to encourage German expansion westwards, hoping that the struggle would last for a long period, during which Russia might be left in peace to develop its own potentially enormous resources. In 1914 a number of leading conservative figures in Russia, headed by Peter Durnovo, begged Nicholas II to adopt the latter option, warning him that if he failed to do so the inevitable war with Germany would probably bring about socialist revolution and the total destruction of the existing Russian social order.[2] Instead the emperor chose to follow the advice of those advisors who urged that alliance with the French and British would probably deter the Germans and that a deal with Berlin would fatally undermine Russian security. The result for Russia was a catastrophe, in which world war was followed by civil war, famine, and terror.

In 1939, facing the same dilemma as Nicholas II, Stalin chose the alternative option. He no doubt did so in part because of a justified fear that if he ganged up with London and Paris they would leave him to do most of the fighting. Like Durnovo he believed that war between the Germans and the Western allies would last a generation. To the surprise of not just Stalin but also of French, British, and most German generals Hitler knocked France out of the war in six weeks and at minimal cost, leaving Russia in the same situation that Alexander I had faced in 1811 when forced to confront, without effective allies, an enemy who could mobilize the resources of all of Europe against him. Hitler's stupidity helped Soviet Russia to survive his onslaught, but at appalling cost. The moral of the story is not that Nicholas II acted foolishly in 1914 or that Stalin was necessarily wrong to act as he did in 1939. The key point is that for the Russians the choices were very uncertain and the stakes terrifyingly high.

In 1917–18 Russia was defeated, though mostly as a result of internal political collapse rather than military failure. In principle this provided Wilhelm II with a real possibility to become Europe's true hegemon.

---

[2] Peter Nikolaevich Durnovo was the tsarist elite at its toughest but also most intelligent. He served as head of the Police Department until 1893 and as Minister of Internal Affairs in 1905–06 and was more responsible than any other individual for the successful repression of the 1905 revolution. Subsequently he headed the Right (i.e. most conservative group) in the State Council, Russia's upper house under the constitutional regime.

The winter of 1916–17 was a key moment in modern history. Had German miscalculation not brought the USA into the war at the very moment when revolution was beginning the disintegration of Russian power, a real opportunity would have opened up for German hegemony in Europe. On their own the French and British could never have defeated Russia or reversed the Treaty of Brest-Litovsk, which confirmed the disintegration of the Russian Empire and laid the foundations for German domination of Eastern Europe. Of course, foundations are not the same as buildings. Where the creation of empires is concerned, military conquest is often easier than political consolidation. In 1919–22 the British had considerable difficulty and some failures in regard to consolidating their empire in Ireland, Iraq, and elsewhere, despite the fact that they had no local rival powers with which to contend and much experience of rule in these areas. The Germans had a harder task on both counts in Eastern Europe. Their empire-building strategy would have needed to show more coherence and guile than had been the norm in German government since Bismarck's demise. Nevertheless, the possibility of pan-European hegemony was there: a Germany that dominated all of Mitteleuropa and Russia's former borderlands (especially Ukraine) possessed potentially overwhelming power.

The case of Russia in 1917 also offers an insight into one key element of Michael Mann's chapter: the extent to which nationalism motivated soldiers. He asks why soldiers fought in the two world wars, so it is interesting to think about why many Russian soldiers refused to do so in 1917. Lack of nationalist spirit was very far from the only issue but it probably was salient. Peasants called up to serve against Napoleon in general held to a traditional Orthodox and monarchist conception of legitimate authority. They also entered a professional army whose scaffolding of veteran cadres and regimental loyalties was never destroyed. The Russia and the army of 1914–17 were very different. Modernity had invaded the villages and was changing peasant mentalities. As important, the old army cadres had largely been destroyed in 1914–15. The officer corps of 1915–17 was very mixed both in its origins and in its loyalties. The army of 1915–17 was in fact a species of militia. In the absence of the old army's regimental spirit this new army needed a sense of nationhood and citizenship. Tsarist Russia did not provide that to peasants before 1914. The country was too poor and too vast to create an educational system capable of inculcating the regime's version of Russian patriotism into the peasantry. Nor (correctly) did the government trust most Russian teachers to do this.

In addition, however, in comparison to 1812 or 1941–43 the tsarist regime in the First World War was the victim of its own relative "success." Both Napoleon and Hitler invaded the heart of Great Russia, causing huge destruction and thereby making it easier to mobilize Russian patriotism against them. It was harder in the First World War to motivate peasant soldiers fighting in Lithuania and Western Ukraine to die for the rights of Serbia and for the European balance of power. This was particularly true as the war dragged on and final victory seemed so distant. In February 1917, Russia had been fighting for two and a half years. Victory was still not in sight. Less than two years after Napoleon invaded Russia in 1812 the Russian army reached Paris. Thirty months after Hitler invaded the Soviet Union there remained much terrible fighting to eradicate Nazi Germany. But Stalingrad and Kursk had already happened and confidence in final victory was strong.

The chapters of John Darwin and Michael Mann discuss issues of empire and ethnicity, nationalism and war. Their focus is on problems of geopolitics and political identity in what one might describe as the first era of Anglophone liberal globalization, in other words, the years between 1850 and 1939. To what extent do their chapters and the questions raised in my own chapter remain relevant today, in the midst of a significant crisis in the second era of liberal globalization, this time led by the United States?

It seems to me that much of what has been written about geopolitics and imperial ethnic identity remains very relevant. The British and German imperial projects failed, above all, because Europe was a poor geopolitical base for empire but also because the British and Germans fatally wounded each other's imperial projects. But imperial power merely departed to other continents where traditionally no balance of power existed and continental-scale hegemony was much easier. The immediate successors of the European empires were the United States and Soviet Russia, fulfilling de Tocqueville's prophecy. In 1991 the Soviet Union collapsed, partly because its version of imperial ethnicity lost its hold on the population. A key point here was that Soviet imperial identity was closely entwined with the attempt to create a successful socialist modernity and suffered badly when the latter's failure became apparent. After a brief interlude when the United States seemed to aspire to global hegemony, potential rival regional hegemons came over the horizon in the shape of China and India. None of these three countries are empires in the traditional sense, but nor are they nations as these were envisaged by nineteenth-century European nationalists. As with John Darwin's British imperial example, to flourish and to sustain their power these polities needed to create political identities and loyalties of continental scale.

So much has been written in recent years on the United States as empire that one hesitates to join the fray. A key reason why the United

States is a nation rather than an empire is because that is what most Americans always imagined it to be. Nor was this just a matter of imagination. Immigrants became citizens, not subjects. Territories became states, not colonies. But the USA is a peculiar and imperial nation, partly because of its continental scale and resources, and partly because American identity is nowadays rooted in ideology rather than ethnicity. That ideology is in principle universal, and the contemporary United States is increasingly like the chameleon, able to present itself in various ethno-racial colours to the outside observer. No potential rival can do this and in that sense the USA is a more plausible global hegemon than any other twentieth-century polity. It remains to be seen whether the American polity will be able to mobilize and channel sufficient resources in sufficiently coherent and intelligent fashion to meet the external challenges of the coming decades. This always was and will remain the key test of any imperial polity.

China appears to be a likelier empire than the United States. It is the heir to the oldest and greatest continuous imperial lineage on earth. Like almost all historical empires, the People's Republic of China(PRC) is not a democracy. It rules over a range of often dissatisfied non-Chinese subjects, who although only 6 percent of the total population, live in vast territories containing much of China's energy and raw materials. It holds almost all the territories conquered by the Qing and claims the rest. But a comparison with the Qing polity shows why contemporary China is not an empire. The Qing gloried in the fact that they conquered and ruled a range of peoples. They kept these peoples apart, using this effectively as a system of government. Manchu and Chinese balanced each other, and the emperor presented a different face and legitimacy to Manchu, Mongol, Han Chinese and Lamaist Buddhists. He alone was the sovereign. Typically, too, of pre-modern polities, the Qing bureaucracy was tiny by contemporary standards and penetrated shallowly into Chinese society. There is a strong contrast with the contemporary PRC, which uses a modern bureaucracy to inculcate a common national language and political identity into its people. China is more of a nation than an empire. Nations differ greatly, however, and it is the ingredients of a specific national identity that matter most because they will largely determine how it acts. Given its power and its historical identity China is likely to be a distinctly imperial nation.

The obvious comparison is between Germany's role in the first era of liberal globalization and China's in the second. In both cases the rise of a potential challenger creates fears, temptations, and insecurities on all sides. Power pervades almost all international relationships. As it shifts, many established norms and expectations are threatened. Nerves jingle.

In some respects it ought to be harder to integrate China into the current era of liberal globalization than was the case with Germany. The traditions and values of Protestant Germany were not that far removed from those of the Anglo-Saxons. There is in principle a bigger gap between Chinese and American values. Integrating China into the commanding heights of contemporary globalization reverses three centuries of Western domination. On the other hand, Germany dreamed of conquering continents, whereas China already rules over one. In principle it is much closer to being a satiated power. But as in the late nineteenth century, technology creates temptations for expansion. The ability to exploit the seabed leads to conflicts over East Asian islands and seabeds in a way that would never have occurred in previous generations. To the extent that energy and other resources begin to shrink, these conflicts can only get worse.

China seeks to join liberal globalization, not to destroy it. Imperial Germany was similar and benefited at least as much from liberal globalization before 1914 as China does now. In July 1914 the Russian minister of finance could not believe that Berlin would risk destroying an international economic order from which it gained so much and through which it had become the leading economic power in Europe. The First World War hugely damaged liberal globalization, but it partly recovered after 1918 and only perished in the 1930s. To an extent the collapse of the global financial system was owed to shifts in global power: the British no longer had the means to control in pre-1914 style and a Washington dominated by Middle America's representatives lacked the will or the knowledge to do so. At that point closed trading blocs and political direction of economies became rational, even essential. The British Empire was more important as an economic unit in 1930–50 than at any time since the early nineteenth century. In a scenario in which the contemporary world economy followed the downward curve of the 1930s, a similar logic would begin to obtain. Unlike in 1929, however, the crisis of liberal capitalist globalization would not come at a time when anti-liberal ideologies were already in power in two major European countries.

Of the topics touched on by John Darwin and Michael Mann, war is probably the one in which most has changed since 1900. Empire and war are closely linked. Wars largely determined the rise and fall of empires. Military power was at empire's core. As already noted, the rulers of great powers before 1914 put much effort into thinking about war and preparing their citizens to fight it. Berlin's decision for war in 1914 was wholly irrational in economic terms. For a polity that saw the promotion of the individual citizen's life and prosperity as its highest duty, such a decision was absurd and evil. But few empires thought this way, and in purely imperial and geopolitical terms Germany's decision was risky but not wholly illogical. This was a world in which it was still possible to believe Clausewitz's view that war was the pursuit of politics by other means. Victory in war could be meaningful. Even in 1939 Hitler was rightly convinced that only war could secure the world power he sought for Germany. Trying to sort out the crazy from the merely evil in Hitler's mind goes well beyond the terms of this chapter, but in the era of nuclear weapons it would clearly require a degree of insanity to apply Clausewitz's reasoning to relations between nuclear-armed great powers. Of course miscalculation and risk taking could still bring catastrophe, but a cold-blooded option for nuclear war as an element of grand strategy seems barely credible when faced with other nuclear states. Given the catastrophic suffering and chaotic consequences of the two world wars it is of course hugely reassuring that the chances of all-out war between great powers have been so reduced.

That is especially the case given the scale of the problems likely to face us in the near to medium future. These include a shift in the global balance of power; the proliferation of nuclear weapons, and the risk even that other weapons of mass destruction could find their way into private hands; the radical impact of globalization on societies in both the First and Third Worlds, including the hollowing-out of part of the middle class in many First World societies; the fragility of some of the financial and commercial systems that underpin liberal globalization; the probability of intensified competition for shrinking resources, above all water, in some regions of the world; and the looming threat of ecological crisis. There is no certainty that any of today's great powers will be able to rise to these challenges, which together pose a major threat to the existing global order.

REFERENCE

Fischer, F. 1967. *Germany's Aims in the First World War*. London: Chatto & Windus.

9   Is nationalism the cause or consequence of the end of empire?

Wesley Hiers and Andreas Wimmer

This chapter addresses the question of whether and to what degree nationalism was the cause or the consequence of imperial collapse. We go about this task in four steps. The first three steps use quantitative data that cover most of the world since 1816. In the first step, we simply analyze the temporal relationship between the transition from empire to nation-state and the foundation of nationalist organizations. We find that in the overwhelming majority, the latter precedes the former. We then proceed to a more fine-grained analysis and ask whether these nationalist organizations were perhaps inspired by imperial retreat from other parts of the empire, such that a partial imperial breakdown would further fuel the flames of nationalism elsewhere. No such effect emerges, however. In the third step, we determine whether nationalist mobilization is a cause for the individual transitions from empire to nation-state observed in the history of today's countries and find this to be the case, even if we take a host of other factors into account (including the weakening of empire through wars).

In the fourth and most important step, we go beyond these coarse quantitative analyses and shift to empires as units of analysis, asking to what degree nationalism caused imperial collapse. Discussing the demise of the Ottoman, Habsburg, French, British, Portuguese and Soviet empires, we assess the varying degrees to which nationalist movements contributed to each imperial collapse and the extent to which each transition was due to other, unrelated factors, including the voluntary retreat of empire or the breakdown of empire due to defeat in international wars. We find that in all cases of imperial collapse nationalist movements played an important, and sometimes, crucial role (for the opposing view, see Betts 1991; Burbank and Cooper 2010; Flint 1983; Sked 2001; Solnick 1998). There is little evidence – with a handful of exceptions such as the Central Asian republics and some African countries – for the idea that imperial breakdown produces nationalist movements or nation-states without a previous agitation for them. We conclude that the rise and global proliferation of nationalist movements has been a crucial factor in reshaping the structure of the state system over the past two hundred years.

Nationalism and the shift from empire to nation-state: some quantitative evidence

We first evaluate the temporal order of the relationship between nationalism and the dissolution of empires. If nationalism was indeed a significant cause of imperial breakdown, it should emerge beforehand. If imperial breakdown produces nationalist movements, the reverse should hold, at least if we follow traditional Humean notions of causality. While certainly crude, such an analysis can take advantage of a global data set that stretches over long periods of time. The following graph is based on the data set assembled for Wimmer and Feinstein (2010). The data set takes today's countries as units of observation and traces developments in these units back in time to 1816. Thus, the data set has "Bosnia" or "Ivory Coast" as units, though Bosnia and Ivory Coast did not exist as independent states in 1816. This data set contains two variables that are of interest for the present purpose.

The first variable indicates the year of the foundation of the first national organization, defined as a formal institution (rather than a loosely organized movement or the following of a political leader) that claims to represent the population (or a segment thereof) of a territory. In other words, it represents the first year in which the nation of one of today's countries was "imagined" by a significant group of people, to use Anderson's (1991) well-known formulation. This variable is obviously less than ideal for investigating the relationship between nationalism and nation-state formation because it contains no information on the relative political power of nationalists – their organizational strength, internal unity, or external alliance partners – or on the diffusion of nationalist frames of meaning and political demands among the population at large – the degree to which such frames and demands have been adopted and taken for granted by peasants, merchants, townspeople, army officers, clergymen, and so forth (see Hroch 2000 [1969]). On the other hand, information on the year of the foundation of a national organization can be traced very precisely and for all territories of the world. Investigating whether the shift to national modes of imagining community – independent of its political power and degree of diffusion – precedes or follows imperial breakdown represents a first step that we then will complement with a more refined analysis of the shift in the balance of power between nationalists and the old regime that opens the path toward independent nation-statehood.

The second variable of interest is the year of the transition from empire to nation-state. More precisely, we coded the year of adoption of a constitution that stipulated a nationally defined group of equal citizens as the sovereign in the name of which the state should be ruled – in contrast to rule in the name of God, dynastic succession, and the like. This second variable thus conforms to the point in time when an empire had lost control over a territory and national sovereignty was achieved. Given that the following analysis focuses on territories that were once controlled by empires, we are less concerned with the more gradual transitions to nation-statehood such as in the case of Britain or Sweden, which obviously do not conform as well to an event-year coding. In the overwhelming majority of former imperial domains, the transition to nation-statehood took the form of a political rupture – such as a declaration of independence, or the assembly of a constitutional convention – that can be located clearly in the flow of calendar time. Note also that the units of observation in this analysis are territories, not polities, and that we code the mode of political control (imperial, nation-state, etc.) for each of them separately. The British Empire (a polity) is thus composed of territories ruled as a nation-state (Britain) and as imperial dependencies (eg. Ghana).[1]

Figure 9.1 relates these two moments in history to each other. It is based on data for 135 of today's countries that were ever part of an empire, thus excluding countries such as Switzerland, Japan, Afghanistan, or Thailand. It also does not contain information on small states such as the island states in the Caribbean (eg. Saint Lucia) or Pacific (Samoa). On the x axis, we plot the years before or after the transition out of empire has been made. The year 0 on this axis thus refers to different points in chronological time: 1991 for Bosnia, but 1832 for Belgium. On the y axis the percentage of territories that had already developed a national organization is shown. The results are straightforward: the overwhelming majority of territories developed nationalism before the dissolution of empire and their transition to national sovereignty. The exceptions are Honduras, El Salvador, Nicaragua, Costa Rica, Panama, Bolivia, Romania, Bulgaria, and Albania. In relation to the Central American republics, this is because the national movements that did indeed exist before the dissolution of the Central American Republic were largely informal and consisted of the followers of various *caudillos*, rather than well-defined organizations with formal membership and leadership structures. The same goes for the former Ottoman domains in Europe.

---

[1] For more detail on data and definitions, see the online appendix to Wimmer and Min 2006.

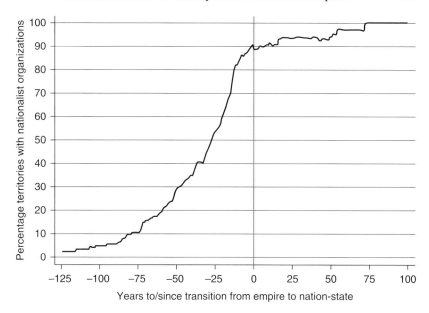

Figure 9.1 Timing of nationalism and the transition to the nation-state for 135 of today's countries, 1816–2005

Is it possible, however, that these national organizations did not appear independently of one other, but rather emerged in response to the success of nationalism in one part of the empire (where "success" means the end of imperial rule and the establishment of an independent nation-state), which then inspired provincial elites elsewhere in the empire to adopt the national template themselves? In this diffusionist version of the empire-to-nationalism argument, imperial breakdown in one part of the empire produces nationalism in other parts of the empire. Rather than a cause of imperial breakdown, nationalism is at least in part its consequence. We evaluate this argument with slightly more advanced statistical techniques.

In Table 9.1, the foundation of a national organization is the dichotomous dependent variable (0 if none was founded in a particular territory during a particular year, 1 if the first organization was indeed founded). We use logistic regression, i.e. we evaluate whether increasing the values of independent variables makes the foundation of a national organization more likely. The analysis includes a series of key variables that may account for the emergence of organized nationalism. While a full account of the rise of nationalism is beyond the scope and focus of this chapter, we need to take these other political forces into account when assessing the role of partial imperial breakdowns. These other variables are indeed

Table 9.1 *Explaining the foundation of national organizations, 1816–2005 (logit analysis)*

	Model 1	Model 2	Model 3	Model 4
% of territories in empire that are already nation-states	−0.01 (0.012)			
Total no. of territories in empire that are already nation-states		−0.05 (0.036)		
No. of nation-states created in the empire during past 5 years			−0.04 (0.087)	
No. of nation-states created in the empire during past 10 years				−0.16 (0.090)
No. of nationalist wars of liberation in the empire in previous year	0.52** (0.132)	0.54** (0.128)	0.51** (0.132)	0.58** (0.124)
Size of the largest ethnic group in country (1996)	1.00* (0.416)	1.01* (0.411)	0.99* (0.412)	1.02* (0.407)
% of adult population that is literate	0.02** (0.005)	0.02** (0.005)	0.02** (0.005)	0.02** (0.005)
No. of national organizations founded among neighbors in past 5 years	0.50** (0.181)	0.47* (0.182)	0.50** (0.181)	0.46** (0.179)
Time controls (natural cubic splines) and size of the territory	Yes	Yes	Yes	Yes
Number of observations	12,004	12,004	12,004	12,004
Number of territories	124	124	124	124

Notes: Robust standard errors in parentheses. ** $p < 0.01$, * $p < 0.05$

significantly associated with the emergence of nationalism, as Table 9.1 shows: the size of the largest ethnic group in the country (which according to Anthony Smith [1986] should make it easier to transform existing ethnic memories into modern nationalist doctrines), literacy rates (which relate to Anderson's [1991] theory of nationalism as a product of the rise of literacy in vernacular languages), and regional diffusion effects (nationalism in one territory inspiring nationalism in neighboring territories). We also add three control variables: two for the passing of chronological time and one for the geographic size of a territory.

The imperial-collapse-causes-nationalism argument is evaluated with four different variables: In Model 1, we measure the percentage of imperial territories that have already transitioned to the nation-state. In Model 2, it is the absolute number of such territories. In Models 3 and 4, we evaluate the effects of the number of nation-state creations within an imperial domain over the past five or ten years respectively, thus moving to a more dynamic analysis. Nevertheless, however we code partial imperial collapse, there is no statistically significant association with the likelihood of the foundation of a national organization in a territory. We conclude that there is no evidence for a partial-imperial-breakdown argument, at least not on the level of these coarse statistical analyses.

We do find, however, that the number of nationalist wars of liberation fought in the empire significantly affects the likelihood that a national organization is founded. It seems that independent of the outcome – whether these wars of liberation succeed in establishing new nation-states – they inspire nationalists in other parts of the empire. This, however, represents a diffusion of nationalism effect, not a partial imperial breakdown effect. The same goes for the number of nationalisms founded in neighboring territories, which also significantly affects the likelihood of nationalism's emergence in a given territory. Nationalism thus spreads among neighbors and also within empires that experience wars of national liberation widely publicized and followed in the entire imperial domain.

In the third step of analysis, we seek to answer the question of whether nationalism was indeed a force that propelled the transition from empire to nation-state on individual territories. Can we show that nationalism was responsible for a successful breakaway from empire? Or was it the case that although it preceded imperial retreat, as shown above, nationalism was largely irrelevant for the process of nation-state formation itself? Some of our preceding work (Wimmer and Feinstein 2010) answered this question as part of a global analysis of all transitions to nation-statehood. Here, we limit our purview again to territories that had ever been under imperial rule, and we offer some more fine-grained analysis of the role of nationalism in this process. In the following statistical analysis, the dependent variable is whether a territory shifted from empire to nation-state in a given year. We test three possible causal effects of nationalism on the transition from empire to nation-state, one direct and two indirect.

The direct effect is two-pronged, encompassing both the emergence and the increasing strength of nationalism. In order to test for a direct effect, we can evaluate whether the temporal sequence uncovered in Figure 9.1 is causally relevant when assessed within the framework of a multivariate analysis that also takes other factors into account: does the emergence and increasing strength of nationalism still explain nation-state formation? The first part of this conjecture refers to a simple temporal sequence. If a territory already saw the formation of national organizations (expressed by a simple, dichotomous variable of whether or not this was the case), nation-state formation should be more likely to follow. A slightly more demanding, second part of this analysis hypothesizes that the likelihood of transitioning out of empire depends on the strength of nationalism. As discussed above, we do not have reliable and traceable data on the political appeal and power of nationalist movements. Collecting such data for the entire world would represent a formidable task. For the time being, we assume that nationalists who had more time to mobilize the population and organize followers should be politically more powerful – assuming a monotonic increase in the strength of nationalism over time. We measure the duration/strength of nationalist mobilization with a simple year count since the establishment of the first national organization, which should increase the likelihood of a transition to the nation-state. Since we also include a "dummy" variable (coded 0 or 1) relating to the presence or absence of national organizations, this year count variable is independent of and in addition to the effect that the mere presence or absence of nationalism has on the likelihood of nation-state creation. It is also independent of the mere passage of chronological time, which is again captured by adding time control variables to the model.

These two variables (emergence and duration) together relate to a direct effect of nationalism on the transition from empire to nation-state. We can also envision two indirect effects: the consequences of nationalism and nation-state formation taking place in *other* parts of the empire and therefore not directly linked to the nationalist struggle on a specific territory. The first of these indirect effects refers to the role of war in the transition from empire to nation-state. Are nationalist wars of liberation in other parts of the empire, which as we saw above inspired the creation of nationalist organizations across an imperial domain, also a relevant factor that helps explain when a territory manages to break away from imperial rule and become a sovereign nation-state? Do such wars fought by other nationalists absorb the military and political energy of the imperial center enough to make it easier to escape imperial rule and successfully declare national sovereignty? Or do we find evidence supporting the realist view that the transition to nation-statehood is a consequence of imperial breakdown in the wake of great power wars that are unrelated to nationalism? We evaluate these two hypotheses with two count variables, one relating to ongoing nationalist wars of liberation fought in other parts of the empire and the other to all non-nationalist wars in the imperial domain.

The second indirect effect occurs when nation-states are created in other parts of the empire. This weakens the center by making the imperial project appear less feasible and by reducing the relative power of the empire as a whole, such that nationalists can more easily get rid of what they portray as the imperial yoke. We try to capture this second indirect role of nationalism in the creation of nation-states by measuring the number of previous nation-state formations within the same imperial domain over the past five years (other time windows produce very similar results).

As in the previous analysis, we include other control variables that according to our previous research also affect the likelihood of nation-state creation. For the present context, these additional factors are less theoretically interesting; we include them for control purposes only. First, a weak international standing of the imperial center, measured by its share of global military and economic power, will make a transition from empire to nation-state more likely. Second, the previous creation of nation-states in the neighborhood (but outside of the imperial domain) will spur nation-state creation on a territory, for a variety of possible reasons. Finally, wars fought on a territory itself, whether related to the nationalist project or not, will again weaken the grip of the imperial center and make transitioning into nation-statehood easier.[2] Table 9.2 presents the results.

Table 9.2 shows that the likelihood of nation-state creation depends not only on the existence of national organizations on a territory (as already suggested by Figure 9.1), but also on the duration of nationalist mobilization, which we interpret as a rough proxy for the strength of nationalist mobilizations. Besides this direct and unequivocal effect of nationalism on the transition from empire to nation-state, Table 9.2 also shows that the two indirect effects discussed above are at work: nationalist wars of independence fought in other parts of the empire increase the probability of nation-state creation, and the more territories that have broken away from the empire to form sovereign nation-states, the more likely it is that remaining territories are undergoing this transition as well. Nationalist mobilization in other parts of the empire, whether in the form of an ongoing war of "national liberation" or in the form of a successful project of nation-state creation, thus indirectly enhances the prospects of further nation-state creation.

There is thus considerable evidence for the causal role of nationalism in bringing about the nation-state, both directly and indirectly. The results reported in Table 9.2, however, also support a "great power war" argument of nation-state creation: non-nationalist wars fought in the empire also significantly increase the chances of nation-state creation. As additional analysis shows, these results are mostly (but not exclusively) brought about by World War I and the collapse of the Ottoman

---

[2] Previous research (Wimmer and Feinstein 2010) has shown that none of the well-known modernization arguments are supported by quantitative analysis: neither industrialization (proxied by railroad length), nor mass literacy in vernacular languages (proxied by adult literacy rates), nor the shift from indirect to direct rule (proxied by government expenditures per capita) affect the likelihood of nation-state creation in significant ways.

Table 9.2 *The transition from empire to nation-state, 1816–2005 (logit analysis)*

Existence of a national organization on the territory	1.06**
	(0.355)
Years since the foundation of first national organization in the territory	0.01*
	(0.003)
No. of nation-states created in last 5 years within empire	0.12**
	(0.035)
No. of nationalist wars of independence fought on other territories of the empire	0.25**
	(0.068)
No. of non-nationalist wars fought on other territories of the empire	0.30**
	(0.077)
No. of nation-states created in past 5 years in the neighborhood	0.54**
	(0.130)
Center's share of global military and economic power	−3.28*
	(1.506)
No. of wars fought on the territory	0.47*
	(0.189)
Time controls (cubic splines) and Continental dummies	Yes
Number of observations	15,469
Number of territories	127

Notes: Robust standard errors in parentheses. ** $p<0.01$, * $p<0.05$

and Habsburg empires. We thus conclude that while important, great power wars are neither the sole nor the most important drivers of the process of nation-state formation. Nationalist movements, wars of liberation, and the weakening of empire through preceding nationalist breakaways play a crucial role in the transition from empire to nation-state.

Nationalism and imperial collapse: assessing the historical evidence

The preceding analysis helps to rule out that nationalism is the consequence of imperial breakdown. If this were true, nationalism would historically develop *after* such breakdown or it would at least be the consequence of imperial retreat in other parts of the empire. We further demonstrated that the duration of nationalist mobilization and agitation helps to explain the successful breakaway from empire, and that the weakening of empire by previous nation-state formations or nationalist wars of liberation in other parts of the empire further promote the creation of nation-states.

However, it may still be that nationalism is only a minor force in the collapse of the overall imperial structure. Nationalism might profit, as shown above, from the weakening of empire brought about by other political forces, such as the great power wars lost by empires or the nationalist wars of liberation fought elsewhere in the empire. But does nationalism play a role in the final demise of empire itself? Or is this imperial breakdown entirely due either to military defeat in great power wars or to the abandonment of the imperial project by its center – not under the pressure of nationalist movements, but because of geopolitical reasons that made holding on to empire unattractive? To evaluate this argument, we now shift the analysis away from the question of what makes nation-state formation more likely on a particular territory and toward an assessment of the causes of imperial breakdown: how important have nationalist movements been for the collapse of empire? Obviously enough, the units of analysis for answering this question need to be empires, not their individual dependencies as in the previous analysis. Statistical tools are therefore less suited to answer this question, since the number of empires is too small to allow for meaningful quantitative analysis. In what follows, we therefore proceed through qualitative historical analysis and answer this question for each of the major empires separately. For the sake of space, we leave out the Spanish Empire as well as the smaller Dutch, Japanese, Italian, Belgian, and German colonial empires.

The Habsburg Empire

The role of nationalism in the demise of the Austro-Hungarian Empire during World War I has been sharply contested. As Mason observes, "[t]he nationality question stands at the center of the historical controversy over the causes of the downfall of the Habsburg Monarchy" (1997: 88). According to Himka, for several decades leading up to and including World War I, "the nationality problem dominated, transformed, and contributed to the destruction of the Empire," an interpretation that has many adherents in the literature (Himka 1992: 80; see also Jászi 1961; Kann 1977; Okey 2001; Stone 1966; Taylor 1965; Wank 1997a; Wank 1997b; Zeman 1961).

Other scholars, however, offer a mostly war-centric view of the empire's collapse. Sked (2001) argues that after some problems linked to ethnic nationalism in the middle decades of the nineteenth century, the empire recovered and was stable by the eve of World War I. Many nation-states emerged from the empire's collapse, but it was the war, not nationalism, that caused this collapse, according to Sked. Burbank and Cooper agree and observe that "[t]he different 'nations' within the Austro-Hungarian Empire in 1914 did not take war as an opportunity to separate themselves" (2010: 363–64). In general, even the most radical within the empire did not advocate independence: "Surprisingly few of even the most fervent nationalists ... favored a formal dissolution of their joint community into its ethnic components, until the course of World War I induced them to espouse such a policy" (Rusinow 1992: 254). This is a point illustrated by Roshwald's (2001) discussion of the Czechs, who ultimately did play a key role in the Habsburg dissolution, but who did not display any overt nationalist agenda until 1917–18. Indeed, a coalition of the main Czech political parties rejected the Allies' January 1917 call for Czech national liberation. It was only after the Russian tsar's overthrow and US entry into the war in March/April of that year that the Czech party coalition shifted its position, first demanding self-government and then secession by 1918. Thus, in this geopolitical, "realist" interpretation, ethnonational identity's role in bringing down the empire was limited to the latter part of the war, a war that itself contributed to the politicization of ethnicity (Roshwald 2001: 90).

However, this great power war-centered view underestimates the role of ethnopolitics and nationalism in the empire's demise for the following three reasons. First, the great power war-centered view of the empire's demise indicates that World War I brought down the empire and sparked nationalism because the Allies strategically encouraged nationalist agitation. This argument obscures the degree to which, until World War I, the geopolitics of Europe acted as a stabilizer of the Habsburg Empire, including by suppressing the secessionist inclinations among its diverse populations. The Austro-Hungarian Empire was part of Europe's precarious balance of power. It acted as a buffer between East and West, and unlike the leaders of the Ottoman Empire, the Habsburg monarchy was Christian. Thus, any secessionist move within the empire would have meant staring down the barrel of not one gun – that of the formidable Habsburg army – but, at a minimum, two (that of the Germans also). Nationalists in the Ottoman Balkans had the blessings and aid of major European powers when they sought independence from the Ottoman Empire, but no such powerful allies were available to nationalists within the Habsburgs' domain. Rather than being the major geopolitical development of World War I that brought down a stable empire, therefore, it was geopolitics that for decades sustained an otherwise unstable empire (Bridge 1990; Kann 1977; Wank 1967). As will become clearer below, these ethno-national tensions were the main reason for the empire's instability. In this context, then, nationalism was a relevant force well before the war, but the nationalists were quite rationally non-secessionist. The Czech leader Thomas Masaryk explained his reformist, non-revolutionary approach just one year before the outbreak of the war that would prove him wrong: "[B]ecause I cannot indulge in dreams of its [the Habsburg Empire's] collapse and know that whether good or bad, it will continue, I am most deeply concerned that we should make something of this Austria" (quoted in Wank 1997b: 46).

To be sure, the above affirms that geopolitics were indeed crucial to the demise of the Habsburg Empire: as of the second decade of the twentieth century, nationalists alone could not have brought down the empire. But World War I in no sense created the empire's nationality problem – the second omission in the realist, great power war-centric school of thought. In fact, to treat World War I and the empire's nationality problem as altogether distinct is to ignore the intimate connection between them. The stability of the empire was foundering on growing separatism among its Slavic population, which itself was being promoted by the irredentist nationalism of Serbia. As noted by Mason, "after 1900 the growth of the South Slav movement made the nationality problem a foreign-policy question, which was only resolved by war in 1914" (Mason 1997: 62).

The driving factor behind the empire's decision to go to war with Serbia was that it "had failed to solve its internal problems," at the center of which was the Southern Slav question (Mason 1997: 69; see also Beller 2006; Himka 1992; Kann 1977; Mann 1993: Chapter 21; Okey 2001; Rusinow 1992; Stone 1966; Taylor 1965; Wank 1967). The German ambassador to the empire understood this well. He described the Habsburg elites thus: "They see with astonishment and anguish the sudden swelling of the Slav wave and on all lips is fluttering the anxious question, what will happen to Austria?" (quoted in Jászi 1961: 427). The ambassador himself was not optimistic, as the empire's internal structure did not seem fit to deliver what was required: "great wisdom and energy of the central government to maintain the centrifugal forces of the strongly developing Slav peoples ..." (quoted in Jászi 1961: 421–22). In this crucial respect, "the war was not an accident, of which the collapse of the Habsburg Empire was an unfortunate by-product; rather it was a symptom of the systemic crisis of the imperial structure" (Wank 1997c: 109).

Thus, while it was indeed World War I that caused the collapse of the Habsburg Empire, the empire's ethno-national problems were central to the process leading to its demise. This is the second reason why an entirely geopolitical interpretation of the empire's collapse is misleading. This point's relevance becomes all the more clear in light of the third one, which concerns how the long-term ethnic structure of the empire precluded a peaceful solution to the problems posed by the peripheral nationalism of the Slavic population. The Southern Slavs of the early twentieth century did not represent the Habsburg Empire's first major ethno-national problem; the Magyars of Hungary did. Out of war and conflict came the Compromise of 1867 (the *Ausgleich*), which accorded Hungary and thereby the Magyars considerable autonomy and prestige within the empire as a formally equal kingdom with its own parliament. Magyar nationalism had not reached beyond the nobility before 1844, but its reach became broader by the time of the Compromise, and it would become broader still (Jászi 1961; Sugar 1967). After the Compromise, "[t]he rulers of Hungary ... sought to create a nation-state on the Western European model – a state for the Magyar (Hungarian) nation" (Rusinow 1992: 255). These efforts included a full array of assimilation policies – Magyars were not quite 50 percent of the Hungarian population. Over time, "an ideology of independence" increasingly gained hold (Jászi 1961: 364). In the early years of the twentieth century, the head of Hungary's parliament, Count Tisza, could be found referring to the Austrian premier as a "distinguished foreigner," and the minister of public education (Count Apponyi) could be found approving a historical textbook "in which the Habsburg dynasty was portrayed as a foreign conqueror" (Jászi 1961: 364). The general relevance of such statements and policies came through during Hungary's constitutional crisis of 1905–06, which was sparked by the election of a coalition that denied the constitutionality of the 1867 compromise and demanded still greater autonomy within the empire and a more thoroughgoing adoption of Magyarization policies than what already prevailed in Hungary (Sugar 1981).

Thus, for at least the last half-century of the Habsburg Empire, a major portion of it was nationalizing within the imperial bosom. But the significance of Magyar nationalism goes well beyond this point. The power within the empire that the Magyars gained in 1867 by virtue of their own mobilization precluded this famously "multinational" empire from solving future ethno-national problems. Federation within the Austrian half of the empire was the most frequently considered reform to address such problems, but "[a]ny Habsburg federation needed Magyar cooperation and this was never fully given" because Magyars did not want to undermine their own privileged position within the empire (Sugar 1967: 112). It was a similar situation with the South Slavs in the lead-up to World War I. South Slav politics underwent a revolution in 1905, when Serb and Croat leaders throughout the monarchy allied to push for South Slav autonomy within the Habsburg realm (Beller 2006: 180). This autonomist push within the empire was bolstered as Serbia's power grew outside the imperial boundaries. After the Habsburg Empire was caught "framing South Slav leaders" for treason "with forged documents" in the infamous trials of 1909–10, and after Serbia made territorial gains in the 1912–13 Balkan Wars, Habsburg concerns about Serbia's increasing attraction to the empire's South Slav population grew to the point of demanding action (Beller 2006: 182). Yet, the earlier way in which the Habsburgs dealt with Magyar separatism precluded an effective response to the growing South Slav problem. Rusinow succinctly summarizes the long-term ethno-national problems created by the original ethno-national solution: "The *Ausgleich* was an answer to the Magyar question that left other pieces of the Empire's national question (including even the German one) unanswered and in fact harder to resolve. Later attempts to extend this kind of solution to other nations or clusters of nations – as in the idea of 'Trialism' in place of Dualism to accommodate the South Slavs – foundered on Magyar opposition" (Rusinow 1992: 251; see also Beller 2006: 142–47). Even as the war looked increasingly hopeless for the Habsburg Empire, and therefore just as maximal unity was required for its survival, Hungary's leader, Tisza, took a tour of the South Slav lands and "banged the table to tell the regional politicians they would never get Trialism" – thereby adamantly confirming "the propaganda of the exiled Slavs and Romanians about the unreformability of the old empire" (Okey 2001: 392). In short, because of the power of Magyar nationalists, the Habsburg Empire did not have the option of peacefully managing the Slavic movement. Its powers of co-optation sapped by the earlier compromise with the Magyars, the empire instead rode its anxieties about this peripheral nationalism into a perilous war, and, as Kann so memorably put it, "committed suicide from fear of death" (Kann 1977: 519).

In sum, the Habsburg Empire pushed into a war that led to its collapse because of a growing ethno-national problem with the South Slavs. It was unable to solve this through a devolution of power, in part because of its earlier method of solving the Magyar question along ethno-national lines with the Compromise of 1867. The rise of peripheral nationalism, irresolvable due to the empire's ethnic structure, thus led the empire into a disastrous war that eventually produced its collapse.

The Ottoman Empire

Compared to the Habsburg Empire, nationalism played a smaller role in the Ottoman collapse. With the help of European powers, nationalist secession eroded the strength of the empire over time, in line with the quantitative argument made above. This eventually contributed to the Ottoman Empire's loss of the war. Nationalism was also crucial for how specific territories – mostly the European ones – gained independence from the empire, again in line with the above analysis. But in the end, it was World War I, and not nationalism, that eviscerated the empire, in contrast to the Habsburg case.

While scholars debate the stability of the Habsburg Empire on the eve of World War I, there is considerable agreement about its counterpart: if the Ottoman Empire was a prize fighter, then it had been getting pummelled for fourteen rounds before meeting the Great War in the final round. The Ottoman Empire lost a large amount of its territory in the century before the war, much but not all of the loss due to nationalist secession. In North Africa, the Ottomans ceded large tracts to the British, French, and, after their 1911 war over modern-day Libya, to the Italians. Ottoman Europe also was lost to a string of secessionist and interstate wars. The Greeks gained independence after an eleven-year war of national liberation that ended in 1832. Serbians, Montenegrins, and Romanian nationalists engaged in a number of revolts both before and after this time, though successful nationalist secessions came only after the Russian victory in the Russo-Turkish War of 1877–78. This loss amounted to one-third of Ottoman territory at the time (Burbank and Cooper 2010: 358). In the years immediately preceding World War I, the Ottomans lost nearly all of their remaining European territories. In 1908, Bulgaria, which in 1878 had gained autonomy within the empire, declared independence and the Habsburg Empire and Greece, respectively, seized Bosnia-Herzegovina and Crete. Between 1910 and 1912, the Albanians waged successful wars for greater autonomy within the empire, and then became independent after the Ottoman Empire's former European provinces seized the Balkan lands in the 1912 Balkan War. In just a few short years, the empire lost close to 4 million subjects and was deprived of its long-time center of gravity (Findley 2010: 202; Lewis 1961: 351).

Whether these wars against the Ottoman Empire were autonomist, irredentist, or nationalist, most commentators agree that they would not have succeeded without the assistance of the great powers. Discussing the empire's European provinces, Haddad notes that nationalism, "combined with European aid, resulted in their separation from Istanbul," and that "[i]t would have been impossible for all of the Balkans to have gained independence by World War I had it not been for European aid" (Haddad 1977: 12, 22; see also Breuilly 1994; Reynolds 2011; Roshwald 2001). Nationalism's role in eroding the territorial base of the Ottoman Empire, then, was not a significant causal factor in and of itself.

Yet in the process of Ottoman imperial collapse and transition to a post-imperial order, nationalism's causal significance reached beyond the Balkans. We are *not* referring to Arab nationalism. After the loss of its European and North African territories, the Ottoman Empire's geographical scope was limited to Anatolia and the Arab lands that lay to the southeast. Though the Ottoman Empire did lose its Arab territories in World War I, this was not because of a nationalist uprising on the part of the local population (Haddad 1977). According to Roshwald, "the role played by Arab nationalist organizations in the defeat of the Ottoman empire" was "practically nil," and he concludes that "the Arab provinces were lost in battle with the British rather than breaking away in rebellion" (Roshwald 2001: 111–13). Nor were Arab defections behind these British victories: "To the unhappy surprise of British commanders, most Arabs remained loyal to the Ottoman empire until the end of the war" (Burbank and Cooper 2010: 372). Significant Arab nationalism among the masses did not arise until after the British and French took control in the post-war period (Breuilly 1994: 152).

Rather than in the Arab lands, it was in the core of the empire, Anatolia, where nationalism became a significant force in the period before imperial collapse. The wars in Europe and North Africa between 1910 and 1912 were crucial to this development. Before those wars, the Young Turks and the Committee of Union and Progress (CUP) fostered their images as defenders of Ottomanism (the multiethnic state), and "denied or downplayed their adherence to Turkish nationalism" (Üngör 2011: 30). Policies throughout the empire generally conformed to this rhetorical commitment to Ottoman, not Turkish, unity. But this belied the fact, recently revealed by research into party correspondence, that the CUP and Young Turks contained "a radical and activist Turkish-nationalist core" (Üngör 2011: 30). In fact, already by 1908, "the CUP's innermost councils were dominated by figures who were wedded to the narrow Turkish-nationalist agendas" and "Arabs were systematically excluded from positions of power in the CUP" (Roshwald 2001: 63–64). Thus, despite the state's rhetorical commitment to Ottomanism, there was among a large segment of the elite an ideological and organizational infrastructure for a nationalization of the core.

Following Ottoman failure in the wars of 1910–12, the CUP took over the administration of the empire in January 1913 and from that point forward Turkification migrated from the realm of ideas to that of policy (Findley 2010; Hanioğlu 2010; Keyder 1997; Roshwald 2001; Shaw and Shaw 1977; Ülker 2005; Üngör 2011; Zürcher 2000). These Turkification policies were not empire-wide. In fact, in relation to the Arab lands, around 1913 the Young Turks broke with the centralization policies that had characterized the Ottoman approach since the 1870s, which helps to explain why the Arab population did not defect from the Ottomans during World War I (Findley 2010; Roshwald 2001; Ülker 2005). But Anatolia was a different story. "By means of settlement and deportation policies, the Young Turks [between 1913 and 1918] sought to nationalize Anatolia as the base of a Turkish national core" (Ülker 2005: 616–17).

This nationalization of the core was directly linked to the secessionist and irredentist nationalisms of the Balkan territories. The First Balkan War led to catastrophic losses for the Ottomans, including territorial losses of 155,000 square kilometers (Findley 2010: 202). The loss of the predominantly Muslim Albania was a particularly strong blow, as it "convinced the Turks that it would be impossible to conciliate different national interests and attain a unified empire" (Shaw and Shaw 1977: 289). According to Ülker, "[a]bove all, the Albanian revolt acted as a catalyst in transforming the already existing Turkish consciousness of the Young Turks into the policies of nationalization" (Ülker 2005: 622).[3] These losses also led to a flood of Muslim refugees into Istanbul. Together, these developments had a profound impact on Ottoman identity politics (Findley 2010). The Balkan losses produced a "breaking point in the thorny relationship between centralization [the old policy] and nationalization [the emergent one]," with the advantage going to "the nationalist project of Turkification" (Ülker 2005: 621–22). Moreover, it was not only that the Ottomans lost the Balkans, but also *how* they lost them that mattered. According to Roshwald, this process provided an "object lesson in the power of nationalism. Most of the regions lost in the conflict were populated by non-Turks whose own nationalist impulses had clearly undermined the Ottoman grip over those territories" (Roshwald 2001: 106–7). At the same time, throughout these wars it was the local Turkish-speaking population that was most supportive of the empire (Roshwald 2001).

Thus, secessionist and irredentist nationalism in Europe both eroded the empire and stimulated the rise of nationalism and the adoption of nationalization policies in the imperial core. This nationalization of the

---

[3] In their revolts between 1910 and 1912, Albanians did not seek independence, but rather extensive autonomy within the empire. Even the most nationalist-minded of the Albanian rebels wanted the protective umbrella of the Ottoman Empire against the independent Balkan states. Albania declared independence only after it appeared that those Balkan states would defeat the Ottomans in the 1912 war. Consistent with Albanian fears, independence was upheld only because of the intervention of the great powers, particularly the Habsburg Empire, which wanted an independent Albania in order to ensure that Serbia would remain landlocked (Jelavich and Jelavich 1977: 222–34; see also Beller 2006: 183).

core clearly happened before the empire collapsed, but it did not make a significant contribution to its demise. Nevertheless, this development is relevant to this chapter's discussion for two reasons. The first has to do with its implications for a counterfactual posited by those who argue that nationalism was of negligible importance until *after* the empire fell: that if the Ottomans had been on the winning side, then the empire would have survived (Burbank and Cooper 2010; Reynolds 2011).[4]

Even if one assumes the correctness of this assessment, the alternative future it implies is woefully incomplete without an understanding of how the Ottoman Empire changed in the second decade of the twentieth century. The survival of the Ottoman Empire would have meant the survival of a very different kind of empire. Through its Turkification policies, the Ottoman Empire was becoming an altogether different kind of state: one that was both national and imperial. It was therefore becoming more like France and Britain in the early twentieth century (with the Arab lands in the role of France's and Britain's distant colonies) and less like the other major land empires of Eurasia (Russia and Austria-Hungary). The France analogy, in fact, could be pushed a bit further with the use of this counterfactual. The Ottoman Empire was transforming in the 1910s. Due to the war the empire failed, and with it the transformation process. If, however, the Ottoman Empire had prevailed in the war and therefore had been able to complete this transformation, and if we suppose that the name change of 1923 were adopted in 1918, then the year 1918 for "Turkey" would have been similar to that of 1789 for France: crossing this temporal line (i.e. before/after 1789 or 1918) within the core territory (France, Turkey) would have meant crossing from empire to nation-state, with the remainder of the state's territories becoming part of its imperial realm.

The second reason this pre-collapse nationalization of the core is relevant concerns the events after the empire fell. France, Britain, Russia, and Greece all scrambled for the Ottoman lands after the war. In so doing, however, they encountered stiff resistance and eventually a nationalist war for independence led by Ataturk. As the above discussion shows, the roots of that resistance rested firmly in the era before World War I, with the development of ideological nationalism and, eventually, policies of Turkic nationalization.

To summarize, in the process leading to imperial collapse, peripheral nationalism was not important in the Arab lands, but it did play a major role in the conflictive march of the European territories toward

---

[4] For the same claim about the Habsburg Empire see Sked 2001.

independence, in line with the quantitative results discussed above. In this respect, nationalism was an enduring part of the process that ended with the collapse of the Ottoman Empire. A second type of nationalism, state-building nationalism, also became important near the end of this process. The nationalization of the core was not enough to save the Ottoman state, but it did lay the groundwork for successful resistance to European incursion in the aftermath of World War I and the empire's collapse, helping to ensure that a Turkish nation-state, rather than some alternative political form, would emerge where the imperial core once had been.

The French colonial empire

French decolonization played out across two continents and two decades and entailed two major wars of national liberation, in present-day Vietnam and Algeria, and a smaller one in Cameroon. There was also plenty of violent conflict in Morocco, Tunisia, and Madagascar. The worst among them was Madagascar, where a 1947 nationalist uprising was met by repression that produced an official death count of more than 85,000 (T. Smith 1982: 101; Thomas et al. 2008: 258). However, only in Algeria and Vietnam was the nationalist war a direct cause of independence. That represents a small proportion of the universe of French colonial cases, so if one treats these two cases as independent from the other ones, then there is ample support for the notion that the process of French decolonization was generally peaceful, French colonial officials were the main actors on the scene, and nationalist mobilization had at most a negligible role (eg. Betts 1991). But this interpretation misreads the decolonization process in three ways. First, nationalist insurgency in Vietnam and Algeria had effects well beyond these territories: on budding nationalists elsewhere (in line with the statistical analysis of the first section), and also on French colonial policy. Second, though not rising to the level of full-scale war, nationalist violence was significant in the process that led to the independence of Morocco and Tunisia as well. Third, even where decolonization was relatively peaceful, in West and Equatorial Africa, nationalist mobilization was considerably more important to the winning of independence and the eventual collapse of empire than is sometimes thought.

Morocco and Tunisia

Nationalist movements emerged in both Morocco and Tunisia well before independence, each with strong leaders who rallied the people (Betts 1991). Representing himself "as the symbol of nationalism" beginning in the late 1940s, the sultan became the focal point of the Moroccan nationalist movement, which called on him to head a constitutional monarchy that represented the will of the Moroccan people (Betts 1991; Grimal 1978: 347). In Tunisia the movement coalesced around Habib Bourguiba, who issued the first independence manifesto in 1945. The French rejected it, but they did initiate a "co-sovereignty" arrangement that placed an equal number of Tunisians and French in the main parliamentary body, the Chief Counsel. Given that Tunisians comprised the vast majority of the population, this arrangement meant dramatically disproportionate power for the French. Protests, strikes, and other mobilizations followed. The French first tried repression, under resident general Jean de Hautecloque, but met still more resistance. By 1954 the French faced considerable "terrorism" in urban areas and a liberation army that started in rural areas but soon expanded its scope. Bourguiba began to appear quite moderate to colonial officials (Suliman 1987: 50–51). Thus, the French recalled de Hautecloque just two years after appointing him, recognized Tunisian independence, and made arrangements toward this end, including the release of Bourguiba from house arrest in France (Betts 1991; Grimal 1978; Suliman 1987).

A similar pattern of protests and riots, attempted repression (including the exile of the main nationalist leader), and finally capitulation occurred in Morocco. Already by January 1944 the Istiqlal Party was calling for national independence (Betts 1991: 99–100). As the movement gained strength, the French detained the sultan, Mohammed V (the name given to him by nationalists upon his return according to Suliman 1987: 45). After this detention, "a shadowy insurgency gradually took hold across Morocco;" its activities included "[a]ssassinations of notoriously pro-French notables ... [and] mounted attacks on army and police targets" (Thomas et al. 2008: 223). The first anniversary of Mohammed V's detention found the police reporting more than three hundred terrorist-related "incidents" in the cities of Casablanca and Rabat alone (Thomas et al. 2008: 223). This was August 1954. Just a few weeks earlier, the new premier of France, Pierre Mendès-France of the Radical Party, had issued the declaration that granted internal autonomy to Tunisia and promised talks concerning a transition to independence. Leaving Morocco out of this arrangement led to widespread discontent and riots during the first anniversary of the sultan's detention, and conflict and violence continued throughout the next year. The second anniversary of the detention again witnessed widespread rioting in urban areas and numerous killings (Thomas et al. 2008; see also Suliman 1987: 43–45). By this time most French leaders, including those in negotiations with the two main nationalist parties, wanted Morocco to join Tunisia on the fast track to independence. But there were holdouts in the cabinet and nothing happened until they were dismissed. In the end, a relatively peaceful withdrawal was negotiated because Moroccan nationalists, like their Tunisian counterparts, were willing to maintain a privileged, post-independence relationship with France (Thomas et al. 2008). In a pattern that would be repeated in sub-Saharan Africa, the French preferred to work with the moderate nationalists rather than allow the growing power of their radical counterparts to become entrenched. Unlike in sub-Saharan Africa, matters had turned rather bloody before the French adopted this strategy.

Nationalist insurgency was not the entire story behind Moroccan and Tunisian independence, but it was a crucial one. In line with the quantitative evidence offered above, what also mattered were the wars of liberation in other parts of the empire. The loss of Indochina and the outbreak of the Algerian War in 1954 both encouraged Moroccan and Tunisian nationalists and made compromise appealing to French leaders (Thomas et al. 2008: 216–17). In addition to these direct and indirect consequences of nationalist mobilization and confrontation, geopolitical forces played a significant role, foremost among them pressure from the US, which sought the "long-term stability and pro-western orientation of the Arab world in general, and North West Africa in particular" (Thomas et al. 2008: 217). That the US had this orientation and applied this pressure is indisputable. That it mattered very much is more difficult to discern. The US also pressured the French in Indochina – to *maintain* colonial rule – and, indeed, bankrolled their efforts to do so, but without effect. And the French listened to US concerns regarding how to handle the Suez issue only after the French joined Britain and Israel in their 1956 blunder. Nevertheless, it is probably fair to say that Morocco and Tunisia attained independence sooner than they might have, thanks to US pressure.

It is also true that France did not budge on Morocco and Tunisia until the configuration of political power changed at home. After France detained the main leaders of the nationalist movement in Morocco and Tunisia in 1952 and 1953, the Radical Party's gaining of the premiership in June 1954 was followed less than six weeks later by a declaration of internal autonomy and independence talks for Tunisia (Thomas et al. 2008). However much nationalist insurgency and US pressure mattered in the process of decolonization, then, they seem to have been mediated by politics in the metropole (and we will soon see that these political developments in France also mattered for French Black Africa). Metropolitan politics, however, were quite directly influenced by nationalist insurgency in the colonies, particularly in Indochina (see Thomas et al.

2008), while it is very *un*likely that US pressures had any effects on these domestic political developments. Moreover, the liberalizing effects of nationalist insurgency also could be reversed, as they were when the Radical Party-led coalition lost a no-confidence vote in February 1955 due at least in part to "a conservative reaction against [the coalition leader] Mendès-France's willingness to enact colonial reform" (Thomas et al. 2008: 223). Despite this reaction, however, France followed through on its independence promises to Tunisia, and after more violence, did the same with Morocco.

West Africa

The French empire's exit from West Africa was markedly more peaceful than elsewhere. From this peacefulness emerged the scholarly argument that the French withdrawal was long planned and almost entirely voluntary (see Chafer 2002). High Commissioner Messmer promoted exactly this idea in his farewell address before departing Dakar: "My departure is not a sad one, as it marks a new stage in the political development of Africa, preparations for which have been made for many long years, since the end of the Second World War" (quoted in Chafer 2002: 188). This impression of an orderly and managed process, one led by the French and in which nationalists played scarcely a role, is also found in narratives of British decolonization, as we will soon see. As for the French, this "vision of a successfully managed French decolonization in Black Africa, carefully prepared over many years," is only part of the story (Chafer 2002: 188; see also Thomas et al. 2008: 153–54).

It is true that there were no serious political movements for independence in Black Africa in the 1940s (Holland 1985; Person 1982). But there was also no intention to grant it. Scholars have sometimes interpreted matters otherwise, conceiving the Brazzaville Conference of 1944 and then the French Union policy of 1946–58 as the initiation and execution of exactly the sort of plan implied by High Commissioner Messmer. While both leaned in a liberalizing direction, however, neither Brazzaville nor the French Union were meant to initiate an evolution toward independence (T. Smith 1982). Even though Brazzaville "has been erroneously viewed as the beginning of decolonization," for "most of the participants ... the aim of the conference was, on the contrary, to consolidate the colonial system definitively by renovating it" (Person 1982: 144). If one wants to argue that the decolonization process started there, the intentions of French officials cannot reasonably be part of the argument. The Brazzaville Report flatly rejected independence as a goal: "The ends of the civilizing work accomplished by France in the colonies exclude any idea of autonomy, all possibility of evolution outside the French bloc of the Empire: the eventual constitution, even in the future, of self-government in the colonies is denied" (quoted in T. Smith 1982: 89). Three years later, nationalist insurgents in Madagascar learned that the French meant these words when their uprising produced a violent response by the empire that killed tens of thousands. In mainland sub-Saharan Africa, however, the French rarely engaged in such violence (Cameroon was an exception), and thus they have had a more plausible case for their claim that independence was always the plan. In reality, however, the French hoped and endeavored almost to the very end to avoid independence in West Africa.

Events moved more slowly in West Africa than elsewhere in the empire after World War II. On the surface at least, nothing much seemed to happen until 1956–57. The West African political elite was integrated into the metropolitan patronage system by virtue of being representatives of the colonies in Paris (Holland 1985). In order to shore up the empire, the French held out the promise of equality for all peoples under French rule. Whether in education, the labor market, or politics, West Africans directed their activities toward redeeming this promise. In this context, "nationalism ... had only a very tenuous lodgment before 1950 ..." (Holland 1985: 155). Or rather what existed was a more assimilationist version of nationalism aimed at equality of treatment under French law (Chafer 2002). Moreover, beyond 1950 and throughout the remainder of the colonial period "the idea of Greater France and the universalist ideals of French republicanism" continued to shape West African political mobilization (Chafer 2002: 19). To a significant degree, nationalist demands that emerged in the 1950s – actually, the "moderate" kind, as we will see – were "refracted through a prior loyalty to the French metropole" (Holland 1985: 158).

Nevertheless, major changes came to French West Africa between 1946 and 1956 (Person 1982). Suffrage dramatically expanded. Guinea's electorate, for example, increased from 131,000 in 1946 to almost 1.4 million just eleven years later. By the end of 1956, universal suffrage was in place across French West Africa (Chafer 2002). At the same time, major sectors of society became increasingly active. Two major parties, the region-wide Rassemblement Démocratique Africain and the Senegal-specific Union Démocratique Sénégalaise, formed and became increasingly adept at bridging the gap between African elites and masses, as they reached their activities into "the farthest corners of the bush" (Person 1982: 156; see also Thomas et al. 2008: 163–68).

As a consequence of this political mobilization, nationalism emerged as a political movement in French West Africa between 1950 and 1956

(Chafer 2002). Of particular importance were the trade unions and the student/youth movements. The unions had been linked to the French Confédération générale du travail, but they broke away to form autonomous unions in the early 1950s (Chafer 2002). These emerging and transforming collective actors signalled a growing rift in French West Africa between moderate nationalists within the political party elite who took a more patient and conciliatory approach to independence, and radical nationalists among students, youth, and trade unionists who "espoused more anti-colonialist positions and pressed for faster progress towards decolonization" (Chafer 2002: 143).

Such was the scene in 1956 when "the political history of French-speaking Africa accelerated" (Person 1982: 161); the colonies arrived at independence just four years later. In 1956 the French National Assembly passed the Loi Cadre, an act that gave the president the power to reform relations with the colonies. The subsequent decrees granted universal suffrage to the people of French West (and Equatorial) Africa, and granted extensive powers to the elected territorial legislatures in the colonies. The most important of these powers was control over the local budget, which was hardly an unmitigated blessing as it pitted local African politicians against trade unions and civil service workers. Territorial legislatures that once were merely channels through which grievances were aired became the objects of these grievances (Chafer 2002). Still, the French imperial state retained control over major areas such as economic development, internal security, and foreign affairs.

This changed two years later, not long after De Gaulle took the helm in France. Under the new constitution, colonial territorial legislatures were to gain full internal autonomy and membership in a newly minted "French Community." Each colony was also to hold a referendum on whether to join the French Community or opt for independence. All but Guinea opted for the Community, and all but Niger did so with more than 94 percent support (in Niger it was 78 percent), though voter turnout varied from 37 to 97 percent and Holland describes the referenda as "not far from pure farce" because "the existing administrations were usually in a position to rig whatever result they desired" (Chafer 2002: 178–79; Holland 1985: 161). Perhaps it was De Gaulle's belief that these referenda were rigged that caused him to treat newly independent Guinea and its president, Sékou Touré, so harshly: Guinea "received exemplary punishment; cast into the outer darkness, it was denied credit and other facilities" and nearly collapsed (Person 1982: 167).

Whatever De Gaulle thought about Guinea's referendum, his response indicated the desire to hold on to the French Empire, albeit in a new form. But within two years, Guinea was the rule rather than the exception.

Guinea's declaration of independence had an effect on the rest of the region, again in line with the statistical results presented in Table 9.2, putting pressure on the moderate nationalists to choose independence now rather than later (Person 1982: 168). Meanwhile, and also conforming to the quantitative analysis offered above, the Algerian War "dragged on and on" against all expectations, which both "made association with France increasingly unbearable for the African nationalists" and apparently made France rethink its resistance to independence (Person 1982: 169). Then the domino effect took over. Cameroon, Mali, and Senegal went first. By November 1960, nearly "all the French-speaking states of Africa ... proclaimed their independence and ... entered the UN under the sponsorship of France" (Person 1982: 169).

Though the French did not intend the Loi Cadre of 1956 to be the first of a chain of events that ended in independence (it instead was an attempt to remake imperial rule on an indirect rather than direct basis [Chafer 2002]), this is what in fact happened. What forces drove the adoption of this and other policies between 1956 and 1960? First, politics in the metropole were important, though they were hardly divorced from what was happening in the colonies. As discussed above, there was a leftward shift in control of the French government in the mid 1950s. This brought with it a more conciliatory approach to nationalist demands in Morocco and Tunisia, as well as the initiation of plans for a new approach to West and Equatorial Africa. The really decisive political development for Africa was the emergence of the Fifth Republic under De Gaulle, and difficulties with the Algerian War were instrumental in bringing about this change in constitution and leadership. According to Darwin, the Fourth Republic "was overthrown as a direct consequence of the Algerian rebellion" (1988: 251; see also Thomas et al. 2008: 395). Thus, nationalism in one part of the empire helped create regime change in the metropole, which in turn accelerated developments toward independence in other parts of the empire.

As for nationalism's direct influence, French West Africa was not like Morocco, Tunisia, Algeria, and Indochina: nationalist mobilization in the region did not directly drive this process (Chafer 2002; Holland 1985; Person 1982; Smith 1982; Thomas et al. 2008). Yet nationalism certainly played a key role in two ways. First, nationalist insurgency beyond the West African Federation, including "French loss of Indochina in 1954, the Foreign Ministry's reluctant preparations to cede greater autonomy in Morocco and Tunisia, and the outbreak of the Algerian rebellion in November 1954" motivated reform in other colonies where such conflict-ridden situations had not yet but perhaps soon could emerge (Thomas et al. 2008: 171–72). In fact, though the

Loi Cadre was not adopted until 1956, French officials initiated consideration of plans for a new approach to sub-Saharan Africa in 1954, just as the empire was withdrawing in defeat from Indochina and insurgents in the Maghreb were turning ever more to violent tactics in their resistance to colonial rule. Wanting "to avoid major bloodshed in black Africa" (Kahler 1984: 197), French officials aimed to create there "an evolutionary situation … that would make it possible to avert an explosion" (Person 1982: 161).

Second, not just the avoidance of bloodshed was at stake. The French wanted to make sure that they maintained influence in the region after independence, if and when it might come. Gaston Deferre, the Socialist minister responsible for the Loi Cadre policy, "explained it in terms of winning African goodwill *before* constitutional demands emerged to polarize metropolitan–colony relationships" (Holland 1985: 160). Because of the emergence of a radical nationalist movement in West Africa, the French had sound reasons for anticipating the growth of polarization over time and attempting to prevent it. As this movement expanded and as its demands became more expansive, French officials came to see the importance of adopting policies that would enable moderate nationalists – mainly the leadership of African political parties – to hold on to power. In this respect, "the colonial power was forced onto the defensive by African nationalist movements and obliged to make concessions to them … in an effort to defuse nationalist pressure" (Chafer 2002: 19). The final concession was to independence itself, and the French shrewdly made it in enough time to ensure the continued credibility and power of the moderate nationalists, and thus the continuing influence of the French in the post-colonial period. The radical nationalist movement in West Africa thus "played a key role in a victory – political independence – from which it was, ultimately, largely excluded" (Chafer 2002: 217).

The British colonial empire

There was significant violence during the waning years of the British Empire – attested to by the experience of the Kikuyu in Kenya and the Chinese in Malaya – but the picture of British decolonization is not complicated by wars of independence in the way that French decolonization is. It is therefore all the easier to underestimate the role of nationalism and conflict more generally in the process of British decolonization, and to see this process as one of voluntary retreat (Flint 1983). Darwin speaks of a "pervasive myth that in the British Empire, unlike the French, Belgian, Dutch, or Portuguese, the transfer of power was effected over tea in an atmosphere of sweetness and light ..." (1999: 554). The propagation of this myth was in fact an explicit goal of colonial policy. In cabinet discussions regarding Indian independence after World War II, the participants were adamant that this must not be seen as something forced on the British, even though they expected that adherence to the status quo would lead to a serious revolt in which the loyalty of Indian troops, according to Prime Minister Attlee, would be "very doubtful" (quoted in Hyam 2006: 108). "To the world at large, the British would be seen as remaining in control of events. History would record a commitment to self-government that had been planned and fulfilled" (Louis 1998: 329; see also Hyam 2006: 108–09). Later, the Macmillan government (1957–63) continued to portray British withdrawal "as the result of a British initiative" (Heinlein 2002: 176).

But rarely was decolonization so voluntary and harmonious. The French learned this the hard way, from Indochina to Algeria, and then acted in Black Africa to avoid violence and secure an influential role in the post-colonial era – not by undercutting nationalism, but rather by making sure that moderate and cooperative nationalists came to power. What characterized France's decolonization process in Black Africa was a general feature of British decolonization, from Asia to Africa (Heinlein 2002; Louis 1998).

Though the British acceded to independence in some parts of the empire earlier than the French, and though the British also contemplated independence everywhere much sooner, the speed with which independence came to the British colonies far outpaced those expectations. "In 1945 the independence of India could be seen on the horizon, but no one would have guessed that within the next two decades the British Empire would be in a state of dissolution" (Louis 1998: 331). Heinlein observes that under the Attlee government of the late 1940s and early 1950s, independence was generally anticipated but not for at least thirty or forty years (2002; see also Hyam 2006). In 1954, London attempted to identify which colonies would become independent by 1974; only the Gold Coast, Nigeria, the (eventually failed) Central African Federation, a Malayan Federation, and a not-yet-formed West Indian Federation were contemplated (Thomas et al. 2008). In a late 1950s report to Prime Minister Macmillan, several colonies, including Kenya, Sierra Leone, Tanganyika, Uganda, Nyasaland (Malawi), Northern Rhodesia (Zambia), were not expected to get even "internal self-government" within a decade, yet all gained independence within a few years. So, unlike the French, the British were thinking about independence in *some* of their colonies well in advance (and acceded to independence demands, without preceding violence, in several more in the late 1940s). But independence came in *nearly all* the colonies well before the British anticipated. To explain this acceleration, one needs to take into account nationalist mobilization, which according to the statistical analysis presented in Table 9.2 should play a crucial role in the transition to nation-statehood and thus cumulatively in the demise of empire.

According to a number of historians, the experience of the transitions to independence of Ceylon (Sri Lanka) and Burma after World War II had a lasting effect on the British approach to colonial peoples' demands for autonomy and independence (Ashton 1998; Darwin 1988; Heinlein 2002; Louis 1998). In 1948 both Burma and Sri Lanka attained independence, but only Sri Lanka maintained close ties with Great Britain through membership in the Commonwealth. British officials foresaw this outcome in November 1947 and in a Memorandum for the African Governors' Conference called for "more Ceylons and fewer Burmas" (quoted in Louis 1998: 337). If Britain had worked with Burmese independence leader Aung Sang from the start, said Prime Minister Attlee, "Burma would have stayed in the Commonwealth" (quoted in Louis 1998: 338). By the early 1950s, "more Ceylons and fewer Burmas" had become a "motto" for the British (Ashton 1998: 448).

Since British colonial officials never had a master plan for the colonies, which were treated more or less on a case-by-case basis, one might question the reach of this motto. According to Heinlein, in case after case, British accession to decolonization and independence was driven by the desire to make sure that "the right kind of nationalists" came to power (Heinlein 2002: 106). British policy revealed a "habit of considering the goodwill of local nationalists as the best guarantee of its interests" (Heinlein 2002: 6). A 1952 Foreign Office study, "The Problem of Nationalism," argued that cultivating what it called "healthy nationalism" was the best way "to minimize loss to ourselves and to establish new and fruitful relationships at all stages" (quoted in Hyam 2006: 179).

This strategy was evident in Nigeria, where the colonial administration "went out of its way to cultivate a relationship with nationalist leaders like Azikiwe" while it also "single-mindedly sought to isolate and destroy the radical Zikist movement" (Furedi 1993: 99). The official in charge of propaganda said that this approach proceeded "from the assumption that the growth of nationalism in Nigeria is inevitable and natural and that our aim must be, not to dam the flood but to divert it into useful channels" (quoted in Furedi 1993: 99). Sir Charles Arden-Clarke, governor of the Gold Coast, drew on the same imagery to explain his support for Nkrumah, arguing that "you cannot slow down a flood – the best you can hope to do is to keep the torrent within its proper channel" (quoted in Hyam 2006: 182). A similar view was expressed by the Cabinet in the mid 1950s when it considered the Gold Coast's request for independence: if they rejected this request, cabinet members agreed, "we may forfeit the great goodwill which now exists and drive the Gold Coast out of the Commonwealth" (quoted in Hyam 2006: 184). More Ceylons and fewer Burmas.

Indeed, Heinlein (2002) argues that the spread of nationalist mobilization throughout the empire explains the *acceleration* of the decolonization trend under the Conservative government in the 1950s. "Tories and socialists alike agreed that it was essential to retain the goodwill of Africans and Asians in order to safeguard British interests after independence" (Heinlein 2002: 105). A near constant of policy making was the desire to avoid "driving colonial nationalists into more radical positions" (Heinlein 2002: 105). In pursuit of this desire, the British adhered to "a long established doctrine in colonial policy" which held "[t]hat the risks of going too slow were probably greater than the risks of going too fast" (Ashton 2006: 46). This doctrine ran "like the proverbial scarlet thread through the history of [British] decolonization" (Hyam 2006: 120).

Sometimes this concern meant that no powerful mass nationalist movement emerged before officials started to plan for its emergence and significance. This is what happened, for example, in Sierra Leone and Uganda (Heinlein 2002). More often, nationalist politicians mobilized on the basis of political reforms, and thereby compelled colonial officials to devolve, then surrender, power much more quickly than anticipated, as was the case in Ghana after the 1946 constitutional reforms (Darwin 1988). In other cases nationalist mobilization posed a more immediate challenge and British officials perceived that the situation was teetering close to the edge: "The rapid accelerations that occurred in India between 1945 and 1947 and in East and Central Africa after 1959, sprang from the calculation that without prompt colonial withdrawal London faced dangerous crises of local control" (Darwin 1999: 545; see also Ashton 2006; Hyam 2006; McIntyre 1998). And in still other cases, the situation was somewhere between these extremes. In Malaya, for example, colonial officials predicted in 1946 that independence would not come for another thirty years. In 1953, the Colonial Office could at most foresee "a substantial measure of local autonomy" by about 1962 (quoted in Heinlein 2002: 109). But full-fledged independence came just four years later. In the meantime the two main political parties in Malaya, the UMNO and MCA, started organizing around and agitating for independence. The colonial secretary and most ministers agreed that this was the price to be paid to guarantee British influence into the future, and so Malaya became independent in 1957 (Hyam 2006).

None of this is to say that *only* nationalist mobilization, and its anticipation by British officials, mattered. Indeed, throughout the period
nationalism interacted with geopolitical concerns in the shaping of decolonization (Darwin 1999; Heinlein 2002; Hyam 2006). This intimate
connection between the two was perhaps never clearer than when the
military Chiefs of Staff argued for a speedy withdrawal from India after
World War II because "to remain might permanently antagonize the
Indians, which would militate against long-term British strategic requirements, the need for bases and airfields and access to the industry and
manpower of India during war" (Hyam 2006: 108). Not every colony
was as strategically important as India, Ceylon, or Malaya, but in every
colony the British desire to support "the right kind of nationalists" was
part of a Cold War strategy to block the wrong kind: communists and
other "extremists." Throughout it all, however, British officials were
acutely aware of nationalists' power to remake the imperial order, and
the British, therefore, worked to align, to the greatest extent possible, this
reconstruction with their own interests.

The Portuguese Empire

If the British and French doubted the wisdom of their conciliatory
approach to nationalism in Africa, the Portuguese experience with the
end of empire provided affirmation. As all the other European powers
were bending to what Macmillan famously called the "winds of change,"
the Portuguese doubled down. Imperial officials changed the description
of their endeavors, as colonies became "overseas provinces" in the 1960s,
but facts on the ground indicated that conquest and colonization continued to provide the accurate interpretive frame. In the case of Angola
alone, 350,000 Portuguese settlers arrived *after* 1960. By 1974, one in
four Portuguese adult males were in the armed forces (Holland 1985:
293). The empire needed a large army: Portugal's reluctance to relin-
quish the empire produced three wars of national liberation – in Angola,
Mozambique, and Guinea-Bissau. Over the course of a decade these
wars played a major part in bringing down the Portuguese regime at
home, and then the empire.

The wars did not cause battle deaths comparable to those in Algeria,
Vietnam, or Madagascar – they numbered in the thousands, not tens of
thousands – but there is general agreement that these wars of liberation
were crucial to the fall of the empire (Holland 1985; Pinto 2003; Thomas
et al. 2008). The chain of events ran from the fighting of "three intractable African colonial wars simultaneously" to the fall of the regime in
Portugal, and from there to rapid decolonization (Thomas et al. 2008: 395).

A purely metropolitan explanation, focused on regime change in Portugal, misses the crucial first part of the sequence. As we have seen, the fall of the Fourth Republic in France was linked in part to French problems in Algeria. This causal dynamic was more transparent still in the Portuguese case. "Overseas issues in the form of apparently perpetual and unwinnable colonial conflicts of varying intensities in Africa ... did indeed bring about and essentially cause the overthrow of the regime" (Robinson 2003: 5; see also Chabal 1993). Pinto describes the colonial wars as "a specific and determining factor in the overthrow of the Portuguese dictatorship" (2003: 19). After noting that the collapse of the empire was "the inevitable consequence of the successful coup against the dictatorship of President Antonio Salazar," Holland clarifies that "[t]he coup itself, however, was the product of a progressive weakening of the Portuguese position in its African colonies after 1970" (1985: 292). Even MacQueen, who argues that the nationalist insurgencies were not becoming any more effective with time and therefore other factors must also have been at play in the demise of the empire, agrees that "the regime collapsed, in part, because of its perceived intransigence over negotiations with the guerrillas [in Angola, Mozambique, and Guinea-Bissau]" (1997: 71).

Though MacQueen is right that other factors were at work, a point to which we will return, it also is not difficult to see why the colonial wars would have a deleterious effect on the regime's fortunes in the metropole. By the early 1970s the Portuguese government was spending more than half of its budget on the colonial wars, "and military expenses were projected to increase even as investments at home in education and social services were squeezed to free the funds necessary for the war effort" (Miller 1975: 136). Indeed, the force responsible for the coup against Salazar's authoritarian regime, the Armed Forces Movement (MFA), acted "in the name of withdrawal from Africa" and chose "as their figurehead General António Spínola, a top Portuguese military officer who had captured the public imagination by openly going on record as saying that Portugal's African wars were unwinnable" (Miller 1975: 136). This judgment that wars were unwinnable was not simply an assessment calculated for other political ends (like joining the European Community – see below); it was shared well beyond Portuguese circles, including by an interdepartmental group that reported to the United States' National Security Council in 1969. This group predicted "continued stalemate: the rebels cannot oust the Portuguese and the Portuguese can contain but not eliminate the rebels" (quoted in Maxwell 1982: 345).

The fact that wars in the three colonies were not equally intractable, and the fact that the colonies were not of equal value, became clear in the immediate aftermath of the coup. Despite making the wars a central part of the program justifying their overthrow of the Caetano regime, the new regime did not immediately establish a decolonization program but instead expressed the view that a political, not military, solution was the way forward in the colonies. This apparently had to do with coup coalition politics, as Spínola, the new president, agreed with the junior officers of the MFA about decolonization in Mozambique and Guinea-Bissau, but preferred a federal solution to Angola. In the case of Guinea-Bissau, which economically was of little value and where "the military situation was irretrievable," Spínola wanted a ceasefire and then independence. A similar situation existed in Mozambique, where FRELIMO "was firmly in control of much of the country and seemed likely to prove a malleable partner after power was transferred" (Holland 1985: 296). But Angola was more valuable, thanks to its wealth of oil, diamonds, coffee, and rare metals; it was "the only Overseas Province to have aided the metropole through its export surplus," and it had a much more factionalized nationalist insurgency compared to the other two cases (Holland 1985; Robinson 2003: 7). Similarly to Spínola's differentiation of the three cases, Spruyt states that in Mozambique the empire faced "protracted withdrawal," in Guinea-Bissau "imminent defeat," but that in Angola the maintenance of a "stalemate" was possible (2005: 196). Perhaps, then, there was a chance for Spínola's federal solution to Angola to work. In the end, however, he did not prevail, and in accordance with the wishes of the MFA and political parties the new regime adopted a constitutional law for complete decolonization a few months after the coup. Three decades after the fact, Spínola claimed he went along with it because he believed that if Lisbon did not act, then its armed forces in Africa would themselves have ceded power (MacQueen 1997).

Thus nationalist insurgency was a central component of the process that led to the collapse of the Portuguese Empire. The colonial wars sapped the legitimacy of the existing regime and stimulated a coup that in turn led to rapid decolonization. To be sure, this central role of nationalist insurgency in imperial collapse does not mean other factors were not in play. Portugal's efforts to join the European Economic Community (EEC) coincided with the colonial wars, and also motivated the coup that led to decolonization. At the same time, as Thomas et al. (2008) explain, the colonial wars, EEC membership, regime change, and decolonization were all interrelated: "Admission to the European Community, with all its attendant trade benefits, also rested squarely on an end to Portugal's colonial wars. It was the pull of EEC membership which made regime change in Lisbon appear imperative to influential constituencies of domestic opinion, from the educated middle class to business leaders and the junior officers who orchestrated military opposition to Caetano's government" (Thomas et al. 2008: 396).

The Soviet Empire

Of the three major contiguous land empires that entered the First World War, only the Russian one survived, albeit in new form. More than seven decades after the Romanov Empire became the Soviet Empire, it collapsed, bringing an end to a long era of imperial rule. Somewhat ironically, this final exit from the imperial stage was made by an actor that for some time had been keeping the show going while at the same time decrying its content: for decades the Soviet Union combined imperial power with anti-imperialist rhetoric.

Is the realist-great-power-competition perspective at least correct with regard to this most recent episode of imperial collapse? Did interstate war or international interference bring about the end of the Soviet Union – irrespective of nationalist movements? As a great power itself, the Soviet Union was also practically immune from all but the most limited intervention by other great powers. As for war, the last one fought by the Soviets was the Afghan War, which concluded in 1988, just a few years before the Soviet demise. However, rather than itself being the cause of imperial collapse, the Afghan War was symptomatic of a more fundamental determinant, Soviet hyper-militarism, which as we soon will see was indirectly linked to the emergence of nationalist mobilization. Thus, neither war itself nor great power meddling can explain this imperial collapse.

At the same time, thousands of demonstrations across the empire, most framed in nationalist terms, preceded the fall of the Soviet imperial state. Yet a number of scholars contend that nationalism was strictly a consequence, not a cause, of the Soviet collapse (see Beissinger 2009). This is indisputable in the case of the Central Asian republics, where political elites merely "dressed up in nationalist garb" in the final days of the empire in an effort to maintain power after independence (Suny 1993: 141). But in other parts of the empire more relevant to the story of its demise, the sequence was different. The imperial collapse that produced nationalism in the Central Asian republics was itself a product of nationalist mobilization in other parts of the empire.

Nationalist mobilization, to be sure, was not the first or most important mover in the causal sequence that ended with the fall of the Soviet Union. A wide range of analysts agrees that nationalist mobilization was itself an outcome of Gorbachev's reforms (Beissinger 2002, 2009; Brubaker 1994; Lapidus 1992; Suny 1993; Zaslavsky 1992, 1997).

And these reforms in turn were a response to an enduring economic crisis, which itself was the result of the Soviet dedication to hyper-militarism. Thus, the causal chain runs from Cold War hyper-militarism to economic crisis to political and economic reforms, and from there to nationalist mobilization and imperial collapse. As Zaslavsky (1997) and Beissinger (2009) jointly emphasize, the Soviet Union's demise as an empire was distinct from its loss of superpower status and fall as a specifically communist regime. Certainly the superpower status and perhaps the communist character of the regime were doomed by the mutually reinforcing hyper-militarism and economic crisis. But it was nationalist mobilization that destroyed any chance of the state's surviving in the imperial form inherited from the Romanov era. It was nationalist mobilization that was responsible for "transforming the collapse of a regime into the disintegration of a state" (Brubaker 1994: 48). Economic and political reforms intended to solve the economic crisis of the imperial state instead opened the political space in which nationalist and then secessionist mobilization could emerge and expand. "From 1988 to 1991 … [the Soviet] state exploded, largely under the pressure of its ethnic problems" (Beissinger 2002: 1). To view this explosion (or perhaps, rather, implosion) as the inevitable consequence of deep economic crisis is to ignore the many other cases where states, and even communist regimes, have been resilient in the face of similar crises (Beissinger 2009).

When launching perestroika and then glasnost, neither Gorbachev nor his fellow reformers foresaw that "the revolution from above would be hijacked by nationalist revolutions from below" (Suny 1993: 132). These reforms "unleashed an unprecedented tide of protests and demonstrations across the entire territory of the USSR in which national grievances, fueled by economic unrest, occupied a central place" (Lapidus 1992: 45). Beissinger's (2002) careful research shows that characterizing these mobilizations as "nationalist" is amply justified. In the thousands of demonstrations analyzed by Beissinger, the three basic types of grievances were economic, democratic, and nationalist in character. But nationalist demands were the dominant ones, which becomes clear when one compares their frequency with that of demands for political liberalization (the second most important). Among the 6,663 demonstrations in Beissinger's sample, about one quarter made both nationalist and liberalizing demands, and 16 percent made liberalizing but not nationalist demands. Demonstrations in which nationalist demands stood alone were far more common: 42 percent of demonstrations made nationalist demands but not liberalizing ones. The difference is more dramatic when one shifts the focus from demonstrations to participants. One third of the demonstrators participated in actions that made both nationalist and liberalizing demands, but just 6 percent participated in demonstrations where liberalizing but not nationalist demands were made. In contrast, nearly three out of every five (57 percent) demonstrators participated in actions that made nationalist but not liberalizing demands (Beissinger 2002: 75–79). Put another way, 90 percent of all participants took part in demonstrations that made nationalist demands, but only 39 percent were involved in demonstrations making liberalizing demands. Moreover, "[a] similar but even more pronounced difference occurred between mobilization over nationalist demands and mobilization over economic demands – in spite of the enormous decline in living standards that occurred during this period" (Beissinger 2009: 336).

In the midst of all these nationalist mobilizations, the local elites also became increasingly less reliable collaborators with the imperial state. The economic crisis and reforms intended to address it instead activated a latent structural weakness of the imperial system: the local elite owed their positions of power to the central imperial state, but also to their membership in a "titular nation" linked to each of the republics (Brubaker 1994; Szporluk 1997). "The Soviet Union was built on the principle of nominal national-territorial autonomy with ethnoterritorial units as its basic structural elements" (Zaslavsky 1997: 86). Prior to the crisis, a system of co-optation kept the lid on this ethno-national element. Leaders of the titular nationalities had power only by virtue of appointments made by the central state. Titular nationalities also received preferential treatment in other domains as well, including higher education. Thus, the ethnic structure of the empire was not a problem for imperial viability so long as the central state could continue to deliver the goods.

With economic decline "it was no longer possible to protect the occupational interests of ethnic educated classes" (Zaslavsky 1997: 89). This emerging crack in the imperial structure, the result of a blow struck by the economic crisis, was actually made worse by the political reforms designed to address that crisis. The spring of 1988 brought a new stage of reform that focused on competitive elections and democratization. This led to the formation of various organizations in support of reform. An example is the People's Front in Support of Perestroika, which emerged first in Estonia and then Latvia and Lithuania, "and then spread – in a Soviet version of the international demonstration effect – to Moldova and the Transcaucasus" (Lapidus 1992: 55). These were not originally nationalist groups, but they became nationalist in a short period of time. Local political elites, who now depended for their power on territorial elections rather than appointments from the center, promoted this change by acting in their own interests. Forced to appeal to local peoples rather than party leaders after the passing of perestroika reforms, politicians shifted direction and started "viewing and presenting themselves as the defenders of republic interests against the center" (Lapidus 1992: 58).

Though Gorbachev and his allies did not anticipate the impact that reforms would have on the Soviet Union's ethno-national structure, they soon recognized this effect. By the end of 1988, Gorbachev identified "nationality policy as 'the most fundamental vital issue of society'" (Lapidus 1992: 46). This was at a time when nationalist mobilization was only beginning to take hold. Though the satellite states of Eastern Europe and the Baltic republics most famously turned against the Soviet state early on, nationalist – though not originally secessionist – mobilization emerged in Azerbaijan first, during the Karabagh Crisis (Beissinger 2002; Suny 1993). On and off since the 1960s, Armenian activists in both Armenia and Azerbaijan made attempts to incorporate Karabagh into Armenia, but the Soviet state refused. Then in mid-February 1988, "[s]uddenly, unpredictably … the Karabagh Armenians, inspired by the rhetoric of *perestroika* and encouraged by regime attacks on old-style party rule, began a series of demonstrations in favor of union with Armenia" (Suny 1993: 133). Gorbachev's efforts to placate the activists were clumsy and ineffective, and by the end of the month "hundreds of thousands were marching in Erevan in continuous demonstrations" (Suny 1993: 134). Then the Azerbaijanis countermobilized, leading the Soviet state to take over Karabagh for more than a year starting in July 1988. But disorder continued, and after a series of arrests of leaders in fall 1988 and then their release in spring 1989, by the end of the year "the nationalist movements had all but displaced the official power structure in the Transcaucasian republics," including Azerbaijan (Suny 1993: 136).

Nationalist mobilization started in the Karabagh Crisis in winter 1988, but it was not based on an "anti-imperial secessionist frame" until nationalist mobilization emerged elsewhere, "developing first in the Baltic in the summer and fall of 1988 and then spreading in a massive way to Georgia, Armenia, Azerbaijan, Moldova, Ukraine, and even eventually to Russia itself" (Beissinger 2002: 160). Already by late 1988 and early 1989, the Baltic republics were declaring sovereignty. Roughly in line with the quantitative analysis presented above, this emboldened the nominally independent states of Eastern Europe, whose break from the Soviet system in turn rebounded on movements within the USSR proper (Beissinger 2009). That these nationalist mobilizations occurred in waves was key to their success: "the disintegration of the Soviet state could not have taken place without the effects of tidal influences of one nationalism on another"; if "these nationalist revolts [had] occurred in isolation from one another," then the empire would not have collapsed (Beissinger 2002: 36). This certainly was the self-understanding of nationalist activists.

Nationalists across the empire not only imitated one another, they encouraged this imitation in the hope that mobilization in other republics would increase the chance of success in their own. The first to make the secessionist move, Baltic nationalists held fast to the proposition that their own liberation depended on the liberation of other republics. As one such nationalist, Edgar Savisaar, put it, "there cannot be a sovereign Estonia if Lithuania, Latvia, and other republics are not sovereign" (quoted in Beissinger 2002: 161). Such activists might as well have said "Nationalists of the Communist World Unite!" In all, 3.9 million people participated in 210 demonstrations "in which members of one nationality expressed solidarity with the secessionist demands of another" between late 1988 and 1991 (Beissinger 2002: 161). This wavelike character of nationalist mobilizations further highlights the crucial causal role of nationalism in the Soviet imperial collapse.

Nationalist mobilization was not simply a last link in a chain of causes that brought down the Soviet Empire. The preceding links in the causal chain – hyper-militarism, economic crisis, reforms – were insufficient to create nationalist mobilization on the large scale that it occurred. As Beissinger argues, the first nationalist upsurges were indeed "strongly advantaged by pre-existing structural conditions" (2002: 38–39). But this was not true for later waves of mobilization; they built on earlier ones. In this respect, nationalist mobilization at time k in context x became a major cause of mobilization at time m in context y. "Institutional change evoked a tide of nationalism into being; but institutions were quickly outstripped by the dizzying pace of events" (Beissinger 2002: 95; for quantitative evidence of such contagion effects see Hale 2000). Again in line with the quantitative analysis offered above, then, nationalism in one part of the empire stimulated the emergence of nationalisms elsewhere.

It should be noted that as nationalist mobilizations emerged, spread, and ultimately produced the collapse of the empire, the Soviet imperial state was until the very end an unwilling participant in the rapidly unfolding drama. During the Karabagh Crisis, the Soviet state declared a state of emergency, arrested movement leaders, sent troops, and near the end tried to use the military "to restore authority to the discredited Azerbaijani Communist party" (Suny 1993: 137). When demonstrators took to the streets in Tbilisi in April 1989 the military used force and killed more than a dozen people. And when Lithuania's legislature issued a declaration of independence in March 1990, the Soviet state attempted a military coup. "But the crackdown backfired," as "[h]undreds of thousands" took to the streets in Lithuania, followed by "huge demonstrations" of solidarity in other parts of the empire (Zaslavsky 1997: 74). To be sure, the Soviet state was generally reluctant to use violence against demonstrators, what became known as the Tbilisi syndrome, after the event mentioned above (Beissinger 2002; Suny 1993). Then again, the counterfactual that force would have worked and therefore that the Soviet imperial elite simply lacked the will to hold the empire together does not conform to the historical lessons learned from the final days of other empires, for instance, of Portuguese control over Angola and Mozambique, or French control over Algeria and Morocco, where violence was met with violence and the empire exited in the end.

Conclusion

The storylines of each imperial collapse entailed distinctive causal sequences, but consistent with the quantitative evidence earlier in this chapter, nationalist mobilization appeared on stage in every case. To be sure, the extent and precise nature of nationalism's causal role differed across these dramas. In increasing order of causal significance, the role of nationalist mobilization in imperial collapse was as follows:

- The Ottoman Empire: Nationalist breakaways led to the weakening of the empire, and this weakened empire then lost the war caused by inter-imperial rivalries, which in turn produced imperial collapse.
- The Habsburg Empire: The nature of the response to Hungarian nationalism made accommodating Slav nationalism impossible, which, combined with the pan-nationalist agitation of Serbia, produced the war that the empire lost for other reasons, which in turn produced imperial collapse.
- France and Britain: Nationalist wars of liberation in Indochina and Algeria, plus nationalist violence and rioting elsewhere (Morocco, Tunisia, Malaya, Kenya, Nyasaland), showed the imperial center that upholding its imperial domain was difficult, costly, and potentially injurious to longer-term economic and geopolitical interests. This prepared the ground for accepting the idea of independence in principle (in the French case) or accepting independence decades earlier than planned (in the British case). Combined with increasingly nationalist and rapidly radicalizing demands by a new generation of African leaders, this brought about the end of both colonial empires through a series of cascading declarations of independence.
- The Soviet Union: Great power economic and military competition led to economic crisis, which prompted political reforms that in turn

produced waves of contagious and mutually reinforcing national mobilizations that then brought the collapse of the empire.

- Portugal: Nationalist wars of liberation in most remaining colonies brought about regime change in the center and the collapse of empire.

Whereas the inferential statistical analysis in the first section of this chapter suggested a relationship between nationalist mobilization and nation-state creation in individual imperial dependencies (see Table 9.2), the historical analysis indicates that nationalism also played an important role in the collapse of the imperial center itself. This is clearest in the Portuguese and Soviet cases, and still quite evident with regard to the British and French empires. In the case of the Habsburg Empire, nationalist mobilization per se was less directly important than the ethnic structure of the empire and the way in which earlier solutions to national problems impeded later ones and thereby triggered a war in which the empire met defeat and collapsed. Only in the Ottoman case can one say that nationalism played merely a minor role in imperial collapse during World War I. It was limited to the previous weakening of the empire through a series of nationalist break-aways, aided by Western support, in the Balkans.

To be sure, geopolitical forces also played an important role both in explaining individual transitions from empire to nation-state and in bringing about imperial collapse. As we have seen in the quantitative section, great power wars unrelated to nationalist independence movements increased the likelihood of such transitions, while imperial strength in the global military and economic arena decreased it. And great power wars played an important role in the collapse of the Habsburg and the Ottoman empires, while geopolitical rivalry stands at the beginning of the causal chain leading to the demise of the Soviet Union, and also helps explain why French and British colonial offices eventually gave in to the idea of African independence. However, none of this amounts to an argument that these geopolitical forces created either nationalism or the cascades of nation-state creations that washed away one imperial domain after the other. Rather, one could conclude, geopolitics variously triggered, accelerated, or delayed a global transformation process whose emergence could not have been avoided and whose subsequent development could not have been suppressed: the rise of a new principle of political legitimacy – self-rule in the name of a nationally defined people – that was embraced by more and more politically ambitious leaders across the world and by ever larger segments of the population. Nationalism, in other words, represents a prime historical force that has reshaped the political outlook of the globe over the past two hundred years.

REFERENCES

Anderson, B. 1991. *Imagined Communities: Reflections on the Origin and Spread of Nationalism*. London: Verso.

Ashton, S.R. 1998. "Ceylon." Pp.447–64 in *The Oxford History of the British Empire*. Vol. IV *The Twentieth Century*, edited by J.M. Brown and W.R. Louis. Oxford University Press.

2006. "Keeping Change within Bounds: A Whitehall Reassessment." Pp. 32–52 in *The British Empire in the 1950s: Retreat or Revival?* edited by M. Lynn. New York: Palgrave Macmillan.

Beissinger, M.R. 2002. *Nationalist Mobilization and the Collapse of the Soviet State*. Cambridge University Press.

2009. "Nationalism and the Collapse of Soviet Communism." *Contemporary European History* 18(3): 331–47.

Beller, S. 2006. *A Concise History of Austria*. Cambridge University Press.

Betts, R.F. 1991. *France and Decolonization 1900–1960*. New York: St. Martin's Press.

Breuilly, J. 1994. *Nationalism and the State*. 2nd edn. University of Chicago Press.

Bridge, F.R. 1990. *The Habsburg Monarchy among the Great Powers, 1815–1918*. New York: Berg.

Brubaker, R. 1994. "Nationhood and the National Question in the Soviet Union and Post-Soviet Eurasia: An Institutionalist Account." *Theory and Society* 23(1): 47–78.

Burbank, J. and F. Cooper. 2010. *Empires in World History: Power and the Politics of Difference*. Princeton University Press.

Chabal, P. 1993. "Emergencies and Nationalist Wars in Portuguese Africa." *Journal of Imperial and Commonwealth History* 21(3): 235–49.

Chafer, T. 2002. *The End of Empire in French West Africa: France's Successful Decolonization?* Oxford and New York: Berg.

Darwin, J. 1988. *Britain and Decolonization: The Retreat from Empire in the Post-War World*. London: Macmillan.

1999. "Decolonization and the End of Empire." Pp. 541–57 in *The Oxford History of the British Empire*. Vol. V *Historiography*, edited by R.W. Winks and A. Low. Oxford University Press.

Findley, C.V. 2010. *Turkey, Islam, Nationalism, and Modernity: A History*. New Haven: Yale University Press.

Flint, J. 1983. "Planned Decolonization and Its Failure in British Africa." *African Affairs* 82(328): 389–411.

Furedi, F. 1993. "Creating a Breathing Space: The Political Management of Colonial Emergencies." *Journal of Imperial and Commonwealth History* 21(3): 89–106.

Grimal, H. 1978. *Decolonization: the British, French, Dutch and Belgian Empires 1919–1963*, trans. S. De Vos. Boulder, CO: Westview Press.

Haddad, W.M. 1977. "Nationalism in the Ottoman Empire." Pp. 3–24 in *Nationalism in a Non-National State: The Dissolution of the Ottoman Empire*. Columbus: Ohio State University Press.

Hale, H. 2000. "The Parade of Sovereignties: Testing Theories of Secession in the Soviet Setting." *British Journal of Political Science* 30: 31–56.

Hanioğlu, M.Ş. 2010. *A Brief History of the Late Ottoman Empire.* Princeton University Press.

Heinlein, F. 2002. *British Government Policy and Decolonisation 1945–1963: Scrutinising the Official Mind.* London and Portland, OR: Frank Cass.

Himka, J. 1992. "Nationality Problems in the Habsburg Monarchy and the Soviet Union: the Perspective of History." Pp. 79–94 in *Nationalism and Empire: The Habsburg Empire and the Soviet Union,* edited by R.L. Rudolph and D.F. Good. New York: St. Martin's Press.

Holland, R.F. 1985. *European Decolonization 1918–1981: An Introductory Survey.* Macmillan.

Hroch, M. 2000 [1969]. *Social Preconditions of Patriotic Groups among the Smaller European Nations.* New York: Columbia University Press.

Hyam, R. 2006. *Britain's Declining Empire: The Road to Decolonization, 1918–1968.* Cambridge University Press.

Jászi, O. 1961. *The Dissolution of the Habsburg Monarchy.* Chicago and London: University of Chicago Press.

Jelavich, C. and B. Jelavich. 1977. *The Establishment of the Balkan National States, 1804–1920.* Seattle and London: University of Washington Press.

Kahler, M. 1984. *Decolonization in Britain and France.* Princeton University Press.

Kann, R.A. 1977. *A History of the Habsburg Empire 1526–1918.* Berkeley: University of California Press.

Keyder, C. 1997. "The Ottoman Empire." Pp. 30–44 in *After Empire: Multiethnic Societies and Nation-Building,* edited by K. Barkey and M. von Hagen. Boulder, CO: Westview Press.

Lapidus, G.W. 1992. "From Democratization to Disintegration: the Impact of Perestroika on the National Question." Pp. 45–70 in *From Union to Commonwealth: Nationalism and Separatism in the Soviet Republics,* edited by G.W. Lapidus, V. Zaslavsky, and P. Goldman. Cambridge University Press.

Lewis, B. 1961. *The Emergence of Modern Turkey.* London and New York: Oxford University Press.

Louis, W.R. 1998. "The Dissolution of the British Empire." Pp. 329–56 in *The Oxford History of the British Empire.* Vol. IV *The Twentieth Century,* edited by J.M. Brown and W.R. Louis. Oxford University Press.

MacQueen, N. 1997. *The Decolonization of Portuguese Africa: Metropolitan Revolution and the Dissolution of Empire.* London and New York: Longman.

Mann, M. 1993. *The Sources of Social Power.* Vol. II. *The Rise of Classes and Nation-States, 1760–1914.* Cambridge University Press.

Mason, J.W. 1997. *The Dissolution of the Austro-Hungarian Empire, 1867–1918.* London and New York: Longman.

Maxwell, K. 1982. "Portugal and Africa: the Last Empire." Pp. 337–85 in *The Transfer of Power in Africa: Decolonization 1940–1960,* edited by P. Gifford and W.R. Louis. New Haven and London: Yale University Press.

McIntyre, W.D. 1998. *British Decolonization, 1946–1997: When, Why, and How Did the British Empire Fall?* London: Macmillan.

Miller, J.C. 1975. "The Politics of Decolonization in Portuguese Africa." *African Affairs* 74(295): 135–47.

Okey, Robin. 2001. *The Habsburg Monarchy, c. 1765–1918: From Enlightenment to Eclipse*. London: Macmillan.

Person, Y. 1982. "French West Africa and Decolonization." Pp. 141–72 in *The Transfer of Power in Africa: Decolonization 1940–1960*, edited by P. Gifford and W.R. Louis. New Haven and London: Yale University Press.

Pinto, A.C. 2003. "The Transition to Democracy and Portugal's Decolonization." Pp. 17–36 in *The Last Empire: Thirty Years of Portuguese Decolonization*, edited by S. Lloyd-Jones and A.C. Pinto. Bristol, UK: Intellect.

Reynolds, M.A. 2011. *Shattering Empires: The Clash and Collapse of the Ottoman and Russian Empires 1908–1918*. Cambridge University Press.

Robinson, R.A.H. 2003. "The Influence of Overseas Issues in Portugal's Transition to Democracy." Pp. 1–16 in *The Last Empire: Thirty Years of Portuguese Decolonization*, edited by S. Lloyd-Jones and A.C. Pinto. Bristol, UK: Intellect.

Roshwald, A. 2001. *Ethnic Nationalism and the Fall of Empires: Central Europe, Russia, and the Middle East, 1914–1923*. London and New York: Routledge.

Rusinow, D. 1992. "Ethnic Politics in the Habsburg Monarchy and Successor States: Three Answers to the National Question." Pp. 79–94 in *Nationalism and Empire: The Habsburg Empire and the Soviet Union*, edited by R.L. Rudolph and D.F. Good. New York: St. Martin's Press.

Shaw, S.J. and E.K. Shaw. 1977. *History of the Ottoman Empire and Modern Turkey*. 2 vols. Vol. II *Reform, Revolution, and Republic: The Rise of Modern Turkey, 1808–1975*. Cambridge University Press.

Sked, A. 2001 *The Decline and Fall of the Habsburg Empire, 1815–1918*. 2nd. edn. London: Longman.

Smith, A.D. 1986. *The Ethnic Origins of Nations*. Oxford: Blackwell.

Smith, T. 1982. "Patterns in the Transfer of Power: A Comparative Study of French and British Decolonization." Pp. 87–116 in *The Transfer of Power in Africa: Decolonization 1940–1960*, edited by P. Gifford and W.R. Louis. New Haven and London: Yale University Press.

Solnick, S.L. 1998. *Stealing the State: Control and Collapse in Soviet Institutions*. Cambridge, MA: Harvard University Press.

Spruyt, H. 2005. *Ending Empire: Contested Sovereignty and Territorial Partition*. Ithaca, NY: Cornell University Press.

Stone, N. 1966. "Army and Society in the Habsburg Monarchy, 1900–1914." *Past and Present* 33 (April): 95–111.

Sugar, P. 1967. "The Rise of Nationalism in the Habsburg Empire." *Austrian History Yearbook* 3: 91–120.

1981. "An Underrated Event: the Hungarian Constitution Crisis of 1905–6." *East European Quarterly* 15: 281–306

Suliman, H.S. 1987. *The Nationalist Movements in the Maghrib: A Comparative Approach*. Research Report No. 78. Uppsala: Scandinavian Institute of African Studies.

Suny, R.G. 1993. *The Revenge of the Past: Nationalism, Revolution, and the Collapse of the Soviet Union*. Stanford University Press.

Szporluk, R. 1997. "The Fall of the Tsarist Empire and the USSR: The Russian Question and Imperial Overextension." Pp. 65–93 in *The End of Empire? The Transformation of the USSR in Comparative Perspective*, edited by K. Dawisha and B. Parrott. Armonk, NY and London: M.E. Sharpe.

Taylor, A.J.P. 1965[1948]. *The Habsburg Monarchy, 1809–1918: A History of the Austrian Empire and Austria-Hungary.* New York: Harper & Row.

Thomas, M., B. Moore, and L.J. Butler. 2008. *Crises of Empire: Decolonization and Europe's Imperial States, 1918–1975.* London: Hodder Education.

Ülker, E. 2005. "Contextualizing 'Turkification': Nation-Building in the Late Ottoman Empire, 1908–18." *Nations and Nationalism* 11(4): 613–36.

Üngör, U. 2011. *The Making of Modern Turkey: Nation and State in Eastern Anatolia, 1913–1950.* Oxford University Press.

Wank, S. 1967. "Foreign Policy and the Nationality Problem in Austria-Hungary, 1867–1914." *Austrian History Yearbook*, Vol. III.

1997a. "Some Reflections on the Habsburg Empire and Its Legacy in the Nationalities Question." *Austrian History Yearbook* 28: 131–46.

1997b. "The Habsburg Empire." Pp. 45–57 in *After Empire: Multiethnic Societies and Nation-Building*, edited by K. Barkey and M. von Hagen. Boulder, CO: Westview Press.

1997c. "The Disintegration of the Habsburg and Ottoman Empires." Pp. 94–120 in *The End of Empire? The Transformation of the USSR in Comparative Perspective*, edited by Karen Dawisha and Bruce Parrott. Armonk, NY and London: M.E. Sharpe.

Wimmer, A. and Y. Feinstein. 2010. "The Rise of the Nation-state Across the World, 1816 to 2001." *American Sociological Review* 75(5): 764–90.

Wimmer, A. and B. Min. 2006. "From Empire to Nation-state: Explaining Wars in the Modern World, 1816–2001." *American Sociological Review* 71(6): 867–97.

Zaslavsky, V. 1992. "The Evolution of Separatism in Soviet Society under Gorbachev." Pp. 71–97 in *From Union to Commonwealth: Nationalism and Separatism in the Soviet Republics*, edited by G.W. Lapidus, V. Zaslavsky, and P. Goldman. Cambridge University Press.

1997. "The Soviet Union." Pp. 73–96 in *After Empire: Multiethnic Societies and Nation-Building*, edited by K. Barkey and M. von Hagen. Boulder, CO: Westview Press.

Zeman, Z.A.B. 1961. *The Break-Up of the Habsburg Empire 1914–1918: A Study in National and Social Revolution.* London: Oxford University Press.

Zürcher, E.J. 2000. "Young Turks, Ottoman Muslims and Turkish Nationalists: Identity Politics 1908–1938." Pp. 150–79 in *Ottoman Past and Today's Turkey*, edited by K.H. Karpat. Leiden: Brill

10 Obliterating heterogeneity through peace
Nationalisms, states and wars, in the Balkans

Siniša Malešević

Despite general recognition that not all nationalisms end up in violence and that wars can be waged without nationalist hysteria there is a tendency to assume that nationalism and warfare are deeply linked. Moreover many social analysts believe that the most important research task is to explain the causal relationship between the two. Hence some gauge the impact of warfare on the development of nationalist sentiments while others are concerned with the question "What types of nationalism are most likely to cause war?" (Van Evera 1994: 5). In this chapter I argue that nationalism and warfare have a very complex and unpredictable relationship that can neither be adequately captured, nor properly understood, by focusing on the narrow causal connection between the two. Rather than causing one another or being a key effect of each other's actions, both nationalism and war emerge, develop, and expand as the outcome of many *longue durée* processes. Hence, in order to explain the relationship between wars and nationalisms it is crucial to analyze the long-term organizational and ideological transformations that have shaped the world in the last two hundred years. In this context I argue that (coercive/ bureaucratic and ideologized) periods of peace matter much more for the growth, expansion, and popular reception of nationalism than times of war. Nationalisms often witnessed in war contexts usually have not brought about these wars, nor have they been forged on the battlefields. Instead, both wars and nationalisms are multifaceted processes that emerge, develop, and are sustained by the continuous organizational and ideological scaffoldings created and enhanced in times of prolonged peace. Since the Balkan Peninsula is often perceived as the epitome of a region teeming with nationalism and warfare I use this case to assess the strength of my general argument.

Has nationalism caused war?

Traditional historiography tends to reinforce popular views of nationalism as being one of the principal causes of warfare. The violence of the French and American revolutions is regularly linked to nationalist aspirations. The Napoleonic Wars are often interpreted through the prism of rising French nationalism and the counternationalisms of Germans and others that developed "in response to French invasions" (Calhoun 2007: 136). In particular the twentieth century has persistently been described as the period when competing nationalist ideologies caused total wars: "European nationalism was a major force in the origins of both world wars of the twentieth century. The peoples of Europe went to war in 1914 in an outburst of nationalistic fervour – the French 'à Berlin,' and the Germans 'nach Paris'..." (Snyder 2009[1968]: 71). This "naturalist" approach often presumes that cultural similarity by itself is a principal driver of violent conflict (Malešević 2011: 143–46). "War is," in the words of one of the main representatives of this perspective, "an expression of culture, often a determinant of cultural forms, in some societies the culture itself" (Keegan 1994: 12). However, as decades of sociological research show, not only is there no significant causality between violence and cultural difference (Brubaker 2004; Fearon and Laitin 1996; Laitin 2007), but cultural similarity by itself is a poor predictor of most social action (Banton 2008; Brubaker et al. 2007; Malešević 2006). Furthermore, since warfare is a substantially older social phenomenon than nationalist ideology, nationalism cannot explain the outbreak of most wars throughout history. If we agree that warfare originated at least ten thousand years ago (Fry 2007; Otterbein 2004) and that fully fledged nationalist ideology is barely two to three hundred years old (Breuilly 1993; Hobsbawm 1990; Mann 1986), then a rough estimate would indicate that even if nationalism is a principal cause of war it can only account for less than 0.3 percent of wars fought through history.

Nevertheless, even the more moderate version of this argument, which posits nationalist ideology as a key generator of warfare only in the modern era (Snyder 2009[1968], 1990: 248–50), cannot explain instances of large-scale modern wars where popular nationalist sentiments were not a decisive force for initiating or waging wars such as the Crimean War (1853–56), the Austro-Prussian War (1866), the Second Boer War (1899–1902), or even World War I and World War II (Burbank and Cooper 2010; Mann 2013).

The Balkan region provides an excellent testing ground for this thesis as the southeast of Europe experienced a progressive acceleration of organized violence through the nineteenth and twentieth centuries. For this very reason the Balkans have regularly been singled out as the embodiment of a case where nationalism was (and some would argue remains) the main source of violent conflict. For example, writing about late-nineteenth- and twentieth-century Balkan warfare Richard Hall argues that "each Balkan people envisioned the restoration of the medieval empires on which they based their national ideas" (2002: 2). Similarly Andre Gerolymatos believes that "at the heart of all the Balkan wars is the clarion call of ethnic hatred served up as cultural heritage," (2002: 5) whereas most traditional historiography interprets the popular uprisings at the beginning of the nineteenth century in southeast Europe as "national revolutions" and the "awakening of nationalities" (Jelavich 1999; Pavlowitch 1999). However, not only is there no reliable evidence to suggest that nationalism was behind violent conflicts in the early nineteenth century Balkans, but it seems plausible to argue that nationalist ideology played little or no part in these early uprisings (Kitromilides 1994, 2010; Malešević 2012a, 2012b; Meriage 1977; Stokes 1976).

The Ottoman, and to a lesser extent Habsburg, imperial legacy posited aristocratic lineage and religious affiliation firmly ahead of any "ethnic" attachments which, if they existed at all, were shared by a miniscule number of elite enthusiasts. The millet system reinforced confessional divides, most of which crisscrossed cultural and linguistic communities.[1] Hence, the rebellions and uprisings of the early nineteenth century, such as the First and Second Serbian Uprisings (1804–13 and 1815–17), Hadži Prodan's Revolt of 1813, or the Wallachian and Cretan insurrections of 1821, were not nationalist revolutions aimed at the overthrow of the Ottoman Empire and the establishment of the independent nation-states of Serbia, Greece and Romania, but were essentially social revolts not very different from the peasant rebellions of the previous centuries. In all of these Balkan uprisings, just as in the Greek War of Independence (1821–29) nationalist ideology played a marginal role or no role at all in the mobilization of social action for violent conflict. Instead of implementing a coherent program of national self-determination these violent events were a highly contingent, disorganized, and messy product of different individuals and groups motivated by diverse and often mutually incompatible interests. For example, the Serbian Uprisings were led by opportunistic merchants and outlaws who utilized the social discontent of peasants to expand their economic and political influence in the

---

[1] The millet system was complex but its key feature was the division into semi-autonomous confessional communities. For more information see Hanioğlu 2010.

region. Both Đorđe Petrović Karađorđe and Miloš Obrenović, the leaders of the two uprisings, were large-scale pig traders initially motivated to establish a monopoly on pork trade with the Habsburg Empire and showing little inclination towards Serbian nationalism. Rather than fight the Ottoman Empire they offered "to restore the order on behalf of the Sultan" and to remove the disloyal ayans and ill-disciplined janissaries (Djordjević 1985; Meriage 1977; Roudometof 2001: 231; Stokes 1976). Similarly the Greek War of Independence originated far away from contemporary Greece (in present-day Romania) as a violent social conflict between two groups of Christian elites. In contrast to latter-day nationalist reinterpretations, this was a far cry from organized national revolution bent on establishing an independent nation-state. Instead it comprised a chaotic and messy series of events involving prolonged internal strife among different groups of "Greeks" with the final outcome decided exclusively by the direct involvement of the great powers (Glenny 1999; Mazower 2000).

The social bandits in the Balkans – *hajduks*, *uskoks*, *khlepts*, and *armatoloi* – later glorified in nationalist historiography as the heroes of national independence, were for the most part driven by economic self-interest, were essentially ignorant of national projects, would easily switch sides during the violent conflicts, and would rob Christians just as much as Muslims (Glenny 1999; Hobsbawm 2000[1969]; Pavlowitch 1999). The notion of shared Greek heritage meant nothing to most bandits, whose worldview was extremely parochial. For example, when a visiting scholar flatteringly compared leading klepht Nikotsaras to the ancient Greek hero Achilles, the klepht was angered by this comparison: "What rubbish are you talking about? Who is this Achilles? Handy with a musket, was he?" (Kakridis 1963: 252). In a similar vein, the Balkan peasantry, who constituted an overwhelming majority of the population, had no understanding of nationalist ideals and tended to identify with the local (village) or much broader religious community of Orthodox Christian believers. Instead of looking towards the establishment of an independent and sovereign nation-state they were much more inclined towards believing in the religiously inspired prophecies that linked the collapse of the Ottoman Empire to the Second Coming of Christ and the consequent restoration of the Byzantine Empire (Roudometof 2001; Stoianovich 1994).

Hence nationalist ideology could not possibly be a principal cause of warfare in the early nineteenth century Balkans as there was very little if any nationalism in the region at that time. What was much more important was the changed geopolitical context where the weakening of the Ottoman Empire created a fierce power struggle between the remaining European empires who extensively encouraged (and in the Greek case even fought for) the establishment of the new political entities in the Balkans (Burbank and Cooper 2010; Meriage 1977).

Has war caused nationalism?

Although the view that nationalism causes war is still highly popular among journalists and the general public, most social scientists subscribe to the opposite view: rather than causing war, nationalism itself is a product of war experience. Violent conflicts are seen as the crucible of cultural and political identity: they sharpen group boundaries, externalize social divides, heighten the polarization of in-groups and out-groups, and internally mobilize social action. In other words, protracted warfare is understood as leading towards forging a strong sense of national attachment whereby nations are conceptualized either as moral communities created through "blood sacrifice" (Hutchinson 2007; Smith 1981, 2003), or as an institutional outcome of coordinated social action involving agents who amplify their cultural markers for individual self-benefit (Hechter 1995; Laitin 2007), or as the historical product of geopolitical competition between state-making rulers (Posen 1993; Tilly 1995).

The problem with this perspective is not its factual inaccuracy, as it is quite easy to demonstrate instances where the direct external threat has led to internal homogenization, but its reluctance to look at the long-term organizational and ideological processes that make this quasi-causal relationship possible. Not all wars are able to generate social cohesion: some protracted conflicts, such as the devastating Peloponnesian wars or the tragic experience of the Habsburg Empire in World War I, entirely shatter group solidarity while other violent conflicts, such as the Mexican–American War (1846–48) or the recent Libyan and Syrian civil wars, just reveal the intensity of existing group polarization. More importantly, historical timing matters a great deal: as pre-modern wars were generally fought by warrior strata that excluded the majority of the, essentially peasant, population there were no structural conditions for the emergence of nationalism as a mass phenomenon. It is only with the gradual expansion of nearly universal conscription, since the late eighteenth and early nineteenth centuries, that nationalist ideology could be forged on the battlefields. Nevertheless, even in this radically changed historical context, warfare did not automatically generate strong national attachments, but it took long-term organizational and ideological transformations to foster a sense of solidarity that would surpass family-based, local, and other face-to-face micro groupings (Malešević 2010, 2011).

The history of the nineteenth-century Balkans was often utilized to verify the argument that the experience of warfare is a key generator of nationalist sentiments. From the Greek War of Independence (1821–29) to the Balkan Wars of 1912–13, the southeast of Europe has been singled out by historians and social scientists as the perfect example of a region where persistent warfare forged strong national consciousness (Biondich 2011; Gerolymatos 2002; Glenny 1999; Stavrianos 2000). Nevertheless, just as wars do not automatically and inevitably create states, the historical record is full of cases where protracted warfare has proved highly destructive to nation formation and nationalism (Malešević 2011; Smith 1981). Much of early nineteenth-century Balkan warfare did not create lasting nationalist ideologies. Not only was it that the outcomes of the Greek War of Independence, the Serbian uprisings, and the similar violent episodes in what are today Romania, Bulgaria, and Bosnia were not more nationally conscious populations, but in most instances these violent rebellions generated deep internal divides in supposedly "national societies." For example, the Greek War of Independence left the legacy of a deeply polarized and antagonistic society as the infighting and massacres committed during the war had a profound impact on the political life of future generations (Jelavich 1999; Roudometof 2001). Similarly, the Serbian Uprisings of 1804–13 and 1815–17 were led by two mutually hostile camps, represented by their leaders, Karađorđe and Obrenović, both of whom were determined to stake their legitimate claim to the throne of Serbia. The direct outcome of these uprisings was a deeply divided society. Hence, instead of bringing more national cohesion, independence resulted in protracted clan-based feuds, internal conflicts, and occasional assassinations (Glenny 1999; Pavlowitch 1999).

More important, as Balkan polities emerged not through well-organized nationalist movements but as a consequence of the geopolitical games of the great powers and the gradual collapse of the Ottoman Empire, the overwhelming majority of their populations were not particularly committed to the new states, nor were they fully aware of their nationhood. While in the early nineteenth century the top Orthodox clergy, wealthy merchants, bankers, and Phanariot families were still fully loyal to the empire and the majority peasantry were equally distrustful of all elites (Christian and Muslim, national and imperial), the intensive state building witnessed in the second half of the century generated new forms of internal conflicts (Kitromilides 1994; Roudometof 2001). The wars fought in the latter half of the nineteenth century and the early twentieth century fostered a degree of nationalist euphoria, but this sentiment would rarely spread beyond the narrow circles of the military establishment, state administrators, top clergy, the royal courts, and cultural elites (Roudometof 2001: 174–75). These wars, such as the Serbo-Bulgarian War of 1885, the Greco-Turkish War of 1897 and the two Balkan Wars of 1912–13, were an integral part of the instant and historically unprecedented state building projects whereby the political and military elites embarked on the gigantic transformation of their polities with a view to creating state structures resembling their Western European counterparts. The unintended consequence of this process was highly polarized societies with a substantial administrative, urban-based stratum loyal to the new polities and supportive of the grand national projects that stood in direct opposition to the huge swathes of peasants, many of whom did not identify with the new states and had great difficulty in differentiating between their religion and their nation (Kitromilides 1994, 2010).[2] In other words, while the wars waged in the early nineteenth century were too small-scale, too short, too localized, and too disorganized to forge strong national attachments, the more intensive, protracted, and large-scale warfare of the late nineteenth and early twentieth centuries reinforced already existing, but very narrowly based, nationalism of the elite; however, it proved too destructive to turn peasants into nationally self-conscious Bulgarians, Greeks, Serbs or Albanians. Despite various attempts to appease rural populations by granting them land and the right to vote and in this way "secure their participation in the First World War" (and the Balkan Wars), many peasant recruits were reluctant to fight in these wars and were often ignorant of nationalist rhetoric (Biondich 2011: 43, 61; Mungiu-Pippidi 2010: 63). For example, the largest political party in Bulgaria, the Bulgarian Agrarian National Union, which represented the peasantry, reflected this mood in its firm opposition to Bulgarian involvement in the 1912–13 Balkan Wars and World War I. The party's leader, later the country's prime minister, was released from prison "in an effort to assuage the mutinous soldiers," but upon his release he "joined the agitation against the war" (Hall 2010: 156). In a similar vein, and despite the excessive prevalence of nationalist propaganda in the military, Serbian and Greek peasant soldiers were not particularly enthusiastic about the nationalist projects

---

[2] On his trip to Macedonia in 1903, British journalist Henry Brailsford (1906: 102) documents well this plasticity of collective identification in the region. When asking a local peasant in Greek if his village was Greek or Bulgarian he received the following reply: "Well, it's Bulgarian now, but four years ago it was Greek … We used to have a Greek teacher [and priest] … but he was very unpunctual and remiss. We went to the Greek Bishop to complain, but he refused to do anything for us. The Bulgarians heard of this and they came and made us an offer. They said they would give us a priest who would live in the village and a teacher to whom we need pay nothing. Well, sirs, ours is a poor village, and so of course we became Bulgarians."

that included the capturing and carving up of Macedonia (Glenny 1999; Roudometof 2001). Hence, neither the sporadic rebellions and uprisings of the early nineteenth century nor the fully fledged warfare of the late nineteenth and early twentieth centuries automatically produced mass-scale nationalisms in the Balkans.

The cumulative bureaucratization of coercion in the Balkans

To say that one should be wary of projecting direct causality between nationalism and warfare in the Balkans does not mean that the two phenomena are completely unrelated. Of course in the modern age nearly all interstate wars (as well as many civil wars) are augmented with and legitimized through nationalist ideologies. Nevertheless, to explain how and why nationalism becomes a key component of warfare in modernity, in contrast to the rest of pre-modern history, it is not enough simply to assume either that a mere cultural similarity inevitably generates national cohesion, or that shared war experience will automatically create strong and durable nationalist feelings. Instead, the focus of analysis should shift to the *longue durée* processes that create institutional and societal conditions where nationalisms and wars appear as ontological twins. Among these large-scale structural processes two stand out: the cumulative bureaucratization of coercion and centrifugal ideologization. As argued in my previous work (Malešević 2010, 2011) these two inter-related processes constitute the key social mechanisms for understanding how nationalism and warfare often become conjoined in the modern era. The cumulative bureaucratization of coercion is an ongoing historical process that involves the constant increase of organizational capability for coercion and the internal pacification of social order through the monopolistic threat of the use of violence. Although the cumulative coercive power of social organizations has been on the increase over the past ten thousand years, its full potency – visible in its territorial scope, infrastructural reach and societal penetration – has acutely accelerated in the past two hundred years (Malešević 2010: 5–8, 92–130).

Although in some respects this region had a slower takeoff in terms of its organizational development, southeast Europe was not impervious to these large-scale structural transformations. On the contrary, the Balkans is a region where the cumulative bureaucratization of coercion has been particularly vivid in the past two centuries. While at the beginning of the nineteenth century most Balkan polities lacked nearly all organizational prerogatives of statehood, by the second half of the twentieth century all of them have become pervasive bureaucratic machines. For example, in

1813 the entire civil service of the new Serbian quasi-state amounted to no more than 24 administrators (Stokes 1975: 4). In the same period the population of around 2 million people inhabiting the Dunabian Principalities (i.e. Romania) were administered by just 1,000 office-holding boyars, whereas even as late as 1879 the entire Bulgarian polity had at its disposal only 2,121 civil servants. Even more striking is the case of Bosnia and Herzegovina, which at the time of its occupation by the Habsburgs (1878) was administered by just 120 bureaucrats (Glenny 1999: 268; Pavlowitch 1999: 31; Roudometof 2001: 163). Similarly, the new polities were well short of the proper military and police apparatuses. The "national" uprisings and wars of "independence" were fought by disorganized, decentralized, undisciplined, and poorly armed bandits, foreign-based volunteers and, often coerced, peasantry (Glenny 1999; Malešević 2012a; Meriage 1977; Stokes 1976). Hence it took some time to transform such units into effective military and police forces.

The direct legacy of the declining Ottoman Empire was the poor or nonexistent road and communication networks, lack of sizable urban congregations, highly decentralized power structures, undeveloped banking sectors, and virtually no industrial base. For example, even in the mid 1850s Serbia and Greece had only 800 and 168 kilometers of paved roads respectively; they had no cities with a population over 30,000 until the second half of the nineteenth century, no national banks or factories until the mid to late nineteenth century, and no proper railways until the late nineteenth century (Beaver 1941; Roudometof 2001; Stoianovich 1994).

The extremely intensive and, for the most part, highly coercive state building programs brought about spectacular organizational changes so that by the end of the nineteenth century and the beginning of the twentieth, most Balkan states had changed beyond recognition. The increased cumulative bureaucratization of coercion resulted in the creation of massive state apparatuses: all Balkan polities had introduced universal conscription, established military academies, increased military budgets and set up large armies. For example between 1872 and 1895 the Greek officer corps expanded by 240 percent and the size of its army was constantly rising so that by the beginning of the twentieth century it amounted to 150,000 soldiers; in Serbia in just ten years (1893–1903) the military grew fourfold, while the Bulgarian army was exponentially increasing. The result was that by the beginning of the First Balkan War (1912) these three small states were able to mobilize up to a million soldiers (Bell 1977; Hall 2002; Pelt 2010).

These huge structural transformations were particularly visible in the administrative sphere, with nearly all Balkan states generating enormous civil service apparatuses. Hence by the beginning of the twentieth century the administrative strata became the largest sector of the urban population. Whereas in 1837 Serbia still had a miniscule bureaucracy consisting of 492 civil servants, by 1902 over 22 percent of Belgrade households consisted of administrators and their families (Stokes 1976). The same pattern of intensive bureaucratization emerged in Greece and Bulgaria, where by the end of the 1930s civil servants with their families constituted one third and one fourth, respectively, of the entire urban population (*c.* 650,000 people in both cases) (Roudometof 2001; Stoianovich 1994). Despite the fact that these were still overwhelmingly rural societies, the administrative strata were so enlarged that by the early twentieth century civil servants constituted over 5 percent of the labor force, which was significantly higher than in much more urbanized societies. For example, in the same period administrators accounted for 2.4 percent of the labor force in Germany, 1.5 percent in Britain and 0.31 percent in Italy and Belgium. On top of that, between 25 and 40 percent of the state's budget was allocated for the salaries of civil servants (Pippidi 2010: 130).

The governments also invested heavily in the development of infrastructure, with Serbia in 1883 having five times more roads than it had twenty-five years earlier, Greece dramatically expanding its transport and commercial shipping, and most Balkan states relying on railways as the engine of development so that by 1913 the Balkan region was in possession of over 8 thousand kilometers of rail tracks (Mirković 1958). The strengthening infrastructural powers of Balkan polities were also visible in the greater centralization of state power underpinned by the adoption of new constitutions (modeled on the highly centralized French 1830, Belgian 1831 and Prussian 1850 constitutions) (Pippidi 2010: 125). In contrast to the messy, decentralized, makeshift polities of the early nineteenth century when the monarchs and administrators lacked reliable military and police forces and had no option but to share power with the local dignitaries and warlords (*knezovi, kodzabasides, vojvode* and *kapitanaioi*), by the century's end the rulers were in full control of their territories (Bechev 2010: 138–50).

In Serbia both the liberal oligarchs (*ustavobranitelji*) who ruled between 1842 and 1858 and Prince Mihailo Obrenović (until his assassination in 1868) managed to enhance the authority of the central state by expanding the coercive and bureaucratic apparatuses of the state. This enhancement included enforcement of the laws that curtailed the power of municipalities, which were replaced by French-style district prefects, the introduction of tenured administrative posts and established civil codes, the legal protection of civil servants, registers of land ownership, and statewide censuses. The state was now heavily involved with industrial output, which increased substantially so that by 1906 there were close to five hundred large industrial enterprises in Serbia, and for the first time the authorities were able to provide statewide services such as health care, public hygiene, cultural development, policing, and land management (Djordjević 1970; Draganich 1974; Vucinich 1968).

The same developmental, centralizing and state building processes were just as visible in Greece, Bulgaria, Romania and the rest of Southeast Europe where the rulers largely imitated the French and Prussian top-down models of state organization (Bechev 2010; McGrew 1985; Mouzelis 1978). In the words of a Bulgarian minister at the time, the principal ambition was to "arrange an omnipotent state machine on the French model, ruled by the centre with thousands of officials paid by the state and depending on it" (Bechev 2010: 142). The administrative build-up went hand in hand with the modernization and expansion of the military and police apparatus, and the Balkan states spent vast amounts on armaments, military materiel and policing. For example, in 1905 more than one third of Bulgaria's budget was spent on the military (Pelt 2010: 240).

These highly vigorous processes of bureaucratization of coercion were further intensified throughout the twentieth century. The outcome of large-scale warfare (including the Balkan Wars of 1912–13, World War I and World War II) was an even greater bureaucratic penetration of societies in southeast Europe. Despite the enormous human and material casualties of these wars the post-war authorities were able to concentrate and further expand state power in its both administrative-organizational and coercive sense. Although this was never a unitary, linear and teleological process, as the economic and organizational booms and busts of the 1920s versus the 1930s, or the 1960s versus the 1980s clearly show, all Balkan states, regardless of their political systems, economic development, or level of external openness, have continued to expand cumulatively their organizational and coercive reach. In this sense there was no substantial difference between a communist state such as Yugoslavia and democratic/ authoritarian Greece. In both communist and non-communist contexts the state remained the main employer, the provider of social provisions, and the protector of social order. The post-1945 Balkans saw further expansion of administrative apparatuses accompanied by accelerated urbanization and the decline of traditional, rural lifestyles. For example, in Yugoslavia by the early 1980s the percentage of those involved in agriculture had dropped from 67 percent (in 1948) to only 20 percent (JSP 1986: 12), and the same trend could be observed in the rest of the Balkans (Biondich 2011; Glenny 1999; Jelavich 1999).

The second half of the twentieth century was by far the most stable and most significant period in state development in southeast Europe. The states became involved in nearly every aspect of social life, providing cradle-to-grave welfare provisions that included guaranteed employment, housing, childcare, pension schemes, free health care, and cultural and sport activities. Furthermore, the omnipotent state machine became the key generator of mass urbanization (building large new cities), industrialization, militarization and cultural production (setting up numerous theatres, concert halls, libraries, museums, etc.). The post-World War II Balkan states have, to use Mann's (1986) concepts, dramatically increased their infrastructural powers, including the ability to raise revenue regularly and efficiently, to collect and store information on their citizens, to control the economy, police and military, and substantially to expand the transport and communication networks. The building of this enormous bureaucratic apparatus resulted in the continuous proliferation of the administrative, military, and police sectors.

The communist states were well known for their huge coercive and bureaucratic state apparatuses, and the Balkan states were no exception. For example in the 1950s the Bulgarian army had over 200,000 soldiers and by the late 1980s the Yugoslav People's Army had over 600,000 active personnel (Brown 1970: 275; Gow 1992). However, non-communist Greece boasted just as large a civil service, military, and police (Close 2002). In consequence and despite their official proclamations, the mid to late twentieth-century Balkan states remained dominated by the administrative strata. For example, for all its rhetoric of proletarian society, workers' councils, and self-management participatory economy, communist Yugoslavia was largely governed by, and for the benefit of, state civil servants. Not only was it the case that apparatchiks rather than workers ran the state, but white-collar strata were dominant in all sectors of society including the Communist Party. The overwhelming majority of membership in the Yugoslav League of Communists consisted of middle-class administrators and professionals: in 1976, out of 1.3 million, 41.8 percent were white-collar workers, 28.1 percent were blue-collar workers and only 5.1 percent were peasants (Jelavich 1999: 343). Hence, when the political and economic crisis reached its peak in the 1980s it was again the bureaucrats and the intelligentsia that spearheaded, and the military and police that allowed for, the revolutionary transformations of the states to take place. While in Yugoslavia the competing party and state bureaucratic machines ultimately found themselves on a collision course that ended in brutal warfare, the rest of the communist Balkans embarked on a slow and painful organizational (and ideological) transition, which brought about even more extensive state apparatuses. The Yugoslav Wars of the 1990s were not simply manufactured by calculating politicians who were able somehow quickly to infest the masses with nationalist sentiments. Instead, both wars and nationalisms emerged as an (in part unintended) outcome of long-term coercive bureaucratization (Malešević 2006: 168–226)[3].

As a recent comparative study of administration systems in southeast Europe demonstrates, all states in the region continue to have a very large core civil service ranging from a staggering 5.52 percent of all the employed population in Montenegro[4] to around 2–3 percent in most Balkan states (Cohen 2010: 47). Hence, regardless of the character of the political or economic regimes involved, the nineteenth- and twentieth-century Balkans saw a continuous increase in the organizational and coercive capacity of the state, which is a crucial precondition for waging large-scale prolonged wars.

Centrifugal ideologization in the Balkans

To understand fully why and how nationalism and warfare often appear so connected in the modern era it is not enough just to focus on the power of coercive/administrative organizations. As human beings are much more willing to follow organizational rules and demands if they are perceived as being legitimate, the cumulative bureaucratization of coercion is regularly accompanied by legitimizing ideologies. As I have argued in an earlier work (Malešević 2010: 8–11, 130–41), in the modern age, organizational developments create the conditions for the emergence and proliferation of centrifugal ideologization as the principal mechanism for the justification of coercive-bureaucratic power. Since modernity gives birth to large-scale social organizations that are inevitably composed of highly diverse individuals and interest groups, it becomes necessary to develop and utilize a particular ideological cement that would transform these heterogeneities into quasi-homogenous units. Hence in this context centrifugal ideologization is understood as a historical, mass-scale organizational process that is able to gradually project, and temporarily forge, ideological unity out of this enormous diversity. As this is a very complex and unpredictable process it is only in modernity, when ideological

---

[3] This, of course, does not mean that the cumulative bureaucratization of coercion inevitably leads to war, nor that this process alone can explain the outbreak of the wars of Yugoslav secession. On the complexity of this particular case see Malešević (2002, 2006).

[4] As late as 2009, tiny Montenegro with a total population of slightly above 600,000 had over 50,000 people working in the public sector, which represents 23 percent of the total employed population (Cohen 2010: 47).

doctrines have to compete with other doctrines and acquire the organizational means to do so, that, when successful, ideologies are able to link effectively diverse pouches of micro solidarity into a reasonably coherent, believable, and comprehensive macroideological narrative (Malešević 2010, 2011).

Despite the fact that the Balkan region has been in the whirlpool of religious and civilizational collisions for much of its history, cultural difference was not an object for mass political mobilization. While the Ottoman Empire was ruled in the name of Islam and privileged its Muslim over its non-Muslim subjects, neither religion nor ethnicity were conceptualized in the horizontal, cross-class sense. Instead the Ottoman Empire was a strictly vertical, highly hierarchical, order that clearly distinguished between different social strata and positioned the Sultan as the absolute owner of the entire empire. Rather than politicizing cultural and religious differences the sultans integrated the conquered Christian and Jewish elites into established Ottoman hierarchies. In this process they made existing religious authorities the leaders of their respective millets, thus turning them into the civil servants of the empire. In this process they also appropriated existing dynastic and religious titles so that all post-1453 Ottoman sultans were also automatically Caesars of the Roman Empire and supreme rulers of the Ottoman Christians (Mazower 2000; Roudometof 2001). At the same time, the overwhelming majority of the Ottoman population were peasants who, regardless of their religious affiliation, were confined to the very narrow world of the kinship and village universe whose worldview combined parochial attachments with elements of ritualistic official monotheism and still-strong pagan beliefs (Meriage 1977; Paxton 1972; Stojančević 1966).

The establishment of quasi-sovereign political entities in the early nineteenth century Balkans did not dramatically transform existing belief systems and practices. For much of the first half of the nineteenth century, religion and local attachments mattered much more for peasant populations than did national and other designations (Meriage 1977; Stokes 1976). The strong kinship structures were often reinforced by clan memberships and, among the South Slavs, the presence of extended patrilocal family units (*zadruga*) (Erlich-Stein 1964). In addition, popular comprehension of Orthodox Christianity tended towards syncretism (with widespread pagan practices and strong Ottoman/Muslim cultural traditions) and religious millenarianism (Roudometof 2001: 14)

Even elite groups such as merchants, bankers, and intellectuals involved in the conspirational plans to rise against Ottoman rule conceptualized their revolt much more in religious than in national, liberal, or secular terms. As Roudometof emphasizes "it was religious and not ethnic solidarity that shaped popular attitudes vis-à-vis the revolt ... the 1821 revolts were conceived of as a revolution of the Orthodox millet against the Ottoman authority structure" (2001: 64). Hence until the second half of the nineteenth century, modern ideological discourses such as nationalism, liberalism, socialism, or even coherent conservative ideology had very little or no impact on popular behavior.

Nevertheless, intensive state building accompanied by the cumulative bureaucratization of coercion throughout the late nineteenth and twentieth centuries eventually created organizational conditions for the emergence and proliferation of mass ideologies. However, for the successful dissemination and reception of ideology it was necessary to establish elementary prerequisites such as full literacy, the standardization of vernacular languages, mass publishing, functioning and comprehensive education systems, access to affordable mass media outlets, and the creation of institutions of "high" culture. While all the southeast European societies started with an almost completely illiterate population, by the second half of the twentieth century nearly full literacy had become the norm. For example, even in 1864 just 4.2 percent of Serbia's citizens were literate and as late as 1880 only 3.3 percent of Bulgarians, 13 percent of Romanians, and 14 percent of the Greek population were able to read and write (Ekmečić 1991: 333; Pippidi, 2010: 127–28; Roudometof 2001: 165). In 1830 there were fewer than 800 pupils and 22 teachers in the entire Serbian polity, and the first primary schools in Montenegro and Albania opened as late as 1834 and 1887 respectively (Roudometof 2001: 149; Stoianovich 1994: 208). The "national" vernaculars were standardized quite late and it took a very long time for mass book publishing to develop. For example between 1806 and 1830 only 17 books were published in Bulgarian, and the first Bulgarian language newspaper did not appear until 1844 (Quick 2003; Roudometof 2001). Even when the new polities were well established and had significantly increased the development of the national press and publishing this did not automatically translate into increased demand. So even in the mid nineteenth century "the appeal of publications in local languages was minimal given that the majority of educated readers tended to read German, Italian, English, or French media" (Case 2010: 282).

Hence, apart from the peculiar religious belief systems and practices mediated through local, clan, family, and village-based interpretations, there was very little ideological penetration in the mid nineteenth-century Balkans. For this to change it was essential to expand state building simultaneously with the development of civil society networks, both of which were decisive in the gradual politicization and thus ideologization of the masses. In other words, the intensive bureaucratization of coercion went hand in hand with the mass ideologization of populations. Sometimes this was a deliberate process led by the state authorities interested in turning peasants into loyal Greeks, Serbs, Romanians or Bulgarians, but often this intensive modernization created unintended consequences with the development and spread of diverse Western ideologies including liberalism, socialism, conservatism, communism, and fascism, which have often metamorphosed into local syncretic variations (Biondich 2011; Glenny 1999; Pavlowitch 2002).

The new states invested enormous resources in the development of cultural apparatuses. Hence literacy rates dramatically improved, the education systems were substantially expanded to include entire populations, and institutions of high culture such as theatres, museums, concert halls, national academies, and universities quickly sprang up all over the late nineteenth-century Balkans. For example, in just twenty-two years, between 1879 and 1911, the Bulgarian budget for public instruction grew by no less than 650 percent and the number of newspapers and periodicals nearly tripled, from 110 to 291 (Case 2010: 286; Pippidi 2010: 128). By the 1930s, newspaper production had reached staggering levels so that in Yugoslavia there were 50 main daily papers in 1936 with a combined circulation of over 400,000 and in Romania by 1938 the leading daily, *Universul*, reached a circulation of 200,000 (Case 2010: 294). This cultural production only intensified after World War II, and all Balkan states further expanded their educational, intellectual and information base. For example, by the 1970s Yugoslavia had 19 universities with outpost departments in 74 cities so that by the early 1980s more than one thousand Ph.D. students graduated each year. In addition, by 1984 there were 1,474 academic and cultural journals, 202 radio stations, and 3,063 daily newspapers (JSP 1986: 113–20).

The inexorable state building of the late nineteenth and the twentieth century inevitably created winners and losers. Regardless of the political systems involved, the clear winners were the civil servants, military and police establishments, and the state intelligentsia, while the principal losers were the peasantry and later, with the advent of industrialization, the blue-collar laborers. The uncontrolled overproduction of educated strata that were later unable to find employment in state institutions fostered ideological discontent and the proliferation of both right- and left-wing extremism. For example, many highly educated but unemployed young Romanians joined the far right Iron Guard as "the uncontrolled development of bureaucracy fed extreme right-wing movements" (Pippidi 2010: 133). In this sense southeast Europe was not an exception to the wider European trend for disenchanted intellectuals, university students, and unemployable professionals to be at the forefront of extreme right- and left-wing radicalism (Mann 2004). What differentiated this part of Europe from its western counterpart was the outcome of the speedy and severe structural transformation: state-led organizational modernization did not create independent middle-class sectors. Instead, the new states emerged and continued to exist as highly polarized social orders divided between city-based administrative strata and the small landholding peasantry. Despite the gigantic political and economic changes that shaped the Balkan Peninsula in the late nineteenth and the twentieth century there was a great deal of continuity in the patterns of the region's social stratification. Not only was there an uninterrupted increase in the size of the administrative, military, and police apparatuses from the mid nineteenth century until the end of the twentieth century, but there was a substantial degree of continuity in the principal ideological conflicts waged in the past 150 years. The ever-increasing organizational and coercive powers fostered the prolife-ration of several potent ideological discourses. Civil servants, military officers, and state intelligentsia became the vanguard of irredentism, state nationalism, etatism, and conservatism in a variety of guises; the peasantry was most receptive to agrarian populism, often infused with hefty religious rhetoric; and blue-collar workers were initially sympathetic to variations of socialist and communist ideas but in the wake of World War II state socialism became more conservative (Biondich 2011; Glenny 1999; Zupanov 1985). To circumvent agrarian populist and leftist movements dissatisfied with the dominance of the urban administrative and coercive strata, the late nineteenth- and early twentieth-century state authorities, together with rightist civil society groupings, often deployed xenophobic and chauvinistic rhetoric in order to displace internal conflicts outside state borders. Hence anti-Semitism, Islamophobia, and ethnic chauvin-ism, often accompanied by concrete policies of ethnic cleansing (i.e. "population exchanges") and periodic pogroms, became a crucial ideo-logical tool for forging national homogeneity (Biondich 2011; Glenny 1999; Mazower 2000). It is important to emphasize that much of this protracted organized ideologization of the masses took place long before any major wars.

Nevertheless, despite concentrated efforts to turn peasants (and the urban proletariat) into nationally conscious Serbs, Bulgarians, Albanians, or Greeks, the majority of the population remained resistant to nationalist appeals well into the twentieth century (Malešević 2012b; Meriage 1977; Stokes 1975, 1976). Even the Balkan Wars of 1912–13 and World War I did not dramatically change this attitude as many peasant soldiers were inclined to desert or deliberately injure themselves to avoid the draft

(Biondich 2011; Glenny 1999; Roudometof 2001). The wars could not create nationalist sentiments where they did not exist; the outbreak of warfare could only ignite the spark among already nationalist administrative, military, and intellectual strata. The aftermath of World War II was much more significant in nationalizing masses and transforming peasants into fully fledged nationalists. The combined influence of the cumulative bureaucratization of coercion and centrifugal ideologization fostered the creation of literate, heavily urbanized, informed, and schooled populations highly receptive to the different articulations of nationalism. In this sense there was no substantial difference between communist states such as Bulgaria or Yugoslavia and anti-communist Greece. All twentieth-century Balkan states, just like the rest of the modern world, relied on nationalism as the principal operative ideology for the justification of rule. Despite the official rhetoric of internationalism and universal proletarian solidarity, all communist states utilized nationalism as the most important source of political legitimization. The official Soviet formula of establishing societies that would be "national in form but socialist in content" could not conceal the actual reality of social orders that were quasi-socialist in form but deeply nationalist in content (Brubaker 1996; Malešević 2002, 2006). Regardless of whether a particular form of state socialism was very rigid (such as in Albania and Romania) or more liberal (as in Yugoslavia) they all invested heavily in the nationalization of the masses and deployed nationalist ideology as the key glue of popular legitimacy. As Enver Hoxha put it bluntly: "The religion of Albanian is Albanianism" (Glenny 1999: 560). Hence nationalism in the Balkans was neither a cause nor a product of the various wars fought over the last two hundred years. Instead its development owes much more to the processes taking place in time of prolonged peace: centrifugal ideologization and the cumulative bureaucratization of coercion.

Conclusion

It is difficult to deny that in the modern era most, if not all, interstate wars and other organized violent confrontations entail intensive nationalist mobilization. This is easily confirmed whenever a particular nation-state is challenged by other political actors: from the reaction of the British public to the 1982 Argentinian invasion of the Falkland Islands, to the spontaneous outbursts of US nationalism in the wake of the 9/11 terrorist attacks, to the popular outrage of Russian public opinion that followed the 2008 Georgian military offensive in South Ossetia. However, the fact that two phenomena, nationalism and war, often emerge together does not mean that one inevitably causes the other. For if this were the case, nationalism would accompany many more wars throughout history than it actually has. Hence, rather than causing each other, both nationalism and war require long-term ideological and organizational work to materialize fully. The historical experience of the Balkan Peninsula clearly demonstrates the structural difficulties in deploying nationalist ideologies to support a war effort where and when they do not exist. Instead of rampant nationalisms fuelling organized violence one often encounters historical contingencies, the geopolitical games of large empires, reluctant peasantry, and opportunist local elites. Not only did nationalist ideologies not cause wars in the Balkans for much of modern history, but nationalism also remained a rather weak social force until well into the twentieth century.

In a similar vein, taking part in large-scale wars does not automatically make human beings into stringent nationalists. On the contrary, as many examples of Balkan warfare show, experiencing devastating and prolonged wars is often likely to make large sections of the population resentful towards grand, national projects. The stunning victories of the Serbian and Greek armies in the Balkans Wars of 1912–13 did not make the Greek and Serbian peasants more enthusiastic about the *Megali Idea* or the *Načertanije*. Hence, when nationalisms and wars appear to set each other off, this often has less to do with the advent of a particular war and much more to do with long-term historical – organizational and ideological – macro processes developed far away from the battlefields.

REFERENCES

Banton, M. 2008. "The Sociology of Ethnic Relations." *Ethnic and Racial Studies* 31(7): 1,267–1,285.
Beaver, S.H. 1941 "Railways in the Balkan Peninsula." *Geographical Journal* 1,107(5): 273–94.
Bechev, D. 2010. "The State and Local Authorities in the Balkans, 1804–1939." Pp. 135–52 in *Ottomans into Europeans*, edited by W. Van Meurs and A. Mungiu-Pippidi. London: Hurst.
Bell, J. 1977. *Peasants in Power: Alexander Stamboliski and the Bulgarian Agrarian National Union, 1899–1923*. Princeton University Press.
Biondich, M. 2011. *The Balkans: Revolution, War and Political Violence since 1878*. Oxford University Press.
Brailsford, H. 1906. *Macedonia: Its Races and Their Future*. London: Methuen.
Breuilly, J. 1993. *Nationalism and the State*. Manchester University Press.
Brown, J. 1970. *Bulgaria under Communist Rule*. New York: Praeger.
Brubaker, R. 1996. *Nationalism Reframed*. Cambridge University Press.
   2004. *Ethnicity without Groups*. Cambridge, MA: Harvard University Press.

Brubaker, R., M. Feischmidt, J. Fox, and L. Grancea. 2007. *Nationalist Politics and Everyday Ethnicity in a Transylvanian Town*. Princeton University Press.

Burbank, J. and F. Cooper. 2010. *Empires in World History*. Princeton University Press.

Calhoun, C. 2007. *Nations Matter*. London: Routledge.

Case, H. 2010. "The Media and State Power in South-East Europe to 1945." Pp. 277–304 in *Ottomans into Europeans*, edited by W. Van Meurs and A. Mungiu-Pippidi. London: Hurst.

Close, D. 2002. *Greece since 1945: Politics, Economy, Society*. New York: Pearson.

Cohen, L.J. 2010. "Administrative Development in 'Low-Intensity' Democracies: Governance, Rule-of-Law and Corruption in the Western Balkans." *Simons Papers in Security and Development*, 5(1): 1–48.

Djordjević, D. 1970. "Projects for the Federation of South-East Europe in the 1860s and 1870s." *Balkanica* 2: 119–46.

   1985. "The Serbian Peasant in the 1876 War." Pp. 305–18 in *War and Society in East Central Europe: Insurrections, Wars and the Eastern Crisis in the 1870s*, edited by B. Kiraly and G. Stokes. Boulder, CO: Social Science Monographs.

Draganich, A. 1974. *Serbia, Nikola Pasic and Yugoslavia*. New Brunswick, NJ: Rutgers University Press.

Ekmečić, M. 1991. "The Emergence of St. Vitus Day as the Principal National Holiday of the Serbs." Pp. 331–42 in *Kosovo: Legacy of Medieval Battle*, edited by W. Vucinich and T. Emmert. Minneapolis: University of Minnesota Press.

Erlich-Stein, V. 1964. *Porodica u transformaciji*. Zagreb: Naprijed.

Fearon, J. and D. Laitin. 1996. "Explaining Interethnic Cooperation." *American Political Science Review* 90(4): 715–35.

Fry, D.S. 2007. *Beyond War: The Human Potential for Peace*. Oxford University Press.

Gerolymatos, A. 2002. *The Balkan Wars*. New York: Basic Books.

Glenny, M. 1999. *The Balkans 1804–1999: Nationalism, War and the Great Powers*. London: Granta.

Gow, J. 1992. *Legitimacy and the Military: The Yugoslav Crisis*. New York: St. Martin's Press.

Hall, R. 2002. *The Balkan Wars 1912–1913*. London: Routledge.

   2010. *Balkan Breakthrough: The Battle of Dobro Pole 1918*. Bloomington: Indiana University Press.

Hanioğlu, M.Ş. 2010. *A Brief History of the Late Ottoman Empire*. Princeton University Press.

Hechter, M. 1995. "Explaining Nationalist Violence." *Nations and Nationalism* 1(1): 53–68.

Hobsbawm, E. 1990. *Nations and Nationalism since 1780*. Cambridge University Press.

   2000 [1969]. *Bandits*. New York: New Press.

Hutchinson, J. 2007. "Warfare, Remembrance and National Identity." Pp. 42–54 in *Nationalism and Ethnosymbolism: History, Culture and Ethnicity in the Formation of Nations*, edited by A. Leoussi and S. Grosby. Edinburgh University Press.

Jelavich, B. 1999. *History of the Balkans*. Cambridge University Press.

JSP. 1986. *Jugoslavija 1945–1985. Statisticki Prikaz*. Belgrade: Savezni Zavod za Statistiku.

Kakridis, J. 1963. "The Ancient Greeks of the War of Independence." *Journal of Balkan Studies* 4(2).

Keegan, J. 1994. *A History of Warfare*. New York: Vintage.

Kitromilides, P. 1994. *Enlightenment, Nationalism, Orthodoxy: Studies in the Culture and Political Thought of South-Eastern Europe*. Brookfield, VT: Variorum.

2010. The Orthodox Church in Modern State Formation in South-East Europe. Pp. 31–50 in *Ottomans into Europeans: State and Institution Building in South Eastern Europe*, edited by W. Van Meurs and A. Mungiu-Pippidi. London: Hurst.

Laitin, D. 2007. *Nations, States, and Violence*. Oxford University Press.

Malešević, S. 2002. *Ideology, Legitimacy and the New State: Yugoslavia, Serbia and Croatia*. London: Routledge.

2006. *Identity as Ideology: Understanding Ethnicity and Nationalism*. New York: Palgrave Macmillan.

2010. *The Sociology of War and Violence*. Cambridge University Press.

2011. "Nationalism, War and Social Cohesion". *Ethnic and Racial Studies* 34(1): 142–61.

2012a. "Wars that Make States and Wars that Make Nations: Organised Violence, Nationalism and State Formation in the Balkans." *European Journal of Sociology* 53(1): 31–63.

2012b. "Did Wars Make Nation-States in the Balkans? Nationalisms, Wars and States in the 19th and Early 20th Century South East Europe." *Journal of Historical Sociology* 25(3): 299–330.

Mann, M. 1986. *The Sources of Social Power*. 4 vols. Vol. I *A History of Power from the Beginning to AD 1760*. Cambridge University Press.

2004. *Fascists*. Cambridge University Press.

2013. "The Role of Nationalism in the Two World Wars" (Chapter 7 of the current volume).

Mazower, M. 2000. *The Balkans: From the End of Byzantium to the Present Day*. London: Phoenix.

McGrew, W. 1985. *Land and Revolution in Modern Greece, 1800–1881*. Kent, OH: Kent State University Press.

Meriage, L.P. 1977. "The First Serbian Uprising (1804–1813): National Revival or a Search for Regional Security." *Canadian Review of Studies in Nationalism* 4(2): 187–205.

Mirković, M. 1958. *Ekonomska historija Jugoslavije*. Zagreb: Ekonomski pregled.

Mouzelis, N. 1978. *Modern Greece: Facets of Underdevelopment*. London: Macmillan.

Mungiu-Pippidi, A. 2010. "Failed Institutional Transfer? Constraints on the Political Modernisation of the Balkans." Pp. 51–74 in *Ottomans into Europeans: State and Institution Building in South Eastern Europe*, edited by W. Van Meurs and A. Mungiu-Pippidi. London: Hurst.

Otterbein, K.F. 2004. *How War Began*. College Station: Texas A&M University Press.

Pavlowitch, S. 1999. *A History of the Balkans 1804–1945*. London: Longman.

2002. *Serbia: The History behind the Name*. London: Hurst.

Paxton, R. 1972. "Nationalism and Revolution: A Re-examination of the Origins of the First Serbian Insurrection, 1804–7." *East European Quarterly* 6(3): 337–62.

Pelt, M. 2010. "Organised Violence in the Service of Nation Building." Pp. 221–44 in *Ottomans into Europeans: State and Institution Building in South Eastern Europe*, edited by W. Van Meurs and A. Mungiu-Pippidi. London: Hurst.

Pippidi, A. 2010. "The Development of an Administrative Class in South-East Europe." Pp. 111–34 in *Ottomans into Europeans: State and Institution Building in South Eastern Europe*, edited by W. Van Meurs and A. Mungiu-Pippidi. London: Hurst.

Posen, B. 1993. "Nationalism, the Mass Army, and Military Power." *International Security* 18(2): 80–124.

Quick, A. 2003. *World Press Encyclopaedia*. Detroit: Gale.

Roudometof, V. 2001. *Nationalism, Globalization and Orthodoxy: The Social Origins of Ethnic Conflict in the Balkans*. Westport, CT: Greenwood Press.

Smith, A. 1981. "War and Ethnicity: The Role of Warfare in the Formation, Self-Images, and Cohesion of Ethnic Communities." *Ethnic and Racial Studies* 4: 375–97.

2003. *Chosen Peoples: Sacred Sources of National Identity*. Oxford University Press.

Snyder, L.L. 1990. "Nationalism and War." Pp. 248–50 in *Encyclopedia of Nationalism*. Chicago: St. James Press.

(2009)[1968]. The New Nationalism. New Brunswick: Transactions.

Stavrianos, L.S. 2000. *The Balkans since 1453*. London: C. Hurst.

Stoianovich, T. 1994. *Balkan Worlds: The First and Last Europe*. New York: M.E. Sharpe.

Stojančević, V. 1966. *Milos Obrenović i njegovo doba*. Belgrade: Prosveta.

Stokes, G. 1975. *Legitimacy through Liberalism: Vladimir Jovanovic and the Transformation of Serbian Politics*. Seattle: University of Washington Press.

1976. "The Absence of Nationalism in Serbian Politics before 1840." *Canadian Review of Studies in Nationalism* 4(1): 77–90.

Tilly, C. 1995. *Coercion, Capital, and European State Formation*. Cambridge: Polity Press.

Van Evera, S. 1994. "Hypotheses on Nationalism and War." *International Security* 18(4): 5–39.

Vucinich, W. 1968. *Serbia between East and West: The Events of 1903–1908*. New York: AMS Press.

Zupanov, J. 1985. *Samoupravljanje i drustvena moc*. Zagreb: Globus.

Part 4

Empty shells, changed conditions

11 Internal wars and Latin American nationalism

Miguel Angel Centeno, Jose Miguel Cruz, Rene Flores, and Gustavo Silva Cano

During several months in 2010, a very peculiar story dominated global news, culminating in 24-hour coverage October 12–14. Trapped for several months and at one point presumed dead, 33 Chilean miners were rescued on global TV. The narrative arc of the rescue was a typical media spectacle of fortitude, technological know-how, and human dignity, topped off by incredible success. From the beginning, the Chilean story took on a nationalistic air. When the miners were discovered alive, their first spoken message to the world was the Chilean national anthem sung in unison. From that day onward, there were scantily few images of the site and the rescue process that did not include a Chilean flag.

For audiences in many parts of the world, the conjunction of tragedy, triumph, and jingoistic celebration would appear perfectly normal, and very much in line with similar events such as the 9/11 and 7/7 terrorist attacks. What could be more typical than an expression of national solidarity in the face of a common threat? Yet for many Latin American observers, the Chilean response seemed somewhat odd. In fact, in country after country in the region, common threats do not soothe internal divisions, but actually seem to deepen them. One could have imagined many other political narratives in the region accompanying the original accident and subsequent rescue focusing on class divisions, regional complaints, or ethnic claims; to stand with the miners as workers is one thing, to stand with them as co-nationals is another. The very exceptionalism of the way Chileans came together behind their government during the mine rescue highlights the particular nature of state–society relations in much of Latin America and serves to bring forth a series of questions about nationalist sentiment in the region. Two issues deserve special attention: first, what is the nature of Latin American nationalism and, second, how does its development correspond to the kind of stimuli associated with it in other parts of the world? The first can help us to understand the specific region better, while the second might improve our analysis of the process of state and nation making throughout the developing world.

Nations and identity in Latin America

How nationalist is Latin America? As with many such questions, it all depends on how one defines nationalism. Based on the often-portrayed seas of flags accompanying national football (soccer) teams and the often irascible public response to perceived transnational (and especially American) encroachments on national sovereignty, we might classify Latin America as extremely nationalistic. Reversing Walker Connor's (1978) nomenclature, we believe these manifestations are better understood as expressions of *patriotism*. This is a general sentiment emphasizing a "love of a place." In general, there is a distinctive and strong *patriotismo* in the region based on pride in folklores, natural beauty, and culture. In fact, several authors have noted the strong link between a sense of place or territory and nationalist sentiment in the region.[1] There is also a strong tradition of anti-imperialist feeling concerned with national sovereignty. Patriotism does include a psychological bond between people and a conviction of their identity and differentiation from others; it refers to a perceived and identified community (Connor 1978: 377–83). Nationalism is a very different political animal and as a political force it must be understood in reference to a state. It is the identification with a state and the recognition of no higher duty than advancing its interests.[2] This is less a matter of celebration of identity and more of what Anderson (1991) notes as "colossal sacrifices" made in the state's name. The notion of sacrifice is also central to Joseph Strayer's (1966) view of the development of nationalism: he noted the critical step in the thirteenth century when people were more willing to sacrifice "lives and property" for the state than for the Church.

We emphasize this statist component because only then can we (following Connor again) understand the process through which the primary loyalty of a population is transferred to a set of political institutions. It is this loyalty (and corresponding actions) much more than any set of sentiments that makes nationalism a potent political force. Obviously, this nationalism may also be expressed negatively: as a rejection of a set of institutions as deserving of loyalty or representing a community. In this chapter, we are less concerned with contending claims for such loyalty and obedience and more with the genesis of loyalty and obedience in general. This has been one of the most important aspects of political development in much of the world and particularly Latin America.

---

[1] See work by Luis Alberto Romero and Fernando Lopez Alves.
[2] On this distinction we follow George Orwell 2002. See also Gerth and Mills 2007; Fevre, Denney and Borland 1997: 560.

Consider the results of two questions from the Latin American Public Opinion Project at Vanderbilt University (LAPOP 2008). In one, respondents are asked about their sense of pride in being of a certain nationality. In the other they are asked about their pride in the political system of that country. Consistently, over 90 percent express a great deal of pride in being of a certain nationality, while the numbers for the political system are a small fraction of this (with exceptions such as Chile and Costa Rica). We want to suggest that the first is a measure of what we call patriotism, while the second is closer to what may be called nationalism, or at least state nationalism. Obviously, this is no more than suggestive, but in the absence of concrete data on nationalist or patriotic sentiment, the consistent gap between the two represents the peculiar status of Latin American national consciousness. There is broad agreement in contemporary scholarship that the link between any national community and the state as an institution was and remains weak and that the legitimation of political authority as the voice of the nation has been limited at best.

The dominant characteristic of Latin America from the very beginning of its modern history through today has been its social and political fractionalization; Latin America is a permanently divided region. We do not deny the existence of a multitude of collective identities based on ethnicity, class, region, etc.,[3] nor are we arguing for an extreme individualized atomization, but we contend that few of these identities have been able to embrace the entire nation or society (or even existed in opposition to the state as such in favor of a different definition of the territory). We need to recognize the essential absence of seemingly primordial identities that parallel those of nation-states. Obviously we can find a broad spectrum in the region, with Costa Rica at one end and Paraguay at the other. Nevertheless, there is enough commonality to make discussion of a regional phenomenon reasonable.

Latin America is defined by intra-statal divisions much more so than by inter-statal ones. We can begin with the obvious racial/ethnic legacy of the Conquest that still defines so much of Andean and Mesoamerican societies, and that of plantation agriculture, which characterized much of the Atlantic Coast. There are also the regional gaps that pervade practically every country: plains and mountains, coasts and interior, capital and provinces. There are also the class gulfs in this most unequal of regions, that help define the rhetoric and struggles of

---

[3] The work of Florencia Mallon (1995), Peter Guardino (2002), David Nugent (1997), and others clearly has demonstrated that such a community arose in the nineteenth century.

politics. Finally, there are the ideological gulfs of Left and Right and in between. That many of these divisions are congruent and interact makes the schisms even starker.

This is not a new phenomenon. In many ways, these divisions are what defined the post-independence projects whereby a form of liberalism was attempted without the concomitant creation of a state able to impose unity or a sense of nation to inspire cohesion. The nineteenth-century liberal project floundered precisely because it refused to do one of two things: impose an absolute order or open the society to redefine what that order should be (Centeno and Ferraro 2012). Over much of its history, the explicit hope of a variety of political projects has been that "progress" of one sort or another would lead to a social convergence. One version of this vision saw the historical mingling of groups as inevitably leading to a new form of nation. This is best epitomized by the Mexican ideology of the *raza cosmica* arising from the various conflicts, or the creation of a generic "post-racial" *guajiro* identity in the Andes and the Caribbean. A more "liberal" vision expected that with enough economic progress, these fissures would be closed. This was at the very heart of the *Concertación* discourse in Chile. But in actuality material, social, racial, and political progress have yet to close these gaps in the present.

We argue that in the case of Latin America, this fractionalization is a reflection of the failure of a post-Conquest national hegemonic project on the continent. No side of any of the various divisions has been able to so defeat the others as to impose its own worldview or domination. Note that this is not necessarily a bad thing. The imposition of a hegemonic project and of a true class or racial domination is not a pretty sight and leaves destruction around it, but such imposition may be the only way to achieve the imagined national community. And perhaps no social process so facilitates the creation of a communal hegemony as war.

War and nationalism

Most of the discussion on the relationship between war and nationalism is based on or makes references to a relatively limited set of cases. These are largely restricted to the "usual suspects" of historical sociology (the North Atlantic, Russia, and Japan), mostly deal with international wars (or, if civil conflicts, between institutionalized opponents as in the US 1861–65), and are concentrated in the era defined by the predominance of the nation-state (1815–2000). These experiences are of limited analytical relevance for the most common type of armed conflict today, which occurs outside of the OECD core and involves actors that are either not politically institutionalized, or fairly weakly so. This chapter questions the extent to which the old adages of nationalism and wars hold in these circumstances.

The centrality of war in nation making was recognized by the German idealists of the nineteenth century. Herder defined the origins of the German people (*Volk*) in the battle of the Teutoburg Forest, Fichte celebrated the spirit of Jena, and Hegel compared war to an ocean wind purifying the health of the people from the "corruption" of perpetual peace. The great historian of war Michael Howard claims that, for much of nineteenth-century Europe, "war was the necessary dialectic in the evolution of nations" (1992: 39). Georg Simmel could celebrate the start of World War I as an opportunity to consolidate national sentiment and cohesion: "the war heralded a purging in the Augean stables of the urbanized money cultures of the West, rooting out all that was ephemeral, superfluous, excessive and inessential in the experience of life" (Harrington 2005: 64).

The experience of war is generally central to the creation of national identity, providing it with the most passionate forms of expression. The more people become involved in domestic or international wars, the more they become aware of their membership in a political community and of the rights and the obligations such membership might confer. A call to fight wars in the name of the nation transforms a citizen from "a passive object into an active subject of political participation" (Holsti 1996: 119). War gives an idea not only of what we are not (the enemy, the "other"), but also of what we are defending, who we are, and what we collectively represent. Violence and national identity are also connected by issues of legitimacy, of how government is perceived by its citizens. If a state or a government is weak in terms of popular perceptions and legitimacy, or in terms of sovereignty, it remains vulnerable to instability, internal conflict, and violence. To the weak state confronted by powerful opposition, the appeal of arguments of national identity is that it both offers a degree of political legitimacy and is seen (at least by those in power) to legitimate and justify the use of coercion, repression, and violence.

Latin America has largely defied this tradition as political violence has not traditionally served as the handmaiden of such communities, nor have such sentiments helped to account for the level and type of conflicts seen in the region. One of the authors has already noted the failure to link historically martial prowess or even danger with a strong sense of nation in the region (Centeno 2002). In contemporary Latin America, we do have some cases where the classic war–nationalism dyad appears to have played out. On April 2, 1982, for example, Argentinians almost unanimously signalled their support for the invasion of the Malvinas/Falklands. Despite its low legitimacy and support, the military regime appeared to have one more gasp of life as it sought to portray itself as the defender of national patrimony. This euphoria, however, did not last very long and, like the military dictatorship, could not survive the defeat.[4] Similar popular sentiment may have helped bring down the Sanchez de Losada government in Bolivia in 2003 when it appeared to be accepting the now century-old Chilean control of the Pacific coastline. A much longer-term dynamic has existed in revolutionary Cuba. While many thought that the regime would follow its Soviet supporters into the dustbin of history, it has been able to survive four US presidents since the fall of the Berlin Wall. It is now widely accepted that it is precisely the American opposition and the nationalist core of the Revolution that best helps to explain its longevity.

As in much of the developing world, however, contemporary political violence in Latin America does not consist of conflicts between states, but struggles within them. In particular, the pattern in the region over the past few decades has been that states are confronting not well-articulated and institutionalized oppositions that seek to replace national govern-ments but instead more amorphous forces that challenge the authority of the state without necessarily offering an alternative project. It is this form of threat that most developing nations face.

In the rest of this chapter, we discuss three cases: Colombia's battle against FARC, Salvador's with the *mara* gangs, and Mexico's with the *narcos*. Obviously there are other possibilities in the region (and many, many more outside of it) including Peru's experience with Sendero Luminoso, the Contra wars in Nicaragua, and the military repression of various groups in the 1970s. Our account seeks to provide a basic narrative of the form of conflict involved. In the absence of agreed-on measures of extent and intensity of nationalist sentiments, we refer to public opinion polls and public demonstrations of support. In the final section, we propose some ways to begin to understand the relationship between this form of war and nationalism.

Colombia and FARC

Over the past decades the levels of violence in Colombia have shown significant fluctuations (Bushnell 2007). The madness of La Violencia (1948–58) was followed by the apparent reconciliation of the National Front. The anti-government groups Fuerzas Armadas Revolucionarias de Colombia (FARC) and Ejército de Liberación Nacional (ELN) were

---

[4] Of much longer (if not larger) import was the boost that the victory gave to Margaret Thatcher.

founded in 1964 and the Movimiento 19 de abril (M-19) in 1970, but their scope of action remained limited. By the early 1970s, Colombia enjoyed its lowest homicide rates in the twentieth century (21 per 100,000). In the 1980s, however, Colombia saw a steep and continued increase in bloodshed, and the intensification of violence was intertwined with the rise of cocaine trafficking.

Throughout the 1980s, Colombia lived a *bonanza coquera* that transformed the country into a hotspot for cocaine production (Díaz and Sánchez 2004: 9). A prospering cocaine business, as well as the relatively high prices of that drug, meant that Colombian traffickers saw their profits skyrocket (Frechette 2007). As a result, their power vis-à-vis the Colombian state also increased dramatically, and the drug cartels soon became important participants in the country's political conflicts. The government stepped up its anti-narcotics operations, and the cartels responded with overwhelming force, unleashing a wave of violence that the country had not seen since La Violencia. Between late 1985 and the early 1990s, Colombia experienced a series of bomb attacks, kidnappings, and high-profile political murders related to the drug trade (Thoumi 2003: 205). Between 1985 and 1992, the murder rate almost doubled from 43 to 77.5 per 100,000 inhabitants. In the face of a growing threat from stronger, wealthier drug cartels, the Colombian state increased its efforts against these organizations. In the 1990s presidents César Gaviria (1990–94) and Ernesto Samper (1994–98) made it their priority to capture or hunt down the leaders of the Medellin and Cali cartels, respectively (Thoumi 2003: 208–27). By 1996, both cartels had been dismantled, their leaders either dead or in prison.

The dismantling of the Medellin and the Cali cartels opened the door for new, smaller syndicates to take over the business. In time, FARC and the ELN also became involved in the drug industry in order to finance their actions against the state, and right-wing paramilitary groups, originally and nominally created to fight the guerrillas, quickly followed suit (Díaz and Sánchez 2004: 22–23, 64–68). The guerrillas and the paramilitary groups started their involvement in the drug business by means of taxing the production of coca leaves and coca paste in the areas where they operated. However, eventually, insurgencies from both Right and Left became direct participants in coca cultivation, cocaine production, drug transportation, and sales (Thoumi 2003: 107–08). The drug trade and the internal conflict, initially two separate phenomena, had become powerfully intertwined.

Elected president in 1998, Andrés Pastrana agreed to establish a 42,000 square-kilometer demilitarized zone for peace negotiations with FARC, by then Colombia's largest guerrilla group (Bushnell 2007: 399).

During those four years FARC took over the production of cocaine in the zone, which allowed the group to obtain a significant amount of financial resources (PNUD 2003: 285). Realizing that his government was unable to succeed against the cartels and the insurgencies on its own, President Pastrana sought help from the United States, the single most important consumer of Colombian drugs. The result was Plan Colombia, a multi-year strategy of US counternarcotics aid that began in 2000, with the aim of reducing the production of drugs in Colombia (Frechette 2007: 11–15). When the fight against terrorism became a prominent topic in American politics, the Colombian government persuaded the US to allocate Plan Colombia funds to military expenditures against the insurgencies. Soon after 9/11, the United States declared FARC, the ELN, and the paramilitary group known as Autodefensas Unidas de Colombia (AUC), as Foreign Terrorist Organizations (Congressional Research Service 2004). Drugs and internal conflict had merged into one common war.

As a candidate and as President, Alvaro Uribe (2002–10) took a hard-line approach, which was well received by the voters. He increased defense spending considerably, intensified efforts in aerial and manual coca eradication, and made frequent use of extradition to the US for drug traffickers (Ministerio de Defensa 2007). The government's strategy began by retaking control of the country's main roads, as well as those areas with significant guerrilla presence that surrounded important cities (Bushnell 2007: 414–15). Uribe's security strategy produced a series of important military victories against FARC. According to government figures, FARC had about 26,000 members in 2002; by 2010, the estimate was 8,000 (El Espectador 2010a). FARC also lost many of the most important hostages that they had kept for years as bargaining chips.

The Uribe administration also dealt with the paramilitary threat, but in a very different fashion. In 2003, negotiations with right-wing paramilitary groups started, leading to the demobilization of some of their main structures in exchange for reduced sentences (Pearl 2010).[5] The negotiations were marred by controversy due to the flagrant human rights violations these organizations had committed, and to the reduced sentences the law ordered for them. Moreover, some paramilitary units remained active. The government's treatment of paramilitary groups became even more controversial due to the scandal commonly called *parapolítica* and involving close ties between Uribe allies in various government branches and the paramilitary groups. The general perception was that the government had been much more lenient with the

---

[5] See also Hernández 2010.

paramilitary groups than with those on the nominal Left. The campaign against the guerrillas was also stained by a significant increase in human rights abuses by government forces and the failure to deal adequately with the hundreds of thousands of people displaced by the anti-guerrilla campaigns.

In spite of the controversy, Uribe had important results to show by the end of his eight-year presidency. In 2009, Colombian annual cocaine production was at its lowest level in twelve years (about 400 tons), while coca cultivation was reduced by almost two thirds from its 2001 level, reaching 68,000 hectares (UNODC 2010: 6). Under the Uribe administration, the homicide rate also went down to levels not seen since the early 1980s and comparable to those of the first years of the National Front: 35 per 100,000 in 2009 from 69 in 2001. The number of kidnappings per year, another major concern at the beginning of the 2000s, was lower than 200 in 2009, down from 2,882 in 2002 (El Espectador 2010b). All these statistics were hailed as successes by the Uribe administration and the Colombian mainstream media. Overall, the notion that drug cartels and the insurgencies were inexorably on the rise was dramatically challenged during the Uribe era.

In part, this was a product of a very consistent and powerful campaign on behalf of the government. Throughout the Uribe presidency, the government's rhetoric was self-righteous, Manichaean, optimistic, and tough. The insurgents were invariably qualified as "terrorists," and as enemies of both the state and the Colombian people. The topos of narcotrafficking was usually brought up in order to describe FARC, the ELN, and paramilitary groups, to the extent that "narco-terrorists" became a common compound noun used to refer to these organizations. This conveyed the idea that the insurgencies were not only perpetrators of attacks against civilians, but also criminals who manufactured and exported drugs in order to finance their war. The dichotomy between good and evil was thus easily created, as the insurgencies were taken to stand for violence, destruction, and the expansion of the drug trade, while the government and its military stood for exactly the opposite.

The idea of a noble fight for the protection of democratic values was a common theme in government rhetoric. The government often juxtaposed the concepts of democracy and violence, democracy and terrorism, and democracy and crime, and there was no question of what side the state was on. The idea of security, defined as a frontal fight against insurgencies and crime, was defended as a fundamental democratic value without which Colombia could not survive. Not in vain was the government's defense strategy called Democratic Security.

The government also used the words "liberty", "peace," and "prosperity" as the objectives of its policies, while the insurgencies were portrayed to symbolize the contrary. FARC's use of kidnapping as a strategy to gain notoriety and bargaining power allowed the government to point to them as the enemies of freedom. Similarly, when the military regained control of the main roads around the country, the government hailed this as a victory for the citizen's liberty to travel within Colombia. The military and police were depicted as heroes and as the defenders of democracy and the constitution. Those soldiers and officers who died in action had an important place in the government's discourse, while those wounded in action usually took part in military ceremonies and parades on national holidays.

One of the elements that defined the Uribe presidency was the high approval rating that he and his policies enjoyed. When compared to the ratings of previous governments, the popular support for the Uribe administration is astounding (Semana 2010). According to polls by Gallup, President Samper reached a maximum approval rating of 69 percent at the beginning of his government, although this level fell quickly to the 40s and 30s (Gallup 2010). President Pastrana's maximum approval rating was a mere 43 percent during the first months of his administration, but his ratings soon fell to around 20 percent, where they stayed for the rest of his administration. In contrast, Uribe started his presidency with an approval rating of 72 percent, and he reached a maximum of 86 percent well into the sixth year of his administration. Throughout the eight years under President Uribe, his approval ratings never fell below 68 percent.

These opinion polls suggest that the majority of Colombians were strongly in favor of many of the government's policies. According to polls by Gallup, solid majorities (consistently between 61 and 83 percent) approved of the way the Uribe administration handled drug trafficking throughout his presidency. Regarding the internal conflict, the Uribe administration also managed to obtain strong support for his policies. During the first years of the Pastrana presidency, up to 59 percent of Colombians believed that the military was unable to destroy the guerrilla groups; by 2008 that percentage had shrunk to 8 percent, given the significant resources dedicated to the defense strategy. Similarly, during the Pastrana administration up to 63 percent of Colombians thought that it was possible for the guerrillas to take power by force, but that number fell significantly during the Uribe era, reaching 10 percent in 2008. It is also noteworthy that throughout the past decade, Colombia's police had an average approval rating of 70 percent, while the military forces' rating was about 78 percent.

Support for the government culminated in the massive *marcha* (demonstration) of February 4, 2008 with 12 million participants. Importantly, while previous *marchas* had been in support of negotiations or generic peace, this one was very much in favor of the dissolution of FARC, even if it had to be achieved by force (El Tiempo 2008b). Former president Cesar Gaviria said that the demonstration "was an expression from civil society that the country had not known in all of its history. An expression that went beyond political parties, labor unions and institutions" (El Tiempo 2008a). This massive demonstration was the culmination of a dramatic shift in popular opinion. In 1999, FARC was still not considered a "terrorist group" but an armed group with a political status, and many still believed that a negotiation process with the state was a realistic solution to the conflict. By 2008 the situation was markedly different. Six years of Democratic Security had convinced large portions of the public that military pressure against FARC was the best option. The government's rhetoric of a fight against terrorism had already been assimilated by the media and the Colombian public.

What can we learn from the Colombian case? First (and as in all the cases below) we lack adequate measures of the form of nationalist legitimacy we are studying. We admit to the imprecision of any judgment based on poll data and the like. Nevertheless, the Colombian case would seem to be one where the Manichaean framing of a conflict did have popular resonance and where apparent success did generate political support. Are Colombians more nationalistic in 2011 than in 2000? We cannot say, but we can infer that the relationship between state and national community was at least temporarily transformed by the internal war.

El Salvador and the *maras*

In the early 2000s, El Salvador was one of the most violent countries in the Americas (UNODC 2007). A society historically shattered by poverty, social inequality, and political violence, it had suffered from decades of a bloody civil war and was far from solving the structural problems that contributed to the violence.[6] In addition, the long civil war had left a fragmented and traumatized civil society, with tens of thousands of internally displaced inhabitants, and the flooding of the streets with military-grade weapons.

Gangs existed in this country long before the end of the civil conflict, but before the mid 1990s they represented a minor problem of public

---

[6] By the early 1990s, 65 percent of the population lived below the poverty line and the poorest 20 percent received only 3.2 percent of the national income (PNUD 2003).

security as their activities yielded only sporadic violence (Smutt and Miranda 1998). The pattern of turf-based youth gangs started to change after the end of the civil war in 1992, when many Salvadoran refugees living in the United States began to return to El Salvador, often through forced deportation (Thale and Falkenburger 2006). The influx of young gang members allowed for the diffusion of US patterns of gang membership including norms, values, and organizational and managerial knowledge. The infusion of newcomers also precipitated the consolidation of several smaller territory-based groups into the MS-13 and the 18th Street gangs, which together account for 84 percent of all gang members in El Salvador (Cruz and Peña 1998). These two gangs soon escalated their drug-trafficking operations and eventually transformed into more ambitious criminal groups (Carranza 2005). As these organizations grew in size, violence escalated throughout the country. By 1998, 27 percent of the Salvadoran population pointed out street gangs or *maras* as the most important issue of public security the government should tackle (Instituto Universitario de Opinión Pública 1998). As the violence escalated, the newly elected government of Francisco Flores in 1999 pledged to address the problems of crime and gangs. Shortly after taking office, President Flores launched an emergency plan called Public Security Comprehensive Strategy, which increased police street patrols along with the use of military units and the involvement of community organizations (Laínez 1999). However, the campaign met with very low public support. In a survey conducted three months after the implementation of the plan, only 10 percent of the population viewed the plan positively; most Salvadorans believed it plainly was not working (Instituto Universitario de Opinión Pública 1999). In 2002, 50 percent of the population said that crime and violence had worsened during the previous year; only 17 percent said that crime had decreased (Instituto Universitario de Opinión Pública 2003a). By May 2003, the percentage of people saying that crime had worsened climbed to 76.3 percent. Opinion polls also revealed poor public assessments of the overall performance of the government. Over three quarters of the population believed that the situation of the country had worsened or stayed the same with the administration of Francisco Flores (Instituto Universitario de Opiníon Publicá 2003b).

On the evening of July 23, 2003, at a nationally broadcast press conference from a poor neighborhood in San Salvador, President Flores launched the Plan Mano Dura. Using a wall covered with graffiti as a backdrop, the president declared that he had "instructed the National Civilian Police and the Armed Forces to work jointly and *rescue these territories* and put the leaders of these gangs behind bars"

(Alvarenga and Gonzalez 2003).[7] President Flores was speaking from the heart of a neighborhood controlled by the 18th Street Gang. As the president spoke live, flanked by the army chief and the police director, the broadcast intermittently flashed scenes of gang members and their tattooed faces. He first announced the enactment of a national state of emergency by declaring that "all legitimate means will be used [to detain gang members] *including those emergency measures included in the Constitution*" (Alvarenga and González 2003: 3). Second, he pledged to send an anti-gang law to the legislature, asking congressmen to support the law without hesitation. Third, he announced that all gang members and people linked to them would be swept from the streets. President Flores finished his presentation by asking the Salvadoran people to support the plan.[8]

The Anti Gang Law penalized membership in the gangs – independently of there being an actual offense – and it allowed for persons under 18 to be tried under a newly codified felony of "illicit association" (*asociación ilícita*) and gang membership. In both cases, the new rulings gave complete authority to the police, and in some cases to military personnel, to carry out arrests often based on arbitrary decisions and thin evidence. Additional reforms restricted the rights of detainees and limited the capacity of the judges to order provisional measures other than detention. The hard-line plan also included the creation of special police squads to carry out mass raids against gang members (Cruz and Carranza 2006). Police could use the presence of tattoos, hand signals, dress codes, and a myriad of physical attributes as evidence of gang membership.

While the plan initially consisted of focused raids on gang-ridden neighborhoods in the capital, police operations were also expanded to small towns in the countryside (Martínez 2003). After the first thirteen months of *mano dura* operations, the police reported that 19,275 suspected gang members had been arrested. However, not all detentions translated into formal imprisonment and court sentences. For instance, 91 percent of the gang members detained during the first year of the crackdown were released within days, usually because state prosecutors lacked the necessary evidence to convict them (Gutiérrez 2003a). The administration was also unable to convince Congress to pass the provisions to suspend constitutional rights. As a result, many gang members were repeatedly imprisoned and released, turning jails into revolving doors (Beltrán 2003).

---

[7] Italics are ours.
[8] The Salvadoran Plan Mano Dura was not the first plan of gang suppression launched in Central America. In fact, neighboring Guatemala and Honduras had already enacted similar programs in 2000 and 2002.

This did not prevent the Flores administration from continuing the crackdowns and raids against gangs. Police units continued sending suspected gang members to jail, while the courts and even the Procuraduría General (Attorney General) offices refused to present charges due to lack of evidence (López and Sánchez 2003). These events submerged the Executive, Congress, and the courts into a bitter public dispute over the *mano dura* plan. The president called opposition to his plans "irresponsible" (El Diario de Hoy 2003), and the government started to lay blame on the courts for the high rate of dismissals of gang-related charges and accused judges of protecting gang membership (Gutiérrez 2003b; López 2003). In the midst of elections, the Supreme Court then decreed that the new policies were unconstitutional.

The apparent failure of the *mano dura* plan did not deter the next president, Antonio Saca, from launching his own version of the plan just three months after taking office in 2004 (La Prensa Gráfica 2004). This new plan, which was called Super Mano Dura, did not rely on a special anti-gang law, but on targeting gang leaderships through intelligence gathering and focal raids. The plan also included prevention and rehabilitation measures that complemented the suppression effort conducted by the police and the military. However, as with the first plan, the main focus revolved around gang imprisonment and a gang "manhunt" (Marroquín et al. 2004). This plan included the deployment of more than twelve thousand police officers (65 percent of the police force), five hundred special investigators and a thousand soldiers across the country (Salamanca 2004). A report by the National Civilian Police detailed that between July 23, 2003 and July 8, 2005 the police captured 30,934 alleged gang members. Although most of detainees ended up being acquitted by the courts, the intensification of the *mano dura* operations led to a serious overflow in the country's corrections system (Beltrán et al. 2004). The Salvadoran jails not only became a problem of humanitarian proportions, but also, since many new inmates were gang members, the *mano dura* crackdowns provided the opportunity for an expansion in gang organization and membership. By placing all youth gang members together, the *mano dura* policies nourished a sort of long-term national gang assembly and facilitated communication among gang members both nationally and internationally (deportees with contacts in the US also served sentences inside the Salvadoran jails).[9]

[9] In 2001, a prison policy was implemented that separated gang members by their gang identity to prevent outbreaks of violence inside the prisons. In practice, this has led to certain jails being known as Mara Salvatrucha prisons and others as 18th Street jails. See Valencia 2009.

Ironically, the rate of homicides did not decline. Homicide rates in El Salvador rose from 40 per 100,000 inhabitants in 2003, the start year of the *mano dura* plans, to 49 in 2004. When the *mano dura* plans were abandoned in 2006, the country had reached a homicide rate of 65 murders per 100,000 inhabitants.

Despite their ultimate fates, the *mano dura* galvanized public opinion into considering gangs as the main national threat to the country. The overtly political nature of these plans required not only intensive advertising of the anti-gang strategy, but also a media campaign promoting a particular framing of the crime situation and the best way to handle it. Immediately after the first proclamation of the plans, the headline of one of the major national newspapers read "All-out war against Maras."[10] The government would spend thousands of dollars publicizing the number of police raids and arrests of gang members in the national media. Newspapers and television newscasts promoted the notion that gangs were the major perpetrators of violence in Central America (Parducci and Amparo 2007). During the Plan Mano Dura and the Super Mano Dura, the police carried out their commando-like operations in front of cameras to be broadcasted later on prime time television.

The anti-gang programs and subsequent publicity promoted the public idea that youth gangs were the main national problem. A compilation of IUDOP surveys shows that before the *mano dura* plans only 2 percent of Salvadorans considered gangs as the main national problem. This percentage increased tenfold in August 2003, just one month into the implementation of the plan. Although three months later these percentages quickly decreased to 7–8 percent, national concern about gangs experienced another modest boost with the launch of the Super Mano Dura plan in August 2004. This increase, nonetheless, did not reach the levels of 2003, and public anxieties about gangs dwindled as time passed.

However, the war against gangs received initial broad support from the population. According to IUDOP surveys, nearly 90 percent of Salvadorans supported the program during the first two years of implementation. This high level of support remained relatively stable despite mounting evidence that the plan was not working as expected and even after the plan had been abandoned in 2006. In December 2006, for instance, 66 percent of the population still agreed with the *mano dura* plans. Ironically, while the programs were popular with the public, they were also seen as ineffective. For instance, in September 2003, just two

---

[10] "Guerra total contra las maras."

294 of the population believed

months into the crackdowns, only 55 percent of the population believed that the Plan Mano Dura was successful in controlling gangs; one year later, this percentage had dropped to 45 percent. Similarly, in September 2005, only one third of the population believed the Super Mano Dura plan was effective, and by September 2006, less than 20 percent believed so.

As in the Colombian case, the El Salvador government saw its monopoly over the means of violence consistently challenged in the 1990s and 2000. Its response was the creation of anti-crime programs full of bellic references. All indications are that the *mano dura* campaigns and the anti-drug efforts have not fostered any closer identification of the national community with the state. In part this may be because such campaigns have been widely recognized failures and El Salvador (like the other Central American states) sees itself more threatened today than a decade ago. Another important factor was that *mara* membership was never as finely delineated as that in FARC and the like. The identity of the enemy (and even the relevance of the threat) remained diffuse.

Mexico and the *narcos*

After the bloody years of the Mexican Revolution (1910–20), Mexico enjoyed a long period of relative stability, at least compared to its Latin American neighbors where revolutionary wars and coups were frequent throughout the twentieth century. While there were some isolated cases of insurrection against the government (most recently the 1994 Zapatista rebellion), they were quickly repressed by official forces. Nevertheless, starting in the late 1980s and especially after the year 2000, Mexican society has come to experience record levels of violence, mostly linked to the rise of powerful drug cartels that are increasingly challenging the state.

Beginning in the 1970s much of the Mexican drug business congregated around Miguel Angel Felix Gallardo, also known as "The Godfather" (*El Padrino*). During these years, the Sinaloa cartel's near monopoly of the drug market in Mexico reduced competition for territory. The Sinaloa cartel had a pyramidal structure, and internal differences were worked out through Gallardo's intervention. His arrest on April 8, 1989 led to increasing tensions between his remaining lieutenants. The first contest was between the Arellano Felix brothers in Tijuana and Joaquin "El Chapo" Guzman, a leading boss of the Sinaloa cartel. El Chapo Guzman sought to reorganize the drug business under his control within a Blood Alliance including the Sinaloa, Tijuana and Gulf cartels. Violence across the country escalated when the Sinaloa Blood Alliance disintegrated in 2004, opening new war fronts amongst quarrelling factions as they fought bitterly over control of *plazas* (gateways for drug transport, especially into the US) and other powerful cartels began challenging the old syndicates, including Los Zetas in Tamaulipas and La Familia Michoacana in Michoacan.

Until the 1980s, the "rules of the game" that governed the activities of drug dealers and their relationship with state actors relied on a few key principles: discretion, not using Mexico as a market, and respect for government authority (Grayson 2010: 32). Criminal organizations were born, from the beginning, out of agreements with state actors at different levels: local police, state military commanders (and sometimes directly with state governors), and federal police agents. Having an alliance with the right government actors could be the difference between success and failure (Ravelo 2007).[11] Through these agreements, drug dealers had to provide payments to public officials (which would make their way up the chain of command). They also had to show deference to public figures and help the state political party (PRI) retain electoral control (often by linking opponents to drug trafficking). In Mexico, drug dealers did not seek public office (unlike in Colombia), but typically maintained a tight web of political contacts and allies.

This "live and let live" pact was in part broken by the sheer amount of profits available. US pressure on Colombian activities in south Florida forced the Cali and Medellin cartels to look for alternative routes to reach the lucrative US market, and they began forming alliances with Mexican groups (Grayson 2010: 56). Soon, Mexican gangs began taking their cut in cocaine (as opposed to cash) and began operating their much more lucrative networks north of the border (Cockburn and St. Clair 1998: 361). The status quo was also transformed by the growing party competition, which meant that elected officials would come from parties other than the PRI. During the late 1990s the PRI sustained continuous defeats at the ballot box and these losses weakened its hegemony. The increasing electoral victories of opposition parties provided structural openings for drug dealers to become more independent from state actors. As one analyst pointed out, "local power fell outside the corruption network, a situation that facilitated more autonomous actions of traffickers, federal agents, local police and corrupt officials, thereby increasing the probability of violent actions to impose new rules of the game" (Astorga 2001: 135).

The 1990s were characterized by growing violence amongst crime syndicates, high-profile political assassinations and kidnappings, and a

---

[11] This was the case of the Arellano Felix brothers.

growing perception of insecurity amongst Mexican society in general. Beyond the previously untouchable high echelon, sections of the population began experiencing acts of violence (Trueba Lara 1995: 135). The hopes of many Mexicans that the electoral defeat of the PRI in 2000 would bring change and stability were quickly dashed as the crime rate kept increasing and larger sections of the population, including the middle class, were touched by it. The Vicente Fox administration (PAN, 2000–06) sought to combat the cartels by confiscating drug shipments and arresting top capos (Grayson 2010: 51), but as before (and as in Colombia) the government policy of arresting bosses did not lead to smaller and more manageable cartels, but to more numerous and violent ones, and an intensifying crime wave in virtually every region of the country (Shirk, quoted in Grayson 2010: 85). Furthermore, there was evidence that the Sinaloa cartel had penetrated the Fox administration itself.

In response, as governor and then as president, Fox used militaristic language against the cartels: "For us it is a war and it is a war that we will take to its ultimate consequences" (Sarmiento 2005). He promised to wage the "mother of all battles" against organized crime, drug trafficking, corruption and impunity (Delgado 2005) and would also use terms such as *combat*, *battle*, and *struggle* (Melgar 2004). Soon, Fox and other top government officials made public declarations calling for a "total war" using "all resources of the state" to "the bitter end" (*hasta las ultimas consecuencias*) (Aguayo 2005).

Fox's successor and fellow PAN member Felipe Calderon began his presidential campaign in 2006 facing a formidable candidate from the Left and struggling to create distance between his candidacy and the deeply unpopular Fox. Elected by a minimal (and contested) margin, Calderon faced a deeply divided nation. He continued using the war metaphor but refined it and employed it in a more consistent way. On September 22, 2006, three months before his inauguration, Calderon presented what would become his administration's framing of the "war": "Public safety is now an issue of national security. Not only are the people, their lives and possessions, their families, being threatened, but insecurity and organized crime now threaten the Mexican State." He added that organized crime "is a threat to peace, to stability and to the life of our nation" (Núñez 2006). Months later he would add that "we have no alternative other than acting and it is a war, it is an issue that I know will be very long, that probably I will not see come to an end as President. ... We are waging this war precisely to have a safer Mexico, a Mexico that has public spaces for our children, for our families. And this implies risks and costs" (Núñez and Herrera 2007a, 2007b).

He added that "we need for society to participate, we need that society sides with us, a society that recuperates the society in itself." From being a presidential directive with Fox, the "war on drugs" became perhaps the most important state policy during the Calderon administration.

The call for national unity did not go unanswered. Antonio Martinez, the attorney general from Baja California, responded: "Mexicans to the call of war. Yes, Mr. President, we are at war and the members of the National Conference of Attorney Generals will be standing by the cannon (*al pie del canon*) ... this war belongs to everyone and it benefits everyone" (Núñez and Herrera 2007a, 2007b). On December 21, 2007, Calderon clearly identified that organized crime was not only a priority of the government (as Fox had maintained) but that it was "the enemy of Mexico." "The enemy of Mexico seeks to maintain its power through violence and intimidation, but the more violence, the tougher will be the response of the Mexican State to punish them," he claimed (Gomez 2007). Other top government officials and public figures also echoed Calderon's war rhetoric and called for citizens to close ranks against the drug cartels. National newspaper columnist German Dehesa wrote that: "Felipe is at war – and we are with him ... I think that in this battle, everybody, all Mexicans ... have to be with our president with all the means at our disposal" (Dehesa 2006). The archdiocese of Mexico published a message in January 2008 to its followers in which it praised Calderon's initiative against the drug cartels calling it a "true war" and asked Catholics to assume their responsibility in the fight against drug traffickers, organized crime, and corruption on many fronts (Gomez 2008).

Calderon's framing of the conflict resonated with the general public. In a national interview conducted by Grupo Reforma in 2007, 69 percent of respondents agreed with Calderon's portrayal of the government's effort against the drug cartels as a "war" (Mancillas and Moreno 2007). Indeed, Calderon's early decision to deploy the army against the drug cartels in Michoacán and then in other regions appears to have boosted his approval ratings. According to a series of interviews conducted by BGC/Ulises Beltrán, 70 percent of Mexicans believed that public safety in Mexico was "bad" or "very bad" in July 2006 (during one of the last months of the Fox administration). By May 2007, this number came down to 47 percent despite the fact that the actual homicide rate had increased. In 2006, 54 percent of respondents believed that drug trafficking was rising. During the first year of Calderon's administration, in 2007, only 37 percent believed drug trafficking was growing. In commenting on these numbers, the political analyst Sergio Sarmiento wrote that "at least in the short run, Calderon's strategy has worked: maybe not to decrease violence or drug trafficking, but its perception ... The big question is whether Mexicans will continue to treat Calderon with such benevolence" (Sarmiento 2007b).

However, Calderon's popularity proved to be ephemeral. By 2008, the confidence of Mexicans in the Calderon administration was rapidly eroding even if the number of people who considered drug trafficking and crime the biggest problem of Mexico (over economic issues) increased. In an open-ended question, Grupo Reforma has asked Mexicans since the beginning of the Calderon administration what is the worst problem facing the country. The percentage of people who believe that "crime" is a worse problem than "the economy" went up to 46 percent in 2010 from 39 percent in 2007. Nevertheless, a majority of Mexicans in 2010 considered that the government was losing the war against drug dealers. In other surveys, Calderon's collapse in popularity ratings is more dramatic. According to a weekly telephone survey conducted by BGC/Ulises Beltran, the percentage of Mexicans who had a lot of confidence in Calderon was only 6 percent by May 2008. Those who trusted him moderately numbered 22 percent, and 35 percent of respondents had zero confidence in him. In the same survey, the proportion of Mexicans that had a lot of confidence in presidents Fox and Calderon had traditionally oscillated between 27 and 38 percent (Sarmiento 2008).

Why have people failed to rally around the government beyond the initial surge of support for Calderon's administration? In part because of its cost. Since 2007, Mexico has seen not only an increase in violence, but also its transformation into a special kind of savagery resulting in almost 40,000 deaths by mid 2011. Drug cartels routinely behead and chop up their rivals' bodies or dissolve them in acid. On September 15, 2008, hundreds of people who had congregated in the main square of Morelia, the capital of Michoacán, to celebrate Mexico's independence were attacked with grenades. There were 9 fatalities and 132 injured people. It was considered by many as the beginning of openly "terroristic" actions against civilian populations. The developing intra-gang wars highlighted the incapacity of the Mexican government to control even its most protected spaces, and the corruption and inefficiency of its prison system was a constant reminder of the futility of the anti-drug enterprise (Sarmiento 2005). As part of the "war against drug traffickers," Calderon had deployed more than 45,000 soldiers by 2009 (Llana 2009). The militarization of drug enforcement in Mexico has stretched the armed forces "to the limit" (Camp, quoted in Grayson 2010: 156). Aging equipment and shortages of ammunitions are widespread throughout the armed forces. Army desertions (close to 150,000 between 2000 and 2008 including thousands from elite outfits) have become a significant problem. While many of these soldiers went to work for the booming private security industry in Mexico, others could have been recruited by the drug cartels (such as in the case of Los Zetas) (Hanson 2007). Many believe that the Mexican army has become "a highly unstable corporation. Just like it recruits elements en masse, it also expels them in the opposite direction" (Cota Meza 2009).

According to Sergio Sarmiento (2008), another key element could be the decreasing levels of trust in several justice and security agencies in Mexico. According to a survey conducted by BGC/Ulises Beltrán, only 10 percent of Mexicans have "a lot" of trust in the state's Attorney General (Procuraduriá General de la República) and only 7 percent of Mexicans trust the federal police (Policía Judicial) "a lot." Congress (the parliament) and the unions are trusted a lot by a mere 5 percent of the population while only 3 percent trust political parties "a lot" (Sarmiento 2008). Indeed, it seems like the lack of legitimacy of several key institutions in Mexico could be imperilling Calderon's call for national unity. Other critics have pointed at the increasing number of human rights violations in which the Mexican army and security agencies appear to be involved. A famous example was the killing of two college students in the northern city of Monterrey. Many have also condemned the "militarization" of the country and criticized the army's involvement in crime enforcement. However, in the same survey, 48 percent of Mexicans say that they have a lot of confidence in the army.

Some critics have questioned Calderon's strategy of declaring war against criminals and drug traffickers in a setting where there are blurry boundaries. For Ximena Peredo, writing in *El Norte*, the war that was declared by Calderon is "delirious because it is impossible to distinguish the good guys from the bad guys" (Peredo 2007). In some famous cases of military corruption, many top police chiefs have been charged with selling protection to drug cartels or actually running extortion and kidnapping rings (Peredo 2007). Several drug cartels have tried to exploit the blurred boundaries between organized crime and government agencies. Indeed, there is some evidence that some cartels have promoted public demonstrations against the army and have also engaged in limited (but very visible) development and welfare efforts in their communities.

As in Colombia, there have also been recurrent mass demonstrations against insecurity and crime. On June 27, 2004, hundreds of thousands of people marched in Mexico City to demand "a Mexico without violence and the end of impunity for criminals" (Ortega 2008). These mass demonstrations highlighted the public's exasperation with increasing violence and with the inability of the Mexican political system to prevent it. Indeed, many participants have pointed out the common links between criminals and corrupt officials.

The Mexican case may be the most perplexing of all. The levels of violence have led to rumblings of "state failure" and a collapse of public order. Yet all indications are that despite the brutal assaults, the government has not come to be perceived as the institutional glue holding the country together or leading in its fight against a clear evil. In part this may be because whatever political or institutional honeymoon occurred immediately after the victory of 2000 is over. In part, the continuing challenge to the electoral legitimacy of Calderon's presidency makes it even more difficult for his government to claim to speak for "all Mexicans." The popularity of *narcocorridos* and the romanticized image of the outlaw also suggest that the "otherness" of the enemy remains unclear.

Internal war and nationalism

Despite the violence recounted above and government efforts to declare a war against the internal enemy, be it FARC, the *maras*, or the *narcos*, it is remarkable how little shift we may see in our (admittedly imperfect) measure of nationalist sentiment across the years in question. According to the Americas Barometer, pride in the nation and the political system remains fairly flat. There is some minimal movement upwards in the case of Colombia and down in the case of El Salvador, but nothing resembling, for example, the kinds of shifts associated with perceived national emergencies.

Polls and anecdotal indications would lead us to believe that Colombia's Uribe has been more successful in creating the "us–them" dynamic with the state as the legitimate representative of the "us" – or at least has done so in significant parts of the population. It is impossible to tell at this point to what extent this marks a structural shift in Colombians' attitudes toward their government and how much it is a temporary, personality-driven phenomenon. The Mexican and Salvadoran cases indicate, however, that internal wars without popular support and with ambiguous enemies certainly do not guarantee the development of nationalist sentiment. If any comparative lesson can be drawn from these it is that it helps to win (or at least be seen as winning).

Rather than the distinction between them, what we believe is most remarkable about these cases is the extent to which an internal war can appear to become "normalized" and almost accepted, and not generate the kind of expected classic responses of growth in solidarity and increased legitimation of the state. Mexico may be the most extreme example: the country has suffered an estimated 40,000 deaths and yet the state does not appear to have received any long-term benefit of supportive sentiment. It is remarkable that whether against criminals or guerrillas, these states have not been able to create a more solid connection with their own population.

Two possible causal avenues suggest themselves. The first is a particularistic story involving the divisions that Latin America has suffered from since independence and that may represent an apparently permanent chasm between the state and large parts of the population (again, noting the exceptions of Chile and Costa Rica). To the extent that the state is perceived as belonging to and obeying some internal "them," it may be impossible to forge the kind of expected solidaristic ties even under the pressure of military conflict.

The second alternative does not look to the nature of these societies, but rather to that of the conflicts themselves.[12] The very ambiguity of the enemy in all of these cases (with Colombia perhaps offering the clearest opportunity for contrast), the possibility that large parts of the population may not feel that the groups representing the threat are illegitimate (but just the opposite), and the absence of a clear successful trend (again, the case of Colombia may be an exception) make it difficult to use this kind of protracted internal struggle in the same manner as the classic bellic nationalisms. Given that these kinds of struggle will most likely represent the military norm for some time, this means that classic forms of establishing state–society solidarity may no longer be available in the "nation-building" toolkit.

REFERENCES

Aguayo, S. 2005. "Las guerras del narco." *El Norte*, January 26.

Alvarenga, A. and D. Gonzalez. 2003. "Barreran a las maras." *El Diario de Hoy*, July 24.

Astorga, L. 2001. "The Limits of Anti-Drug Policy in Mexico." *International Social Science Journal*, 53(169): 427–34.

Beltrán, J. 2003. "PNC recapturaría a pandilleros." *El Diario de Hoy*, July 27.

Beltrán, J., O. Iraheta, and W. Salamanca. 2004. "Crisis carcelaria," *El Diario de Hoy*, September 21.

Bushnell, D. 2007. *Colombia: Una nación a pesar de sí misma*. Bogotá: Editorial Planeta.

---

[12] An interesting contrast may be with the response to the killing of Osama bin Laden by US troops, but while this shared some of the tactical characteristics of internal struggles, the enemy in this case had been more than demonized and his "otherness" was never in question.

Carranza, M. 2005. "Detención o muerte: hacia dónde van los niños pandilleros en El Salvador". Pp. 1–22 in *Ni guerra ni paz. Comparaciones internacionales de niños y jóvenes en violencia armada organizada*, edited by L. Dowdney. Río de Janeiro: Viveiros de Castro Editora.

Centeno, M. 2002. *Blood and Debt: War and the Nation-State in Latin America*. University Park, PA: Pennsylvania State University Press.

Centeno, M. and A. Ferraro. 2012. *The Republics of the Possible*. Cambridge University Press.

Cockburn, A. and J. St. Clair. 1998. *Whiteout: The CIA, Drugs and the Press*. New York: Verso.

CRS (Congressional Research Service). 2004. *Foreign Terrorist Organizations*. Washington, DC: Federation of American Scientists. Accessed at: www.fas. org/irp/crs/RL32223.pdf.

Connor, W. 1978. "A Nation is a nation, is a state, is an ethnic group, is a ..." *Ethnic and Racial Studies* 1(4): 377–400.

Cota Meza, R. 2009. "Contingentes de sangre: el ejército y las deserciones." *Letras Libres*, October 2009.

Cruz, J.M. and M. Carranza. 2006. "Pandillas y políticas públicas: El caso de El Salvador". Pp. 133–76 in *Juventudes, violencia y exclusión: Desafíos para las políticas públicas*, edited by J. Moro. Guatemala: MagnaTerra Editores.

Cruz, J.M. and N. Portillo Peña. 1998. *Solidaridad y violencia en las pandillas del gran San Salvador. Más allá de la vida loca*. San Salvador: UCA Editores.

Dehesa, G. 2006. "La gran Guerra." *Mural*, December 14.

Delgado, R. 2005. "Sobreaviso/Disparos y disparates." *Palabra*, June 18.

Díaz, A.M. and F. Sánchez. 2004. "Geografía de los cultivos ilícitos y conflicto armado en Colombia." Ph.D. thesis, Universidad de los Andes – Facultad de Economía. Accessed at http://economia.uniandes.edu.co/publicaciones/ D200418.pdf.

El Diario de Hoy. 2003. "Flores dice que la decisión es un acto irresponsable." *El Diario de Hoy*, July 31.

El Espectador. 2010a. "A las Farc sólo le quedan 8.000 hombres." *El Espectador*, April 27.

    2010b. "Las cifras históricas del secuestro en Colombia." *El Espectador*, February 6.

El Tiempo. 2008a. "La marcha que pasará a la historia." *El Tiempo*, February 5.

    2008b. "Marcha contra las FARC, mayor movilización en la historia del país." *El Tiempo*, February 4.

Fevre, R., D. Denney, and J. Borland. 1997. "Class, Status, and Party in the Analysis of Nationalism: Lessons from Max Weber." *Nations and Nationalism* 3(4): 559–77.

Frechette, M. 2007. "Colombia and the United States – The Partnership: But What is The Endgame." Strategic Studies Institute – United States Army War College. Accessed at www.strategicstudiesinstitute.army.mil/pdffiles/ pub762.pdf.

Gallup. 2010. "Gallup Poll Bimestral." *Semana*. Accessed at http://www.semana. com/documents/Doc-2085_2010729.pdf.

Gerth, H.H. and C.W. Mills. 2007. *From Max Weber*. New York: Routledge.

Gomez, F. 2007. "Calderón: no habrá tregua contra crimen." *El Universal*, December 21.

Gomez, L. 2008. "Elogian batalla contra narco." *Mural*, January 28.

Grayson, G.W. 2010. *Mexico: Narco-violence and a Failed State?* Piscataway, NJ: Transaction Publishers.

Guardino, P. 2002. *Peasant Politics, and the Formation of Mexico's National State.* Stanford University Press.

Gutiérrez, E. 2003a. "Liberan 101 mareros por falta de pruebas." *El Diario de Hoy*, July 30.

   2003b. "Quedan libres primeros detenidos con nueva ley." *El Diario de Hoy*, October 17.

Hanson, S. 2007. "Backgrounder: Mexico's Drug War." Paper published by the Council on Foreign Relations, June 28. Accessed at: www.proceso.com.mx/rv/modHome/detalleExclusiva/81429.

Harrington, A. 2005. "Introduction to Georg Simmel's Essay 'Europe and America in World History'," *European Journal of Social Theory* 8(1): 63–72.

Hernández, C.L. 2010. *Y refundaron la patria. …* Bogotá: Random House Mondadori.

Holsti, K.J. 1996. *The State, War, and the State of War*. Cambridge University Press.

Howard, Michael. 1992. *Lessons of History*. Yale University Press.

Instituto Universitario de Opinión Pública. 1998. *Encuesta de opinión sobre delincuencia*. Serie de informes 70. San Salvador: IUDOP-UCA.

   1999. *Encuesta de evaluación de los primeros 100 dias de gestión de Francisco Flores*. Serie de informes 79. San Salvador: IUDOP-UCA.

   2003a. *Encuesta de evaluación del año 2002*. Serie de informes 97. San Salvador: IUDOP-UCA.

   2003b. *Informe de evaluación de gobierno 03 y poselectoral*. Serie de informes 100. San Salvador: IUDOP-UCA.

La Prensa Gráfica. 2004. "Nuevo impulso a lucha antimaras. El presidente Saca lanzó anoche su plan 'Súper Mano Dura.'" *La Prensa Gráfica*, August 31.

Laínez, L. 1999. "Ofensiva contra el crimen." *El Diario de Hoy*, May 30.

LAPOP. 2008. *The Americas Barometer by the Latin American Public Opinion Project (LAPOP)*.

Llana, S.M. 2009. "Briefing: How Mexico is Waging War on Drug Cartels." *Christian Science Monitor*, August 19.

López, A. 2003. "Presidente no consultó con Sector Justicia." *El Diario de Hoy*, July 29.

López, A. and M. Sánchez. 2003. "Piden pruebas para procesos contra maras." *El Diario de Hoy*, August 7.

Mallon, F. 1995. *Peasant and Nation*. Berkeley: University of California Press.

Mancillas, M.A and A. Moreno. 2007. "Encuesta/Sube apoyo a mandatario; Encuesta Grupo REFORMA: Segunda evaluación al Presidente Felipe Calderón." *El Norte*, 1 June.

Marroquín, D., G. Morán, and A. Henríquez. 2004. "Inicia cacería de pandilleros. Saca anuncia nuevo plan antidelincuencial." *La Prensa Gráfica,* August 31.

Martínez, W. 2003. "Mano dura en cantón El Tablón." *El Diario de Hoy,* September 11.

Melgar, I. 2004. "Ve el Presidente en ciudadania pieza clave contra delincuencia." *Mural,* July 13.

Ministerio de Defensa, Gobierno de Colombia. 2007. *Política de Consolidación de la Seguridad Democrática.* Bogotá: Ministerio de Defensa de Colombia.

Nugent, D. 1997. *Modernity and the Edge of Empire.* Stanford University Press.

Núñez, E. 2006. "Ofrece Felipe una guerra contra narco; Solicita apoyo de la sociedad para combatir la criminalidad." *El Norte,* September 22.

Núñez, E. and R. Herrera. 2007a. "Llama el Presidente a recobrar confianza; Cierra filas con Procuradores. Pide promover la participación de la ciudadanía en lucha antidelincuencia." *El Norte,* March 31.

   2007b. "Revela Calderón recibir amenazas; Admite que lucha antinarco será a largo plazo. Asegura Presidente que asume costos y los riesgos del combate." *Mural,* March 23.

Ortega, O. 2008. "Descuidan seguridad; Persiste clamor por delincuencia, a cuatro años de la 'megamarcha'." *El Norte,* June 15.

Orwell, G. 2002. "Notes on Nationalism." Pp. 865–84 in his *Essays,* edited by John Carey. New York: Knopf.

Parducci, M. and M. Amparo. 2007. "Indiferencias y espantos. Relatos de jóvenes y pandillas en la prensa escrita de Guatemala, El Salvador, y Honduras." Pp. 41–62 in *Los relatos periodísticos del crimen,* edited by G. Rey. Bogotá: Centro de Competencia en Comunicación, Fundación Friedrich Ebert.

Pearl, F. 2010. "Buscando un equilibrio entre la justicia y la paz." *Corporación Pensamiento Siglo XXI: Bogotá, 2010.* Accessed at: http://idejust.files. wordpress.com/2010/07/colombia-buscando-un-equilibrio-entre-la-justicia-y-la-paz-2010.pdf.

Peredo, X. 2007. "Al grito de Guerra." *El Norte,* 21 May.

PNUD. 2003. *El Conflicto, Callejón con Salida. Informe Nacional de Desarrollo Humano.* Bogotá: United Nations Development Program.

Ravelo, Ricardo. 2007. *Herencia maldita. El reto de Calderón y el nuevo mapa del narcotráfico.* Mexico City: Grijalbo.

Salamanca, W. 2004. "Un plan con armas legales." *El Diario de Hoy,* August 31.

Sarmiento, S. 2005. "Guerra perdida." *El Norte,* January 18.

   2007. "Popularidad." *El Norte,* May 16.

   2008. "Caida de Calderon." *Reforma,* May 20.

Semana. 2010. "¿Cuál era la magia?" *Semana,* July 31.

Smutt, Marcela and Lissette Miranda. 1998. *El fenómeno de las pandillas en El Salvador.* San Salvador: UNICEF/FLACSO Programa El Salvador.

Strayer, J. 1966. "The Historical Experience in Europe." Pp. 22–23 in *Nation-Building,* edited by K. Deutsch and W.J. Foltz. New York: Atherton Press.

Thale, G. and E. Falkenburger. 2006. *Youth Gangs in Central America. Issues on Human Rights, Effective Policing, and Prevention.* WOLA Special Report. Washington, DC: Washington Office on Latin America.

Thoumi, F. 2003. *Illegal Drugs, Economy, and Society in the Andes.* Baltimore: Johns Hopkins University Press.

Trueba Lara, J.L. 1995. *Política y narcopoder en México.* Mexico City: Grupo Editorial Planeta.

UNODC, United Nations Office on Drugs and Crime. 2007. *Crime and Development in Central America: Caught in the Crossfire.* New York: United Nations.

   2010. *Colombia: Coca Cultivation Survey 2009.* Accessed at www.unodc.org/documents/crop-monitoring.

Valencia, D. 2009. "Los alegatos de Frankestein. Entrevista con Carlos Ernesto Mojica Lechuga, alias 'El Viejo Lin'." *El Faro,* April 13.

12 War and nationalism
The view from Central Africa

René Lemarchand

[T]he clue to an understanding of nationalism is its weakness at least as much as its strength. It was the dog who failed to bark who provided the vital clue for Sherlock Holmes. The numbers of potential nationalisms which failed to bark is far, far larger than those which did, though *they* have captured all our attention.
Ernest Gellner, *Nations and Nationalism* (1983: 43)

The most obvious conclusion to be drawn from these wide-ranging inquests into the nexus between nationalism and war is the indeterminacy of the relationship. This is made reasonably clear in a number of chapters in this book. Chapter 7 by Michael Mann is one example among others: on the basis of the evidence from the First and Second World Wars, he points to the importance of the time frame and identity of the protagonists as major variables. In one instance nationalism was the product rather than the cause of the hostilities, and in the other Japan and Nazi Germany were the most obvious exceptions to the rule.

More directly relevant to the case at hand, however, is the proposition set forth in the previous chapter, in the multi-authored discussion of internal wars and Latin American nationalism: "contemporary political violence in Latin America does not consist of conflicts between states, but struggles within them" (Centeno et al. 2013). The same could be said of many other parts of the world. Nowhere, however, is the observation more appropriate than in former Belgian Africa (i.e. the Congo, Rwanda, and Burundi) where our field of vision is consistently blurred by the opaqueness of the two major concepts that set the parameters of our reflection.

Exploring the relationship between war and nationalism begs many questions. Should the frame of reference for the analysis of nationalism be ethnic or territorial? Can one envision (*pace* Andreas Wimmer) the birth of a nation-state in the absence of nationalism (the examples of Belgium and Switzerland are cases in point)? Of the varieties of nationalism observable, historically, which is the one most likely to cause war? And, one might add, what kind of war? One should remember that pundits and policy makers were scarcely able to decide whether the campaign against Gaddafi was recognizable as war.

Africa is where national identities are conspicuously challenged by competing solidarities, and where the art of war dissolves into the fog of bitter ethno-regional feuds. What was once hailed (or reviled) as the "rising tide of nationalism" – "those pestilential syllables," in Lord Hailey's memorable phrasing – today looks more like an ebbing current, leaving in its wake a variety of dangerous shoals, labelled *ethnicity, regionalism, irredentism, factionalism, warlordism*, and so forth. Nor is war anything like a straightforward concept where civil strife and interstate conflict intermingle, where cross-border violence is the harbinger of territorial invasions, and the invading force quickly mutates into a genocidal army. All of this and much more can be read into the recent history of the Great Lakes region of Central Africa. But before turning our comparative lens to Central Africa, some general comments are in order about the specificity of nationalism on the continent.

The weakness of African nationalism

As elsewhere in Third World countries, and this is also true of much of Eastern and Central Europe in the nineteenth century, African nationalism was first and foremost the expression of a sustained effort to cast aside the chains of imperial bondage, and, second, an attempt to forge unifying bonds among the diverse communities enclosed in colonial boundaries. The more sustained the anti-colonial struggle, the greater the chances of aspirations to unity becoming reality. With the exceptions of Kenya, Algeria, and the Cameroon, independence was granted with relative ease. Nationalism in such circumstances was a slender reed on which to build a nation. Joseph Nye hits the nail on the head when he writes, "African nationalism was more of an ideology held by an elite wishing to call a nation into being rather than a widespread sentiment of community … The problem lies not in the intensity of African nationalism (in the sense of a widespread national consciousness) but in the weakness of African nationalism" (1975: 165). Unsurprisingly, the approach of independence heightened awareness of sub-identities, clustering around the clan, the tribe, or the region. In many instances a widespread "fear of domination" by one group over the other helped to further weaken nationalist impulses.

As a subject of academic discourse nationalism proved correspondingly short-lived. Thomas Hodgkin's landmark (1956) study of nationalism in colonial Africa was followed two years later by James S. Coleman's (1958) brilliant exploration of the same theme in Nigeria. Seen at the time as major intellectual breakthroughs, both works inspired valiant efforts at replication in other parts of the continent. Yet the 1960s were barely over when new and more depressing titles came into fashion, evocative of the burdens of nation building, political fragmentation, and conflict, collapsed states and warlord politics, genocide and civil war. Writing in the mid seventies, Coleman (1975) felt the need to rethink and ultimately rephrase his earlier definition of nationalism, drawing attention to "protonationalism," "subterritorial nationalities," and "ethnic nationalisms." But with the growing salience of warlordism and factions as key features of the African landscape, many began to wonder about the pertinence of such labels. Similar doubts were cast upon the concept of the nation-state as the end point of a linear progression to modernity. In 1993, in an exemplary spirit of self-criticism, Crawford Young retrospectively admitted the excessive optimism of his earlier projections: "The sunny hues of optimism pervading my manuscript concerning the collective capacity of nation-states and civil societies to harmoniously manage cultural pluralism now seem several shades too bright" (1993: 4).

Europe and Africa: contrasting trajectories

If the fragility of African states mirrors the precariousness of national identities, both are inscribed in a historical trajectory that departs in fundamental ways from the European model. War, it has been argued, was a blessing in disguise for European nation-builders. For Samuel Huntington, "war was the great stimulus to state building," a statement that finds an echo in Charles Tilly's much-quoted remark that "war made the state, and the state made war" (both quoted in Herbst 2000: 112). The evidence from Africa, however, suggests otherwise. What makes the history of state building in Africa different, according to Jeffrey Herbst, is the absence of the transformative side-effects elsewhere engendered by war, ranging from tax collection and bureaucratization to social mobilization – all of which, in addition to fostering a strong awareness of "us" versus "them," contributed decisively to the rise of modern state systems (Herbst 2000: 15). The reason for this, presumably, lies in the low population densities of the continent, along with the abundance of vacant land. Both factors help to explain why Africa never experienced wars of conquest of the kind that shaped the growth of European states. Such wars, Herbst argues, "create[d], quite literally, a life and death imperative to raise taxes, enlist men as soldiers, and develop the necessary infrastructures to fight and win battles against rapacious neighbours" (2000: 14). Entirely different was the experience of the African continent, where fighting over one's turf seldom proved worth the effort.

But if Africa has experienced so few battles – at least nothing like the equivalents of Crécy and Iena, of Valmy and Sedan – this is no reason to ignore the many massacres it has endured, and continues to suffer, and this precisely where population densities are the highest in the continent, and land hunger is most acute. What does this tell us about the relation between war and nationalism?

The least that can be said is that it calls for a reconsideration, if not demolition, of the Herbstian thesis. To begin with, for all the bloodshed, European attempts at state building rarely met with success. Charles Tilly's assessment is worth bearing in mind: "Most of the European efforts to build states failed. The enormous majority of the political units which were around to bid for autonomy and strength in 1500 disappeared in the next few centuries, smashed or absorbed by other states-in-the-making. The substantial majority of the units which got so far as to acquire a recognizable existence as states during those centuries still disappeared. And of the handful which survived or emerged into the nineteenth century as autonomous states, only a few operated effectively" (1975: 38). So much for the contribution of the battlefield to the construction of viable states.

The next point is that in contrast to the European experience, varied as it is, state systems in Africa were all imported, and with little or no attention paid to the fit of traditional polities into the larger frame imposed by the colonizer. It took Europeans centuries to develop a common awareness of belonging to a state, and to this day many would like nothing so much as to opt out (think of Belgium). Under the far more limiting circumstances facing African state builders, the surprising fact is that so few are willing to challenge the boundaries of the colonial state. The break-up of the Sudan is the exception that confirms the rule.

Yet another reservation refers to the counterfactual evidence against Herbst's argument: as noted earlier, even where high population densities and scarcity of land are key features of the social landscape, as is the case in eastern Democratic Republic of the Congo (DRC), warfare has had the opposite effect of what has been observed in Europe. To repeat, it is not because warfare is endemic that it carries the seeds of state building; where the context of warfare is that of a failed state, and where the stakes involve access to mineral wealth, the privatization of sovereignty (Mbembe 2001: 93) is all too predictable, along with the proliferation of private armies. Mbembe's description of how "a new form of organizing power" takes shape on the debris of broken polities is worth quoting at length:

A new form of organizing power resting on control of the principal means of coercion (armed force, means of intimidation, imprisonment, expropriation, killing) is emerging in the framework of territories that are no longer fully states. For, in these states, orders are poorly defined or, at any event, change in accordance with the vicissitudes of military activity, yet the exercise of the right to raise taxes, seize provisions, tributes, tolls, rents, tailles, tithes, and exactions make it possible to finance bands of fighters, a semblance of civil apparatus, and an apparatus of coercion while participating in the formal and informal international networks of interstate movements of currencies and wealth (such as ivory, diamonds, timber, ores). *This is the situation in those countries where the process of privatizing sovereignty has been combined with war and has rested on a novel interlocking between the interests of international middlemen, businessmen, and dealers, and those of local plutocrats.* (Mbembe 2001: 92–93; my emphasis)

What the author goes on to describe as "new systems of coercion and exploitation" (2001: 93) is nowhere more dramatically illustrated than in the recent history of the Great Lakes region.

Foreign-linked factionalism: warfare, genocide, and ethnic cleansing

No other region in the continent has been more consistently ravaged by violence than the three states of former Belgian Africa that make up the core area of the Great Lakes, Rwanda, Burundi, and the DRC. No state has experienced the disasters of war more cruelly than the DRC; nowhere else in the continent has genocide taken a heavier toll than in Rwanda in 1994 and Burundi in 1972; in no other area has ethnic cleansing been conducted with such savagery as in eastern Congo. So far from promoting a sense of "We Congolese" in the face of armed invasion, the result has been the surge of factional conflict and fragmentation on an unprecedented scale.

As a point of entry into our discussion it is useful to consider briefly the contrasts and paradoxes inscribed in the history of the region. Irrespective of certain criteria – size, mineral wealth, or social structure – Rwanda and Burundi, each a hundred times smaller than the Congo, and both among the poorest of the poor, are as different from their huge neighbor to the west as any other two states in the continent. Again, the contrast between the binary, rank-ordered social structure of Rwanda and Burundi, both riven by Hutu–Tutsi polarities, and the vastly more complicated pattern of ethnic identities found in the Congo is only the most obvious – and politically consequential – of such differences.

As for the paradoxes: although eastern Congo offered a fertile ground for ethnic confrontations long before the Rwanda bloodbath, the roots of the Congo Wars are in Rwanda; they are, in a fundamental sense, a spinoff of the 1994 genocide. Again, while the disintegration of Mobutu's army greatly facilitated the penetration of Kagame's Rwanda Patriotic Front (RPF) into eastern DRC, against all odds it is in tiny, poverty-stricken Rwanda that there has emerged the most efficient, professionally trained and disciplined military establishment anywhere in Central Africa. In addition to being a major recipient of foreign aid – a gesture of atonement for the inaction of the international community during the genocide – Rwanda has derived enormous wealth from its long-standing armed "protectorate" in eastern Congo. In practical terms this means that Rwanda's wars in the Congo have been self-financing. The same can be said of Uganda. According to William Reno (2000), the huge profits derived from the illicit trade of the Congo's gold enabled Museveni to pay off the whole of Uganda's foreign debt to the International Monetary Fund and the World Bank.

The resulting fragmentation of the Congo state, along with the determination of its neighbors to keep it fragmented, explains why, despite its enormous mineral wealth, 80 percent of its population lives below the poverty line. As has been emphasized time and again, the Congo's mineral resources served as a magnet for attracting the predatory activities of its neighbors: with few exceptions, all shared a vested interest in making sure that the Congo would remain a failed state, as it has to this day. Chris Dietrich underscores the underlying motives: "A failed state can offer substantial opportunities to a neighbouring sovereign. Extraction of the resources of a country such as the FDRC can provide rich pickings for others who, through the deployment of their armed forces, can control and exploit mining ventures that they would otherwise not be able to access" (Dietrich 2001: 3). To put it in a nutshell, the rise of privatized sovereignties is traceable to the predatory intrusion of neighboring sovereigns.

Unlike what happened in other parts of the continent, where clientist and patronage networks were instrumental in consolidating the state, foreign-linked clientelism has been the dominant relational pattern introduced by the penetration of external forces into the Congo. So far from helping consolidate the state, the result has been precisely the opposite. What is involved here is best described in Alan Dowty's words as: "an alliance or cooperation between internal factions within a state and that state's external 'enemies.' This has been termed foreign-linked factionalism, and might be more fully defined as the presence within a state of a competing faction that seeks or accepts aid from other states in order to seize or wield power by non-legitimized means" (1971: 431). The phenomenon is by no means unique to the Congo. Historical parallels can be found in the Classical world as well as in India, Europe and Latin America. Nonetheless, that a state the size of the Congo should become "clientelized" by neighbors many times smaller and vastly less well endowed runs counter to Rosenau's observation that "small polities are more vulnerable to penetrative processes than super ones" (quoted in Dowty 1971: 435). Equally worth noting is the unique combination of military and ethnic linkages at work in sustaining this type of power configuration.

The Congo Wars: rebel armies and foreign patrons

The first (1996–97) and second (1998–2003) Congo Wars are major watersheds in analyzing the interplay between internal violence and interstate hostilities.[1] The first was a by-product of the Rwanda genocide (1994), the second a continuation of the first, but with Rwanda's ornery client and former ally, Laurent Kabila, now turned into Kigali's foremost enemy. In both instances Rwanda was the principal orchestrator, with Uganda playing second fiddle. Even though the 1998 war brought into view a new cast of protagonists, now as before Rwanda's allies were masterminded in Kigali. That President Kagame's strongest supporters in his fight against his former-client-turned-renegade happened to be Tutsi elements indigenous to the Congo, usually referred to as ethnic Tutsi in North Kivu and Banyamulenge in South Kivu,[2] is of course crucial to an understanding of the enduring hostility of "native" Congolese towards all Tutsi, irrespective of their national origins. Nonetheless, anti-Tutsi sentiment, though responsible for much of the ethnic violence that has swept across North and South Kivu, has yet to translate into a lasting national consciousness.

This is not the place for an extensive discussion of the Congo Wars; by way of a background, however, the following points are worth emphasizing:

• While economic motives later came into play, security concerns were the driving motivation behind Kagame's decision, taken jointly with Uganda's Museveni, to give maximum support to the Alliance des Forces Démocratiques pour la Libération du Congo (AFDL), a loose

---

[1] For an outstanding analysis, see Reyntjens 2009); for a more discursive treatment see Prunier 2009).
[2] See Willame 1997.

coalition of anti-Mobutist forces formally led by Laurent Kabila; the aim was to eliminate the threats posed to Rwanda by the remnants of the Rwandan génocidaires, the so-called *interahamwe*, and Former Forces Armées Rwandaises (FAR) soldiers, dispersed in eastern Congo. Once this was accomplished the next step was to orchestrate the overthrow of Mobutu and replace him with a trustworthy client; no one seemed more qualified for the job than Laurent Kabila.

- Regime change in Kinshasa meant the enthronement of Kabila as the new "King of the Congo," but left the king-makers with few resources (least of all legitimacy) with which to fill the resulting political void into which rushed all sorts of fissiparous forces, including foreign and domestic militias.

- Despite massive support from Rwanda and Uganda the AFDL was never able to overcome the internal rifts arising from the circumstances of its birth: the movement came about as a merging of four pre-existing anti-Mobutu parties; as a result of bitter disagreements among their leaders, notably over Rwanda's role, further tensions surfaced, leading to murderous settlings of accounts.

- The crunch came in August 1998 when Kabila, ignoring the risk of a backlash, notified his Rwandan advisors in Kinshasa, including the Rwandan Chief of Staff, James Kabarebe, that their time was up. While the expulsion of the Rwandans (and their Banyamulenge auxiliaries) was the occasion for joyful celebrations in Kinshasa, Kabila's fateful move was the precipitating factor that led to the Second Congo War, and the division of the country into three regional fiefdoms, headed respectively by the Mouvement Pour la Libération du Congo (MLC) in the north, the Rassemblement Congolais pour la Démocratie (RCD) in the east, and the Kinshasa-based Kabila government in the rest of the country.

What came to be dubbed "Africa's First World War" involved a dizzying array of protagonists, domestic and foreign, whose rivalries led to the outbreak of further conflicts within each of the main warring factions. Commenting on the "magnitude and impact of war" in his testimony before the US House Sub-committee on Africa in 1998, Peter Rosenblum did not mince his words:

The war underway in the Congo is one of the most unsettling and destructive events to occur in Africa in the past decades ... The war is undermining the delicate fabric of society [...] by creating incentives for military opportunists, violating taboos and traditions that gave the Congolese a sense of order and self-respect – including the use of child soldiers on both sides – and inflicting scars that are likely to divide ethnic communities in the years to come. (Rosenblum 1998: 1)

Thirteen years and millions of casualties later the scars have yet to heal.

By early 2000 the key rebel groups and their foreign allies were the following:[3]

1. *Forces loyal to Laurent Kabila:*
   Angola, 2,000 troops
   Namibia, 2,000 troops
   Zimbabwe, 10,000 troops
2. *Forces allied against Kabila:*
   Uganda, 9,000 troops
   Rwanda, 10,000 troops
   Burundi, unknown
3. *Militias loyal to Kabila:*
   Hutu ex-FAR and *interahamwe*
   Mai-Mai
4. *Rebel militias fighting against Kabila*:
   MLC (Jean-Pierre Bemba)
   RCD-ML (Ernest Wamba)
   RCD-Goma (Emile Ilunga)

The listing above can only convey a highly simplified picture of the playing field. Keeping track of factional splits and realignments is beyond the scope of this discussion. What needs to be emphasized is the profoundly divisive impact of foreign military involvement. In contrast to situations where war against a common enemy helps to crystallize national identities, the relationship of dependency between domestic factions and their foreign patrons only served to exacerbate internal enmities in the Congo. The Congo Wars thus mutated into a war by proxies, where local protagonists were increasingly seen as tools in the hands of their foreign patrons.

Second, serious disagreements soon emerged within, and among, client factions over the costs and benefits of their dependence, thus causing breakaways and the proliferation of new rebel groups. The phenomenon lies at the heart of the splits suffered by the RCD-Goma; to this day many Banyamulenge of South Kivu bitterly admit to having been "instrumentalized" by Rwanda. This helps to explain the long-standing conflict between the Munzunzu faction of the RCD and the Rwandan Patriotic Army (RPA) in the Itombwe high plateau of South

---

[3] Troop estimates are rough approximations borrowed from Fisher and Unishi 2000.

Kivu. Anti-Rwandan sentiment is still very much in evidence among those Banyamulenge of South Kivu who feel that they were little more than tools in the hands of Kagame.

Third, factional disputes over access to the mineral resources of Eastern Congo injected yet another element of discord among rebel groups while fuelling similar rivalries among their foreign sponsors. This is nowhere more dramatically illustrated than in the violent clashes that erupted between Rwanda and Uganda in Kisangani in 1999, 2000, and 2001, each claiming a monopoly of the rich diamond and gold deposits. At a later stage, Uganda would play a crucial role in playing one group of rebel forces off against the other, as happened in Ituri in 2003.

Fourth, in the course of the small wars being fought in the midst of bigger ones, countless atrocities were committed, more often than not with the encouragement if not the active participation of external patrons. This is nowhere more painfully evident than in the bitter Hema–Lendu strife in Ituri, where the involvement of Rwandan and Ugandan armed forces on opposite sides of the conflict contributed in no small way to its savagery.[4] But perhaps the most shocking example of mass atrocities committed in the course of the anti-Mobutist crusade, and largely concealed by the greater salience of that crusade in public perception, is the mass killing of Hutu refugees by units of the Rwandan army and AFDL in eastern Congo in 1996 and 1997. What could be seen as a sideshow in the AFDL march to Kinshasa is more accurately described as genocide.[5]

Fifth, insofar as the integration of former rebels into the Forces Armées de la République Démocratique du Congo (FARDC) has been the standard strategy for security sector reform (SSR), the result has been to inject new sources of internal tension within the armed forces. There are few equivalents anywhere in Africa for the levels of incompetence, indiscipline and rampant corruption for which the FARDC has become notorious.[6] In contrast to states where the military has gained the respect

[4] For an extensive discussion of the Hema–Lendu drama, see Reyntjens 2009: 215–19.

[5] On the extensive human rights violations committed by the Rwandan army see the so-called "UN Mapping Report" (UNHCR 2010), which concludes that such violations constitute crimes against humanity and war crimes. An excellent critical commentary on the report can be found in "L'ombre d'un génocide en RD-Congo" (2010). See also Reyntjens and Lemarchand 2011.

[6] The appropriation of troops' salaries by commanding officers, a recurrent practice since the birth of the FARC, goes far in explaining the predatory behavior of Congolese soldiers. To cite but one example, shortly after the inauguration of the transitional government in 2003, the local media in Goma reported that the deputy commander of the 8th military region had pocketed $200,000 intended to pay his troops, which he later denied, saying the money had been purloined by a thief who later fled to Rwanda.

of the citizenry for its performance in combat and become a source and symbol of national pride, no other army has attracted as much discredit to itself as the FARDC. A closer look at its performance explains why.

The FARDC: division, integration and defection

Attempts to turn the Congolese army into a coherent force to protect civilian lives were doomed from the start by the circumstances of its restructuring, when, in accordance with the Global and Inclusive Accord of 2002, the transitional government appointed military commanders to each of the eleven newly established military regions. The majority were drawn from the belligerent groups that were the signatories of the peace accord.[7] As if to add to the potential for conflict, the same pluralist approach governed appointments *within* each region. The situation described by Stephanie Wolters in 2004 foreshadowed impending disasters: "Currently the senior ranks of each military zone are filled by an assortment of officers from the various groups, who were appointed following discussions and compromises between the parties" (2004: 1). By early 2004 the 8th and 10th military regions, covering respectively North and South Kivu, were rife with internal tensions.

The crisis point was reached in May 2004 when a serious dispute broke out between the recently appointed military commander of the 10th region, General Mbudja Mabe, and the Banyamulenge second in command, Colonel Mutebutsi. Violence soon erupted in Bukavu, causing the death of at least fifteen civilians, most of them Banyamulenge. This was the signal for the notorious Colonel Laurent Nkunda to move his troops into Bukavu. "Once in occupation," writes Stephanie Wolters, "Nkunda ravaged the town" (2004: 2).[8] A week later, after the belated intervention of the UN mission in the Congo, MONUC, Nkunda was forced to withdraw. Meanwhile, thousands of Banyamulenge residents of Bukavu fled across the border to Burundi, where over a hundred were killed by Hutu extremists.

The brief and bloody encounter between Mabe and Nkunda should have given the top brass in Kinshasa pause to reconsider the wisdom of their recruitment policy. Instead the integration of rebel groups into the

---

[7] These were the MLC, RCD-Goma, President Kabila's party, the Parti pour la Reconstruction et le Développement (PPRD), the Rassemblement Congolais pour la Démocratie-Kisangani-Mouvement de Libération (RCD-K/ML), the Rassemblement Congolais pour la Démocratie-National (RCD-N), and Mai-Mai militias.

[8] Wolters adds that, according to witnesses and a Human Rights Watch report, "Nkunda's men went from door to door, raping and looting when the occupants of houses could not find sufficient cash to pay them off" (2004: 2).

army grew apace. According to one count, "56 rebel groups had been successively 'integrated' since the 1980s" (Jacquemot 2010: 7). Kabila's policy of "recuperation" led to the appointment of a number of former warlords and renegade officers to high-ranking positions. All were rewarded by swift promotions: overnight, majors became colonels, and colonels became majors. Examples abound of rebels-to-colonels-and-generals stories.[9] The integration of turncoats into the FARDC did little to discourage claimants to their succession; as more rebel commanders decided they would rather switch than fight, others rose up to replace them, thus further enlarging the pool of potential candidates for future reintegration.

One of the most spectacular of such "switches" occurred in 2009, after the sacking of Nkunda from the presidency of the Conseil National pour la Défense du Peuple (CNDP) by Kagame, largely under pressure from the State Department, and his replacement by Bosco Ntagunda, an extremely brutal warlord who now stands as one the FARDC's pre-eminent commanders in North Kivu. The game-changing event followed the decision by the governments of Rwanda and the DRC to join hands in rooting out the remnants of Rwanda's Hutu *génocidaires*, formally known as the Forces Démocratiques pour la Libération du Rwanda (FDLR). In return for Rwanda's military assistance in hunting down the FDLR, the armed wing of the CNDP (estimated at 18,000 men) would be integrated into the FARDC, and the civilian wing would be transformed into a political party.

Under the Swahili code name of Umoja Wetu (Our Unity), joint operations were conducted in North Kivu by elements of the Rwanda Defence Forces (RDF) and FARDC against FDLR positions, but with mixed results.[10] After the withdrawal of the RDF, much of the ethnic cleansing of Hutu was done by units of the FARDC in which the "integrated" CNDP played a major role. By then the anti-FDLR man-euvers had been expanded to the whole of North and South Kivu under the code name Kimia II – *kimia* in Swahili meaning "calm." That the word turned out to be a sad misnomer became clear when reports came out describing the extensive human rights violations committed by the FARDC in the course of armed raids conducted against the FDLR, in turn unleashing widespread revenge killings by Hutu elements.[11]

---

[9] For some samples, see Lemarchand 2009: 111.
[10] For an excellent discussion of the background to Umoja Wetu and its sequel, see International Crisis Group 2010.
[11] By October 2009 an estimated 1,000 civilians had been killed, 7,000 women had been raped, and 6,000 dwellings had been destroyed, for which both the FARDC and the FDLR were held responsible. See "Les conséquences désastreuses des opérations anti-FDLR sur les civils" 2009.

The integration of the CNDP into the FARDC can hardly be described as a resounding success. The first massive desertion of ex-CNDP elements occurred in late 2009 with the defection of Lt. Col. Emmanuel Nsengyumva. Concurrently, a number of integrated Mai-Mai groups followed suit and joined the FDLR. The motives for defecting vary, ranging from non-payment of salaries to the more attractive prospects of participating in the trade of illicit mining, to personal grudges against commanding officers. But perhaps the most serious source of division within the CNDP stems from the continuing influence of Nkunda over his former unit commanders. Rivalries between pro-Ntaganda and pro-Nkunda factions show no sign of abating. If anything the involvement of anti-Kagame dissidents in the intra-CNDP squabbles promises to further aggravate tension between the two warlords. What impact if any such intra-mural disputes may have on the stability of the provincial governments is as yet impossible to assess.

Concluding thoughts

To return to the main theme of this discussion: for reasons that have as much to do with the divisive impact of colonial authorities as with the social landscape of the region, nowhere in the Great Lakes has nationalism been a powerful unifying force. At best it has been an ephemeral phenomenon (as in the Congo), at worst a source of continuing ethnic enmity.

The early post-independence years are instructive in this regard. In Rwanda, nationalism as a broadly based, inter-ethnic movement became the principal casualty of the Belgian-backed 1959 Hutu revolution, two years before independence (1962). From then on, and until 1994, the Rwandan nation became identified with Hutu domination, in much the same way as it has now become synonymous with Tutsi rule. In Burundi, unlike what happened in Rwanda, at first the monarchy served as a powerful symbol of national unity, but with the projection of the Rwandan model onto the country's social map and the death of Prince Rwagasore in 1961, Hutu–Tutsi antagonisms, fuelled by the rise of Tutsi hegemony, set the tone of Burundi politics for the next forty years.[12]

In the Congo no sooner was the threshold of independence crossed than the army mutinied, followed by the Katanga and Kasai secessions, in turn paving the way for the first UN peace-keeping operation in the Congo. The decisive blow to the rise of a strong national sentiment came in early 1961 with the CIA-engineered and Belgian-assisted assassination of prime minister Patrice Lumumba, the only leader who could claim a

---

[12] See Lemarchand 1970, 1994.

credible national stature. Although Mobutu never achieved such stature, and went out of his way to disclaim culpability for Lumumba's death, his authenticity campaign did create an incipient sense of national identity among a large proportion of the population. What neither Mobutu nor either of his followers were able to achieve was to overcome the resentments and prejudices arising from the historic rift between Kinyarwanda speakers – and more specifically those Tutsi elements indigenous to the Congo – and the so-called "native" Congolese.

To this day the "us" versus "them" polarity looms large in the minds of many "authentic" Congolese who feel that ethnic Tutsi are at best the carriers of divided loyalties, at worst the source of subversive intentions. The phenomenon is traceable in part to the carryover of colonial mythologies into the context of eastern Congo, and the history of inter-ethnic tensions in the years following independence. The decisive factor, however, was the involvement of a large number of Congolese Tutsi in both Congo wars on the side of the Rwandan army. In the politics of foreign-linked clientelism, ethnic Tutsi provided a crucial linkage. Perceived by many Congolese as the architects of an unholy alliance with Rwanda, the Tutsi minority remains to this day a minority at risk.

War is the central, irreducible fact that has shaped ethnic identities in all three states of the Great Lakes. Besides injecting a strong element of distrust between communities, it has had a devastating impact on the fabric of society. In addition to the sheer number of lives destroyed it has torn to bits the fragile social ties that sustained life among the living. It has created hatreds where none previously existed, it has unleashed predatory instincts on an unprecedented scale, and it has sown the seeds of a failed state. Its shoots will continue to flourish for a long time to come.

REFERENCES

Centeno, M., J.M. Cruz, R. Flores, and G.S. Cano. 2013. "Internal Wars and Latin American Nationalism." (Chapter 11 of the current volume).

Coleman, J. 1958. *Nigeria: Background to Nationalism*. Berkeley: University of California Press.

1975. "Tradition and Nationalism in Tropical Africa." Pp. 3–36 in *New States in the Modern World*, edited by M. Kilson. Cambridge, MA: Harvard University Press.

Dietrich, C. 2001. "The Commercialisation of Military Deployment in Africa." Unpublished manuscript.

Dowty, A. 1971. "Foreign-Linked Factionalism as a Historical Pattern." *Journal of Conflict Resolution* 15(4): 429–42.

Fisher, I. and N. Unishi. 2000. "Rival Armies Ravage Congo in Africa's 'World War'." *International Herald Tribune*, February 7: 1–2.

Gellner, E.A. 1983. *Nations and Nationalism*. Oxford: Blackwell.

Herbst, J. 2000. *States and Power in Africa: Comparative Lessons in Authority and Control*. Princeton University Press.

Hodgkin, T. 1956. *Nationalism in Colonial Africa*. London: Frederick Muller.

International Crisis Group. 2010. *Congo: Pas de Stabilité au Kivu Malgré le Rapprochement avec le Rwanda*. Report No. 165, 16 November.

Jacquemot, P. 2010. "The Dynamics of Instability in Eastern DRC." *Forced Migration Review* 36: 6–7.

Lemarchand, R. 1970. *Rwanda and Burundi*. London: Pall Mall Press.

   1994. *Burundi: Ethnocide as Discourse and Practice*. Washington and New York: Wilson Center Press and Cambridge University Press.

   2009. "Reflections on the Crisis in the Congo." Pp. 105–22 in *L'Afrique des Grands Lacs, Annuaire 2008–2009*, edited by S. Marysse, F. Reyntjens, and S. Vandeginste. Paris: L'Harmattan.

"Les conséquences désastreuses des opérations anti-FDLR sur les civils." 2009. *Le Monde*, October 14.

"L'ombre d'un génocide en RD-Congo." 2010. *La Croix*, August 23.

Mbembe, A. 2001. *On the Postcolony*. Berkeley and Los Angeles: University of California Press.

Nye, J. 1975. "Nationalism, Statesmen, and the Size of African States." Pp. 158–70 in *New States in the Modern World*, edited by M. Kilson. Cambridge, MA: Harvard University Press.

Prunier, G. 2009. *Africa's World War: Congo, the Rwanda Genocide and the Making of a Continental Catastrophe*. Oxford University Press.

Reno, W. 2000. *"Debt and the Role of Pretending in Uganda's International Relations."* Occasional Paper, Centre of African Studies, Copenhagen.

Reyntjens, F. 2009. *The Great African War: Congo and Regional Geopolitics, 1996–2009*. Cambridge University Press.

Reyntjens, F. and R. Lemarchand. 2011. "Mass Murder in Eastern Congo." Pp. 20–36 in *Forgotten Genocides, Denial, Oblivion and Memory*, edited by R. Lemarchand. Philadelphia: University of Pennsylvania Press.

Rosenblum, P. 1998. Testimony. In "Democratic Republic of Congo in Crisis: hearing before the Subcommittee on Africa, of the Committee on International Relations, House of Representatives, One Hundred Fifth Congress, second session 15 September 1998, Volume 4." Washington, DC: US Government Printing Office.

Tilly, C. 1975. "Reflections on the History of European State-Making." Pp. 3–83 in *The Formation of National States in Western Europe*, edited by C. Tilly. Princeton University Press.

UNHCR. 2010. *DRC: Mapping Human Rights Violations 1993–2003*. Geneva: UNHCR.

Willame, J. 1997. *Banyarwanda and Banyamulenge: Violences ethniques et gestion de l'identitaire au Kivu*. Paris: L'Harmattan.

Wolters, S. 2004. "Continuing Instability in the Kivus: Testing the DRC Transition to the Limit." Institute for Security Studies Occasional Paper 94.

Young, C. 1993. "The Dialectics of Cultural Pluralism: Concept and Reality." Pp. 3–35 in *The Rising Tide of Cultural Pluralism: The Nation-State At Bay?* edited by C. Young. Madison: University of Wisconsin Press.

13 Victory in defeat?
National identity after civil war in Finland and Ireland

Bill Kissane

War can accelerate state building, and so too can civil war. Following independence Finland and Ireland saw a sharp reduction of their territories coincide with a rapid assertion of central authority during civil war. These civil war victories – by Finnish "Whites" and Irish "Free Staters" – provided the bases for their evolution as the two "successor states" which emerged during and after the First World War to retain their independence throughout the twentieth century. The victories resolved fundamental issues to do with statehood and also strengthened the respective states. Yet both also needed to reconstruct a common sense of national identity afterwards. This was problematic. International wars often lead to unifying narratives of conflict, but those of civil wars are divisive. Such was the case in Finland and Ireland, despite the integration of the losers into the systems afterwards. In Finland, the Social Democrats' participation in the political system saw no lessening of the dominance of the White interpretation of the civil war as "a war of liberation" before the 1960s. In Ireland, the losers had nationalism on their side, and came to monopolize the definition of what was national. Success at nation building did not automatically follow success at state building.

National identity has often been strengthened by the experience of solidarity during interstate wars. Ideological resources and bureaucratic control of coercion by the state are two critical variables (Malešević 2011: 141–61). This chapter explores the connection between state strength and national identity after civil wars. While in Finland there was a connection between the assertion of state strength in 1918 and the molding of national identity afterwards, in Ireland the combination of strong coercive state power and the moral support of the Catholic Church were insufficient. The victors monopolized state power and the losers, the definition of what was national. Yet the losers had played no role in state building before 1932, and were marginalized during reconstruction. The state was no less powerful than in Finland, but the losers still found victory in defeat. What explains the difference – the apparent disconnect between state and nation building – in Ireland?

One approach is simply to distinguish between the capacity to build strong states and that to mold identity on the basis that national identity is an independent variable. Yet in Ireland the losers had lost the propaganda battle in 1922–23: the public first chose the 26-county state over the 32-county nation. Another approach is to see identity as a proxy for class, and to explain outcomes in terms of cleavages that gave civil war divisions more substance. Yet the social bases of the Social Democrats' support were much stronger. The connection between state strength and national identity after civil war is obviously complex. Political scientists often reduce the challenge of post-conflict reconstruction to one of state capacity, and are then surprised to find that identities remain rooted in conflict. This was so in Finland and Ireland, which experienced mixtures of civil war, independence struggle, and revolution. The way these elements combined shaped identity. In Finland national identity thrived on victory, in Ireland on defeat. One difference is that the Irish victors aborted a national revolution to focus on the task of state building, and could not base national identity on their victory for this reason. In contrast the Finnish Social Democrats aborted a socialist revolution and faced historical oblivion in the first decades of the state's existence (Alapuro 1988: 150–97).

The civil wars

The very moment Finland and Ireland asserted their claims to independent statehood revealed the depths of their internal divisions. The Finnish conflict followed soon after the Bolshevik seizure of power in October 1917, and the Irish Civil War resulted from divisions over the Anglo-Irish Treaty of 1921. These conflicts, totally unexpected, were experienced as a profound shock. One aspect of this shock was the feeling that not all of society shared similar fundamental values. Struggles over who had the right to define what was national emerged. In Finland "Reds" were treated as traitors. In Ireland "Pro-Treatyites," who supported the Irish Free State in place of the Republic, were also considered traitors. Nationalists externalized the source of these internal divisions. White Finns claimed that the socialist movement had been contaminated by its exposure to Bolshevik Russia. Hard-line Irish republicans thought the "Free Staters" corrupted by their exposure to British high society during the treaty negotiations. The names, "Reds" versus "Whites," and "Free Staters" versus "republicans," reflected the stronger social basis of the Finnish conflict.

In demonstrating what "we" were really capable of, civil war disappointed hopes once vested in independence. Cultural nationalism had been initiated by Swedish-speaking elites in Finland, while early enthusiasts for Gaelic revivalism in Ireland were often Protestants. They had built up a positive image of "the people," to be shattered by civil wars whose destructiveness they blamed on the character of "the people" (Hämäläinen 1979; O'Callaghan 1984). The Irish state had to protect large Protestant estate owners from being burnt out by the Irish Republican Army between 1922 and 1923. The Swedish-speaking elite in Finland supported the Whites. Within the majority communities, struggles over who had the right interpretation of "the people" and the right to represent them gave the Finnish Civil War particular bitterness (Liikanen 1995). This bitterness continued after 1918 as the Whites persisted in representing the Reds as people "with no fatherland." In Ireland, nationalists derided "sectional interests" and "rotten politics" in a community with a long tradition of electoral monopoly (Kissane 2002: 147). The civil war was fought between two wings of Sinn Féin who both legitimized their actions as defenses of "the nation." Yet each side's definition of the nation excluded the other. The two parties that eventually emerged from the split, Fine Gael and Fianna Fáil, would continue to compete into the twenty-first century over the claim to be representing the nation.

The First World War had provided the context for growing radicalization. Neither country was a theatre of war, but British and Russian troops were stationed on their respective territories. In Ireland the war averted a conflict between Catholics and Protestants over the issue of Home Rule. The 1916 Rising, and the execution of its leaders, transformed the conflict into one between the British state and Irish republicanism. Constitutionalism became discredited. In Finland the Social Democrats had been the largest party since 1907, but lacked the legislative power to achieve social reforms. With economic conditions deteriorating during the war, frustration with parliamentary politics grew. After its 1918 general election victory, Sinn Féin demanded that Britain recognize the Republic proclaimed in 1916 and redeclared in 1919. The IRA began a war of independence in January 1919 that continued until June 1921. Internal opposition was concentrated in the northeast of Ulster, where Unionists were in the majority. Partition in 1920 placated thousands of demilitarized "loyalist" soldiers, but was followed by another electoral victory for Sinn Féin in 1921.

In both countries parliaments were an important symbol of independence, but became polarized by constitutional crises. Such was the status of the Eduskunta and Dáil parliaments that all parties attended them right up to the start of the civil wars. The Finnish Social Democrats passed a Power Law in 1917 aimed at legislative independence. Power would be transferred from St. Petersburg to Helsinki, and from the senate to parliament (Jussila et al. 1999: 97). The law would have made Finland politically independent, but left some foreign policy powers to the Russians. Both the bourgeois parties and the Russians opposed the law. The Finnish Russian Provisional Government rejected the Power Law and ordered fresh elections in October 1917, in which the Social Democrats lost their majority. The Social Democrats refused to accept the election as legitimate. The new bourgeois senate declared independence on December 6, 1917, and proceeded to assert its authority over Russian troops in Ostrobothnia. The next step was to disarm the Red Guards.

With partition an established fact by 1921, nationalist Ireland soon became divided between those for whom the Anglo-Irish Treaty was a sell-out, and those for whom it was a "stepping stone" to full independence. The issue of status proved more divisive than that of partition. The treaty gave 26 counties of Ireland internal autonomy, but their continued subordination to Britain as an imperial dominion was symbolized by provisions such as the oath to the Free State constitution and to the British Crown required of parliamentarians. The treaty mandated fresh elections, which on June 16 saw the anti-treaty republicans lose many seats. The Irish Provisional Government then claimed a mandate to implement the treaty. Its decision to attack the IRA on June 28 followed an ultimatum delivered by the British government two days previously. Just as the Social Democrats referred to the Power Law as the basis for an alternative political order, republicans continued to maintain that the June election had not disestablished the 32-county Republic. Situations of "multiple sovereignty" emerged, with governmental authority fragmented into two blocs, each claiming exclusive legitimacy (Alapuro 1988: 160–67; Coakley 1986: 187–207).

Civil war victory came quickly in both cases. The two governments forcefully asserted their legal authority, disarming the Russian soldiers in Ostrobothnia and attacking the IRA in Dublin. The quick defeat of the IRA in Dublin, the support of the press, and the backing of the Catholic Church enabled the Irish Provisional Government to project its authority in the capital, labelling the IRA "irregulars." With a constant supply of arms from Britain, the National Army soon grew to over 50,000 men and achieved a rapid advantage in the war's conventional phase in the summer (Kissane 2005: 64–99). The Catholic Church strongly backed the government, and IRA men were prevented from receiving the sacraments. Guerrilla resistance continued into April 1923, but reprisal executions and weak public support demoralized the IRA, which declared a ceasefire on April 30, 1923. Overall casualties were less than a thousand. However, pacification required extraordinary measures; the internment of over 10,000 people, rigorous censorship, and reprisal executions designed to discourage resistance. Prosecutions for civil war offences were discontinued in 1924 (Kissane 2005). Thousands of IRA men emigrated in 1923–24 (Foster 2009).

The Finnish Civil War, which lasted from January 27 to May 15, 1918, was more conventional, with the Reds (*punaiset*) at first controlling the more urbanized Southwest. The White (*valkoiset*) counteroffensive in early March, supported by the Baltic Sea Division of the German army, was successful. The Bolsheviks supported the Reds mainly through arms supplies. White victories in the battles of Tampere and Viipuri and the German occupation of Helsinki ensured victory. Over 37,000 people lost their lives, most of them after the fighting had ended. Atrocities were common on both sides, but since most people lost their lives in prison camps – through cold, hunger, and executions – the Reds suffered the most (Alapuro 2002: 169). Memories of the Red and White terrors lingered long after a conflict that was as violent as the Spanish Civil War. After its victory the Finnish Senate decided to appoint a German crown prince as monarch in 1918. After the German defeat in World War I, Finland became a democratic republic in 1919. To the Left however, the civil war inaugurated the "White Finland" of the inter-war era, a state that maintained a parliamentary facade, but used an array of legislation to drive the Communists underground. The Left's attitude remained basically defensive, and the Social Democrat premier of a short-lived coalition in 1926, Väino Tanner, was forced to take a salute at a White victory parade. The institutional symbol of the White Victory was the semi-official Civic Guard, which had over 100,000 members.

Abortive revolutions

The White and pro-treaty victories established platforms for these states' subsequent evolution, but a common national identity could not be based on these victories. In contrast to a case like Israel, where deep internal divisions did not fracture the independence movement, independence was achieved through outright civil war, so no common myth of the state's origins emerged. In contrast to a classic revolution, like the French Revolution, the Finnish and Irish revolutions had been defeated, and for this reason could not provide a stable basis for later political values and identities (Alapuro 2010). In Finland the Communists quickly split from the Social Democrats, while in Ireland the victors were accused of having sold out the revolution. The same accusation was made after the anti-treaty Fianna Fáil came to power in 1932.

Political traditions shaped how politicians responded to the experience of revolution. Alapuro argues that the Social Democrats responded by continuing to follow the path they had been taking in the previous decade. In 1907 they had gained access to power by legal means, their focus was on legislative reforms, and after achieving a majority in 1917 they passed the Power Law in accordance with legal precedents (Alapuro 1988: 169). They were Finnish nationalists and Finnish democrats. If they had an orientation towards radical action it was that of the general strike. Yet when they organized such a strike in October their aims were restorative, aiming to restore the political gains they had made the previous year (Alapuro 1988: 167–68). The real revolutionary impetus came from below, as worsening economic conditions polarized class relations and the Red Guards became impatient with parliamentary tactics.

In Ireland there *was* a longstanding tradition of revolutionary violence. The 1916 Rising had no popular mandate, but the executions of its leaders had galvanized public opinion behind the republican cause. Moderate and radical nationalists accepted the necessity of physical force until the Treaty. In 1922, a radical wing of the IRA was determined to renew the conflict with Britain rather than allow an opportunity for the Free State to consolidate. Some believed that more heroic action would return the support of a war-weary public to their cause. The crucial point is that once the civil war had begun, the anti-treaty politicians supported the IRA. Rather than abort the revolution, even when defeated in conventional hostilities, they supported a guerrilla war led by the IRA. They also formed a republican government in October 1922 and committed themselves to the defense of the "isolated Republic" outside the empire (Kissane 2005: 99–125). After inconclusive negotiations they buried their arms and returned home in May 1923. There was no surrender.

It would be easy to explain the different aftermaths simply in terms of contrasting types of civil war. The Finnish Civil War has been attributed to worsening social conditions and the Irish Civil War to the elite split following the treaty. Yet perceptions of social radicalism led to a reaction in both cases. Rural soviets, strikes, and "land grabbing" had punctuated the Irish War of Independence, leading ministers to conclude in 1922 that only the vigorous assertion of central authority would prevent the disintegration of the social fabric. By January 1923, mass executions were being proposed to prevent the possibility of a land war, and the army was used to crush "land grabbing" and labor unrest (Regan 1999: 120). In wartime Finland, food shortages, land evictions, and unemployment meant that the socialist movement eventually became radicalized. It had little actual contact with the Bolsheviks, but after the Bolshevik Revolution in October 1917 the bourgeois parties were determined to prevent its extension to Finland. Some Finns, believing in activist resistance to Russian rule, had already escaped to Germany and had received military training. Russian troops remained on Finnish territory into 1918 and the Germans intervened on the White side in the civil war. Although the Red Guards were drawn more clearly from the poorer classes than were the Irish republicans, anxiety about the social fabric fed into the urgency with which both governments regarded the "public order" question. At least a hundred Irish soviets had been established between 1917 and 1923 (Kostick 2009). Yet in return for electoral advancement and a place in parliament, the Irish Labour leadership also aborted the revolution in 1922, leaving the field to republicans who cared more about nationalist symbols than class politics.

A crucial factor had been the absence of state institutions specifically tasked with the maintenance of public order. Until the end of 1917, Finland had neither a properly constituted police force nor a body that was capable of protecting individual rights and the property order (Alapuro 1988: 152). In a largely spontaneous process on the workers' side, militias, later called Red Guards, and civil guards were formed with increasing rapidity in 1917. The former saw themselves as protectors of workers' rights and the latter were motivated partly by the need to protect bourgeois interests against a radicalized labor movement (Jussila et al. 1999: 108). By the end of 1917, there were about 40,000 civil guards and 30,000 Red Guards in the country (Jussila et al. 1999: 108). The rapid growth of the former in the second part of 1917 was a crucial factor drawing even the most devoted parliamentarians in the Social Democrat Party toward the Red Guards (Rintala 1962: 11). On January 25, two days before the revolution was launched, the senate declared the civil guards to be government troops, despite strong opposition from the Social Democrats. The order for the Red Guards to mobilize on January 27, which came from the executive committee of the Social Democrats' trade union organization, coincided with the spontaneous clashing of Red Guards with civil guards in the Viipuri area on the same day.

Imperial collapse also created a power vacuum in Ireland. The traditional police force, the Royal Irish Constabulary, had been discredited during the War of Independence and the new Civic Guard did not begin operating until after the civil war began. In the meantime, most of the countryside was under the control of the IRA, but the provisional government was slowly building up the National Army. This was a threat to the IRA, which controlled most of the territory of the state. In the spring of 1922, two rival armies existed side by side. The Provisional

Government's decision to attack the Four Courts on June 28 followed the British ultimatum, but also reflected the failure of efforts at maintaining unity that had been going on since February. The provisional government's justification for the attack on the Four Courts was the IRA's kidnapping of its assistant chief of staff on June 26. The revolution, and the IRA's central role therein, had been served notice.

In 1918 the Finnish Reds had no military training, got little outside help beyond arms, and took no real military initiative. Rather, the Social Democrats wanted to consolidate their administrative grip on the more urbanized southwest of Finland where life for the bourgeoisie initially went on much as it had in 1917 (Alapuro 1988: 174). The Finnish Democrats carried out only "a defensive revolution," since the expectation had been that parliamentary means would lead to power (Alapuro 1988: 175). Had they been revolutionary it would have been logical for them to oppose the bourgeois parties' Land Reform Bill in January 1918, which they didn't. Moreover, the peasantry, which largely voted Social Democrat, had not supported a revolution in the way that peasants in Russia and the Baltic states did at that time. Nor did the Social Democrat leadership apply the term "revolution" (as opposed to "class war") to the civil war in 1918, and it actually adopted a democratic constitution, based on the Swiss model, during the fighting (Alapuro 1988: 175). While the urban workers seldom fought on the White side, the peasantry was found on both sides in 1918 (Alapuro 1988: 195–96).

The Social Democrat leaders' aim was thus to preserve what had been achieved since 1917. Democracy had been won in 1906 not for a class, but for the Finnish people or *kansa*, (which also meant nation) (Kurunmäki 2008: 355–71). After the civil war, with the leadership in the hands of men like Väino Tanner, who renounced the revolution, the leaders again worked for the consolidation of representative institutions and class peace (Alapuro 1988: 207). Like other European Social Democrat parties that had to come to terms with the power of the Right, this meant that a clear distance emerged between them and the Communist Party. Guaranteed the right to contest elections by the 1919 constitution, the Social Democrats secured 80 seats in March 1919 and again became the largest party in parliament. They also controlled a total of 160 localities, including industrial cities such as Tampere (Haapala 2008). They soon succeeded in forcing through an amnesty bill that allowed for the release on probation of some 3,600 prisoners and the conditional restoration of civil rights to more than 40,000 prisoners released earlier.

In Ireland the treaty split, initially about means and not ends, became a division over the legitimacy of revolutionary nationalism. The IRA had opposed a vote on the treaty since they knew it would register a majority for peace. After the election on June 16 their opponents claimed a clear victory and began to use the language of majority rule to delegitimize the IRA. At stake now was not simply the treaty, but how Irish republicanism could be reconciled to a democratic, but 26-county state. The President of the Executive Council, William Cosgrave, once exclaimed that he would not stop at executing ten thousand republicans if the state were to live. He refused to enter negotiations that involved the reunification of the IRA, or revision of the treaty (Kissane 2005: 99–126). He believed that good relations should be maintained with London, and in 1925 his government accepted the findings of a Boundary Commission, in return for a financial settlement, that copper-fastened the border with Northern Ireland.

The Pro-Treatyite rejection of revolutionary nationalism led to a focus on the practical tasks of state building. Most of the state's senior civil servants had taken little part in the war of independence. The elites who accepted the treaty were more likely than their opponents to have had senior experience at running things before 1921 (Regan 1999: 82). The years between 1923 and 1927 proved ones of legislative achievement: a major land act, local government reorganization, and judicial reform. A new constitution was introduced in 1922. Measures such as the insistence on meritocratic standards throughout the public service established Cosgrave's as the party that "built the state" (Meehan 2010). Like the Finnish Social Democrats the government responded to the revolutionary situation by returning to gradualist traditions. As in Finland arguments about the character and rights of the people were polarizing. To radical nationalists the experience of revolution had brought out the best in the Irish people. To the pro-treaty elite it showed their unfitness for self-rule (MacArdle 1951; O'Hegarty 1998). The desire to establish a state, firmly autonomous from what some regarded as a "corrupting" native culture, reflected this conviction (Kissane 2005: 174). That, in the aftermath of civil war and revolution, Irish statehood was first conceived in terms of a strong set of institutions clearly differentiated from society, was remarkable. Yet often seeing politics "simply as administration," it was hard for those who had aborted the revolution to create a popular identification with the state. This gave a symbolic advantage to the losers.

National identity after civil war

After major wars or national crises, small states, perhaps more so than larger states, need to assert an identity. For big states this may not be a problem. Smaller countries face the specific task of locating conflicts to do with their origins in a national context (Alapuro 2002: 181). This was harder in Finland and Ireland, where these conflicts were bound up in external events. Both civil wars had come "from the outside in," and were first incorporated into national political traditions by being regarded as wars of independence or liberation. Finnish independence had come about only as a consequence of the First World War, and the Whites believed that nation building was incomplete in 1917. The roots of independence were thought of as originating deep in the past, and the White victory was seen as the culmination of a long-term development (Haapala 2008). The White interpretation suited the post-civil war context, and monuments celebrating their victory soon dotted the land. The border with the Soviet Union and the position of the Aland Islands were not settled before 1921, and Finland had closer ties with the very nationalistic Baltic states in the 1920s than with Scandinavia.

In Ireland the victors spent little money commemorating their victory, and public monuments to their fallen heroes, such as Arthur Griffith, were allowed to lapse into desuetude (Dolan 2003). In contrast, the losers had a richer tradition of commemorating nationalist defeats. The 1916 Rising, not the civil war, was commemorated by both sides as the real founding event for the state. Defeat, not victory, was the source of stronger symbols. The state's legitimacy rested in no small measure on the extent to which it was seen as being faithful to traditional symbols (Garvin 1981). The name for the pro-treaty party Cumann na nGaedheal (family of the Gael), and of the parliament Dáil Éireann, suggested this. The image the victors promoted of the state was revivalist: symbols (such as postage stamps) would stress its roots in the pre-British Gaelic order. Yet such symbols could serve any state, not specifically the one founded by the treaty. Key treaty provisions, such as the oath, symbolically underscored the state's subordination to Britain. Hence the Free State was seen as incomplete, its symbols a token of national failure. The Republic, in contrast, remained a meta-constitutional ideal that inspired those who wanted, for very different reasons, to change the status quo. The sense of provisionality that accompanied the treaty created a climate wherein many forms of opposition, including in the arts, flourished (Allen 2009). It also meant that both of the civil war sides would compete over "unfinished business." De Valera's *Fianna Fail: the Republican Party* competed with *Fine Gael: The United Ireland Party*. The Republic, and an end to partition, were not simply political objectives or tokens of nationalist commitment, but were metaphors of a provisional attitude to the state that actually remains today. In this state of unfulfilment, it is precisely those who actually built the state whose legacy becomes insubstantial.

Identity wars may be a stronger source of symbolism than class wars, but both civil wars were rich in symbolic possibilities. The Finnish Right interpreted their civil war in national terms, as a "war of liberation" (*vappausota*) against Leftist forces contaminated by their exposure to the Soviet Union. This implied that the Reds' position was anti-national. The Left, in contrast, interpreted the war in social terms, as a defense of the gains for the Social Democrats that had followed the October Revolution (Alapuro 2002: 169). After 1918 the Social Democrats continued to believe that their fight had been for social justice, while the Communists viewed the civil war as a class war (*luokkasota*). Both found it harder to represent their cause as a national one. In Ireland it was the losers who interpreted the civil war in national terms. In 1922 the anti-treaty IRA had seen the fighting not as a civil war, but as a continuation of the war of independence against the British that began in 1916 (Kissane 2005: 1). There was no real difference here between those who entered the parliament in 1927, and Sinn Féin and the IRA. This interpretation naturally appealed when the state saw the national revolution as incomplete. Dorothy MacArdle's canonical republican text *The Irish Republic* represented the republican defeat as an interruption of a revolution, still ongoing in 1935, the year of its publication (MacArdle 1951). She had close relations with the Fianna Fáil leader, de Valera, who introduced a constitution two years later. Later radical historians developed her view that the civil war was not something new, but a continuation of a longer-term revolution (Gallagher 1965; Greaves 1971). The Pro-Treatyites saw the conflict in *social* terms, as a defense of majority rule and the property order. This view, key to their successful civil war propaganda, became less effective once society demobilized in the mid 1920s.

The Irish Civil War also had a marked social dimension, but the losers did not embrace it as a part of their cause. Just as the Labour Party became marginalized in the war's aftermath, the social agitation which lasted into 1923 was downplayed. The marked imbalance of power encouraged this. Before 1931, when the anti-treaty Irish press was formed, the losers faced hostile newspapers, the Catholic hierarchy, and constant vilification by the governments. In 1922–23, government propaganda had stressed the economic cost of the "irregular" tactics, and "Red scare" tactics marked elections into the 1930s. Among the leaders for the September 1927 election were: "Help the Government to Finish the Job," "Who Are the War-Makers?" "Now They Are Shocked," "The Making of Ireland – or Its Undoing," "They Took the Oath to Save Their Party – They Would Not Take It in 1922 to Save Their Country from Civil War," "De Valera in the Dumps and the Voters on the Warpath," "Economy – by Torch And Petrol Can," "Digging Freedom's Grave in 1922" (Moss 1933: 126). In other words, Fianna Fáil was forced to remake its image to recover ground electorally. In September 1927 de Valera publicly announced that "the sinister design of aiming at bringing about a sudden revolutionary upheaval with which our opponents choose to credit us, is altogether foreign to our purpose and programme" (quoted in Kissane 2005: 189). Fianna Fáil played the green, not red, card on their way back to power. Social radicalism was forsaken.

In Finland the losers were inhibited from stressing the national, not the social, aspect of their civil war experience. Most Finnish political parties had a distinct social profile, economic reform had been on the agenda since 1906, and the Social Democrats had sister parties in Scandinavia. For the names used for the civil war, the Finnish Social Democrats' preference was for *kansalaissota* (peoples' war) while the Communists preferred *luokkasota* (class war). The neutral term *sissällisota*, also preferred by some Social Democrats, translates as "internal war" (Alapuro 2002: 172). All suggest the civil war's social character. Articulating their cause as a national one was more difficult. The White interpretation prevailed at a time of great Russophobia, cultural revivalism and external threat. It was only after the relationship with the Soviets changed after 1945 that the Left's perspective was gradually accepted. In Ireland, change in the external context would also allow the social interpretations of the civil war to return. The pro-treaty cause had a conservative logic, harder to represent in nationalist terms when the revolution was seen as "interrupted" by their victory. In the 1920s and 1930s a cottage industry grew for biographies of Michael Collins, the lost military leader. His life and politics also had the advantage of being unfulfilled, while his successors were more and more tied to the treaty that symbolized the limits of nationalism. Only after the republican cause was abandoned between 1969 and 1972, and partition was practically accepted during the Northern Irish conflict, did the centrality of democracy to the conflict begin to be stressed. Since then, its internal dimension has been stressed by different themes: the divide between autocrats and democrats within Sinn Féin, the role of factional and local divisions behind the treaty split, and the existence of social radicalism in the Irish countryside in 1922.

Both nationalist interpretations were Hegelian in that the nation was seen as a cultural essence unfolding itself through time. Yet there was a key difference between the two, which brings out the contrasting connections between state power and national identity in the two countries. In Finland the essence became substance when the White victory established the state. In Ireland the dream of revolution was seen to have died the moment the state was born (Allen 2009: 2). The gap between essence (nation) and substance (state) remained to be closed. Whereas in Finland victory resonated in terms of identity, in Ireland defeat was more portentous. Yet more prosaic readings of state formation were also available. The story of the Irish state was generally read in two ways. One looked upon the war against the British as the near satisfaction of the 1916 act of national redemption, with the unification of the island remaining the ultimate goal (McCarthy 2006). The civil war was a tragic diversion. The second view sees the substance of nationhood having been virtually realized in the late nineteenth century with the successful alliance of Charles Stewart Parnell, the Irish Parliamentary Party, and the Catholic hierarchy. In this view, the violence between 1916 and 1923 was an exception in a story of constitutional evolution towards self-government, to which path Ireland returned with the conclusion of the civil war (McCarthy: 2006). It was to this evolutionary interpretation that the two pro-treaty leaders, Griffith and Collins, explicitly appealed in 1922 (Kissane 2005: 55–61). In Finland, too, the nation could have been conceived of not as cultural essence, but as political practice, slowly emerging from complex matrices of law and institutions. The autonomous Grand Duchy of the Tsar, created in 1809, had created a political roof under which the Finns gradually built up a connection between people and nation before 1914. To this day 1809 is seen as a foundation for Finnish independence. The capstone of this process for the Left was the achievement of equal suffrage under a democratic parliament in 1906. The Social Democrats contributed to this change, and referred to it as a source of their values after the civil war. The civil war was a tragic breakdown, and the country returned to the practical business of politics with the 1919 constitution.

Yet while both states had these pre-war roots, violence remained key to national identity. In post-1945 Europe the influence of paramilitary formations on state formation was crucial. In Finland the White civil guards were semi-incorporated into the state. In Ireland the IRA was marginalized, but at the symbolic level a struggle for legitimacy continued: *Oglaigh na hEireann* remained the official name for both the National Army founded during the civil war and the IRA. In this context, the losers were better able to place their civil war defeat in a longer national telos. The 1916 Rising would be celebrated by both the state and the IRA into the 1970s. In Finland there had been no popular tradition of political violence, so the Left's revolution could not easily be incorporated into a national tradition. Internal political violence was actually specific to 1917, although labor agitation was not. The names of Finnish parties denoted their distinct social profiles; purely ideological parties did not flourish. Up to the 1960s silence enveloped memories of both the White and Red terrors. Alapuro sees the Finnish Civil War as an "exceptional event," which did not change institutions or social

structures (Alapuro in press). Neither did it change the Social Democrats' gradualist approach to politics. After 1918 the Red Guards were no
longer part of the Social Democrat movement, but such were the IRA's
claims in Ireland that the state eventually banned the press from using
this name in its reference to the organization.

Positive and negative reintegration

The different reconstructions of identity reflect the different ways in
which the losers were integrated after the civil wars. By being identified
with an incomplete national revolution the Irish losers staged a remarkable comeback. The leftist position on the Finnish Civil War led to
second-class citizenship within "White Finland." Yet neither state
was completely tied to the interests of the victors. Indeed, both quickly
deradicalized, notably in terms of the size of their militaries. Similar
nation-building measures were implemented: democratic constitution-
making, land reform, and the promotion of an image of the nation as an
inter-class community. They suggested that state power was used to
promote general reconciliation. The legitimacy of the Irish losers' cause
in the wider nationalist culture, and the electoral strength of the Finnish
Left, encouraged this approach. Yet the Irish losers experienced a more
positive form of integration.

Alapuro contrasts two strategies of integration in Finland: one based on
the promotion of an inter-class cultural-nationalist community, and the
other based on national integration through conciliation (1988: 204–06).
In Finland the conservative strategy could not reconcile the losing side,
since it implied the suppression of class differences. The Finnish Socialist
Labor Party (a split-off from the Social Democrat Party in 1920) was
banned after having contested the 1922 election. It contested the 1924,
1927, and 1929 elections as the Workers and Smallholders Party, but
was banned again after 1929. The second, conciliatory approach was
espoused by the Agrarian Union and the National Progressives, and
prompted the passing of Land Reform Bills, and amnesties for the rank-
and-file Reds. Yet further anti-communist laws, introduced in October
1930, almost led to the suppression of the Social Democrats as well.
Employing violent tactics, the quasi-fascist Lapuas wanted these laws to
extend to the Social Democrats: "its activists saw themselves as making a
valiant attempt to safeguard the achievements of the civil war and restore
the White Finland that had emerged from it" (Jussila et al. 1999: 155).
The movement was eventually suppressed. The crisis showed that the
Agrarian Party had no sympathy for efforts to extend the repression to
the Social Democrats. To the Social Democrats the crisis underlined

their dependence on parliamentary institutions. In 1937 the two parties negotiated a coalition based on the protection of democracy and resistance to fascism (Karvonen 2000: 150–51).

In Ireland the idea of the inter-class cultural nationalist community was so strong that class politics were subsumed by it. Politics became dominated by two wings of Sinn Féin that both promoted cultural revival. Labour quickly lost ground, having remained neutral in the civil war. By 1932 it was supporting a minority Fianna Fáil government. Since the social bases of the civil war split were less structured than in Finland, it was easier for this conservative model of integration to work. It appealed to the loser's ideological self-image, and implied the second-order nature of Labour's challenge in 1922–23. After all, both civil war parties were offshoots of Sinn Féin. Yet the state was initially exclusive. The ranks of the security forces had been screened for their political sympathies. Employment in reconstruction projects was open only to those who had served in the National Army, and discrimination in private employment was also encouraged. The oath to the crown, an exclusive device, remained in place until 1933. Yet rapprochement was encouraged by the emergence of Fianna Fáil from the ranks of Sinn Féin in 1926. Fianna Fáil (reluctantly) took the oath, and became the parliamentary opposition from 1927 on. It also deliberately sought the approval of the Catholic Church. The victors then distinguished between the interests of the state and those of their party, when they relinquished power in 1932. Fianna Fáil remained in power for the next sixteen years and used its parliamentary strength to undo the treaty. By 1938, with partition outstanding, most of the treaty grievances had been resolved.

In Finland, the Social Democrats experienced a more "negative integration" (Kirby 1979: 96). Their leader, Tanner, was not associated with the revolution, while the leader of Fianna Fáil, de Valera, President of the republican government during the Civil War, was personally blamed for it by his opponents (Valiulis 1986). Yet Fianna Fáil formed single-party governments, while the Social Democrats governed through coalition. Fianna Fáil's protectionist policies alienated their civil war opponents and when the Blueshirt movement emerged in protest, a Fianna Fáil government repressed it (the Blueshirts' President had been a senior commander in the National Army in 1922). In contrast, in Finland much of bourgeois society had initially been responsive to the Lapuas. Integration in Ireland was also more positive in symbolic terms. Fianna Fáil's 1937 constitution replaced that of 1922, renamed the state, made no mention of Britain, and claimed authority over the whole island. Presented as a fait accompli through the referendum, this constitution was bitterly opposed by Fine Gael (Kissane 2011).

One indication of the different modes of integration was that the nationalist intelligentsia embraced the losers only in Ireland. Given the absence of a strong bourgeoisie, this group was pivotal in both countries. Civil war creates a deep rift between state and society, and reconciliation requires that this rift be healed. The nation, severed from the intellectuals during the civil wars, had to be reconstructed. Yet in Finland the Left had developed no real critique of Finnish society, and the intelligentsia and students, who had provided the cultural images of the nation before 1918, were on the White side, as were the Swedish-speaking elites (Alapuro 2012). The Lutheran Church was also strongly opposed to the Left in the civil war. This meant that no intellectual group championed the socialist cause as a national one. In Ireland the nationalist intelligentsia had also provided the rationale for independence before 1921 (Hutchinson 1987). Yet the main cultural organizations had been neutral in 1922 (Kissane 2005). The Gaelic League, the Irish National Teachers Organisation, or the Gaelic Athletic Association would only have regarded the treaty as a temporary measure. The Catholic hierarchy was committed to the social order in 1922, not to the treaty per se. Thus, for the intelligentsia too, the treaty and partition were provisional and the anti-treatyites were rehabilitated in a way that a class-based movement would never have been.

Hence the different modes of political integration also reflected the different social bases of the losers' cause. On the one hand, the Finnish Left had a stronger subculture than the anti-treaty republicans, with its own educational, social, sporting, and welfare organizations for workers (Alapuro in press). Hostility to the Lutheran Church was pervasive, and the Left's unions were at the forefront of labor disputes. Yet the Social Democrats were not independent of the dominant nationalist ideas of Finnishness. In their civil war narratives, the ideal worker was actually imbued with the same qualities that characterized the non-socialist Finn, and these qualities derived from rural traditions (Alapuro in press). With more autonomy but less independence, the Left experienced a deep "cultural isolation" (Alapuro in press). While Red Guardists could be portrayed as "duped" countrymen, the Communists could not operate openly until after 1944, when their party was legalized. In Ireland such was the integrative power of the mainstream culture that even those who continued to reject the Irish state (Sinn Féin and the IRA) became a dissenting current, not a separate subculture (Bell 1972). They were not isolated. The Anti-Treatyites' immediate response to the Civil War had been to build up an underground state (with its own army and parliament) in order to keep the losers untouched and uncorrupted by the Free State (Pyne 1969–70: 40). This project quickly failed. As in

Finland, conceptions of the model citizen were deeply influenced by rural culture, but the losers had a strong electoral presence in the west of Ireland.

Thus "positive integration" in Ireland reflected the more fragmented social basis of civil war politics. The question after 1923 was not whether to put class before nation, but which civil war party would succeed in championing the nationalist cause. The civil war, "Green against Green," reinforced the dominance of nationalist conceptions of politics (Hopkinson 1988). In Finland, party politics was more structured by class. Its party system usually consisted of six political groupings. Most had a distinct social profile and it was harder for any one to become nationally hegemonic (Soikkanen 1987: 29). The Social Democrats were thus socially, not nationally defined, and developed no populist critique of the state. While Fianna Fáil represented its opponents as lackeys of the British, and in 1936 abolished a Senate intended in 1922 to provide representation for the Anglo-Irish minority, the Social Democrats regarded language as a second-class issue. The bitter arguments about the claims of Finnish versus Swedish (the language of the elite) in the 1930s were conducted within the victorious camp. The Social Democrats addressed civil war grievances through reform. The Anti-Treatyites in contrast championed the small farmer, changed the symbolic aspect of the state, while after 1932 using all the techniques of state power, such as its repressive laws that their opponents had developed in the 1920s.

Conclusion

In terms of the relationship between state power and national identity the Finnish experience was not unique. Most contemporaneous European civil wars had a class dimension. The Finnish losers were not alone in being excluded from the nation afterwards. Negative integration has been the common experience of the European Left after civil wars. The Whites were not unusual in using the familiar trope of army, church, and nation to identify the state with their victory. Malešević's connection between coercive strength, ideological resources, and the monopoly of national identity existed. Unlike in Ireland, where the nationalist elite long possessed the tools of popular incorporation, democratic politics had come suddenly in 1905. When the scale of social disaffection was revealed in 1917–18, the response was to consider the Reds "those with no fatherland" (Alapuro in press). Only in 1966 did Väinö Linna's trilogy of novels, *Under the Northern Star*, give a sympathetic account of the Reds by stressing their social grievances. Linna's work helped to integrate the Reds into the Finns' self-conception.

The Finnish state did deradicalize after 1918 and was autonomous from the victors' interests to some degree, but at the symbolic level it remained identified with the White victory. This was expressed by the official position of the civic guards. In Ireland state institutions proved more neutral. The Gardai, an unarmed police force sent into the countryside during the civil war, was accepted by both sides. Yet the achievement of state autonomy gave a symbolic advantage to the losers. Success in the practical tasks of state building could not satisfy the pride of revolutionary destiny, and the restive search for identity gave the initiative to those who had not compromised in 1922. Their integration into the polity was positive in two senses: it allowed them to vindicate their civil war cause through revision of the treaty, and also to bridge a gulf between state and society that long preceded independence. In 1931 Cosgrave lamented "the absence of a state sense" among the Irish people (Kissane 2004). By 1945, after the experience of neutrality in the war, there was no longer any doubt that most people identified with the state. Indeed in both countries national unity, which had been destroyed in one (civil) war, was restored in another (international) war. United in the Winter War (November 1939 to March 1940) and its Continuation (June 1941 to September 1944), against the Soviets, Finland began the integration of the Communists into the system.

This suggests that generalizations about state strength and national identity must distinguish between different types of war. Civil war has two distinct consequences. Since coexistence within a state is required after civil but not international war, reconciliation is more an imperative. Yet after civil wars, the reconstruction of national identity has to accommodate competing, not unifying, narratives. As a result, both Finland and Ireland could only accomplish "reconciliation without truth" (Forsberg 2007). Under the common roof of institutions relationships were healed, while historical understanding of these civil wars was obstructed by silence and the political use of civil war memories. Yet state strength *was* at work in two ways. Reconciliation followed the security provided by military victory in the civil war, and cooperation was encouraged by the existence of strong traditional political institutions. This points to at least an indirect connection between state strength and national identity. The problem is that such indirect relationships do not make for strong symbols of identity. These symbols remained rooted in war. Nonetheless, Finland was not simply created by the White victory, nor Ireland by revolution. Indeed, while unequal in the symbolic struggle for identity, the two historic approaches to state formation were reconciled in practice. In the shadow of the Soviet Union, the Whites could lord it over the Left, knowing that the Social Democrats had abandoned revolution in favor of a constructive engagement with the state. Only the security provided by the Free State and the disengagement of Britain in the 1920s led the public to hand power back to de Valera in 1932. One can only observe that the existence of such tacit understandings does not rule out a strong role for symbolism in the expression of national identity.

REFERENCES

Alapuro, R. 1988. *State and Revolution in Finland.* Berkeley: University of California Press.

2002. "Coping with the Civil War of 1918 in Twentieth Century Finland." Pp. 169–84 in *Historical Injustice and Democratic Transition in Eastern Asia and Northern Europe: Ghosts at the Table of Democracy,* edited by K. Christie and R. Cribb. London: New York: Routledge.

2010. "Violence in the Finnish Civil War in Today's Perspective." Paper presented to the History, Memory, Politics Seminar. Helsinki Collegium for Advanced Studies, 19 May 2010.

In press. "The Reconstruction of National Identity in Finland after the Civil War of 1918." In *Reconstructing National Identity after Europe's Internal Wars,* edited by B. Kissane. Philadelphia: University of Pennsylvania Press.

Allen, N. 2009. *Modernism, Ireland and Civil War.* Cambridge University Press.

Bell, J.B. 1972. "Societal Patterns and Lessons: The Irish Case." Pp. 217–29 in *Civil Wars in the Twentieth Century,* edited by R. Higham. Lexington: University of Kentucky Press.

Coakley, J. 1986. "Political Succession and Regime Change in New States in Interwar Europe: Ireland, Finland, Czechoslovakia, and the Baltic Republics." *European Journal of Political Research* 14(1–2): 187–206.

Dolan, A. 2003. *Commemorating the Irish Civil War: History and Memory, 1923–2000.* Cambridge University Press.

Forsberg, T. 2007. "Post-Conflict Justice and the Finnish Civil War 1918: Reconciliation without Truth?" Pp. 137–54 in *Finnish Yearbook of International Law,* Vol. 18, edited by J. Klabbers. The Hague: Brill.

Foster, G. 2009. "The Social Structures and Cultural Politics of the Irish Civil War." Ph.D. thesis, University of Notre Dame, South Bend, IN.

Gallagher, F. 1965. *The Anglo-Irish Treaty.* London: Hutchinson.

Garvin, T. 1981. *The Evolution of Irish Nationalist Politics.* Dublin: Gill & Macmillan.

Greaves, D.C. 1971. *Liam Mellowes and the Irish Revolution.* London: Lawrence & Wishart.

Haapala, P. 2008. "The Legacy of the Civil War 1918 in Finnish Historiography." Paper presented to the Joint Conference between Finnish and Estonian Historians 2008: The Difficult Past No. 2.

Hämäläinen, P. 1979. *In Time of Storm: Revolution, Civil War, and the Ethnolinguistic Issue in Finland.* Albany: State University of New York Press.

Hopkinson, M. 1988. *Green Against Green: The Irish Civil War 1922–23.* Dublin: Gill & Macmillan.

Hutchinson, J. 1987. *The Dynamics of Cultural Nationalism: The Gaelic Revival and the Creation of the Irish Nation State*. London: Allen and Unwin.

Jussila, O., S. Hentila, and J. Nevakivi. 1999. *From Grand Duchy to Modern State: A Political History of Finland since 1809*. London: Hurst & Co.

Karvonen, L. 2000. "Finland: From Conflict to Compromise." Pp. 129–57 in *Conditions of Democracy in Europe, 1919–1939: Systematic Case Studies*, edited by D. Berg-Schlosser and J. Mitchell. Basingstoke: Macmillan.

Kirby, D. 1979. *Finland in the Twentieth Century*. London: Hurst & Co.

Kissane, B. 2002. *Explaining Irish Democracy*. University College Dublin Press.
    "Democratization, State Formation and Civil War in Finland and Ireland: A Comment on the Democratic Peace Hypothesis." *Comparative Political Studies* 37(8): 969–85.
    2005. *The Politics of the Irish Civil War*. Oxford University Press.
    2011. *New Beginnings: Constitutionalism and Democracy in Modern Ireland*. University College Dublin Press.

Kostick, C. 2009. *Revolution in Ireland: Popular Militancy 1917–1923*. Cork University Press.

Kurunmäki, J. 2008. "The Breakthrough of Universal Suffrage in Finland, 1905–06." Pp. 355–71 in *The Ashgate Companion to the Politics of Democratization in Europe: Concepts and Histories*, edited by K. Palonen, T. Pulkkinen, and J.M. Rosales. Farnham: Ashgate.

Liikanen, I. 1995. *Fennoman ja kansa. Joukkojarjestaytymsen lapimurto ja Suomalaisen puoleen synty*. Hesinki: Suomen Historiallinen Seura.

MacArdle, D. 1951. *The Irish Republic*, 3rd edn. Dublin: Victor Gollancz.

Malešević, S. 2011. "Nationalism, War and Social Cohesion." *Ethnic and Racial Studies* 34(1): 141–61.

McCarthy, J.P. 2006. *Kevin O'Higgins: Builder of the Irish State*. Dublin: Irish Academic Press.

Meehan, C. 2010. *The Cosgrave Party*. Dublin: Irish Academic Press.

Moss, W. 1933. *Political Parties in the Irish Free State*. New York: Columbia University Press.

O'Callaghan, M. 1984. "Language, Nationality and Cultural Identity in the Irish Free State, 1922–7: The 'Irish Statesman' and 'Catholic Bulletin' reappraised." *Irish Historical Studies* (94): 226–45.

O'Hegarty, P.S. 1998[1924]. *The Victory of Sinn Fein*. University College Dublin Press.

Pyne, P. 1969–70. "The Third Sinn Fein Party: 1923–26." *Economic and Social Review* 1: 29–50, 129–57.

Regan, J. 1999. *The Irish Counter-revolution 1921–1936*. Dublin: Gill & Macmillan.

Rintala, M. 1962. *Three Generations: The Extreme Right Wing in Finnish Politics*. Bloomington: Indiana University Press.

Soikkanen, T. 1987. "The Development of Political Parties: An Introduction and Overview." Pp. 28–34 in *Political Parties in Finland*, edited by J. Mylly and M.R. Berry. University of Turku.

Valiulis, M. 1986. "The Man They Could Never Forgive: The View of the Opposition. Eamon De Valera and the Civil War." Pp. 92–100 in *Eamon de Valera and His Times*, edited by J.A. Murphy and J.P. O'Carroll. Cork University Press.

14   When nationalists disagree
Who should one hate and kill?

Stephen M. Saideman

Events in the 1990s in the Balkans, Central Africa, and elsewhere not only energized the scholarship of ethnic conflict and nationalism, but also brought the word "nationalist" into the mainstream media. The media defined the bad guys in these conflicts as "nationalists," which ultimately proved to be less than helpful. After all, to many people, Slobodan Milosevic was not the most extreme Serb nationalist, if he was even a true believer at all. Indeed, he posed as a moderate nationalist when running in elections, juxtaposing himself with Serbs who seemed to be more passionate defenders of the Serb nation.[1] The problem with this kind of discussion is that it suggests that each nation has a simple political spectrum with one end defined as least nationalist and the other as most nationalist.

Each nationalism is actually more complex than that, consisting of a variety of ideas about what the nation is and should be, who the enemies are, and what should be done. It is not simply an issue of less or more, but to which strands one adheres, how one views the various elements, and how they fit together. This is important because it belies the usual equation of more nationalism = more war. The reality is that being a diehard nationalist may actually also make one less inclined towards aggressive foreign policies.

This chapter borrows and builds on work published elsewhere, including Saideman and Auerswald 2012 and Saideman and Ayres 2008. As a result, I owe many debts, including to the Social Science and Humanities Research Council of Canada, the Canada Research Chairs program, the Security and Defence Forum of Canada's Department of National Defence, and NATO's Public Diplomacy grant program for funding this research. I am also thankful to a team of research assistants including Ora Szekely, Raluca Popa, Ionuț Lăcustă, Sarah-Myriam Martin-Brûlé, Claudia Martinez Ochoa, Vania Draguieva, Michelle Meyer, David Lehman, Suranjan Weeraratne, Lori Young, Chris Chhim, Alex Jablonski, Jenyfer Maisonneuve, Katarina Germani, and Bronwen De Sena.
[1] Much has been written about Milosevic's insincerity, including Gagnon 2004, and Kaufman 1994.

The purpose here is to assert that any nationalism is more complex than averred. Many individuals or parties or countries seeking to be the representatives of a particular nation may or may not share an understanding of what it means to be a member of that nation. The degree of shared or conflicting understandings of what the nation is has significant implications not just for whether a country will go to war but with whom. The focus here will be on the form of nationalism that most directly connects to war: irredentism.[2] Efforts to unify kin by changing international boundaries will cause war, as countries as a rule do not give up territory without a fight. By understanding how nationalisms, rather than nationalism, impact irredentism, we can assess how the content of nationalisms shapes the likelihood of war. We can then take this understanding of nationalism and extend it to the politics of intervention.

This chapter proceeds as follows. First, I consider how we think about identity and what that means for nationalism, including how ties to "the nation" and antipathies to "others" can create a variety of possible nationalisms. Second, I develop the connections between nationalism and irredentism. Third, I then consider Romania to illustrate the conditions under which nationalism might inhibit war. Fourth, I briefly show how various strains of xenophobia can produce different foreign policy stances towards the international effort in Afghanistan. Fifth, I address the role of xenophobia in the reactions to Libya's conflict. I conclude with some implications for future research.

Identity and nationalism

For much of the discussion in the 1990s and beyond, when politicians and journalists referred to nationalism, they meant ethnic nationalism: movements that aimed at creating ethnically homogeneous political units, preferably nation-states. Focusing on half of the classic distinction between civic and ethnic nationalisms,[3] the tendency was to assume not only the coherence of an ethnic group but also that the group had a shared goal: to unify the nation in a single state. This tends to take too much for granted, so starting with identity can help us figure out how nationalisms are actually far more complex.

The starting point is identity, as nationalism is one way in which a person defines who s/he is. Abdelal and his co-authors (2006) clarify

---

[2] See Ambrosio 2001, Saideman and Ayres 2008, and Weiner 1971 for analyses of irredentism.

[3] For various takes on the civic/ethnic nationalism dichotomy see Brubaker 1996, Ignatieff 1994, Shulman 2002, and Smith 1993.

identity by focusing on two dimensions: content and contestation. Our interest here is first on four aspects of content: constitutive norms, social purposes, relational comparisons with other social categories, and cognitive models. That is, who belongs, for what purpose, as opposed to what other ways of identifying, thinking what?

Any kind of identity distinguishes members of the group from non-members (Mercer 1995). While most analysts of nationalism take seriously the identification of who is the "us," identification of the relevant "them" is often overlooked.[4] Who is seen as the adversary to be opposed matters as it may determine who the targets of nationalist policies might be. Extremist politicians choose not only to favor the in-group, but also to discriminate against the *most salient* out-group. Deegan-Krause (2004) documents the multiplicity of "others" that could be and were targeted by varying nationalists within post-Cold War Slovakia.[5] Some out-groups may not be sufficiently important in the nationalism of the day to resonate enough to justify risky foreign policies. That is, politicians using nationalism to gain support either for themselves or for an aggressive foreign policy must be sensitive to who matters in the nationalism they are espousing.

For illustration, consider the US invasion of Grenada. Ronald Reagan defined this expedition as aimed at preventing the scourge of communism from spreading, casting the adversary as belonging to a group that is salient in the American identity as the relevant other (Bostdorff 1991; Eldon 1984). The definition of the Grenadians to be toppled as Cuban/Soviet puppets was deliberate in order to improve the appeal of the mission back home.

To be clear, even the categories of "us" and "them" are not as clear as they often appear to be. One group may see another as kin under some conditions and the "other" under other conditions (Brewer 1991). As important, individuals within a given country may vary in how much they care about the various groups elsewhere. Some will identify those outside of the country as being part of "us" – the same ethnic group – and therefore deserving of support. Some will identify the same group as being "them" – a rival group, undeserving of assistance and perhaps even a source of threat. Yet still others will simply feel no kind of tie, neither amity nor enmity, towards particular groups outside the country.

---

[4] An exception to this has been Freudian psychoanalytic approaches, which regard "us" and "them" categories as intertwined; see Volkan 1999.

[5] Petersen (2002) develops a logic where different sets of emotions lead to different sorts of targets, as fear leads to targeting the most threatening groups, resentment leads to a focus on higher-status groups, and hate centers on historical rivals.

While understanding who is "us" and "them" seems fundamental for understanding the implications of nationalism for war, a second dimension also needs to be addressed: is a group tolerant of coexisting with individuals and groups who have other identities?[6] How accepting is a group of living with and governing with others? That is, how xenophobic are members of the nation in question? Experience ought to matter here, as living in a relatively homogeneous state for decades may cause a group to be less willing to live with other ethnic groups. Hungary, which used to rule jointly a very heterogeneous empire, is now one of the most homogeneous countries in Europe, thanks to the Treaty of Trianon. The idea of returning Transylvania back to Hungary with all of its lost Hungarians is actually an anathema to many Hungarians since such a change would bring in many Romanians as well (Saideman and Ayres 2008).

The general point is that the definition of who is "us" and who is "them" is distinct from the varying of willingness or tolerance for interaction. To say a group is xenophobic means that they are less tolerant of coexisting with the "other."[7] They do not want to live with the "other," they do not want to work with the "other," and they do not want their children marrying the "other." This, obviously, can have political implications. To be clear, this approach is distinct from those that distinguish between patriotism and nationalism. Those who make this move consider the former to be love of country and the latter to refer to enmity towards out-groups (Herrmann et al. 2009). The problem in that formulation is that it suggests a single meaning for a nationalism, whereas the position argued here is that the content of any nationalism can contain a variety of elements, including self-love and other-hate, and that multiple combinations of definitions of "self" and "other" not only can coexist but often conflict with each other.

A quick example concerning recent Quebec politics can illustrate how the same group may have multiple nationalisms that ultimately compete with each other through politics. In the Quebec provincial election in 2007, three parties competed. The Parti Quebecois was clearer than ever that its mandate would be to separate Quebec from Canada. The Liberal Party took a federalist stance, arguing for Quebec to stay in Canada. A third party, Action Démocratique du Québec (ADQ), gained much traction, not by playing up the separatism debate, but by focusing on the "reasonable accommodation" of immigrants. That is, the ADQ essentially became the party of xenophobes by focusing

---

[6] See Brown 1999 for a similar distinction.
[7] Wimmer (2002) suggests that this xenophobia is inherent in the modern state.

much attention on whether Quebec was endangering its identity by bending too much to the perceived demands of immigrants, particularly Muslims. In the aftermath of this election, where the ADQ did surprisingly well, finishing second, the two other parties learned to graft a xenophobic strand to their distinct nationalisms, ultimately marginalizing the ADQ.[8]

Thus, nationalism is rather complex, and attachment to one's nation does not mean that one has to be intolerant towards others.[9] This complexity is relevant for foreign policy, as Herrmann et al. (2009) found not only that nationalism is multidimensional, but also that those dimensions have an impact on foreign policy attitudes, including whether to engage in cooperation or use force. Likewise, Shevel (2010) argues that one can only make sense of Ukraine's law on the diaspora if one takes seriously how different versions of Ukrainian nationalism interacted with political competition. Next, we consider the most direct connection between nationalism and foreign policy: irredentism.

Nationalisms and irredentism

Why does all of this matter? Irredentism, if successful, would change not only the size of the country but also who resides within it. A successful irredentist war would be the equivalent of a massive wave of immigration: a sudden influx of people who had not been citizens or residents. This has the potential for altering not only the balance of political power (Horowitz 1985) but also the distribution of goods and services, especially public ones. So, the questions become: how much do members of the nation care about their kin nearby? How do they identify with them? How do they feel about the other people residing in the desired territory? The irony is that many of the people attached to their kin abroad are also likely to be hostile to the others. The perception of identity with particular people abroad may be combined with an enhanced sense of enmity with the group that governs the neighboring territory.

When we speak of extreme nationalisms, two ideas come to mind: a deep attachment to the idea that all members of a group should have their own nation, *and* a deep intolerance of others. This need not be true. Members of a group may desire to bring their perceived community into one country but may not mind the presence of others. For instance, there were all kinds of Serb nationalists making claims in the 1990s, with

[8] For a discussion of the reasonable accommodation debate in Quebec and its political dynamics, see Bélanger 2009, Mahrouse 2010, and Sharify-Funk 2010.
[9] Davidov (2011) finds that the various threads within a nationalism need not co-vary.

Table 14.1 *Dimensions of nationalism and irredentist inclinations*

| | Attitude towards other | |
Identification with kin	Tolerant/heterogeneity	Intolerant/homogeneity
Weak	Lack of interest	Hostile disinterest
Strong	Irredentism	Only irredentism if "clean"

Source: Saideman and Ayres 2008.

many focusing their attention on the plight of Serbs within Bosnia and Croatia. Unifying pieces of those countries with Serbia did not mean that one wanted to have an ethnically pure Serbia. Indeed, many nationalists resisted the departure of Kosovo, even though its ethnic composition included far more Albanians than Serbs. On the other hand, we tend to consider the ideal of civic nationalists to be individuals who do not identify so much with kin and are more tolerant of others, but again, these two tendencies do not have to travel together. We can imagine people who do not identify with any group, but still do not want to disturb the existing balances in their society. Indeed many, although not all, American xenophobes who oppose immigration lay claim not to ethnic definitions of what it means to be an American, but to civic ones.[10]

With two distinct dimensions, we obviously need a two-by-two (see Table 14.1). These two dimensions not only suggest when we should expect to see support for aggressive foreign policies to unify "lost territories" with the homeland, but also where we might see ethnic cleansing.[11] I would distinguish between the tactical cleansing by the Serbs in Bosnia and the more strategic cleansing by the Croats in Krajina.[12] A Greater Serbia could include Muslims, Croats, and Hungarians, but it seemed to be the case that evicting Serbs from Krajina (in Croatia) was a strategic move to increase the ethnic homogeneity of Croatia. An intolerant nationalist group would only seek irredentism if its identification with its kin abroad were particularly strong, such as when the kin abroad actually have key positions within the government. The cases of Armenia and Croatia are instructive here, where the

---

[10] Of course, many American xenophobes do identify themselves and America as Christian and white, but the anti-immigration crowd is not so homogeneous.

[11] For more on ethnic cleansing, see Mann 2005.

[12] An interesting project would be to do content analyses of speeches by Franjo Tudjman and Slobodan Milosevic to see if one was more xenophobic than the other.

irredentist policy was developed and implemented by politicians who were from the targeted territory and/or depended politically on those who were from the desired areas.

The punchline here is that groups who hate may actually be opposed to international adventures because they might bring into the country more of the "others" that they despise. Xenophobia may actually serve as a brake on irredentism. As important, with any nationalism containing multiple strands of identification and opposition, there is much room for politics. Rather than being an exercise of simply whipping up hate or playing up the risk to one's kin, the competition among politicians, including among nationalist politicians, involves agenda setting and issue framing. With multiple identities and perhaps multiple "others" as well, it is a matter not just of more and less, but also of which and where. Adept politicians will frame the discussions to highlight the identities and adversaries that unify the most relevant audiences. They will understand that not all adversaries are the same, with some providing not only more resonance, but also solidarity among otherwise disparate groups.

The meaning of Greater Romania

If one were to lay odds in 1989 about where irredentism might be the strongest in Eastern Europe, most probably one would have bet on Romania. Romania combined the most violent transition with the least significant initial reforms,[13] and Romanian leaders in the 1990s were willing to use force several times against the opposition. The boundary separating Romania from its claimed lost territory of Moldova was drawn by Hitler and Stalin in the run-up to World War II, making it the least legitimate line on the maps of Europe. There was an interest in the Greater Romania project within Moldova among the mobilized groups that had pushed for Moldova's independence from the Soviet Union.[14] Indeed, some saw union as inevitable (RFE/RL 1991: 42).

Yet interest in Romania in an irredentist effort has been surprisingly weak, even as the Greater Romania Party had some success. Why? Is it because Romanian nationalism is weak? Most observers would suggest otherwise. "The predominant features of Romanian nationalism are its general xenophobia (though mainly directed at Hungarians

---

[13] Termed a revolution, it was more a coup at first with members of the existing regime replacing Ceauşescu.

[14] King's (2000) is the definitive effort in delineating the history and contested nature of Moldovan identities, and much of the discussion here is informed by King's work. His Chapter 6 is most relevant for this discussion.

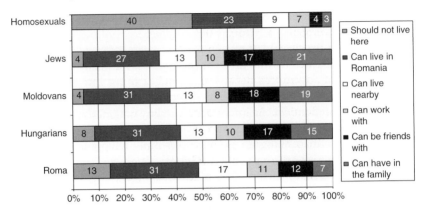

Figure 14.1 Attitudes towards minorities in Romania

and Russians) and particularly virulent anti-Semitism" (Rohozinska 1999: 1).[15] Ceausescu put much effort into reminding Romanians that Romania belonged to Romanians and that foreigners were to be feared (Tismaneanu 1998). So, this raises the question of what is Romanian nationalism? What are the key components of Romanian identity?

While there is much to it, a key element is definition by opposition: Romanians are not Hungarians, they are not Roma (Grigoria 2004),[16] and they are not Jews (Barkey 2000). Politicians can make much of these various "others" and have done precisely that. For instance in 1993, President Iliescu accused the Hungarians of being a "fifth column" (Mihailescu 2005). Indeed, attitudes towards non-Romanians range from hostile to barely tolerant, as Figure 14.1 illustrates.[17]

Thus, the first thing to realize is that any Romanian nationalist has plenty of targets for political stances at home, including immigrants, so focusing on the kin outside of Romania would seem unnecessary. This figure suggests something else as well: that the Moldovans are not nearly as popular as one would expect for a target of an irredentist campaign. They rank somewhere between Jews and Hungarians in terms of how tolerated they are – not exactly beloved. It could be that this survey does not distinguish between Romanians residing in Moldova and the other residents of that new country. Indeed, "welcoming the prodigal cousins back into the pan-Romanian fold,

---

[15] See also Chirot 2005.   [16] See also Bran 1995.
[17] Institutul pentru Politici Publica 2003: 36. The original figure contains data about other groups as well (Arabs, Chinese, blacks, lesbians, Muslims), but I extracted the most relevant ones as well as homosexuals as they are the focus of the most extreme views.

with significant numbers of Ukrainians and Russians in tow, was hardly an appealing proposition" (King 2000: 228).

Moreover, even if we focus just on the Moldovans who do identify with Romanians, we find that they are not seen so much as "us" in Romania. "Moldavians … were simply too marginal and helpless to be good material for nationalist recruiters" (Gallagher 1995: 174). Moldovan students who go to universities in Bucharest live apart, the males are seen as being more violent, and they are generally outsiders (Jura 2004).[18] Even Roma in Romania consider the visitors and immigrants from Moldova to be victims of discrimination (Grigori 2004). Consequently, polls showed only weak support for the irredentist project at perhaps its height of possibility in the early 1990s (Gallagher 1995: 187).

Romania has refrained from pursuing an irredentist policy even though the Greater Romania Party has hardly been marginal. Why? Because the Romanians in Moldova are marginal when compared to other aspects of Romanian nationalism that focus on the "others" in the country's midst, rather than the potential "us" that is abroad.

Xenophobia and intervention

Fear and intolerance of others may not only shape when and where we will see irredentism, but also when and where countries will intervene short of conquest and annexation. While there has been much more at stake in Afghanistan and Libya than the dynamics of xenophobia, we can see even here, with the multiplicity of interests, that identity politics play out in very important ways.

Afghanistan

The discussion thus far has stressed that identity and nationalisms can have multiple meanings that can propel or restrict irredentist foreign policies, causing or preventing war. Fear or intolerance of other groups can serve to deter irredentism because one does not want more "others" sharing the same political space. Yet that suggests that all xenophobic parties might have similar foreign policy stances. Recently, I have discovered an interesting comparison between two anti-immigration, anti-Muslim populist parties in Europe: the Danish People's Party (Dansk Folkeparti) and the Dutch Freedom Party (Partij voor de Vrijheid).[19]

---

[18] The Romanian graduate students serving as interpreters during this research trip concurred, having witnessed these attitudes on more than a few occasions.

[19] This section relies heavily on a series of interviews I conducted in Copenhagen, August 23–27, 2010, and The Hague, January 24–27, 2011.

In both Denmark and the Netherlands, we have seen minority coalitions of centre-right parties rely on these populist parties to maintain their governments. Neither the Danish People's Party nor the Freedom Party is in formal coalitions, but each usually votes with the minority coalition of Liberals and Christian Democrats. So, they play similar roles and have similar ideologies, but they have taken very different positions on their country's participation in the international effort in Afghanistan.

Both Denmark and the Netherlands have been significant participants in the effort led by the North Atlantic Treaty Organization (NATO) to stabilize Afghanistan: the International Security Assistance Force (ISAF). The mission has been less popular in the Netherlands than in Denmark, but is, obviously, a highly salient issue in both countries, especially since each has had contingents working in some of the most dangerous parts of Afghanistan.

In Denmark, the Danish People's Party (DPP) has consistently supported the mission and voted for it when it came up in the parliament. As a populist party, there have been strains of isolationism in its stances, but these were not sufficient to get in the way of supporting the Afghanistan effort. One could suggest that this is because Denmark served as a focal point due to the cartoon crisis when protesters and governments in the Islamic world objected to depictions of Mohammed.[20] This opposition to Denmark and the increased risk of being a target of terrorism could have influenced the position of the DPP on Muslims (Centre of Military Studies 2010). While the crisis may have cemented the party's stance, this position preceded the crisis. The DPP has generally defined the issue as fighting Muslims in Afghanistan rather than fighting them in Denmark. So, the DPP's anti-Muslim component of its xenophobic ideology takes priority over its isolationist stance.

The Dutch government fell in early 2010 over the decision to extend the mission (and for other reasons as well). In early 2011 the new government proposed taking on a new, smaller and less risky mission: police training in northern Afghanistan. This provoked quite an interesting period of political uncertainty as the Freedom Party refused to support the effort, forcing the government to rely on fickle opposition parties, as was also the case in 2006 when the mission to Uruzgan was being considered. While the new mission was finally approved, it

---

[20] In 2005, a Danish newspaper published a series of editorial cartoons depicting Mohammed. This produced some protests within Denmark, which got much more publicity after Prime Minister Rasmussen refused to meet with ambassadors from Muslim-majority countries. He issued a letter saying that the Danish government had no influence on the press. The dispute produced protests around the Islamic world in 2006.

demonstrated that the Freedom Party was much more focused on events in the Netherlands, more focused on a Fortress Holland, than on situations elsewhere.[21]

Thus, two parties that are similar in many ways have both defined a populist appeal, presenting xenophobia as an ideology, and yet have developed different stances towards one of the key foreign policies of recent times. Within the broad category of populist xenophobia, we therefore find multiple strands of identification and opposition presenting the potential for varying priorities leading to different policy positions. Thus not only can nationalisms provoke conflicts and deter irredentism, but they can also shape participation in alliances and their interventions.

Reacting to Libya: humane xenophobia(?)

The ironies accumulate when we consider how nationalist identities have shaped the international reaction to the Libyan Civil War. In March 2011 The United Nations passed a resolution authorizing the international community in the form of NATO to use force to protect the civilians of Libya from Muammar Qaddafi's reprisals against protestors. Yet before all of the votes had taken place, France had already started striking targets in Libya (Willsher 2011). From even before the start of the campaign to the moment this piece was revised, France bore a disproportionate share of the effort, and helped drag its NATO partners into the campaign.[22] Given that France has often been on the wrong side of humanitarian efforts (Rwanda in 1994, Tunisia in 2011) and has not pushed for intervention elsewhere (Bahrain, Syria), to say that France just sought to protect civilians strains the credulity of observers.

Instead, we can observe that intervention in Libya served as an opportunity for President Nicolas Sarkozy to service two distinct nationalist imperatives, old and new, at the same time: for France to be seen as a leader and to limit the flood of immigrants. Harking back to De Gaulle (Cerny 1980), the idea of France as a great power is a key component defining France and the French. By taking a lead in this effort, Sarkozy was invoking this key element of French nationalism: that France is a great country that can make its mark on world events. Acting first and most energetically not only put France in the lead

---

[21] I am indebted to the insights of some of the political analysts at the Canadian embassy in The Hague.

[22] To be clear, France was quite willing to continue the campaign as an ad hoc effort, but agreed to a NATO mission to keep the support of the US and others.

in Libya, but could also be seen as an attempt by Sarkozy to raise his own standing back home (Applebaum 2011).

The second imperative helps to determine why France became so involved in Libya's turmoil but not in that of more distant Arab countries such as Syria. While France has historic ties with Syria, Libya's proximity and the threat of increased refugee flows made it a higher priority. Anti-immigrant and especially anti-Muslim sentiment had been on the rise in France for some time, carrying the National Front party higher in the polls at Sarkozy's expense.[23] The Libyan conflict threatened to send yet more Muslim refugees across the Mediterranean after the earlier waves of Tunisians.[24] Such a flow would undermine Sarkozy's popularity even further.[25] Intervening early to stem the flow before it began would prevent the xenophobic parties back home from having yet more fodder for their campaigns.

Thus, Sarkozy's Libyan effort touched upon two key strands in French nationalism: foreign policy as a place for France to demonstrate its relevance, and the intolerance of yet more heterogeneity, especially via Muslim immigrants. It may not have worked to increase his popularity, but it is clear that xenophobia helps to explain Sarkozy's and France's discrimination here. Grandeur called for leadership, but intolerance pointed towards Libya, not Syria.

Conclusions

The aim of this chapter has been to demonstrate that nationalism is more complex than usually considered, especially by scholars of international relations (like myself). To say that one person is more of a nationalist than another misses the point, as it is the meaning of the nationalism that matters. Politics is often a contest about which elements of the shared identification as a nation should matter and what their implications are. A nation may have shared ties with the residents of a nearby country, but how strong that identification is and whether it competes with other inclinations, such as hatred of others residing in the same territory, will shape the likelihood of war. Xenophobia can serve as a brake on aggressive nationalisms, but xenophobia itself,

---

[23] Sarkozy was not new to xenophobic policies as he deported significant numbers of Roma in 2010.

[24] Of course, an alternative would have been simply to prevent the refugees from reaching Europe, as we have apparently seen in the Mediterranean (Donadio 2011).

[25] Indeed, Sarkozy risked endangering the essence of the European Union – a single marketplace – by blocking the border with Italy to prevent more refugees from reaching France (Trayno 2011).

as the Danish and Dutch comparison suggests, is more complex than previously considered.

Most countries have a great deal of choice about the targets of their policies, as a multi-threaded nationalism can highlight certain kin or adversaries as being more important than others. Politicians with agendas will try to shape the nationalism of the moment to focus on their preferred targets, but they have limited power to do so. They may care a great deal about the kin in state x, but their audience may actually care far more about their kin in state y, or about the others residing within the state (as in the case of Romania). The example of France demonstrates that xenophobia can encourage intervention and violence as states seek quick solutions to limit refugee flows.

Understanding that nationalism and identification are complex processes is the first step to figuring out not just whether war is likely but against whom it is likely. Moreover, appreciating these nuanced dynamics of nationalism can help us to understand the fights among nationalists to define the agenda of the nation. The next steps are to figure out the winning strategies to define the nation and why they are more successful.

REFERENCES

Abdelal, R., Y.M. Herrera, A.I. Johnston, and R. McDermott. 2006. "Identity as a Variable." *American Political Science Review* 4(4): 695–711.

Ambrosio, T. 2001. *Irredentism: Ethnic Conflict and International Politics.* Westport, CT: Praeger.

Applebaum, A. 2011. "Wag Le Chien: Did French President Nicolas Sarkozy Push the Libyan Intervention to Boost His Re-election Bid?" *Slate*, March 28.

Barkey, K. 2000. "Negotiated Paths to Nationhood: A Comparison of Hungary and Romania in the Early Twentieth Century." *East European Politics and Societies* 14(3): 497–531.

Bélanger, E. 2009. "The 2008 Provincial Election in Quebec." *Canadian Political Science Review* 3(1): 93–99.

Bostdorff, D.M. 1991. "The Presidency and Promoted Crisis: Reagan, Grenada, and Issue Management." *Presidential Studies Quarterly* 21(4): 737–50.

Bran, M. 1995. "Romania: Using Nationalism for Political Legitimacy." Pp. 280–94 in *New Xenophobia in Europe*, edited by B. Baumartand and A. Favell. London: Kluwer Law International.

Brewer, M.B. 1991. "The Social Self – On Being the Same and Different at the Same Time." *Personality and Social Psychology Bulletin* 17(5): 475–82.

Brown, D. 1999. "Are There Good and Bad Nationalisms?" *Nations and Nationalism* 5(2): 281–302.

Brubaker, R. 1996. *Nationalism Reframed: Nationhood and the National Question in the New Europe.* Cambridge and New York: Cambridge University Press.

Centre of Military Studies. 2010. Roundtable, August 26. Copenhagen.

Cerny, P.G. 1980. *The Politics of Grandeur: Ideological Aspects of De Gaulle's Foreign Policy.* Cambridge University Press.

Chirot, D. 2005. "What Provokes Violent Ethnic Conflict? Political Choice in One African and Two Balkan Cases." Pp. 140–65 in *Ethnic Politics After Communism*, edited by Z. Barany and R.G. Moser. Ithaca, NY: Cornell University Press.

Davidov, E. 2011. "Nationalism and Constructive Patriotism: A Longitudinal Test of Comparability in 22 Countries with the ISSP." *International Journal of Public Opinion Research* 23(1): 88–103.

Deegan-Krause, K. 2004. "Uniting the Enemy: Politics and the Convergence of Nationalisms in Slovakia." *East European Politics and Societies* 18(4): 651–96.

Donadio, R. 2011. "France to Help Block Tunisian Migrants." *New York Times* April 8.

Eldon, K. 1984. "Grenada as Theater." *World Policy Journal* 1(3): 635–51.

Gagnon, V.P. 2004. *The Myth of Ethnic War: Serbia and Croatia in the 1990s.* Ithaca, NY: Cornell University Press.

Gallagher, T. 1995. *Romania after Ceauşescu: The Politics of Intolerance.* Edinburgh University Press.

Grigoria, D. 2004 Interviewed by Saideman, S. May 12.

Herrmann, R.K., P. Isernia, and P. Segatti. 2009. "Attachment to the Nation and International Relations: Dimensions of Identity and Their Relationship to War and Peace." *Political Psychology* 30(5): 721–54.

Horowitz, D. 1985. *Ethnic Groups in Conflict.* Berkeley: University of California Press.

Ignatieff, M. 1994. *Blood and Belonging: Journeys into the New Nationalism.* New York: Farrar, Straus, and Giroux.

Institutul pentru Politici Publica (Institute on Public Policy). 2003. *Intoleranţă, Discriminare Autoritarism: În Opinia Publică (Intolerance, Discrimination and Authoritarianism in Public Opinion).* Bucharest: Institute on Public Policy.

Jura, C. 2004. Interviewed by Saideman, S. May 13.

Kaufman, S.J. 1994. "The Irresistible Force and the Imperceptible Object: The Yugoslav Breakup and Western Policy." *Security Studies* 4(2): 281–329.

King, C. 2000. *The Moldovan: Romania, Russia, and the Politics of Culture.* Stanford, CA: Hoover Institution Press.

Mahrouse, G. 2010. "'Reasonable Accommodation' in Québec: the Limits of Participation and Dialogue." *Race & Class* 52(1): 85–96.

Mann, M. 2005. *The Dark Side of Democracy: Explaining Ethnic Cleansing.* New York: Cambridge University Press.

Mercer, J. 1995. "Anarchy and Identity." *International Organization* 49(2): 229–52.

Mihailescu, M. 2005. "Dampening The Powder Keg: Understanding Interethnic Cooperation in Post-Communist Romania (1990–96)." *Nationalism and Ethnic Politics* 11(1): 25–59.

Petersen, R. 2002. *Understanding Ethnic Violence: Fear, Hatred, Resentment in Twentieth Century Eastern Europe.* Cambridge University Press.

RFE/RL. 1991. "Weekly Record of Events." *Research Report*, September 6.

Rohozinska, J. 1999. "Romania's Ills: Strays and Stereotypes." *Central Europe Review* 1(11).

Saideman, S. and David P. Auerswald. 2012. "Comparing Caveats: Understanding the Sources of National Restrictions upon NATO's Mission in Afghanistan." *International Studies Quarterly* 56(1): 64–87.

Saideman, S. and R.W. Ayres. 2008. *For Kin or Country: Xenophobia, Nationalism, and War*. New York: Columbia University Press.

Sharify-Funk, M. 2010. "Muslims and the Politics of Reasonable Accommodation: Analyzing the Bouchard-Taylor Report and its Impact on the Canadian Province of Quebec." *Journal of Muslim Minority Affairs* 30: 535–53.

Shevel, O. 2010. "The Post-Communist Diaspora Laws Beyond the 'Good Civic versus Bad Ethnic' Nationalism Dichotomy." *East European Politics and Societies* 24(1): 159–87.

Shulman, S. 2002. "Challenging the Civic/Ethnic and West/East Dichotomies in the Study of Nationalism." *Comparative Political Studies* 35(5): 554–585.

Smith, A.D. 1993. *National Identity*. Reno: University of Nevada Press.

Tismaneanu, V. 1998. *Fantasies of Salvation: Democracy, Nationalism, and Myth in Post-Communist Europe*. Princeton University Press.

Trayno, I. 2011. "Europe Movies to End Passport-Free Travel in Migrant Row." *Guardian*, May 12.

Volkan, V. 1999. *Bloodlines: From Ethnic Pride to Ethnic Terrorism*. Boulder, CO: Westview Press.

Weiner, M. 1971. "The Macedonian Syndrome." *World Politics* 23(1): 665–83.

Willsher, K. 2011. "As France Takes the Reins on Libya, Sarkozy Triumphs." *Los Angeles Times*, March 20.

Wimmer, A. 2002. *Nationalist Exclusion and Ethnic Conflict: Shadows of Modernity*. Cambridge and New York: Cambridge University Press.

Index